D1130891

EARLY VICTORIAN ENGLAND
1830–1865

OLD WESTMINSTER—*DE WINT*

EARLY VICTORIAN ENGLAND

1830–1865

Omnium rerum aut similitudo aut multitudo
stomachum facit, praeter intelligere.

VOLUME I

GEOFFREY CUMBERLEGE
OXFORD UNIVERSITY PRESS
LONDON NEW YORK TORONTO

Oxford University Press, Amen House, London E.C. 4
GLASGOW NEW YORK TORONTO MELBOURNE WELLINGTON
BOMBAY CALCUTTA MADRAS CAPE TOWN
Geoffrey Cumberlege, Publisher to the University

FIRST PUBLISHED 1934
SECOND IMPRESSION 1951

Reprinted lithographically in Great Britain
at the UNIVERSITY PRESS, OXFORD

PREFACE

THE period with which these volumes deal might be variously defined. In political history, it is the age of the ten-pound householder, who rose to power with the Reform Act of 1832 and took a larger electorate into partnership by the Act of 1867. Industrially, it opens with the invention of railway transport and ends with a railway system practically complete. It saw the transformation of the individualist England of the Georges into a modern administrative state. On a larger view, it is the age of expansion, and the British North America Act of 1867 closes one phase of history and opens another of which the end is not yet in sight. The same period includes the transition from sail to steam and the invention of the electric telegraph; it covers the golden age of English agriculture, the summer afternoon of aristocracy. If it had been the Queen and not Prince Albert who died in 1861, the process of English history would have been easier to apprehend. The long life of the Sovereign, the long careers of her most famous subjects, created an illusion which the word Victorian enshrines. The sixties are a decade of swift, decisive transformation. In front of them lies the world in which we were born. Behind them is a world which has passed out of memory, and which it is the purpose of these chapters to call back to life.

The history of the period, in the ordinary sense of the word history, has often been written. The object of the contributors to these volumes has been rather to provide the background of ideas and habits, to recall the sights and sounds of Early Victorian England, and so to create for the reader of the history or literature of the time the atmosphere which will bring their details into perspective or relief. The amount of information available is so vast that it would be far easier to compile an encyclopaedia of the period than to write a book about it; and there are topics, Law being the most conspicuous, which, as they could not be adequately treated without overrunning the limit assigned, are, reluctantly but necessarily, omitted. This is how the age appears to us, each in the sphere with which the writer is most familiar: these are the things which, in our judgement, are significant, and by which, when the surface markings which distinguish the modern from the old-fashioned have been obliterated, the Early Victorian Age will be recognized in history.

G. M. YOUNG.

CONTENTS

VOLUME I

LIST OF ILLUSTRATIONS viii

NOTE ON COSTUME xiv

CHRONOLOGICAL TABLE xvii

I. WORK AND WAGES. *By* J. H. CLAPHAM 1

II. HOMES AND HABITS. *By* MRS. C. S. PEEL . . . 77

III. TOWN LIFE AND LONDON. *By* R. H. MOTTRAM . 153

IV. LIFE IN THE NEW TOWNS. *By* J. H. CLAPHAM AND M. H. CLAPHAM 225

V. COUNTRY LIFE AND SPORT. *By* BERNARD DARWIN . 245

VI. THE NAVY. *By* ADMIRAL G. A. BALLARD . . . 297

VII. THE ARMY. *By* SIR JOHN FORTESCUE . . . 345

VIII. THE MERCANTILE MARINE. *By* BASIL LUBBOCK . 377

VOLUME II

IX. THE PRESS. *By* E. E. KELLETT 1

X. ART. *By* A. P. OPPÉ 99

XI. ARCHITECTURE. *By* A. E. RICHARDSON . . . 177

XII. MUSIC. *By* E. J. DENT 249

XIII. DRAMA. *By* ALLARDYCE NICOLL 265

XIV. HOLIDAYS AND TRAVEL. *By* MONA WILSON . . 283

XV. CHARITY. *By* E. LASCELLES 315

XVI. EXPANSION AND EMIGRATION. *By* D. WOODRUFF . 349

XVII. PORTRAIT OF AN AGE. *By* G. M. YOUNG . . 411

LIST OF ILLUSTRATIONS

Acknowledgements are due in each case to the owner whose name appears below, and in particular to H.M. the King for gracious permission to reproduce Frith's Ramsgate Sands (Plate 126) from the Buckingham Palace Collection.

VOLUME I

PAGE

Frontispiece. Old Westminster. From the water-colour by Peter de Wint in the Victoria and Albert Museum

1. Work. From the painting by Ford Madox Brown in the Manchester Art Gallery . . . . *facing* 8
2. Watch-cases. Coventry, *c.* 1850 . . . *tail-piece* 76
3. Old Gentleman, 1830. (Sir Francis Burdett.) Victoria and Albert Museum . . . . *facing* 80
4. Young Gentlemen, 1834. From the *Gentleman's Magazine of Fashion*. Mrs. Richardson . . . . . . *facing* 82
5. Young Ladies, 1830. From *La Belle Assemblée*. Mrs. Richardson *facing* 84
6. Young Lady, 1835: Concert Dress. From the *Court Magazine*. Mrs. Richardson . . . . *facing* 86
7. Dandies, 1838. From *Modes de Paris*. Mrs. Richardson . *facing* 88
8. Model of 1842, with later accessories (Florence Dombey style). Victoria and Albert Museum . . . . . *facing* 90
9. Young Lady and Maid, 1844. From *Les Modes Parisiennes*. Mrs. Richardson . . . . *facing* 94
10. The Crinoline, 1855. From *La Mode*. Mrs. Richardson . *facing* 96
11. State Bed, 1851 . . . . *facing* 100
12. Dressing Cases, 1851 . . . . *facing* 104
13. Table Lamps and Chandelier, 1851 . . . . . *facing* 112
14. Table Glass, 1851 . . . . *facing* 114
15. Boy of 1856. (*Eric, or Little by Little* style.) Victoria and Albert Museum . . . . *facing* 116
16. Three Generations, 1857. From the *Gentleman's Magazine of Fiction*. Mrs. Richardson . . . . . . *facing* 118
17. Young Ladies, 1860. From the *Journal des Demoiselles*. Mrs. Richardson . . . . *facing* 122
18. Young Lady, 1860. From a photograph in the possession of Mrs. Arnold-Forster . . . . *facing* 124
19. Old Lady and Child, 1860. From a photograph in the possession of Mrs. Arnold-Forster . . . . *facing* 126
20. Young Ladies, 1861: outdoor style. From the *Englishwoman's Domestic Magazine*. Mrs. Richardson . . . *facing* 128
21. The Great of 1865: including Tennyson, Browning, Swinburne, and Longfellow. Victoria and Albert Museum . . *facing* 134
22. Walking Dress, 1866–7. From the *Courrier de la Mode*. Mrs. Richardson . . . . *facing* 138

23. Model Dwellings designed by Prince Albert (Gold Medal, 1851) *facing* 144
24. The Pastry Cook: a valentine. J. Johnson . . . *facing* 146
25. The Cookmaid: a valentine. J. Johnson . . . *facing* 148
26. Sanitary Handbill, 1832. J. Johnson . . . . *facing* 162
27. (1) Jacob's Island (*Oliver Twist*). (2) Fleet Prison, 1848. From the water-colours by Wykeham Archer in the British Museum *facing* 168
28. The Hub of the City, 1851. From Harold P. Clunn, *The Face of London*. Messrs. F. & E. Stoneham, Ltd. . . . *facing* 170
29. Temple Bar, 1846. From the water-colour by Wykeham Archer in the British Museum . . . . *facing* 174
30. Smithfield, 1850. From the water-colour by Wykeham Archer in the British Museum . . . . *facing* 182
31. Newgate, before an Execution. From Harold P. Clunn, *The Face of London*. Messrs. Simpkin, Marshall . . . *facing* 184
32. The Chamber of Horrors: a handbill. J. Johnson . . *facing* 186
33. St. James's Street, 1840. From *Comic Novels*. J. Johnson . *facing* 188
34. Hyde Park near Grosvenor Gate. From a lithograph by T. Shotter Boys, 1842. British Museum . . . . . *facing* 190
35. Making a Club Member. From *Comic Novels*, 1840. J. Johnson . *facing* 192
36. Al-fresco painting of Mount Hecla, Surrey Zoological Gardens. From a Railway Guide. J. Johnson . . . *facing* 194
37. Cowgate, Norwich, *c.* 1830. From an oil painting by Henry Ninham. R. H. Mottram . . . . . . *facing* 208
38. Opening of the Great Exhibition, 1851. From a bas-relief in the Borough of Colchester Public Library . . . *facing* 212
39. Great Exhibition: Refreshment Tariff . . . . *facing* 216
40. Great Exhibition: Her Majesty's Boudoir. From a coloured lithograph . . . . *facing* 218
41. Great Exhibition: Hiram Power's *Greek Slave*. From a coloured lithograph . . . . *facing* 220
42. Modern and Mediaeval Town. From A. W. Pugin, *Contrasts*, second edition, 1841. R.I.B.A. . . . . . *facing* 228
43. The Plymouth Athenaeum. From a print. Royal Institute of British Architects . . . . *facing* 236
44, 45. The Rural Scene, by Birket Foster. Victoria and Albert Museum *facing* 248, 250
46. (*a*) The Club Walking, (*b*) The Waits, by Birket Foster. Victoria and Albert Museum . . . . *facing* 252
47. Country House group, 1855, reading the Fall of Sebastopol. From a photograph in the possession of Mrs. Arnold-Forster . *facing* 254
48, 49. Country House groups, *c.* 1860. From photographs in the possession of Mrs. Arnold-Forster . . . *facing* 256, 258
50. Shrubland Park, Ipswich: garden by Barry. From a photograph in *Country Life* . . . . *facing* 260
51. Cricket. From a Sporting Handkerchief. Sir Jeremiah Colman, Bart. . . . . *facing* 272

52. H.M.S. *Howe*: 120-gun ship of the line, first rate . . *facing* 302
53. (1) H.M.S. *Southampton*: 50-gun frigate, fourth rate. (2) H.M.S. *Osprey*: 12-gun brig-rigged sloop . . . . . *facing* 304
54. (1) H.M.S. *Gorgon*: 6-gun paddle frigate, fifth rate. (2) H.M.S. *Royal Oak* . . . . *facing* 306
55. H.M.S. *Warrior*: 41 guns, armour-plated screw battleship . *facing* 316

Nos. 52–5 are from the Macpherson Collection in the National Maritime Museum

56. Deck of a Corvette, *c.* 1856. From a photograph in the possession of Admiral Ballard . . . . . . *facing* 336
57. Quarter-deck of a Frigate, 1865. From a photograph in the possession of Admiral Ballard . . . . . . *facing* 340
58. 3rd Hussars. Officers in Undress. From a lithograph in colours by and after E. Hull, 1830 . . . . . . *facing* 348
59. Royal Artillery in Action. From a lithograph in colours by A. O. Driscoll after W. Heath, 1840 . . . . . *facing* 356
60. Battle of the Alma. The Guards moving up to the Redoubt. From a water-colour by Orlando Norie . . . . *facing* 358
61. Non-commissioned Officers of the Coldstream Guards. From a lithograph in colours by and after J. A. Vintner, 1856 . *facing* 360
62. Christmas Dinner on the Heights of Sebastopol. From a lithograph in colours by J. A. Vintner after W. Simpson, 1855 . *facing* 362
63. Siege of Sebastopol. A quiet night in the batteries. From a lithograph in colours by Day & Son, after W. Simpson . *facing* 364
64. The Presentation of the Crimean Medal, Horse Guards Parade. From a lithograph in colours by T. Picken after J. Tenniel, 1855 *facing* 366
65. The Grand Review of Volunteer Rifle Corps, Hyde Park, 1860. From a lithograph in colours by C. J. Calliford . . *facing* 370
66. The wreck of H.M.S. *Birkenhead*. From a lithograph in colours by V. Brookes after R. S. Bond (a survivor) . . . *facing* 372
67. (1) The *Thomas Coutts*. From a photograph. (2) Waterford Line Schooners. From an aquatint in colours by Stuart and Reeve *facing* 386
68. (1) P. & O. s.s. *Hindostan*. From a photograph. (2) s.s. *Archimedes*. From an aquatint in colours by Rosenberg after Huggins *facing* 396
69. (1) P. & O. s.s. *Himalayan*. (2) The Race: *Taeping* and *Ariel*. From photographs . . . . *facing* 412

Nos. 58–69 are reproduced by permission of the owners, Messrs. Thomas H. Parker, Ltd.

VOLUME II

Frontispiece. Election Meeting: Wilton, 1865. Photograph. Mrs. Richardson
70. Dickens and his Friends, by D. Maclise. Victoria and Albert Museum . . . . *facing* 4
71. Printing House Square, *c.* 1840. From the water-colour by Wykeham Archer. British Museum . . . . *facing* 16

72. Useful Knowledge: Charles Knight's prospectus, 1847. J. Johnson *between* 40, 41
73. Useful Knowledge: The Pyramids, and The Crystal Palace. J. Johnson . . . . *facing* 44
74. Book-binding, 1860: Tennyson's *The Princess* . . *facing* 92
75. Book-binding: Queen Victoria's *Journal of our Life in the Highlands* *facing* 94
76. Burlington House, 1855. From the water-colour by Wykeham Archer in the British Museum . . . . . *facing* 102
77. Mr. Pips at the Academy, 1849. From *Mr. Pips' Diary*, by Richard Doyle . . . . *facing* 104
78. The Village Choir. From the painting by Thomas Webster. Victoria and Albert Museum . . . . . . *facing* 106
79. The Suffering Husband. From the painting by Augustus Egg. National Gallery of British Art . . . . *facing* 112
80. Hylas and the Water-Nymphs. From the statuary group by John Gibson. National Gallery of British Art . . *between* 118, 119
81. Clocks, 1851 . . . . *between* 118, 119
82. Waiting for the Verdict, by Abraham Solomon. From a print in the British Museum . . . . . . *facing* 128
83. The Crossing-Sweeper, by W. P. Frith. From a print in the British Museum . . . . *facing* 136
84. 'Open your Mouth', by W. Mulready. Victoria and Albert Museum *facing* 142
85. The Sonnet, by W. Mulready. Victoria and Albert Museum *facing* 144
86. Cartoons for the Houses of Parliament, by W. Cope and J. Severn. From prints in the Victoria and Albert Museum . . *facing* 146
87. English Autumn Afternoon, by Ford Madox Brown. Birmingham Art Gallery . . . . *facing* 148
88. Borrowdale, by William Collins. Guildhall Art Gallery, London *facing* 150
89. 'We praise Thee, O God', by Henry Barraud. From a print in the British Museum . . . . *facing* 152
90. The Duet, by Frank Stone. Victoria and Albert Museum . *facing* 154
91. The Carpenter's Shop, by J. E. Millais. (*a*) The picture, in the National Gallery of British Art; (*b*) the reproduction in *The Illustrated London News*, 11 May 1850 . . . *facing* 162
92. Waiting, by J. E. Millais. Birmingham Art Gallery . *facing* 168
93. Photographic Composition, *c.* 1855, by Mervyn Story-Maskelyne. Mrs. Arnold-Forster . . . . *facing* 176
94. The New Victualling Office, Devil's Point, Plymouth. From Brittain and Brayley, *Devon and Cornwall Illustrated* . *facing* 180
95. Destruction of Nash's Colonnade, Regent Street, 1848. From the water-colour by Wykeham Archer. British Museum . *facing* 184
96. Demolition of old London Bridge, 1824. From Harold P. Clunn, *The Face of London*. Messrs. Simpkin, Marshall . . *facing* 186
97. Lansdown Terrace, Cheltenham: J. B. Papworth. From a photograph in *Country Life* . . . . . *facing* 188

98. Highclere House, Hampshire, before and after Sir Charles Barry's reconstruction. R.I.B.A. . . . . *facing* 190
99. St. George's Hall, Liverpool. From a sketch by H. L. Elmes. Royal Institute of British Architects . . . . . *facing* 192
100. Design for Royal Exchange, by C. R. Cockerell. Royal Institute of British Architects . . . . *facing* 194
101. Design for an Insurance Office, by C. R. Cockerell. Royal Institute of British Architects . . . . *facing* 196
102. Railway Stations. (*a*) Functional: Mocatta. (*b*) Romantic (Shrewsbury). Royal Institute of British Architects . . *facing* 198
103. Coffee Room, Paddington, by Philip Hardwick. Royal Institute of British Architects . . . . *facing* 202
104. Town Planning: Harlesden Park. Royal Institute of British Architects . . . . *facing* 204
105. Ball-room, Buckingham Palace, by Sir James Pennethorne. Royal Institute of British Architects . . . . . *facing* 206
106. The Mediaeval Court, Great Exhibition, 1851 . . *facing* 212
107. Vase in Electro Plate, Great Exhibition . . . *facing* 236
108. Fire-place and Coal Vases . . . . *facing* 240
109. Table (designed by the Duchess of Sutherland), and Buffet *facing* 244
110. After the Opera. From a print. Mrs. Richardson . . *facing* 256
111. Erard's Pianoforte, Great Exhibition, 1851 . . . *facing* 260
112. Cottage Piano: Great Exhibition, 1851 . . . *facing* 262
113. Stage Attitudes, *c.* 1830 . . . . . . *facing* 268
114. Phelps as Falstaff, 1846 . . . . . . *facing* 270
115. Midsummer Night's Dream, Act V (Kean) . . . *facing* 272
116. Richard II: Historical Episode (Kean) . . . *facing* 274
117. Playbill of 1846 . . . . *facing* 276
118. Playbill of 1857 . . . . *between* 280, 281
Nos. 113–18 are all from the Gabrielle Enthoven Collection in the Victoria and Albert Museum
119. Title-page for Travel Book, by Birket Foster . . *facing* 284
120. Thames Steamer *Nymph*. From a lithograph in colours. Messrs. Thomas H. Parker, Ltd. . . . . *facing* 286
121. Bonchurch in 1837. From a print. Royal Institute of British Architects . . . . *facing* 288
122. Liverpool Railway: Fares and Regulations. J. Johnson *between* 292, 293
123. 'To Brighton and Back for 3*s.* 6*d.*', by Charles Rossiter. Birmingham Art Gallery . . . . *facing* 296
124. Pegwell Bay, by W. Dyce. National Gallery . *between* 300, 301
125. By the Sea. From a photograph by Mervyn Story-Maskelyne. Mrs. Arnold-Forster . . . . *between* 300, 301
126. Ramsgate Sands, by W. P. Frith. From the original in Buckingham Palace, by gracious permission of H.M. the King . *facing* 310
127. The Last of England, by Ford Madox Brown. Birmingham Art Gallery . . . . *facing* 352
128. Emigrant Ships. (1) *Marco Polo*. From a lithograph in colours by Raymond after Egremont. (2) *James Baines*. From a photograph. Messrs. Thomas H. Parker, Ltd. . . . . *facing* 368

129. Emigrants arriving at Sydney Cove, 1852. From the lithograph by T. Picken after Sir O. W. Brierly. Messrs. Thomas H. Parker, Ltd. *facing* 376
130. Barry's Design for new Government Offices, 1857. Royal Institute of British Architects . . . . . . *facing* 438
131. The Repeal of the Corn Laws. From *The Times*, 4 December 1845 *facing* 448
132. Dizzy the Farmer's Friend. *Mr. Pips' Diary*, by R. Doyle . *facing* 452
133. Death of Sir Robert Peel. From *The Times*, 3 July 1850 . *facing* 480
134. The Fall of Sebastopol. From *The Times*, 11 September 1855 *facing* 484
135. The Fall of Delhi. From *The Times*, 27 October 1857 . *facing* 492
136. Death of the Prince Consort. From *The Times*, 16 December 1861 *facing* 496
137. Death of Lord Palmerston. From *The Times*, 19 October 1865 *facing* 502

COSTUME

THE illustrations of costume have been selected to show the general development rather than the details of fashion. Following on the high-waisted and straight-hanging style of the early nineteenth century (revived as a picture-frock by Kate Greenaway), the waist is lowered and the frock belled. (Mrs. Richardson has with much probability suggested that the re-elaboration of costume reflects the revulsion from the Republican-antique to the Renaissance-Bourbon at the Restoration. Something also must be allowed for the pageantry of the time, largely inspired by Scott, and the taste for fancy-dress balls.) The beginning is seen in Plate 5 (1830) and carried farther in Plate 6 (1835). Plate 8 shows the quiet style of the early forties: the skirt here is naturally full, not padded. Plate 9 shows the high style of 1844. The skirt now comes to be supported on masses of petticoats bunched at the waist, an arrangement which made the crinoline (Plate 10, 1855: Plate 17, 1860) a physical and mechanical necessity. By 1861 the outdoor mind (archery, croquet) is beginning to make itself felt in the tailor-made coat covering a crinoline line (Plate 20). Then (Plates 18, 22; 1860–6) the inflated skirt subsides by way of the flounce, the polonaise, and the bustle, into the more manageable style required by the greater freedom and activity of late Victorian life. The old lady of Plate 19 is wearing the pre-crinoline bunched skirt.

But as women's fashions were mostly derived from France they are not historically of much interest in England, which did on the other hand set the fashion in men's wear. By 1830 the use of black for professional and business wear was established; but for sport, travel, and social occasions a great variety of colour, green, brown, blue, was still permitted. At the Waterbrook dinner, only Uriah Heep seems to be in black, and the standard late Victorian evening dress, black and white with a tie of moderate dimensions, would in the thirties have been taken for the garb of a waiter, an usher, or a Westminster boy.

In 1830 black breeches were still worn by the older men (Plate 3) and, for Sunday wear, the fashion persisted among the yeomanry till the fifties. But trousers (with a flap buttoned across the waist) were normal: they were worn tight (observe the reclining gentleman in Plate 7) and were of every texture, colour, and pattern, from Brougham's tartan cloth, through Disraeli's green velvet to Macaulay's nankeen. Gaiters might be worn over the trousers. The wrist-bands would be turned up over the coat-cuff.

The coat can be reduced to one of two types: the outdoor, close-buttoned against the weather, with a full skirt for riding, and the indoor, with fine drawn tails and lapels rolled well back to display the linen, neck-cloth, jewellery, and flowered waistcoat (Plate 4). The early Victorian male was biologically sound: he liked to display his lines—good calves, slender waist, broad chest, and clustering hair; and the cut of the dandy's clothes conformed to the baroque swagger of his gestures and attitudes (Plate 7). In some of Wykeham Archer's drawings, the 'proud full sail' of the London *bourgeoisie* contrasts almost racially with the bandy and shambling gait of the proletariate.

The social contrast is carried through in the opposition of tails and jacket, which (like the cap or low-crowned hat) is the wear of boys or labourers (Plate 15). The spencer was originally a short double-breasted overcoat, showing the tails. The name was transferred, first to a very short woman's jacket, and then (later forties) to a man's undercoat, parent of the lounge suit. David Copperfield interviews the Aunts in a spencer. Thomas Traddles, Esq., of the Inner Temple, wears a coat. The arrival of the spencer marks the decline of Early Victorian ostentation in clothing (blown upon, perhaps, by the doings of the Swell Mob and Count d'Orsay) and the movement of costume (as of manners) towards what P. G. Hamerton called 'an informal serviceableness'. Shorter hair and the Albert (watch-chain worn across the waistcoat instead of the long thin chain passed over the neck) tend in the same direction.

The two types of coat produce, as a compromise, the morning coat for all wear (Plate 16) (with its vestigial buttons in the small of the back, from the riding coat, but open in front to show waistcoat and shirt). Thus we arrive at two styles of graduated informality—spencer and morning coat; the frock coat for formal wear; and the 'full social dress' which, by 1860 had not been finally differentiated into day and evening. This differentiation—high waistcoat and a continuous curve of the coat from throat to tail, against low waistcoat and cut-away tail, and the final triumph of black and white for the evening—completes the story. This final phase is illustrated by the portraits of the great issued by Samuel Bros., Merchant Tailors of Ludgate Hill, about 1863 (Plate 21). Among the personages represented are Browning, Tennyson, and Longfellow (in morning wear), and Swinburne (in full social dress).

N. R.
G. M. Y.

CHRONOLOGICAL TABLE

CHRONOLOGICAL

Note.—The floruit is taken as the year in which the person give the date of death;

	Floruit.	Died.	Publications.
1830.	Arnold[42] Carlyle[81] Rowland Hill[79] Barry[60]	Hazlitt[78]	Lyell's Principles of Geology; Tennyson's Poems chiefly Lyrical; Milman, History of the Jews; Moore, Life of Byron.
1831.			Peacock, Crotchet Castle.
1832.	Thirlwall[75] Lyell[75]	Scott[71] Bentham[48] Crabbe[54]	Bulwer, Eugene Aram; Penny Magazine (–45); Austin, Province of Jurisprudence; H. Martineau, Illustrations of Pol. Econ. (–34); Tennyson's Poems.
1833.		A. H. Hallam[77] Wilberforce[59]	Sartor Resartus.
1834.	Stanley (Derby)[69]	Coleridge[72] Irving[92] Malthus[66] Lamb[75]	Last Days of Pompeii.
1835.	Pusey[82] Macaulay[59] Chadwick[90] Hudson[71] Decimus Burton[81]	Mrs. Hemans[93] Cobbett[62]	Thirlwall, Hist. of Greece (–47); Paracelsus; Midshipman Easy.
1836.	Newman[90] Tennyson[92] Shaftesbury[85] W. Barnes[86] D'Orsay[52] Mrs. Carlyle[66]	James Mill[73] Godwin[56]	Boz; Pericles and Aspasia; Porter's Progress of the Nation (–43); Pickwick; Pugin's Contrasts.
1837.	H. Martineau[76] Landseer[75]	Constable[76] Grimaldi[79] Soane[53]	French Revolution; Hallam, Literature of Europe (–39); Oliver Twist; McCulloch's British Empire.
1838.	Lytton[73] Borrow[81] Whitworth[87]		Nicholas Nickleby; Proverbial Philosophy (–42); Lockhart's Life of Scott; Gladstone on Church and State; Lane's Arabian Nights; Froude's Remains.
1839.	Disraeli[81] Cobden[65] Kay-Shuttleworth[77]		Voyage of the Beagle.

TABLE

named reached 35. The small figures in the floruit column in the next, of birth.

Art and Architecture.	*Public Affairs.*	*Other Events.*
.. ..	Fall of the Wellington Government. Grey P.M. Committee on London Cabs.	July Revolution. Manchester and L'pool Railway.
Travellers' Club (Barry).	Mrs. Partington. Burning of Bristol.	British Association. Faraday's electro-magnetic current.
.. ..	Reform Act.	
.. ..	Committee on Open Spaces (large towns). Committee on Agriculture. Factory Act Abolition of Slavery.	Keble's Assize Sermon.
.. ..	New Poor Law. Houses of Parliament burnt. Grey resigned; Melbourne P.M. Whigs dismissed; Peel P.M. Committee on Inebriety. Criminal Law Commission (–49).	Fox Talbot's first photograph.
Select Committee on Arts and Manufactures.	Whigs return: Melbourne P.M. Municipal Reform Act.	
Fitzwilliam (Basevi). Reform Club and Highclere (Barry). Landseer's Chief Mourner. London Art Union.		
.. ..	Negro Emancipation completed. Durham in Canada. Committee on Trade Unions. Registrar-General's First Report.	s.s. *Archimedes*. London & Birmingham Railway. *Sirius* crossed Atlantic.
St. George's Hall, Liverpool (Elmes).	Bedchamber Plot. Penny Postage Act. Birmingham Riots. Royal Commission on Police. First Factory Inspectors' Report.	Aden annexed.

	Floruit.	*Died.*	*Publications.*
1840.	Ainsworth[82] F. D. Maurice[72] Brassey[70]	Lord Holland[73]	Old Curiosity Shop; Ingoldsby Legends; Barnaby Rudge; Sordello.
1841.	J. S. Mill[73] Mrs. Browning[61] Cornwall Lewis[63]		Heroes; Punch; Tract XC; Bells and Pomegranates (–46).
1842.	..	Arnold[95]	American Notes; Lays of Ancient Rome; Tennyson's Collected Poems.
1843.	Manning[92]	Southey[74]	Past and Present; Martin Chuzzlewit; Macaulay's Essays; Liddell and Scott; Modern Painters I; Mill's Logic; Bible in Spain; Song of the Shirt; Last of the Barons.
1844.	Gladstone[98] Darwin[82] Kinglake[91] Lady Eastlake[93] Fanny Kemble[93] Monckton Milnes[85]	..	Coningsby; Vestiges of Creation; Cry of the Children; Barnes' Poems of Rural Life.
1845.	M. Tupper[89] Mrs. Gaskell[65] Armstrong[80]	Lady Holland[70] Sydney Smith[71] Mrs. Fry[80] Barham[88] Hood[99] Grey[64]	Carlyle's Cromwell; Jeames de la Pluche; Sybil; Mrs. Caudle's Curtain Lectures; Essay on Development.
1846.	Thackeray[63] Fitzgerald[83] Liddell[98] Livingstone[73] Bright[89]	Haydon[86]	Grote's Greece (–56); Lear, Book of Nonsense; Rawlinson, Behistun Inscription; Strauss's Leben Jesu (trans.).
1847.	Dickens[70] Browning[89] Smiles[04] Pugin[52]	Franklin[86] O'Connell[75] Arnold[95]	Tancred; Eothen; Princess; Comic Hist. of England; Jane Eyre; Vanity Fair; Wuthering Heights.
1848.	Aytoun[65]	Emily Brontë[18] Marryat[92] Melbourne[79] G. Stephenson[81]	Dombey; Layard's Nineveh; Mill's Political Economy; Yeast; Mary Barton; Pendennis.
1849.	C. Reade[84]	Anne Brontë[20] Maria Edgeworth[67] Brunel[69] Etty[87] Lady Blessington[89]	Household Words; Strayed Reveller; David Copperfield; Seven Lamps; Rig Veda (trans. –73); Macaulay's History (–61); The Germ; The Caxtons; Scottish Cavaliers.

Art and Architecture.	*Public Affairs.*	*Other Events.*
Trafalgar Square (Barry). Houses of Parliament begun. Landseer: Dignity and Impudence. Mulready's Envelope.	Opium War. Bombardment of Acre. Health of Towns Committee.	P. & O. incorporated. New Zealand annexed.
Houses of Parliament (Decoration) Committee. Royal Exchange (Tite).	Fall of Whig Government. Peel P.M. Factory Committee. Handloom Weavers Committee.	R.M.S.P. Company.
.. ..	Income Tax. Ashley's Act (Women and Children in Mines). Chartist Riots. Truck Committee. Ashburton Treaty. Committee on Town Housing. Sanitary Condition of Labouring Population (Chadwick).	Hong Kong annexed.
St. George's, Southwark (Pugin). Lincoln's Inn (Hardwick). Cartoons for Houses of Parliament	Rebecca Riots. Clontarf meeting. Smoke Abatement Committee. Rural Allotments Committee.	Disruption of Church of Scotland. Newman left St. Mary's.
.. ..	Bank Charter Act. Railway Act. Royal Commission on Health of Towns. Metropolitan Improvements Committee (–51).	Rochdale Pioneers.
.. ..	Railway Mania. Maynooth Grant. Potato failure.	
Cruikshank's Bottle.	Potato famine. Repeal of Corn Laws. Russell P.M. Andover Workhouse Scandal. Railway Navvies Committee.	Daily News. Evangelical Alliance.
Jenny Lind in England. British Museum (Smirke). Great Hall at Euston (Hardwick).	Fielden's Factory Act. Bank crisis. Smithfield (Removal) Committee.	Hampden controversy. Chloroform first used. Franklin expedition.
P.R.B.	Fleet Prison demolished. Public Health Act.	European Revolutions. Gorham Case.
Doyle's Manners and Customs. Millais: Isabella.	Repeal of Navigation Acts. Free Libraries Committee (–52).	Punjab annexed.

	Floruit.	*Died.*	*Publications.*
1850.	Church[90] Trollope[82]	Peel[90] Wordsworth[70] Jeffrey[73]	In Memoriam (1833–); Alton Locke; Prelude (posthumous).
1851.	C. Brontë[55] Elwin[00] C. Newton[94]	Mrs. Shelley[97]	H. Spencer's Social Statics; Cranford; Stones of Venice; Lavengro; Casa Guidi Windows; Life of Sterling.
1852.	Jowett[93] Layard[94] G. H. Lewes[74] Helen Faucit[98]	Wellington[89] Pugin[12] Moore[79] J. Doe and R. Roe	Empedocles on Etna; Esmond; Hayward's Art of Dining; Bleak House; Oxford and Cambridge Magazine.
1853.	Eliza Cook[89] Froude[94]		Verdant Green; Hypatia; The Newcomes (–55); Villette; Scholar Gipsy; Haydon's Autobiography; Heir of Redclyffe.
1854.	Clough[61] C. Kingsley[75] Q. Victoria[01] George Eliot[80] Frith[09]	C. Kemble[75]	Milman, Latin Christianity; Angel in the House (–62); Hard Times; Firmilian.
1855.	H. Spencer[03] P. Albert[61] Mansell[71] Miss Nightingale[10]	C. Brontë[20] Rogers[62]	Westward Ho!; Men and Women; The Warden; Mecca and Al-Medinah; Maud; North and South.
1856.	Burton[90] Buckle[62] Dion Boucicault[90] Madox Brown[93]	W. Hamilton[88]	Daisy Chain; Froude's History, I and II; Opium Eater (final version: first 1822); Lady Eastlake on *Modern Painters* (Quarterly); It is Never too Late to Mend.
1857.	M. Arnold[88] T. Hughes[96] Mrs. Lynn Linton[98]	D. Jerrold[03]	Aurora Leigh; Coral Island; Two Years Ago; Virginians; Buckle's History, I; Little Dorrit; Barchester Towers; Guy Livingstone; John Halifax; Tom Brown; Romany Rye; Scenes of Clerical Life.
1858.	Max Müller[00] C. Yonge[01] Freeman[92] Patmore[96]	R. Owen[71]	Defence of Guinevere; Ionica; Three Clerks; Mansell's Limits of Religious Thought; Wallace and Darwin on Natural Selection (simultaneous).

Art and Architecture.	*Public Affairs.*	*Other Events.*
Millais: Carpenter's Shop.	Don Pacifico. Papal Aggression.	Gold in California.
Landseer: Monarch of the Glen.	Ecclesiastical Titles Act. Window tax repealed. Great Exhibition. Dismissal of Palmerston. H. Mann's Report on Church Attendance.	French *Coup d'État.* Gold in Australia. Bibby Line. Livingstone reached Zambezi.
Brown: Work. Keene's first drawing in Punch. Millais: Huguenots. Ophelia.	Common Law Procedure Act. Derby P.M.: Disraeli Ch. of Ex. Aberdeen P.M.; Gladstone Ch. of Ex. New Houses of Parliament opened. Draining and Sewerage of Towns Report. Cholera Report (40/9).	
Millais: Order of Release. Frith: Ramsgate Sands.	Competitive exam. for I.C.S. Arbuthnot-Trevelyan reforms of H.C.S. Death Duties. Charity Commission.	
Doyle's Brown, Jones, and Robinson. Illustrated Tennyson (Millais, Rossetti, &c.).	Crystal Palace at Sydenham. Alma, Inkermann, Baláclava. Drink Traffic Report. Cholera Report (54).	Working Men's College.
Brown: Last of England. Church in Gordon Square (Brandon). Leighton: Cimabue.	Palmerston, P.M. Fall of Sebastopol. Limited Liability Act. Metropolitan Board of Works. Adulteration of Food Committee. Met. Communications Committee. Cathedrals Commission.	Daily Telegraph.
Millais: Autumn Leaves. Millais: Blind Girl. Mausoleum of Halicarnassus. Hunt: Scape-goat.	Peace of Paris. Life Peerage controversy.	Bombardment of Canton. Speke on Victoria Nyanza.
Millais: Sir Isumbras. Dorchester House (Vulliamy); Decorations (Stevens). Oxford Union frescoes.	Defeat and return of Palmerston. Indian Mutiny. Divorce Act. Bank crisis. Military Education Commission.	
Exeter College Chapel (Scott). Frith: Derby Day. Stevens: Wellington Monument.	Conspiracy to Murder Bill. Defeat of Palmerston. Government Buildings Report. Derby P.M. India transferred to Crown. Jews admitted to Parliament. Property qualification for M.P.'s removed.	s.s. *Great Eastern.* Ottawa capital of Canada. Oxford and Cambridge Locals.

	Floruit.	*Died.*	*Publications.*
1859.	Wilkie Collins[89]	J. Austin[90] Leigh Hunt[84] De Quincey[85] Macaulay[00] D. Cox[83] H. Hallam[77]	Origin of Species; Adam Bede; Smiles' Self-Help; Richard Feverel; Tale of Two Cities; Omar Khayyam; Mill on Liberty; (Four) Idylls of the King.
1860.	Huxley[95] Blackmore[80] Birket Foster[99] Ballantyne[94]	..	Woman in White; Mill on the Floss; Cornhill; Notes on Nursing; Unto this Last; Great Expectations; Evan Harrington; Essays and Reviews.
1861.	Bagehot[77] R. H. Hutton[97]	P. Albert[20] Mrs. Browning[06] A. H. Clough[19]	Silas Marner; Golden Treasury; Framley Parsonage; Philip; Cloister and Hearth; Gryll Grange; Science of Languages; Mrs. Beeton; Maine's Ancient Law.
1862.	Speke[64]	Buckle[21]	Modern Love; Derby's Homer; Goblin Market; Ravenshoe.
1863.	Meredith[04] Rossetti[82] Lightfoot[89]	Lyndhurst[72] Thackeray[11] Whately[87]	Man's Place in Nature; Kinglake's Crimea; Gardiner's History, I and II; Water Babies; Romola; Lyell's Antiquity of Man.
1864.	Millais[96] S. R. Gardiner[02]	Landor[75]	Enoch Arden; Wives and Daughters; Apologia; Small House at Allington; Dramatis Personae; Atalanta in Calydon.
1865.	Miss Rossetti[94]	Greville[94] Rowan Hamilton[05] Mrs. Beeton[36] Cobden[04] Palmerston[85] Wiseman[02]	Alice in Wonderland; Fortnightly Review; Ecce Homo; Lecky's History of Rationalism; Freeman's Norman Conquest, I; Essays in Criticism; Sesame and Lilies.

Art and Architecture.	*Public Affairs.*	*Other Events.*
Red House, Bexley. Millais: Vale of Rest. Landseer's Lions in Trafalgar Square (–66).	Derby defeated; Palmerston P.M. Gladstone Ch. of Ex.	Franco-Austrian War. Livingstone on Lake Nyassa.
Du Maurier's first picture in Punch. Whistler: At the Piano.	Cobden treaty with France. Volunteer movement. Museums Committee (Sunday opening).	Annexation of Savoy. Garibaldi in Sicily and Naples. Burning of Summer Palace. Brown's armour plate. Source of Nile discovered.
Morris & Co. founded. Whitehall (Scott).	Trent incident. Elementary Education: Newcastle Commission. Elementary Education: Revised Code.	Victor Emmanuel king of Italy. American Civil War.
Frith: Railway Station.	Lancashire Cotton Famine (–64).	Colenso controversy.
Whistler: Symphony in White.		Taiping rebellion.
Albert Memorial (Scott).	Rural Housing Report. Public Schools Commission (Clarendon).	Schleswig-Holstein. Geneva Convention.
St. Pancras (Scott).	Met. Open Spaces Committee. Jamaica Rising.	Antiseptic surgery.

I

WORK AND WAGES

§ 1. THE ECONOMIC BALANCE.

§ 2. AGRICULTURE AND THE COUNTRY.

§ 3. LONDON.

§ 4. THE TEXTILE TRADES.

§ 5. COAL AND IRON.

§ 6. ENGINEERING.

§ 7. THE ORGANIZATION OF LABOUR.

§ 8. THE ECONOMIC RHYTHM.

I

WORK AND WAGES

By J. H. CLAPHAM

§ 1. THE ECONOMIC BALANCE

EIGHTEEN months before Victoria came to the throne, the Corn Law being still intact, the price of wheat dropped to a figure which would have been thought low in the early years of George III. Helped by a succession of splendid harvests, it had been falling year after year since 1831. That was probably why the Whigs did not worry about the Corn Law and why statesmen who knew something of the land, and most statesmen of the thirties and forties did, had hopes that improved farming might keep pace with population, and the country remain economically balanced between agriculture, manufactures, and commerce. They were to be disappointed; but even in the forties, before the potatoes rotted in Ireland, good home harvests could still make reasonable prices; and in the fifties, after Peel's decision had thrown the market doors wide open, only about a quarter of the wheat consumed in the country, and a very much smaller proportion of the other essential foodstuffs, was brought from overseas. Imported food merely stopped the gaps in the home supply and kept prices from rising unduly in years of shortage.

The scales were tilting steadily to the side of manufactures and commerce all through the early Victorian age; but at its close the balance was not even yet upset. 'We come,' the Commissioners for the Census of 1861 in England and Wales wrote, as they approached the agricultural population, 'we come to the great central productive class of the country in which 2,010,454 persons are employed.' To the whole of industry and commerce, in town and country, they assigned less than 5,500,000 persons. Scotland was slightly more agricultural than England; Ireland very much more. The population of 'urban districts' in England and Wales only just got above that of 'rural districts' in 1851. The gap was widening fast during the following decades, with the help of a completed railway system; but not until 1881 would the urban population be more than double the rural. In 1861 it stood to it in the ratio of 5 to 4.

The free traders of the forties and fifties never dreamed that the country could become in any thorough way dependent on foreign food supplies. They quoted a few simple figures to show that, putting all other facts and arguments aside, the fleets of the whole world were not capacious enough to make it so. They supposed, therefore, that the harvest would remain what it always had been, a thing of direct personal economic interest to every Englishman; and for the early Victorian age their supposition was right. It was not merely that bread prices fluctuated with the harvests—they varied in London between 6*d*. and 11*d*. the four-pound loaf in years of peace during the free-trade fifties—but that these fluctuations affected the whole rhythm of the economic life of the country, very much as they had while the Corn Law stood. Indeed, the fluctuations were greater, and the effects on the rhythm possibly more marked, between 1847 and 1865 than they had been between 1836 and 1846. When harvests were bad, and bread was dear, a generation which lived far more nearly by bread alone than its successors find it easy to conceive had its power of purchasing other things curtailed, and the home trade flagged. When harvests were good, and corn was cheap, the situation was reversed. Farmers, it is true, received less per quarter for their wheat; but this was more than compensated on the average by the greater number of quarters which they got from their fields. They looked on the high prices of wet years only as part compensation for losses of crops and increased working costs. For a short spell, in the years 1848–52, after the Corn Law was repealed and the famine years in Ireland, which had made all food dear, were over, they were discouraged by a run of low prices; but the pressure of population on the food supplies, with a little help from the American War and the weather, soon corrected that; and, as the cost of importing corn by sailing-ship was still relatively high, they generally got remunerative prices even in the most abundant years. Besides, the prices of all their other standard products were going up—oats and barley, meat, milk, butter and wool—and this kept them in good humour even when rather unusually low wheat prices recurred, as they did for about a year in 1858–9, and for about two years in 1863–5. Any trifle of discouragement which such years might bring was outweighed by the fact that a man who paid less for his bread probably ate more meat or drank more beer, and certainly spent his saved pence on something which some one, if not necessarily the farmer, had produced.

In less obvious ways also rural prosperity, fluctuating with the harvests, touched the welfare of the manufacturers and the towns. Between the thirties and the fifties, the habit of keeping bank accounts was growing fast among farmers. Their deposits, made more or less all the year round, but most in the autumn, went to swell those of their landlords and of the tradesmen of country towns in the country banks. Gurney or Stuckey of the country bank lent the surplus cash, most abundant when crops were heavy and rents promptly paid, to London bill-brokers—especially to Overend and Gurney, the early Victorian 'bankers' bankers'. With it the brokers discounted the bills of the manufacturing midlands and north, and so furnished circulating capital to industry. Thus the accumulations of 'the great central productive class' helped to finance other groups of producers.

§ 2. AGRICULTURE AND THE COUNTRY

English agriculture was still a model for other countries, as it had been early in the century, when a book about it is held to have opened the modern era in the agriculture of Germany. Coke of Norfolk, an agricultural pioneer to whom all the world made pilgrimage, only died—in an extreme and vigorous old age—in 1842. Englishmen wrote much, and Scotsmen more, about their agricultural shortcomings and the slow spread of enlightened farming. All that they said was true; but so was what a visiting French expert, or rather his somewhat uninspired translator, wrote in 1854: 'The fact is, that English agriculture, taken as a whole, is at this day the first in the world; and it is in the way of realizing further progress.'[1] Success had been attained mainly by the systematic growth of fodder crops on land which had once been left fallow; by intelligent breeding of sheep and cattle, and by the unique success with which sheep-farming and arable farming had been blended; by a proper utilization of the island's great natural advantages for grazing; by the

[1] Léonce de Lavergne, *The Rural Economy of England, Scotland, and Ireland* (1855), p. 2.

ruthless sweeping away of the ancient conservative open-field husbandry, and the inclosure of nearly every cultivable common, which had prepared the ground for the 'improver'; and by what seemed to the visiting expert an extraordinary simplification and standardization of agricultural routine. He was amazed at the breadth of pasture to be found even in districts primarily arable, although imported corn had barely begun to encourage its extension when he saw England. The 'furze and broom and heath' of the Surrey commons seemed to him '*souvenirs* of the ancient state of the country'. Open fields, with their mixed-up, unenclosed strips, so familiar in his north French home, he never mentioned. Probably he never saw one. There had been still a fair number scattered about the country when Victoria came to the throne; though in no district were they then at all general. They had been enclosed, rearranged, and fenced rapidly during the next fifteen years. When an agricultural writer of the sixties came across a few survivors he was distressed, and 'hastened to draw a veil' by saying no more about them.[1] By the late Victorian age they were almost forgotten, except by those who handled documents of title to land; and the surviving commons were being protected, less as grazing ground for village herds, than as 'open spaces' for a crowded people.

The standard agricultural routine, as the French visitor saw it, was thus—plenty of grass, whether natural or artificial; 'two roots—the potato and turnip; two spring cereals —barley and oats; and a winter one—wheat; all these plants linked together by an alternating course of cereals or white crops, with forage or green crops, commencing with roots or plants which require to be hoed, and ending with wheat; this is the whole secret. The English have discarded all other crops, such as sugar-beet, tobacco, oleaginous plants, and fruit'[2] —all but the hops and the Kentish fruits and the Irish flax, that is. They 'are not great consumers of fruit and vegetables, and they are right; for both the one and the other with them are very tasteless'. So the Frenchman, in hard concise outline, and with all the truth that is compatible with such concision.

To him, as to any continental, the concentration of land-

[1] *Journal of the Royal Agricultural Society* (1864), p. 301.
[2] Lavergne, op. cit., p. 64.

ownership in England was astonishing. The census of 1861 would put 30,100 landed proprietors into its 'great central productive class'. That means an average of well over 1,000 acres to each proprietor. But as the class included little squires, miscellaneous small proprietors, and the remnant of the cultivating freeholders, the 'yeomen', one must picture the typical landed gentleman with his several thousands of acres, and the typical nobleman with his many thousands. Perhaps noblemen and gentlemen were not all productive in the strict economic sense; but from them had come the patrons and leaders of the new agriculture. In Britain they were rarely absentees, except when serving the State. They were glad to get back from its service to their field drainage—all progressive landlords were draining—to the farming covenants with their tenants which safeguarded the reformed agriculture, and to their new farm-buildings; yes, and to the partridges and the foxes. Men 'born to hunt and vote and raise the price of corn' the critic from their own ranks had called them; but, as a class, they had always cared about the raising of the corn, whatever the price. John Stuart Mill, who held that non-cultivating landowners could only justify their existence by being land improvers, allowed, in 1848, that 'in Great Britain the landed proprietor is not infrequently an improver'. His added verdict, 'but it cannot be said that he is generally so', was perhaps harsh, though it might certainly be upheld. There was not the improvement that there might have been because, apart from the neglect or extravagance of individuals, the class habit of strict family settlements and charges upon the estate for widows and daughters and younger sons often left the heir, a mere life-tenant, short of free capital. And yet no country had been so generally or so much improved by its landowners.

Through the small squires, there was an economic gradation, but usually with sharp social dividing lines, downwards to what remained of the cultivating freeholders. Prosperous during the great French wars, this class had suffered intensely from post-war price falls and fluctuations, and was described by expert witnesses as being in very low water on the eve of the Victorian age. It had dwindled, but it did not vanish. Almost everywhere remnants could be found, and in some districts—the Fens, the Yorkshire and Cumberland dales, Clun Forest, parts of Suffolk and Kent, and elsewhere

—strong remnants. The cultivating freeholder was usually a poor conservative farmer who 'lived nearly as a workman', as was said of the Kentish type in 1833. Often he suffered, like his great neighbours, from the burdening of his property with jointures, charges, and mortgages. So every now and again he was sold up, and the great neighbour, or, more probably, some new man from the towns, bought. But he and his like still cultivated, in their own way, perhaps 10 per cent. of the land of early Victorian England; of Wales much less; of Scotland really none at all. There it was all landlord and tenant.

A few fortunate yeomen families had bought their way up gradually into the gentry. More often, when fortunate, yeomen had joined the class of the big tenant-farmers, selling their inherited acres to stock a large farm, or adding to them land rented from the neighbouring squire. The average English farm seemed gigantic to visitors from peasant countries. And it was growing bigger, but so slowly that figures taken in 1851 will serve for the whole generation of which that year is the middle. It was then of 111 acres.[1] In many of the western counties, in Wales, and in the crofting parts of Scotland, a much smaller holding was normal. In Lancashire and Cheshire nine-tenths of the farms were under 100 acres, and in Lancashire alone two-thirds were under 40. But that was on the wet, grazing side of the country where, as Cobden used to say, people were not interested in corn laws because they grew so little corn. Half the farmed land of England, including most of the arable area, was in holdings of at least 200 acres; and nearly a sixth was in holdings of 500 acres and upwards. Over them rode the big Victorian farmer whose ''erse's legs' beat out 'proputty, proputty, proputty', the kind of hard-fisted, top-booted man who followed the hounds, voted with squire, served with him in the yeomanry, and with him had perhaps ridden down handfuls of rebellious labourers in 1830; and who could be pictured saying that 'the poor in a loomp is bad'. The farmer in that picture was buying his land—'feyther run oop to the farm, an' I runs oop to the mill';[2] most were content to rent it.

[1] For England and Wales; for Great Britain the figure was 102, because the Scottish average was only 74. The figures are from returns made at the census of 1851.

[2] Tennyson, *The Northern Farmer: New Style.*

WORK—*FORD MADOX BROWN*

By permission of the Manchester Corporation

Yet only a part of the country was cultivated by these men, separated from their labourers by a whole world. The 100- to 200-acre man was a regular employer, but was hardly in their class. Mixed up with these middling farmers almost everywhere, and dominant down the west side of the island, were the small men—small by English standards—who could manage their land with the help of their families and, at most, a hired man or two or a little casual help from migrant Irishmen at haymaking or harvest time. There were 102,000 farmers in England and Wales with less than 50 acres each at the census of 1851; and 142,000 with less than 100 acres. Those with less than 50 would seldom need regular hired labour; those with from 50 to 100 would not need much. There was only a narrow social gap between them and their men, when they had any; and the single labourer still frequently lived 'in' as one of the household. In Wales there were whole counties in which there were more labourers living 'in' than 'out' at the census of 1861. Among the crofters of the Highlands and the Isles wage-workers of any kind were unknown. So imperfectly, even in capitalistic Britain, had the rural holding yet lost the character assigned to it in the very earliest English land-charters: *terra unius familiae*.

One result of this was that in the whole of England and Wales there were only about five labourers or farm servants to every farmer or cultivating freeholder.[1] The five includes the lads, the dairymaids, and the, rather rare, outdoor women agricultural labourers. As most labouring families supplied more than one private to the army of the farm-steads and fields, the ratio of labouring to farming families was between three and two to one, instead of five to one. For though English agriculture may properly be called capitalistic, its organization had not much in common with the growing capitalism of contemporary industry. Farmers were wasteful of labour power and slow to adopt machinery. In some parts of the south slowness had been inculcated as a social duty by their landlords—to avoid anti-threshing-machine riots such as had occurred in 1830. By the sixties you could find nearly everywhere threshing machinery of some kind, even the steam kind—'the endless ladder and the booming wheel'; but in lonely districts the flail still rose and

[1] Corresponding figures for Scotland are not available.

fell winter by winter, and it was forgotten hardly anywhere. All the best farmers drilled their corn in England; but none, good or bad, drilled it in Wales. Before the fifties, a really efficient reaping machine was unknown. Plenty of corn was still reaped with the sickle so near London as Hertfordshire in 1864. A great deal of the Middlesex hay was cut for the mews of London with the scythe. At that time there was much talk about steam-ploughing; but only a few score thousand acres were steam-ploughed. Very likely there was as much ploughed by oxen. Ploughs and other implements were steadily improved; but the economy of labour with them was not great. Yet the most wasteful use of man-power could not easily require much more than one regular worker to every 40 acres—ten or twelve men to a 400-acre farm. And as no part of England was all laid out in 400-acre farms, only in a few big-farm parishes could labourers outnumber farmers by ten or twelve to one.

Wasteful use of labour was easy, especially in the south and east, where most of the big farms were, because labour was—in the phrase of the day—redundant, and cheap. Under William IV the Whigs had stopped that supplementing of wages from the rates which had been generalized, as a social emergency measure for years of scarcity, during the French wars, and continued through legislative timidity or administrative inertia when war was over. They had remodelled the Poor Law in 1834; created the Unions of parishes and the Union Workhouses; and issued to nearly all rural Unions an order forbidding not merely grants in aid of wages, but every kind of outdoor relief, to able-bodied people. (The Scottish law made no provision for any relief to the able-bodied, either before or after its reform in 1845.) Fortunately for farmers and the Government, cheap bread during the years 1834–7 had permitted the final stoppage of rate-aid to wages, and the blunt refusal of outdoor relief to the able-bodied to be enforced, without too great misery in the countryside, or more than a slight rise in wages. After that, through the troubles and political vicissitudes of the forties, wages fluctuated very little. In 1853 they rose sharply; and though they fell again when the Crimean War was over, in the last years of the early Victorian age they were more than 20 per cent. higher than they had been at their lowest during it—in the years of very cheap bread, 1848–52.

These are figures for 'the poor in a loomp', as the northern farmer said. Near London, near the industrial towns, near the coal-mines, the competition of urban and industrial employments had improved their wage position above the national average. *Per contra*, in the most stagnant and backward counties it was necessarily below. Here, in the deep country, 'redundant labour' had been called into being and retained by the old rules of 'settlement' which gave a man the best chance of poor relief in the parish of his birth. Here, too, there had grown up that familiar early Victorian distinction between the 'close' and the 'open' parish—the 'close' all in one man's hands, or dominated by one man, in which a limit could be set to 'redundancy' and to poor-rate liability by control of the supply of cottages; the 'open' where the land was in many hands and there had been nothing to prevent the running-up of cheap cottages by little country speculators in the housing of the poor. It was in open parishes, and from the mean streets of little market towns, that those mixed agricultural gangs—children, women, a few men—were recruited, which were marched out to weed and gather in the stones on east midland farms reclaimed so recently from fen, or heath, or wold, that they lacked resident labour. From the open parishes, too, men often tramped to their work in the close, where they could get pay, but not a roof or a claim on the rates. By the end of the age, legislation had regulated the conduct of the gangs; and cottage-building, with the completion of the first clearing and weeding of newly farmed land, had reduced farmers' need of them. Exactly at its close, in 1865, the Union Chargeability Act took away the temptation for the close parish to use labour from the open without incurring a corresponding liability for poor rates, by making the Union, not the single parish, the unit for all purposes of administration. Hitherto there had been a Union workhouse, but parishes had contributed to it yearly only in proportion to the numbers of their 'settled' poor who were sent there.

Meanwhile, one well-considered project of the Poor Law reformers of 1834 had miscarried. Disgusted by the abuses of those mixed workhouses which were to be found under the old laws in most towns and in some country districts—the workhouse of Crabbe's *Village* or of *Oliver Twist*—they had recommended separate houses in each Union for children, for the aged, for able-bodied men, and for able-bodied women. These could have been administered on different and equitable lines. But it had been found more convenient to amalgamate and centralize; and this had been done universally. The one new, gaunt, brick building held children, sick, and aged, with those destitute able-bodied men and women who were inevitably often of weak or doubtful character. There were rules for separation and segregation; but they were difficult to devise and were often ill kept. And so 'the house', deliberately made 'deterrent' to encourage the able-bodied to shift for themselves, contained also the children, there through no fault of their own, and only too many of the 'redundant' aged and infirm. That was so not only on the land. Prince Albert in 1849 started a movement whose aim was to wipe out the disgrace of half the adult poor in the workhouse of St. George's, Hanover Square, and two-thirds in that of Marylebone, being unemployed or broken-down domestic servants from those most respectable quarters.

Poor Law reformers had always looked to migration or emigration to relieve pressure in the overcrowded parts of the countryside. Under the Act of 1834 Guardians were authorized to help the destitute people to emigrate. They never did much of that. In 1864–5 the number of people so helped was thirty-six—an absolute minimum it is true. An attempt to transfer families from the deep country of the south to the cotton districts, made in the early years of the reformed law, had confirmed Lancashire and the West Riding in the belief that the aim of Poor Law reformers was to punish the poor for their poverty; the appropriate method an import of docile folk accustomed to low pay who would serve, in a time of slack trade and unemployment, as what was already called 'blackleg' labour. Some of the assisted migrants wrote gratefully to the Poor Law Commissioners; but that did nothing to increase the goodwill of the cotton-workers. There was, indeed, little but ill will towards those Commissioners who, besides all this, had insisted on the building of what north countrymen called, not workhouses, but Bastilles, State prisons.

The really effective official help to migration was given, not by the Poor Law, but by the Colonial Land and Emigration Commissioners, from 1847 onwards. They selected and helped, on an average, between 9,000 and 10,000 British emigrants, and several thousands of Irish emigrants, every year—most in the early years, when need was greatest and Australia's demand for men was at its height. Yet this assisted emigration, which was directed mainly to Australasia, was only a fragment of the whole. Between 1853 and 1860, when the flight from Ireland after the famine had already slackened, 36,000 people from Great Britain, and 80,000 from Ireland, went to North America, and 48,000 mixed British and Irish went to Australasia every year. What proportion of the assisted or independent emigrants were countrymen is not known, but it was certainly high.

Emigration alone would never have relieved pressure in any village, for population was growing fast all the time in spite of it. But the first spell of active railway building happened to come immediately after the reform of the Poor Law; and the railway mania proper, when the country was being cut open, banked up, tunnelled, and bridged everywhere with furious energy, coincided with the most difficult years of the Law's administration in the middle forties. The leading 'navigators' were rough professionals who moved about with the great railway contractors, even following Thomas Brassey to make railways abroad; but they were recruited from those who could handle spade and barrow, and their arrival in a district meant a good temporary demand for local labour and a chance of permanent enlistment with them for young men of their sort. When built, the railway offered careers in its service to some countrymen, and, for those who could afford it, a quick easy road up to town, where there was an almost insatiable demand for general labourers; and above them for men who could manage horses; and above them for picked upstanding countrymen to fill the lengthening ranks of the police.

In many of these careers, especially in the humblest, the venturing countryman had to face the competition of the immigrant Irish, with their standard of living well below his own, which was itself low enough. Indeed, he met Irishmen in the fields in certain parts of England, and occasionally in Scotland; but not often in winter. They had been familiar in London and in a few other towns even in the eighteenth century. They had come first as seasonal migrants. In the country, they seldom got beyond that position, arriving for the hay and staying to help with the corn in districts where native labour was not redundant and was relatively dear, like the hayfields of Middlesex and south Lancashire. There was little chance of their obtaining a settlement from the parochial authorities in any village, either before or after the reform of the Poor Law; though sometimes a knot of them established itself in a country market town. Hence their sustained migratory habits. Hence, too, their frequence in navvy gangs, which were not interested in settlement. But in the towns, especially in London, the Lancashire towns, Edinburgh and Glasgow, they had become sessile, as the zoologists say, in great numbers before the Victorian age. There had been attempts to apply Poor Law principles; but the forcible carting and shipping of destitute Irishmen from London towards Connemara had not been a success. It was easier and cheaper to give them a little help to which they were not legally entitled. So they stayed, and their children got settlement in slum parishes. They were general labourers, builders' labourers, dock labourers, in the first generation; labourers in Welsh ironworks also, and in the textile towns weavers, and spinners, and wool-combers. Without them the transformation and expansion of the industries of Lancashire and Wales, and, in a less degree, of Yorkshire, would not have been possible at the rate in fact recorded; though how good that acceleration was for them, or for Lancashire, or for Wales, is an open question.

With the potato famine of 1845–7 the Irish came in at a terrifying rate. By July 1, 1847, not less than 300,000 had landed at Liverpool and a quarter of these had stayed there —destitute, starving, suffering from small-pox and hunger typhus. The rest had drifted inland, mostly to Manchester and the cotton towns. 'In different parts of Liverpool fifty or sixty were found in a house containing three or four small rooms; and in more than one instance upwards of forty were found sleeping in a cellar.'[1] From these nurseries of disease, fever 'gradually crept up among the wealthier classes of society', even into Toxteth Park. Cellar dwelling was an old habit with the immigrant Irish. Wherever the sanitary inquiries of the thirties and forties report it as specially prevalent—in Liverpool, Manchester, Leeds—it is always

[1] From a report of 1847 quoted in Hope, E. W., *Health at the Gateway* (1931), p. 44.

connected with them, though not confined to them. 'Boz's' account of a slum tenement in Seven Dials, published in 1836, ends with 'an Irish labourer and his family in the back kitchen'. (Kitchens in Seven Dials were rarely above ground.) It can hardly be an accident that towns to which the Irish only penetrated in small and manageable numbers —Birmingham, Leicester, Nottingham—were never much troubled with this social disease. Not that any one blames the starving family from a Connaught cabin for huddling into a Liverpool cellar. Where else should they go when 30,000 other such families had landed in the Mersey that year? There were no famine camps for them.

So voracious were the towns and their industries that they absorbed—in a fashion—the Irish, very many English countrymen, and their own surplus children; for, thanks to doctors, hospitals, and drains, a town could now breed some surplus of its own. In the eighteenth century towns had usually, and properly, been classed with armies and navies as devourers of men. Had they not become, if not yet healthy, still very much healthier, and had the Irish not been always there to meet their coarser needs, their drag upon the villages would have been greater and sooner felt—unless, indeed, the villager, however 'redundant' at home, had refused to sell himself at the Irishman's price, and so had slowed down town growth, which might have been for England's good. But that is all speculative. As things happened, the strictly agricultural population had at least become stationary, and may have begun to decline, by 1851. Even the population enumerated in rural districts, a very different group, grew by less than 2 per cent. during the fifties: with the sixties it began to fall. And in the sixties the purchasing power of the agricultural labourer's earnings, his real wage, hitherto almost stationary, moved up a perceptible fraction. Machinery was coming in too slowly to act as a direct threat to the wage level, or as an obvious driver of honest unadaptable men to the workhouse. Migration, emigration, and transfers from agricultural to other kinds of work in the rural districts themselves, had at length given the farm labourers' skill faint beginnings of a scarcity value; though that was hardly appreciated by those most interested in his welfare. No doubt the coming of the Irish had postponed that dim dawn—by how much no one can say.

Some English labourers had recognized the danger, when faced with it directly, long before. Irishmen had first appeared in Lincolnshire in 1831: 'the native labourers assembled in great numbers and drove them away'. But against Irish competition working indirectly through the towns, or through those rural districts relatively short of labour, which but for the Irish must have drawn on other rural districts, such simple methods were not available. Nor had they often been tried. Nine years after the close of the early Victorian age, the drafting in of Irish labour was one of the methods adopted by East Anglian farmers to break the greatest, the only great, agricultural labourers' strike of the century.

But if the English labourer's position was not yet strong, no doubt it had improved. Economists did not any more write of him as redundant. 'Able-bodied pauperism' on the land had greatly declined, though far too many old people there still ended their days in 'the house'. And whenever times were good, sometimes even when they were not, all the greater and better landlords had been building and rebuilding what were known as 'estate cottages', to distinguish them from the small speculative builder's cottages in open villages, or the ancient tumble-down freehold cottages, copyhold cottages, and squatters' cottages of dubious tenure on the skirts of old commons or former forests, which still housed an important group of the labouring families, especially in the south-west. It was from Somerset, just after the close of the early Victorian age, that a Government commissioner sent the depressing report, which might, nevertheless, perhaps have been anticipated, that the worst cottages were generally the small freeholds housing the small freeholder. Such might be bad, indeed—two scanty rooms; walls of wattle-and-daub or, more probably in the west, of 'cob'; roof of thatch, and it leaky, and as many occupants as the family had members. Places no better were to be found, less or more, in every county. There were some particularly bad ones in the Cambridgeshire fens. But the average labourer's cottage was better than that—brick or stone built according to the district, and with three or four rooms. The typical 'estate cottage' was much better, and as often as not it had five rooms. By building the best of these, landlords helped to justify their existence to John Stuart Mill; but some of the lesser owners, poor squires who had not a Duke of Bedford's resources from London rentals to spend on estate improvement, and who found themselves gibbeted by reformers, thought the Dukes had set too hot a pace. And no doubt there were owners who thought very little at all; some of them absentee ecclesiastical and collegiate corporations—Deans and Chapters, Masters and Fellows—whose lands were so let, on long beneficial leases not to farming tenants but to local persons of importance acting as middlemen, that the legal owners' interest in estate matters was intermittent and, therefore, slight.

Few things in England had altered less than the lives of craftsmen and traders in the villages and country towns. The village might have been enclosed, its whole field-map rubbed out and redrawn, since 1760 or 1800, but the smithy was probably just what and where it had always been. True, the village weaver who worked up homespun wool and flax for the farm-houses, the man who was called the weaver as his neighbour might be called the baker, was almost extinct. He had been dying out for a long time, and had survived only here and there to the start of the Victorian age, particularly in the east midlands, where one of the last representatives of the class was drawn by George Eliot in *Silas Marner*. But some other ancient types were wonderfully little changed. From among the blacksmiths and the wheelwrights principally, there had grown up a few large-scale makers of agricultural implements and machinery; but the ordinary day's work, and the ordinary scale of business, among blacksmiths and wheelwrights, and for that matter among saddlers and tanners, was very little changed. Not one blacksmith in seven, of the many thousands who made returns at the census of 1851, employed three men. The average master blacksmith had his mate and perhaps a lad, the ordinary handicraftsman's staff of the Middle Ages. In the wheelwright's business there was more variety and specialization: the staff was normally rather bigger. But even of the wheelwrights, only about one in every five had three men or more under him. The country tanner was a bigger man than the wheelwright, and always had been; yet his normal staff, so far as is known, was only between five and ten; and a good many of those who made returns in 1851 employed less than five. As for technique—but for a little more iron in the wheelwright's shop, there had been no change worth mentioning in any of these trades.

Still less changed, at least in true country districts, was the oldest of mechanical trades, that of the miller. Even in very large towns, although the steam-drive had replaced water or wind, the rest of the mechanism was much what it had been under George II, or even under Edward II. Chaucer's miller from Trumpington would not have been puzzled in the early Victorian King's Mill downstream at Cambridge. And many of the true village mills, most of which survived on or near their ancient sites, were little, if any, bigger than they had been in Edward II's reign. Nearly half the millers who made returns in 1851 said that they employed only one or two men. The steam-drive had facilitated milling in towns where water or wind milling had, for one reason or another, been difficult—in London, for instance, which in the eighteenth century had mainly consumed country-milled flour. Free trade and the heavy imports of wheat which followed it were bringing business to these steam mills on tide water. But neither they nor the wheat imports were yet great enough to encourage and enable England to do without the mills of the villages and country towns. Concentration of milling at the ports, with roller-grinding and the organization of that succession of mechanical processes on which the modern industry depends, was a late Victorian development.

There were rich men among the country millers, not because mills were big, but because the business had often been combined with corn and flour-dealing, or had been subordinated to these as a corn-merchant's side line. Many banking firms had grown out of composite businesses of this sort; and the corn-merchant banker of the country town was a recognized Victorian type. Tennyson's 'wealthy miller' in his meal-laden atmosphere, whose smile 'was full of dealings with the world', though a regular countryman, and so not quite of the type, can hardly have got his wealth from that narrow local dealing and grinding on commission which was the minimum of the rural miller's trade.

Rich shopkeepers also were not uncommon in the country, in the county towns at least. George Hudson, a farmer's son, had made a very comfortable fortune as a linen-draper at York long before he became a king of the new railways.

York was something of a metropolis, as were most county towns, and offered metropolitan opportunities to the retailer. Besides the townsmen, all the lesser gentry, the clergy, and the substantial farmers of the neighbourhood came into them for supplies, seldom dealing with London; so that the retailer's position was stronger in some ways, especially in the home counties, during the thirties and early forties, than it became later, when London was so much more accessible. Compared with other countries, however, it was remarkably strong everywhere: the English, if not a nation of shopkeepers, were a nation of shop-users. Even before 1800 'in the Midland and Southern counties, the [country] labourer in general purchased a very considerable portion, if not the whole, of his clothes from the shopkeeper';[1] and his bread from the baker; and his meat, when he could afford it, from the butcher; and so did those above him. In the north, and in Scotland, at that time home production of clothing had been commoner, and baking at home universal. Pedlars, and occasional visits to markets or fairs, had met the rest of the domestic needs both of labourers and of farmers. But the village shop had been spreading north; even the village bakery a little. Since the roads of England had become good, shops had been encouraged and supplied by the commercial 'bagmen' who drove everywhere in their gigs and made more than half the business and, as contemporaries said, the excellence of the English wayside inn. It was one of these bagmen who told Mr. Pickwick the story of Tom Smart, in the commercial room of the 'Peacock' at Eatanswill.

When *Pickwick* began to appear in 1836, though the air was full of railway projects, England of the roads was almost untouched. Gig and coach, ostler and guard, and the great ritual of changing horses, seemed barely threatened. There were railways; but they were local affairs, mostly on the coalfields, largely engaged in mineral traffic, and some of them still using horse traction. But the projectors and constructors were at work, and their leaders already had clearly in mind not just railways, but a railway system. Ten years later, for Mr. Carker, travelling back from Dijon after his failure with Edith Dombey, there was still, on the French side of the Channel, 'the monotony of bells and wheels, and horses' feet,

[1] Eden, Sir F. M., *The State of the Poor*, Bk. ii, ch. 2.

and no rest'; but on the English side 'the trembling and vibration' of the 'fiery devil, thundering along so smoothly tracked through the distant valley by a glare of light and lurid smoke, and gone'.[1] It was so in every valley of the country along which traffic naturally ran. By December 31, 1848, when people were reading *Dombey and Son*, out that year, there were 5,127 miles of railway open in the United Kingdom, and over 2,000 miles more under construction by an army of about 175,000 navvies and miscellaneous work-people. Coaches were extinct on all the main routes. All thought of making more canals, or of a national road policy, had faded away; for, as some one said not many years later, the traffic on the North Road was now as local in character as that on any common parish highway. Projectors, engineers, and navvies had done their work quickly and well. And already, by that administrative combination of the railway lines first constructed in which George Hudson excelled, the skeletons of the great companies, as they existed down to 1923, were taking shape. By 1865 they had almost reached their final forms.

England, which had been intensely proud of her coaching achievement in 1836, was almost bewildered by the quick success of the railway. 'It is impossible', a most serious student of railway economics wrote in 1850, 'to regard the vast buildings and their dependencies, which constitute a chief terminal station of a great line of railway, without feelings of inexpressible astonishment. . . .'[2] And then the speed! 'So rapid are the communications that it is frequently announced that this or that professor or artist will, on Monday evening, deliver a lecture or entertainment in Liverpool, on Tuesday in Manchester, on Wednesday in Preston, on Thursday in Halifax, and so forth.'[3] These were centres of industry. Through the real country towns professors and artists circulated, no doubt, less freely. The ordinary townsmen there only became acquainted gradually with railway speed: 'Not much in the habit of travelling by rail myself, Sir,' the waiter in the railway inn, which served a small town lying some miles off the line, said to Mr. Carker. At that time many such towns were not linked to the railway

[1] *Dombey and Son* was written in 1846.
[2] Dionysius Lardner, LL.D., *Railway Economy* (1850), p. 122.
[3] Op. cit., p. 18.

system. Linkage went on steadily, however, during the next fifteen years; for any town which the first railway network missed suffered for it, and was eager to be included. The bagmen, and the corn and the coal, were now moving by rail, which was important. By the end, very few towns, even of the third rank, had not got their new railway station. Their business life was quickened. Here and there some structural change in it might be beginning, aided by the railway, as when—towards the end of the age—knitting or shoemaking, carried on hitherto as semi-rural outwork industries, began to gather into factories. Here and there, again, the railways made a town out of nearly nothing—a port hitherto inaccessible, or a colonial town of their own, as contemporaries called it, like Crewe. But in the average country town quickening of the pulse began late and accelerated very gradually. In villages off the rail, and most villages were off it, there might be no more than a throbbing in the ears, a sound of speed far off; though even that was exciting.

§ 3. LONDON

London had been growing by about a quarter of a million a decade before the railway terminal stations were designed. They helped it to double that rate of growth in the decades following 1841. Concurrently, they hastened the dispersion of the more comfortable Londoners into suburbs, a process which had set in more than a generation earlier. But it was not until the end of the early Victorian age that they did anything to spread out thinner the whole London population. Even the emptying of the City, its change from a place of residence to a place of business, did not begin until the fifties. There were more people domiciled in it in 1851 than at any previous census, including many of the clerks in the Bank of England—and the cattle were still driven through its streets to Smithfield Market on a Monday. The emptying began slowly somewhere about 1855, and did not become marked until after 1861, when it was helped by the Metropolitan Railway, 'the underground', opened in 1863. The early emptying was not, effectively, into suburbs or into the country; only into other parts of central London—Seven Dials, perhaps, or St. Giles'; or across the river into the pestilent undrained slums of the Surrey side, which Charles Kingsley described, with no trace of exaggeration, in *Alton*

Locke. It was from about the date of the opening of the Metropolitan that the pressure began to relax a very little in the whole mass of some 1,200,000 people inhabiting the central districts. The early Victorian London workman invariably lived near his work; nothing else was possible. And he took there what housing he could get—which was probably better than in any other great capital city, if yet often infamously bad.

There was, it is true, the omnibus which he might sometimes use. But for many years after the experimental start in 1829, omnibuses were few and dear. They were not for him. A fare so low as 2*d*. was unknown before 1846. In 1855 some Parisian promoters, reversing the process by which French railways had been made with English capital, organized the *Compagnie générale des omnibus de Londres* (*Anglice*, the L.G.O.C.). They bought up existing private lines and started fresh ones. After that, organized road travel 'for all' became rather less of a fiction. But on many routes, and at many times of the day, no buses ran. Dockers and builders' labourers did not go to work on them; nor even masons and carpenters as a regular thing. As for trams—the first experimental lines were only laid in 1861; their rails proved a nuisance and were pulled up.

So the Londoner who had no 'conveyance' of his own went on foot, if he could not afford—in *Pickwick's* day—a hackney-coach, or later, when John Leech was drawing for *Punch* (1841–64) a 'hansom cab' or a 'four-wheeler', or even a twopenny seat on a bus. Meanwhile, the road-users, led in the forties and fifties by the omnibus proprietors, kept up an agitation for the improvement of road surfaces. The streets of the city were often paved; and so were many in Westminster. But the traditional material for London roads, especially for the turnpikes leading into the country—the Old Kent Road, the Edgware Road, the Oxford Road—was local gravel. Very little else had been used where the pavement ended in 1827, when the Metropolitan Road Commission took over all the turnpikes north of the Thames. And even thirty years later not half the roads under its control had been macadamized with broken granite. Omnibus men were complaining in 1856 of the gravel which hurt their horses; of the toll-gates on every road out of London which limited their range; and of the tolls on Waterloo and

Southwark bridges which helped to keep south London apart, distinct, transpontine.

It was a foul river that the bridges crossed. The scour of the tides was now insufficient to cleanse it. London had always drained into it, so far as it had drained at all; for the chief metropolitan sanitary standby had been the cesspool. The city proper had for some time possessed a decently competent body of Sewer Commissioners, who, taking good medical advice, had almost got rid of cesspools by 1850; and to do so had made forty or fifty miles of drains which, of course, discharged into the Thames between Ludgate and Tower Hill. Not until 1852 was burial stopped in those rank city graveyards of which there is a sample in *Bleak House*. (The book began to appear in serial form that year.) Outside the city was a patchwork of local authorities with little power. Cesspools, as private property, and dust-heaps, so called by courtesy, could not be touched summarily by any of these. Such things might be indicted as nuisances at common law, and a court might order a nuisance to be abated. But it could not prevent its repetition; and no court would have called a cesspool or a dust-heap as such a nuisance. Until 1851 any one could open a slaughter-house anywhere. Years later, there was slaughtering in yards off the Strand; and drawing of drinking-water from slum pumps; and cellar tenements sometimes below cesspool level; and, in other cellars, cows; and 'pig keeping . . . to a very considerable extent' in Westminster.[1] There was still a water company whose intake was below Teddington Lock in 1854, though two years earlier the practice had been made illegal.

Irresolute legislation dealing with these things, and some increase of sanitary action by vestries and district boards, had been noticeable since 1848, when the aftermath of the Irish famine and a scare of cholera had made it clear that the improvement in the health of cities which, hard though it may be to believe, had undoubtedly come between 1775 and 1825, had now stopped, or even been reversed. But it is only with a group of Acts passed in 1855 that the modern sanitary history of London begins. One was a Nuisances Removal Act. Another established the Metropolitan Board

[1] Reports of the various Medical Officers of Health quoted in Jephson, H., *The Sanitary Evolution of London* (1907): the Westminster pigs are on p. 115.

of Works. The Board's predecessor, a Metropolitan Commission of Sewers, had taken five years to make one main drain, which in a few more years collapsed. The Board did much better: by 1860 it had built great arterial sewers, north and south of the river, discharging between Woolwich and Erith. It was not too soon. The river had become so offensive at Westminster, in the hot summer of 1858, that there was talk in the clubs about transferring Parliament elsewhere. As for the removal of nuisances, that was necessarily slow. There were competent people in 1864–5 who said that, if it were strictly applied to the London bakehouses, half of them would have to be removed.

With all this, it is not to be forgotten that the London death-rate in 1861 was lower than the national death-rate either of France or of Prussia in the same year. The early Victorians were neither blind nor hypocritical when they talked about progress, which after all means motion not perfection. If they were apt to confuse mere motion with motion in some sense good, there are excuses. They had been given a thundering revelation of physical speed beside which the 'glory of motion' on De Quincey's 'English Mail-coach' was a stagnant thing. And swift communications, they argued, meant easy intercourse; intercourse promoted health, plenty, and peace. 'But if, in spite of this general tendency towards pacific progress and peace, war should occasionally break out, the improved means of communication will aid in bringing it to a prompt close. A single battle will decide the fate of a country, and the longest war will probably be circumscribed within a few months.'[1] That was a reasonable argument when it was put forward in 1850.

The railways brought up to London some, at least, of the wage-earning immigrants upon whose arrival its growth, and in the old days its very existence, had mainly depended. But probably a majority of them still tramped up by stages, as all their predecessors had. The cost of tramping cards, issued by trade clubs and friendly societies to skilled men who were moving about the country in search of work, was a regular, and most valuable, item in the expenditure of those organizations. And when a skilled man, worth 30*s.* a week, had to tramp, an unskilled man, worth 18*s.* or 20*s.* at most, could not count on riding any great distance, even

[1] Lardner, *Railway Economy*, pp. 171–8.

in Gladstone's 'parliamentary' trains, at least one of which every railway company was obliged, since 1844, to run every day except Sunday, charging its third-class passengers not more than 1*d*. a mile. Besides, except for the Irish and some other special groups, a long tramp into London was not normal. Nor was it, in fact, to any growing town. Manchester immigrants came mostly from Lancashire, Derbyshire, Cheshire, and the near side of the West Riding; London immigrants mostly from the home counties; and though the special attractions of the capital no doubt gave it more long-distance men than any other town, a two or three days' tramp, at most, would bring the typical young new Londoner up from Essex, or Hertfordshire, or Berkshire. Once domiciled in his London street, usually, to begin with, as some one's lodger, he, like the waiter who served Mr. Carker in the country inn, was 'not much in the habit of travelling by rail'. There is no scene in a third-class railway carriage in Dickens.

The ordinary Londoner had only been touched lightly and, so to speak, patchily by those mechanical, scientific, and industrial changes which were making a new England. Before the railways came he had hardly been touched at all. Even after, he often escaped contact, living and working very much as his father and his grandfather had worked and lived. The chief things that the railways brought him were cheaper coal and, as time went on, some rather fresher food—though it took them so long to organize the carriage of milk successfully that, to the close of the age, all London's milk came from London, or near suburban, cow-houses and cow-cellars; or from that London pump which provided a stock early Victorian jest. There was hardly a hundredweight of coal burnt in London before 1840 which had not come down the North Sea from the Tyne and the Wear in sailing colliers, whole fleets of which might be held up at the mouth of the Thames when a strong west wind was blowing with the stream. Steam colliers only appeared in the fifties, to meet railway competition; and for many years most of the trade remained to the sailing 'Geordies'.

How close the grip of the north-east coast coal-owners was on the Metropolitan market is shown by the existence, down to 1845, of a committee on Tyneside for 'the limitation of the vend' of coal; that is, the adjustment of the output of the Tyne and Wear collieries to the state of prices in London, in the collieries' interest, of course. The committee broke down, in that year, as such committees will, over a quarrel about the shares in the limited output which the various collieries might claim; but it would certainly have been revived, as it had been several times before after similar squabbles, had not railway competition already threatened the monopoly. It had been hoped, years before, that the Grand Junction Canal might do this; but the 'Paddington coal' which it brought had never amounted to much. For a long time neither Euston, the terminus of the London and Birmingham, nor the new railway Paddington, did much better. Their owners found passenger traffic so profitable that they neglected minerals. In 1850, when Euston had been open for twelve years, only 55,000 tons of coal came into London by rail, against 3,500,000 tons by sea. The sea-coal was handled and broken by keelmen and colliers' crews on the Tyne; and in London by coal-whippers and lightermen, and 'first merchants' and 'second merchants', and coal-heavers in long hats, and by those who peddled it by the half-hundredweight, and even by the stone, in back streets and alleys. It is not surprising that there was talk of a renewed 'limitation of the vend' of coal. But the opening in 1850 of the Great Northern Railway, with its direct line to the Nottinghamshire, Derbyshire, and South Yorkshire fields, soon stopped the talk. By 1860 there were 1,500,000, and by 1865 2,500,000, tons coming in yearly from these fields. Trucks of the 'inland coal' could run from the pithead to the London terminus. Though back streets could not be served without the coal pedlar, the stuff was handled far less often than consumers' sea-coal, and came cheaper. It was soon the fuel of the poor. Comfortable people, however, still mostly demanded, and so invariably received, 'best Wallsend'.

With at least one technical result of the new era every Londoner was familiar—gas-lighting. It had come as a new and glorious wonder in the later years of George III. It had spread as an effective street-light, and a great assistance to Peel's new police, under George IV and William IV. Under Victoria it was being extended continually into courts and alleys, places of business, and every sort of private house. In 1843 it appeared inside the Bank of England. The lamp and the candlestick fade, though slowly, out of the literature of middle- and working-class London. Their decline can be traced in Dickens, from *Pickwick* of 1836 to *Our Mutual Friend* of 1864–5. It is true that in *Our Mutual Friend* Mrs. Wilfer puts down her candle, and does not turn up the gas, in the little hall of the house in Holloway across the 'tract of suburban Sahara where . . . bones were boiled . . . and dust was heaped by contractors'. But Holloway was still half-rural, and perhaps the house was old. Down by the water-side, there was gas-light in the parlour of that ancient 'tavern of dropsical appearance', the Six Jolly Fellowship-Porters; and there was a 'flaring gas-light pendent from the ceiling', pictured as a rather vulgar appliance, in the principal room of Mr. Boffin's Bower among the dust-heaps 'up Maiden Lane, Battle Bridge'.

The gas-works in Horseferry Lane, Brick Lane, and the like—names suggestive of the kind of site originally chosen—had been the first great symbols of the new industrial era shown to all London. The London Gas-light and Coke Company had a capital of £580,000, and 126 miles of gas-mains, fifteen years before Victoria's accession. When John Ruskin cast about for things typical of the age which he disliked he sometimes hit upon a railway station, sometimes upon a gasometer. Here, though he did not say all this, was anonymous capitalistic enterprise, with its great iron gas containers, its iron piping, its points of contact with chemical science, its complete dependence on coal, and its growing crowd of wage-earners. The gas-worker had specialized out as a new industrial type; and every winter pressure at the gas-works, when demand touched its peaks, gave employment to casual workers, Irishmen often, who in summer-time carried for bricklayers or did navvies' jobs. Hence the alliance, in later Trade Union nomenclature, of the gas-workers with the general labourers.

There were other products and symbols of the new industrial age, besides the gasometers and the flaring gas-lights, scattered over London; but they did not dominate the city as the cotton-mills dominated Manchester, or the coal-mines and ironworks the new upland towns of Glamorgan. Long before Boulton and Watt, steam-engines had pumped for the London water-companies. Boulton and Watt themselves had promoted the first steam corn-mill in London, in fact, the first in the world, as a piece of steam-engine propaganda in 1786. It was burnt down by incendiaries a few years later; but it was rebuilt, and it naturally had successors. *The Times* was printed by steam before Waterloo. Bramah, the inventor, worked all his life in London; and so did his pupil Henry Maudslay, who died in 1831, and who probably did as much as any single man to create mechanical engineering as an organized large-scale industry. In later life he had specialized on the building of marine engines; and his two sons, the Maudslay firm of early Victorian times, built the engines for the first screw-steamer ordered by the Admiralty, in 1841. They continued to build for the Navy during the next twenty-five years and more. Yet, at the census of 1851, the whole miscellaneous body of men described as 'engine and machine makers' in the London area was hardly larger than the group of the 'grooms, horsekeepers, jockeys', and was much smaller than that of the butchers.

During the next ten years it seemed that the Thames might become a great home not only for the making of marine engines but for the new and complementary industry of iron ship-building. The pioneer of that industry there, William Fairbairn, who started at Millwall in 1835, had to face every kind of opposition from those Thames ship-builders and ship-wrights, with their friends and sympathizers, who could see no good in iron walls. Though he claimed to have built more than a hundred iron ships, during the next fifteen years, they were mostly rather small, and in the end he gave up discouraged. But in the fifties, for five long years, the whole country followed, with alternations of pride and anxiety, what seemed the great national enterprise of designing and building at Millwall an iron steamer nearly 700 feet long and over 80 feet in the beam. The *Great Eastern*, as she eventually became, ruined the man who built her, and lost the money of those shareholders who paid for her. She was launched in 1858, only after three failures, and was sold before she was fitted out for sea—to another group of to-be-disappointed shareholders. All the same, she was the largest and most remarkable single 'commodity' turned out by the technical thought and organized labour of early Victorian England. It was many years before anything so gigantic was again attempted.

In the year of her launching, a firm established in 1846,

which became the Thames Ironworks Company, set up another milestone when it completed the first British iron-clad, the *Warrior*. But all this came late, and was exceptional. On the Thames, as on those other rivers which did far more than the Thames to set iron ships on the sea and engines inside ships, the iron ship, even the engined ship, was not typical of the age. Down to 1865 the sailing tonnage on the United Kingdom register was growing continuously. It reached its absolute recorded maximum in that year. In 1860 the steam tonnage was not a tenth of the whole; and most of the steamers, with nearly all the sailing ships, were still built of wood. The iron ship only began to win in the sixties; and the ship-building yard which was the glory of the early Victorian Thames, Green's of Blackwall, launched its first iron ship in 1866. It is fair to add that, by that time, and partly perhaps for that reason, ship-building as a Thames industry was on the decline.

From Green's yard came the wooden 'Blackwall frigates', the first of which, the *Seringapatam*, was finished in the year of Victoria's accession. They and their predecessors, the Thames-built East Indiamen—slow sailing, like naval three-deckers, and fit to carry the fortunes of Jos Sedley—were finely constructed of chosen timber by the sort of skilled father-to-son ship-wright who had his close old-fashioned trade club and looked down on those grimy boiler-makers who, because they knew how to drive rivets in iron plates, were turning into iron ship-builders. Such new-comers were no tradesmen. The ship-wright, like his handiwork, had a pedigree and traditions. ('And his father's name before him was Chips, and *his* father's name before *him* was Chips, and they were all Chipses.' That family of ship-wrights had the tradition of selling themselves to the Devil 'for an iron pot and a bushel of tenpenny nails and half a ton of copper and a rat that could speak';[1] but there were other traditions.) No doubt the *Seringapatam*, as viewed by a naval architect, was a great improvement on the *Ramchunder*, East Indiaman. She and her successors could hold the seas with those Yankee clipper fleets which included the world's best ships and most highly trained master mariners. But the 'Blackwallers', like their contemporaries the Aberdeen clippers, were only exquisite products of an old, though still

[1] Dickens, *The Uncommercial Traveller*.

living and adaptable, technique. Samuel Pepys would have understood and admired them. Chips the grandfather could have helped to build them without unlearning anything. To the new technique they owed only some of their fittings—and some great part of the demand for their services.

Scattered over innumerable trades and sub-trades, most of the craftsmen of London were in much the same position as the ship-wrights. They might have mastered some new process since first they had learnt their trade, but they had seldom been called on to unlearn it; had seldom found their skill suddenly made of no value in the market. Take the skilled men and apprentices of the building trade, by far the most important industrial group in London, which numbered over 60,000 in 1851, against the 6,600 'engine and machine makers'. Here were none of the new technical or social revolutions and problems. Houses were built, glazed, plumbed, and painted very much as they had been any time these hundred years; except that there was more plumbing than there used to be, for the water-closet was now pretty well established; and that iron was creeping into new warehouses, hospitals, and even churches, still more into chapels—cast iron for pillars and wrought iron for 'what are called girders', as an expert put it in 1867.[1] These structural uses of iron Ruskin's denunciations failed to stop; but they had not yet interfered much with the building trades. There were big contractors and small speculative builders, who rose regularly from the ranks of master carpenters or master bricklayers—and fell almost as regularly. But this was nothing new. And there was no new problem of child labour, or anything of that sort. There were only a few hundred boys under fifteen in the building trades in all London. The proportion of young boys was rather higher in the country, it is true, because many learnt their trade there and then moved up to town; but everywhere fourteen or fifteen was the ordinary age for regular entry, as it always had been.

Work was intermittent, seasonally, and with the intermittent throbbing expansions of London, especially among the painters, who were the most unfortunate, most unhealthy, and least respected group. They were reputed to be particularly heavy drinkers, no doubt because of their

[1] *Report of the Royal Commission on Trade Unions*, 1868–9; evidence, Q. 10,696.

liability to 'painters' colic', against which no steps had yet been taken to protect them. But there is no reason to think that work had ever been less irregular, or white lead less unwholesome, since London was London. Wages in the building trades, as in most trades, were going up slowly after 1847–8. In the building trades they rose by nearly 40 per cent. between 1840 and 1866; and the four-pound loaf was cheaper in the latter year than in the former. Hours of work remained fairly steady at the pre-Victorian level of about 64 a week in summer and about 52 in winter, until nearly the end of the age. Then, increased prosperity and better organization among the building craftsmen, accompanied by negotiations and a few notable strikes, brought some curtailment and—more important—that unique social creation of early Victorian England, the Saturday half-holiday, *la semaine anglaise*. When the age began, comfortable men went to the city on Saturday afternoon, as often as not; Lloyd's was open, though we are not told how much business was transacted there. When the age closed, by Saturday at 3 p.m. a working carpenter might be strolling round with his pipe to the 'Dog and Duck'.

It was the carpenter's good fortune, with the ship-wright and the engineer, to work away from his home and under an employer who could be resisted or persuaded 'collectively'. A great mass of the skilled and semi-skilled London workmen, and a still greater mass of the workwomen, competed against one another for piece-jobs, which they did in their own homes; others were small shop and garret workers, in little feeble groups, controlled absolutely by master or mistress. Even the most skilled outworkers—high-grade tailors and shoe-makers; specialists in the watch trade of Clerkenwell, one of whom made only dials, another hands, and so on; silk-weavers of Spitalfields, a diminished but still very important group—even these had the old-fashioned handicaps of unregulated, indefinite, or at best self-regulated hours, and all the sanitary and domestic accompaniments of home work in the houses and tenements of a crowded city. Below them lay the long shabby perspective of the all but unskilled out-workers, who took the price they were offered for fear that there might soon be no offer at all; the perspective which led to Tom Hood's stitching-woman making 'seam, and gusset, and band' in her 'poverty, hunger, and dirt'. The arrival of the sewing machine in the fifties suggested possibilities of amelioration in the ancient stitching business; but there was not much change in it ten years later, although pioneer employers, in London and elsewhere, were buying machines and setting girls to work in embryo clothing factories.

The groups of shirt-makers, milliners, and tailors who worked on employers' premises also included some of the least fortunate people in London, except the vagrants and the literally destitute. As a very young man, in 1835, Dickens had thought that the 'milliners' and staymakers' apprentices' were 'the hardest worked, the worst paid, and too often the worst used class of the community'.[1] He was a good observer, if not quite judicially minded. The community had done nothing for them thirty years later. Nor had mechanical invention done anything, and general economic progress not much. They were in the grip of their mistresses. In 'rush' seasons their hours might be almost unlimited. Their pay was always exiguous.

How completely the largest group of workers in London, the domestic servants, were in the grip of master or mistress is hard to say. That many of them were poorly paid and detestably lodged is certain. That the grip was often rather brutal, all the dreary humour, printed and pictured, which turns on the slatternly London 'slavey' is there to witness. But relations were not always unequal, and there were possibilities of retaliation. Dickens's servants, with their cockney elasticity and repartee, knew when the scales were inclining their way. Susan Nipper, it may be recalled, when Mrs. Pipchin spoke lamentably about the better days which she had seen, 'was understood to observe that she pitied the better days which had seen Mrs. Pipchin'. Thackeray's 'gentlemen's gentlemen' usually had the measure of their masters, though Major Pendennis won the last bout with Mr. Morgan. It was easy for Thackeray to make rather snobbish fun of Jeames de la Pluche; but Jeames had a sense of his own dignity and his place in his own world. He was probably conscious neither of oppression nor of wage-slavery.

But average conditions are not to be looked for in the servants' halls and the serving hierarchies of the West End, where most of the 24,000 male domestic servants and of the

[1] *Sketches by Boz.*

39,000 women who classified themselves as housekeepers, cooks, housemaids, and so forth, were to be found in 1851. The centre of gravity lies somewhere among the great army of London 'general domestic servants', numbering 121,000. (There were only six cities in England which had so many *inhabitants*; so the London 'slaveys' must not be dismissed in any casual aside.) Considerably more than half of them were under twenty-five, and barely a sixth were over thirty-five. It was a career which one normally abandoned young. That was possibly one reason, though certainly not the chief reason, why a Government which inquired repeatedly and in detail into the labour of women and girls in factories, and mines, and agricultural gangs, and workshops; into the conditions of hand-loom weavers, nailers, and framework-knitters, and of the navvies with their dubious womenfolk, did not collect any facts about the servant girls. The chief reason, no doubt, was that the very idea of making such a tiresome and almost indecently intrusive inquiry never crossed any governing mind. Inquiry up the backstairs or into the maids' attic! Not the most prurient outside reformer had even suggested it. As a result, not much is known for certain about servant girls' wages; though it is probable that the average London 'general' of eighteen and upwards got less than £10 a year, plus whatever board and lodgings her mistress thought appropriate. It is to be remembered that the wage of a grown woman in regular work at the end of the early Victorian era was in the neighbourhood of 10*s*. a week; and that the feeble or unfortunate made much less. There was very little factory employment available for women in the London area. As a career, service, in its various grades, had not much to compete with except the different stitching trades and rough, heavy jobs, like laundry work and scrubbing. Though seven London women described themselves as merchants in 1851, not one claimed to be a commercial clerk. Few worked in shops, except milliners' shops or beer-shops. Service was the obvious alternative to stitching, pending wedlock; and it is likely enough that the first was, on the average, the more attractive. Perhaps escape from service into wedlock was rather easier than escape from stitching; certainly milliners married later than maidservants. It is true that those who followed the career of service for life had some prospect of dying in the workhouse; but that was a risk against which no wage-earner was fully insured, and to which the single, or isolated, stitching woman was more than ordinarily exposed.

In spite of the dogmatic preference of the 1834 Poor Law reformers for poor-relief in 'the house', indoor relief did not become universal, or even general, either in London or anywhere else. The ratio of those relieved 'out' to those relieved 'in' at any given date throughout the period was usually six or seven to one. Emergency outdoor relief to the sick or the unemployed, and regular relief—of a shilling or two a week—to old folk past work, who had a roof of their own and children who would help maintain them, were the commonest forms. The absence of anything except this scanty, customary, old-age pension to the very poor, useful only to those who had a home, explains the high risk of death in the workhouse for the broken-down celibate domestic servant, or isolated stitching woman past work, who had none.

Little, if any, outdoor relief was given to the most desperate section of the community, a section disproportionately large in London and one to which the Poor Law reformers of the thirties had given no serious thought, the casuals and vagrants—the ragged, often barefoot, crowd who, having no regular domicile or parish, slept in alleys and staircases, and under the new railway arches; lived no one quite knew how; served as a tragi-comic background for early Victorian satirists and cartoonists; and stirred the sympathies of writers like Tom Hood and Henry Mayhew, the man who, besides helping to found *Punch*, wrote the first set study of *London Labour and the London Poor*. If any people from this outcast class, or any vagrants from the country, applied at a London workhouse they might be given a night's lodging on the men's or the women's side; perhaps might be required to do some perfunctory work to pay for it; and might be sent on with a few pence to find food. In this way some 'casuals', those who would trust themselves to Bumble and the Guardians, circulated about the London workhouses, overcrowding them with an unwholesome element distasteful to the more decent inmates. There were as yet no regular casual wards. Plans which were drawn up in 1857–8 for the establishment of special metropolitan 'asylums for the homeless poor' were still only plans when Henry Mayhew began to write in the early sixties. And so, behind those who worked in London, came the tattered companies who could get no work, or wanted none, and in either case were becoming increasingly unfit to do any—the despair of priest and prophet and utilitarian reformer.

§ 4. THE TEXTILE TRADES

Foreigners who thought of work in England usually had before their mind's eye either some picture of the Thames and the financial and commercial crowds of the city—merchant, banker, financier, stockbroker, and merchant's clerk—with a background of the building, clothing, supply, and luxury trades of the world's greatest capital; or else a smoky picture of manufacturing districts in the north which were claiming the leadership of English economic life, and with some reason. If the foreigner wished to study the new England he went first to south Lancashire. He seldom liked it. Friedrich Engels, who knew Manchester well, concluded in 1844 that 350,000 working people of the town and its environs 'lived, almost all of them, in wretched, damp, filthy cottages; that the streets which surrounded them were usually in the most miserable and filthy condition, laid out without the slightest reference to ventilation'; and so on.[1] He gave plenty of evidence in support, with much exact unsavoury detail. Ten years later, to Léonce de Lavergne, the French student of English agriculture, south Lancashire seemed 'an immense morass, shut in between the sea and the mountains; stiff clay land, with an impervious subsoil . . . a most gloomy climate, continual rain, a constant cold sea-wind, besides a thick smoke, shutting out what little light penetrates the foggy atmosphere; lastly, the ground, the inhabitants, and their dwellings completely covered with a coating of black dust—fancy all this, and some idea may be gained of this strange country, where the air and the earth seem only a mixture of coal and water'.[2] Perhaps he was there in November; but as a rule he was a good observer of soils and climates, and those who know the strange country can recognize at least a defensible caricature.

In this environment and climate, or in something like

[1] *The Condition of the Working Classes in England in 1844*, p. 43.
[2] Op. cit., p. 261.

them, lay the main head-quarters of those textile manufactures which employed directly more people than any group of associated industries except agriculture. The numbers were so great—actually greater in 1851 than in 1901; and proportionately, of course, far greater—because the conditions of the world, and England's commercial strength, had facilitated continuous rapid expansion of the exports, principally of cotton yarns and goods, while the progress of machinery, though devastatingly swift, had not been nearly swift enough to limit the aggregate demand for labour. The possibility of ultimate limitation was just coming into sight in the sixties, with the final defeat of hand-loom weaving in the cotton industry; but down to the fifties the fact that the final manufacturing process had been only mechanized in part, while the demand for the products of the thoroughly mechanized spinning processes, either for export as yarn or for weaving, was continually expanding, had attached to the associated industries one person out of every thirteen or fourteen of ten years old and upwards in the whole country.

At the time of Victoria's accession the lamentable condition of the domestic cotton weavers was already a matter of common knowledge. They had petitioned Parliament, and a parliamentary committee in 1834 had reported its pity and amazement at their sufferings and 'patience unexampled'. There were at that time about 100,000 cotton power-looms and about 200,000 cotton hand-looms in the country. The English hand-loom weavers had clung to their trade, proudly and foolishly, and had usually brought up their children to it. Immigrant Irish, in scores of thousands, had taken to it in south Lancashire and the Glasgow area. Their coming was probably the main cause of the acute distress. In times of slack trade the mill-owner naturally ran the power-looms, in which he had sunk capital, and let the hand-loom weavers 'play'. Those who did plain weaving—specialists were in a rather better position—thus constituted, in the most precise sense, what Marx, following Chartist writers of the thirties, called the capitalists' reserve army of labour. Between 1835 and 1850, death and desertion thinned its battalions. By 1850 there were 250,000 cotton power-looms at work, and perhaps some 40,000 or 50,000 hand-looms still available. The second figure went on dwindling. When civil war in America cut off the main supply of cotton in the sixties, the hand-loom weavers were so small a class that little is heard of any special hardships which they may have borne. Quotations of their earnings are hard to find after 1850. The remnant in the sixties were specialists. All plain work had been taken over by the clanging looms of iron, and the mechanization of the industry, with its accompanying concentration into factories, was complete.

With the completed transition, and helped by Factory Acts, a still expanding world demand for cotton goods, and their own tenacity and thrift, the cotton families of the strange country of coal and water, recently subjects of national pity and of special protective legislation, were taking the lead in all working-class movements. They were not entirely dependent on cotton: they usually had members working at engineering or some other of the many trades of Lancashire. Their thrift had made them active supporters of Friendly Societies, Building Societies, Savings Banks, and of those Co-operative Stores which began to rise under the gloomy Lancashire sky of the forties, when the long tragedy of hand-loom weaving had reached its penultimate, and perhaps its most sombre, act. By 1863 the North of England Co-operative Wholesale Society had been started to free the stores from grasping wholesalers, as the stores had freed spinners and weavers from untrustworthy local retailers. The cotton people were facing at that time the most formidable danger of the century; but the cutting-off of American supplies had not broken the co-operative movement; it seemed almost to have strengthened it, for co-operation had been a product of adversity. Earnings had been good immediately before war in America began. That type of Lancashire family was developing which was to become normal in late Victorian times. Though the grandfather of the fifties might be a hand-loom weaver past work, the father might be a weaving overlooker at 25*s.* to 28*s.* a week; elder girls power-loom weavers at 14*s.* or 15*s.*; a lad an 'improver' in an engineering shop; and a small boy a 'little piecer' in a spinning-room, at 6*s.* or so. Such families were able to put something aside against the next industrial crisis, if unable to meet unaided such an abnormal emergency as the Cotton Famine. If trade were brisk, as it was at the end of 1865, the money was there to be spent at Oldham or Rochdale wakes, or on a trip to Blackpool; for years before the Famine there had been Sunday excursions by rail to Blackpool from Oldham—return fares '1*s.* for ladies and 1*s.* 6*d.* for gentlemen'.

The story of weaving in that branch of the wool industry which came nearest to the cotton manufacture, the making of light plain 'dress-goods' from combed worsted yarn, was like the cotton story, but dragged behind it. The first experiments with power had come much later: there were only 3,000 worsted power-looms in the whole country in 1835. But there were nearly eleven times that number by 1850. Plain weaving had nearly all gone into the mills, though there was still a fairly active hand-loom trade in 'fancies'. That, too, was sucked into the mills during the next decade, but apparently without causing any great distress. The forties were the difficult decade, as on so many sides of national life. Difficulty was increased in the worsted industry by another delayed revolution—that in wool-combing. The hand combers of the twenties and thirties were a strong and well-organized group of indispensable men. Combing machines existed but they were not efficient. The principal threat to the Yorkshire combers' position had come from the immigrant Irish; for combing had, of course, been practised in Ireland, and was not hard to learn. But the inventors were working without rest during the forties. By 1850–1 the victory of machine combing was certain. Within half a dozen years it was complete: one of the swiftest of known industrial revolutions. Combing, apart from the overlooking jobs connected with it, sank from a high-grade to a low-grade, a mere machine-watching, affair. But the whole industry was active and expanding—unwholesomely active during the American Civil War when, for lack of cotton, there was an exaggerated temporary demand for wool—and Bradford, its capital, was growing up-hill and down-dale, with not much order and, until after 1848–50, less sanitation among its crowded little two- and three-room stone cottages. Visitors, foreign or English, found these Yorkshire towns not more agreeable than those on the Lancashire side of the hills; but they were smaller and easier to get out of, and the windy moors, away from which Emily Brontë could not live, were very near them all. Yorkshire townspeople retained longer and more noticeably than the men of the greater Lancashire towns something of the character and features of the countrymen from whom they sprang.

In the woollen industry proper, the industry which made the sleek broadcloth of respectability, the blankets and flannels, the uniform cloths, 'pilot' cloths, and all those stout heavy things which men wore before tweeds came south, the transformation of an old set technique was far slower than in worsted or cotton. This was partly because the industry was much more scattered than either of the others. Except for the cotton manufacture of Clydesdale and the feeble remnants of the worsted manufacture in Norfolk, they were almost confined to south Lancashire, west Yorkshire, and the adjacent corners of Derbyshire and Cheshire. Though nearly half of the woollen workers were in the West Riding and Lancashire, there was a strong ancient industry on both sides of the Cotswolds, with outliers westward as far as Cornwall; another in the Tweed towns, with outliers, large or small, in every Scottish county; an industry numerically less considerable, but socially important, scattered over the counties of Wales; and remnants of ancient industries in many English counties not usually thought of in connexion with the modern manufacture. In Cardigan or the Scottish Isles rapid transformation was not to be expected: spinning wheel and hand-loom died slow and hard. But even in Yorkshire change came so slowly that there was time for social adjustment. And few immigrants had gone into the trade to disturb its balance. There had always been large employers in it, particularly in the west of England, men who controlled the whole series of processes in cloth-making; though much of the work had been done for them by wage-earning cottagers at home. But in Yorkshire there was a numerous, and famous, body of domestic master clothiers. When power-driven machinery for carding and other processes had first come in, these small employers had combined to set up 'company mills' of their own, in which the new machines were installed; or they had got the machine jobs done for them on commission by 'millers' who had acquired the necessary equipment.

Even the few large factories of the early nineteenth century remained curiously unmechanized, judged by modern standards, until within a few years of Victoria's accession. In 1828 the power-driven spinning mule was hardly known in them. Down to 1850 spinning was mostly done in the Cotswolds on the hand-driven jenny; and after 1865 there were still handicraft operations interrupting the sequence of the machines in many Yorkshire spinning-rooms. In 1835 there were only 2,000 woollen power-looms in the whole country; in 1850 only 9,000. All about Leeds, the chief seat of manufacturing by power, thousands of hand-loom weavers were making a fair living, according to Yorkshire standards of the day, in the fifties and sixties. The small clothier was disappearing—by fall or rise—but was not yet extinct. Out of nearly a thousand woollen cloth manufacturers who made returns of the number of men whom they employed in 1851, more than five hundred put the figure below ten; only eighty-two put it above a hundred. There was a further concentration of employment during the next fourteen years, but it was gradual. No crisis came in the industry itself, though it felt the effects of crises connected with the ebb and flow of the whole economic life of the country, or arising from some external event which, from the English viewpoint, had neither rhythm nor reason. Such was the crisis of the Cotton Famine. This helped the woollen industry, as it did the worsted, but less, because worsteds are nearer to cottons than blankets and broadcloth are. Woollen manufacturing could show neither such rich profits nor such good wages as cotton; but it had a more even course—less wretchedness in the forties; less expansion in the fifties; no disaster in the sixties. Its sales were predominantly at home; those of cotton predominantly abroad. Its raw material was now either native or grown on British territory.[1] More secure than its neighbour, it was also more sluggish.

In the lesser textile industries—flax, with its new deputy, jute, and silk—the sphere of the power-driven machine, though always extending, was more limited even than in woollen. Flax-spinning by power was nearly as old as cotton-spinning. But the power-machine had taken a long time to master the preliminary processes of scutching and heckling the flax, and it never got complete control of weaving the linen. The hecklers, a group of handicraftsmen who had occupied a position similar to that of the hand wool-combers, a controlling position because they were indispensable, only lost control in the Scottish flax industry during the forties—once more, the forties—with the adoption of improved heck-

[1] From 1835 onwards Australian wool was driving all other imported wools out of the English market.

ling machinery. The whole industry was already moving north and north-west, from Leeds, where machinery was first applied to spinning, into Fife, Forfar, and Ulster, where, in its unmechanized state, it was old-established. By the sixties factory spinning was stationary at Leeds and the hand-loom was fast disappearing in Scotland. But in 1850 there had only been 6,000 power-looms in Britain; few, if any, in Ulster, which had now become the head-quarters of the pure linen industry; while Scotland, and particularly Dundee, was turning more and more to the use of jute, a material which had been used very little anywhere when Victoria came to the throne. The jute industry, making nothing but plain goods, was thoroughly mechanized by the end of the period; but fine linen weaving kept much of its ancient character.

For silk-weaving the power-loom had barely been tried in 1837. There were only 1,100 at work in 1850; and all the old types of hand silk-weaving were active during the next fifteen years—fine silks of Spitalfields and the small towns of Essex and Suffolk; silk ribbons of Coventry; silk handkerchiefs of Macclesfield. The primary process of silk-throwing, the oldest textile factory-industry in the country, continued relatively unchanged, except that steam more and more replaced the original water power; but that had no important social or economic effects, beyond the slight encouragement which it gave to concentration of the industry near the coal-fields. Meanwhile, there was developing on the coal-fields the business of combing, spinning, and weaving broken fibres of waste silk as if they had been flax or wool; but this thoroughly mechanized industry was not of importance before the sixties.

The weaving out-workers of all the textile industries were supplemented by the cottage framework knitters of the Midlands, an unhappy people whose physique in 1844–5 was said to be 'much below the average of even the manufacturing districts of the North'.[1] At that time there had been a few experiments with power-driven knitting machinery in factories, but the effective basis of the industry was this cottage out-work. So far from dwindling, the number of hand-worked frames had increased since 1832, and it continued to increase until 1860, or rather later, though not very

[1] R. M. Muggeridge's *Report on the Condition of the Framework Knitters*, p. 7.

fast. There were, in fact, too many frames and too many knitters. The trade was easily learnt, and frames could be rented, at usurious rates, from small speculators in the misery of those who worked them. Factories were beginning to spring up; but in 1862 it was officially estimated that out of 120,000 people connected in various ways with the hosiery industry, of whom about half were the actual knitters, less than 4,500 came within the scope of the Factory Law as then prescribed, that is to say, worked in places where power was used. The rest were in the cottages, or in little 'frame-shops' run by a master knitter or some kind of middle-man.

Except for a few favoured sections, knitting had been and remained a socially unwholesome trade, though conditions were bettering in the fifties. Work was intermittent, ill paid, subject to the abuses of the frame-rent, and sometimes to those of payment in truck—in defiance of the law, ancient and modern.[1] In an industry scattered over remote rural districts, in which the material was given-out to the work-people and the finished goods taken-in by some agent, who might well be a local publican, it was easy for payment to be made in goods, or in credit for goods, at the agent's place of business. And the goods might be bad or over-priced. This abuse was, however, declining in the hosiery trade. By the late sixties it was almost extinct. Nothing did more to kill it than the rise of hosiery factories, in none of which was truck ever attempted.

Lace factories were older than hosiery factories, though lace-machines were not so old as stocking-frames. The application of power to the lace-machines began about half a generation before the Victorian era. By 1865 there were some 200 small factories, mainly in the Nottingham district. But the great majority of the lace-makers were hand workers, like the knitters—makers of Bedfordshire or Devonshire pillow-lace, or whatever it might be, on the land, or out-workers, finishers, embroiderers in the towns where the factory lace-net was made. From one evil of hosiery-making the trade was free. Few men tried to support families by it. But there was room enough for the exploitation of women; and, with hosiery and straw-plaiting, it was one of the last trades in England to employ tiny children. Mere babies of

[1] There had been laws against payment in truck since the fifteenth century. A recent law was that of 1831.

three or four were put to cottage lace-making and straw-plaiting in the sixties. What were called the 'getting-up rooms' or 'Mistresses rooms', in which machine-made lace was finished, were often horribly overcrowded with very young girls. Children were regularly sent to learn how to seam knitted gloves at five years old, sometimes at three and a half. And the 'schools' where these industries for babes were taught were often miserable cramped cottages.

Reporting on child labour in the 'wearing apparel' trades in 1864, a Royal Commissioner noted that 'the "sewing machine" is employed in a great variety of ways and promises to produce a complete revolution'.[1] This wide use was a new thing, dating only from the end of the previous decade, when in London, Norwich, Leeds, Bristol, and other towns, hand-worked sewing machines first began to be collected into small factories. About the same time leather-sewing, sole-riveting, and other machines were being tried in boot-making, a trade which down to about 1855 had been a pure handicraft. There had long been large wholesale boot-makers in Stafford, Northampton, and other places; but no true factories. The employers supplied material and gave work out to various classes of workpeople; to girls and women who stitched the uppers, and to master shoe-makers who soled and heeled and put the boots together, just as they did in the 'bespoke' trade of London. Socially, boot-making was a reasonably healthy trade, free of the worst abuses and oppressions from which the machine was just beginning to relieve some of the stitching women. There was some striking against the new machinery, as was natural, but the trade as a whole was entering its new phase without excessive friction, and certainly without any grave distress. At first, few of the machines were power-driven and they were often served by men who had previously worked without them.

After long discussion, long and rather ineffective experiments with the cotton industry, and a fierce agitation in the north during the difficult years which preceded the Reform Bill, the State had started a comprehensive system for the regulation of the labour of children and 'young persons' in textile factories in 1833. It came fully into force in 1836, and was on its trial during the next ten years. The factory workers and their allies, who had aimed at regulation of the

[1] Children's Employment Commission (1864), p. xlvi.

whole industry by means of a Ten Hours' Bill, not merely at regulation of youthful and child labour, considered themselves betrayed. Their employers, now well represented in Parliament, especially after the arrival of Richard Cobden at Westminster in 1841, believed themselves unjustly victimized. There were employers in the 'factory movement', but they were always a small, though an able and determined, group. The dominant employers' view, which Bright shared with Cobden, was that State 'interference' must be, in some undetermined economico-political sense, wrong; and that, in any event, selective interference was most demonstrably unjust. There was some throwing of *tu quoque* across the floor of the House, when landlords of reputedly insanitary cottage-fulls of overworked rustic children attacked the manufacturing representatives, who had been attacking them in Corn Law debates as bread-taxers, almost as parties to a *pacte de famine*. Meanwhile, very slowly and cautiously, with Peel, who half shared the Bright-Cobden view, in power, the regulation and safeguarding of work in the textile mills was extended; and Parliament was faced with the repulsive and notorious results of that inquiry into the labour of women and children outside those mills, which was undertaken in the early forties partly in response to the protest against selective interference.

The factories had been regulated mainly because they were new and conspicuous, and because, in the early days, men connected with them—the elder Peel and Robert Owen—had demanded regulation. Mines went downwards—the miners had always been something of a race apart—and no mine-owner had ever taken up their cause before the world. So the report of half-naked women underground, girls crawling as draught-animals in the dirt of narrow workings, and little boys sitting solitary, opening and shutting ventilation doors in the gross darkness, all day long where there was no day—these things disgusted even people usually apathetic. The worst things were far from universal. Women and girls did not work under or above ground on the great Northumberland and Durham coal-field, and only exceptionally in a number of other districts. But the evils were not less real because only localized. Parliament at once (1842), driven on by Lord Ashley's prompt use of the general disgust, ordered the women out of the pits; said that boys were not to go down them under the age of ten; and began the inspection and safeguarding of the miners' work. The new law took some years to get into full operation, as was natural with a small and inexperienced inspectorate. But, by 1851, against 216,000 male coal-miners in Britain, of ten years old and upwards, there were only 3,000 women; and these were by that time, probably without exception, the 'pit-brow lasses' of Lancashire and a few other places, whose work was legal under the Act of 1842 because it was not subterranean.

With child labour outside the textile factories and mines the early Victorian Parliament never dealt systematically. The report of 1843, which followed that on the mines, showed that it existed everywhere and was abused in all kinds of ways. Reports of 1863–6 said very much the same. It was on the report of 1863 that Charles Kingsley wrote *The Water Babies*. Abuses were at their worst where the child was an apprenticed drudge to some small master or independent journeyman in an ugly trade, like the chimney-climbing boy or the potters' 'mould runner', who trotted all day in and out of the terrible temperatures of the kilns. It was ascertained in 1843 that the employment of mere babes, as in straw-plaiting, was unusual; but simply because there were so few things that they could do. Those light jobs which could be learnt almost from the cradle were learnt, more often than not—the report of 1843 said 'in all cases', but that was an over-statement—by the child from its own parents. Taking the country as a whole, regular work generally began between the ages of seven and eight; so the attempt of the earlier Factory Acts to standardize the starting age at nine was not merely the rectification of an abuse, but a reform in average industrial practice.

In the twenty years which divided the two inquiries the textile code had been strengthened and extended, but before 1864 only to strictly allied industries, such as print-works, bleach-works, and lace-mills. The code, which began only with children, had been applied, after some controversy, to women. To men it never applied directly; but the male textile operatives were well aware of its indirect applications. They often fought from behind the petticoats. The ten hours' day they never forgot, and in 1848, the year of European revolution, they secured it under an Act of the previous year. To mark their gratitude they asked Lord

Ashley, their friend and advocate in Parliament, to present on their behalf a golden medal to Queen Victoria. Not many crowned heads received gold medals from their humbler subjects that year. Two years later, one of the many early Victorian Factory Acts decided that women and 'young persons' should not start work before 6 a.m. nor cease work later than 7 p.m. On Saturdays they were to stop at 2 p.m. *La semaine anglaise*, which many other trades proceeded to acquire by negotiation or strike during the next fifteen years, was thus created for textile factory workers by a stroke of the parliamentary draftsman's pen. The age closes with reformers and Parliament preparing, on the basis of the reports on child labour of 1863–6, to extend the factory code, and with it the English week, and all that Saturday-afternoon's cricket-playing and football-watching which it was to frame, to every work-place where power was used, and to many where it was not.[1]

§ 5. COAL AND IRON

A mines code, enforced like the factory code by a body of inspectors, had grown up beside it. No amount of inspection could make mining a safe career; but the creation of a body of trained experts whose thoughts were concentrated on safety, and who, like the factory inspectors, were instructed to report regularly to one of Her Majesty's Ministers, was a wholesome innovation. The eighteenth century had had its inspectors, and to spare; but they were not too successful. Adam Smith was inclined to treat them as just so much grit in the national economic machinery. The educated inspectorate of the nineteenth century, with a disinterested standard of professional responsibility and direct access to the highest levels of government, was a structure built by the early Victorians on foundations laid for them by Jeremy Bentham.

Those two hundred and odd thousand miners of 1851, brought for the first time during the previous decade within the view of the ordinary newspaper and novel-reading public, and of the law, seem a rather small body in relation to their national importance. There were more shoe-makers. But the miners, upon whose backs rested, or from whose picks depended, the new industrial England—whichever metaphor

[1] The principal Act was of 1867.

be preferred—already far outnumbered a group of older renown and not less importance, the merchant seamen; for the miners' numbers had more than doubled during the previous twenty-five years, with the rapid ingress of mechanical civilization, while those of the seamen had grown slowly; were, indeed, almost stationary until free trade and steam gave a sudden stimulus to shipping in the forties. But mere numbers have never measured the importance of social groups.

Two generations earlier the bulk of the miners had been in Northumberland and Durham, working the coal that would be shipped away coastwise, largely for domestic use. In 1851 less than a fifth of them were there. They had been increasing in those areas where the local coal was consumed locally. About a fifth were in the west midland shires, among which Staffordshire, in 1855, still made more pig-iron than all Scotland and nearly as much as all Wales and Monmouth together. A quarter of the miners were in Lancashire and the West Riding; nearly a sixth in Scotland. About their work and their life much is known. Precisely what their earnings were, in any year or place, is hard to ascertain. Then, as now, the number of 'shifts' worked weekly fluctuated, and there are no statistics of the fluctuations. The wage was normally a piece-rate, so much per ton. It also fluctuated violently with the course of trade. There might be, and usually were, deductions from it for such things as lights and the sharpening of picks. On the other hand, there were additions in free, or cheap, coal for the miner, and perhaps a free, or cheap, cottage. The highest daily wage recorded, in any district or any year, in the early Victorian era is just over 5*s*., for Northumberland and Durham in 1861. During the thirties and forties the figure there seems to have varied between 3*s*. and 4*s*. No higher figure than this is recorded at any time for Lanarkshire; and only a penny or two higher for south Wales. Lancashire figures fluctuate between 20*s*. and 25*s*. a week, which, on the reasonable assumption that five days' work a week might be somewhere near the average, means again 4*s*. or 5*s*. a day. Such Yorkshire figures as exist are rather worse than those of Lancashire.

In coal-miners' wages an upward movement of that central level, about which fluctuations occurred, set in from about 1852. For many years before that the central level had been remarkably uniform, though the fluctuations about it in a primary producing industry, such as mining, had been frequent and abrupt. The rise during the early fifties coincided with a general price rise and was helped by the Crimean War, after which there was a reaction, though not quite to the old basic level. Later the rise was resumed, until by 1865 the basic level was approaching 20 per cent. above the point at which it had stood during the thirties and forties. The early Victorian miner may thus be thought of working for a wage of between 15*s*. and 25*s*., according to his district, his skill, and his luck in employment; and with this wage moving intermittently upwards, once the forties were over.

There was still a great deal of coal raised from shallow, and some even from open, workings. Much of the south Welsh coal was got by tunnelling into the sides of the steep valleys of Glamorgan and Monmouth. The 'thick coal' of south Staffordshire lay near the surface; and on all the coal-fields there was a considerable amount of coal got from shallow pits at, or near, the surface outcrop of the coal measures. In all these places the conditions and risks were only those of quarrying. It was in the deep pits, some few of which had been sunk before 1845 below what was then regarded as about the practicable maximum of 1,000 or 1,200 feet, that the great risks and new difficult technical problems had to be met. In the Cornish copper mines, some of which were at least as deep, the main problem had been that of pumping, to cope with which steam had first been used. Heat was trying and the air was impure at great depths in Cornwall; but rock-falls were rare, and there was neither 'fire-damp' nor 'choke damp'. Except in a few of the deep and 'fiery' northern coal pits, there had been few serious explosions before the forties. But, as the greater depths were reached, there and on other fields, a series of terribly destructive explosions followed, which were the occasion of the more stringent mining law of the fifties. Lights and ventilation, winding engines, and methods of transport underground, were inquired into and regulated; and the inspectors acquired their technical knowledge.

The early steam-winding engines were only of a few score horse-power, even for deep pits. Shallow pits had horse-winches, or possibly hand-winches, in the forties; while in parts of Scotland, as the report of 1842 told the world, all the coal, even from deep pits, was carried up ladders—sometimes up hundreds of feet of them—on women's backs, the usual load being so great that two men were needed to adjust it. The women often climbed crying, a witness said; but when unloaded they began to sing. And so down again for a fresh load. Ashley's Act stopped all this; and steam-engines replaced the winches almost everywhere.

With the horses and the women was being discarded, during the forties, the hempen cable which had hoisted the coal in great wicker 'corves', and the miner with his leg through a loop hanging from it, or perhaps gripping it with hand and knee. But wire cables, a recent invention, were only found in a comparatively few leading pits by 1850; and the general replacement of the corves by iron 'cages', running on guide rods, and able to lift either coal or men, was long delayed; although the 'cage' was known before Victorian times.

The most essential, most difficult, and so most slowly mastered, problems offered to mine inspectors and to those 'viewers' who were the earliest mining experts, were problems of ventilation. Shallow pits had no special ventilating arrangements and recognized no problem. As the need grew with greater depths, burning cressets of coal had been hung at suitable points in the workings to set up air currents. But the almost universal early Victorian method of ventilation in deep pits was a great furnace near the base of the 'upcast' shaft, which provoked a hot upward current and sucked colder and fresher air through the workings. It was the doors which controlled the flow of these currents that the little boys used to shut and open all day as the underground traffic went by. The furnace, though often very skilfully handled, was a primitive and dangerous device. It might go out for lack of fresh air; or get too much and burn too fiercely. Once it was out, or burning too fiercely, the pit was in a bad way. Inventors and mining engineers considered all kinds of alternatives—fans, air-pumps, and high-pressure steam discharged so as to create air currents. The steam discharge was tried and failed. Fans and pumps were first tried with success in 1849–50 in south Wales; thence they travelled slowly north, the first fan appearing in Durham only in 1860.

But the fan which ultimately persuaded the north-country mining engineers that it really was more efficient than a well-managed furnace was only invented in 1862, by a Belgian. Certainly, the miner's life was becoming rather more secure, rather more wholesome. Risky and hard it remained, but probably both easier and safer than that of the seaman.

If the life of industrial England hung from the picks of the 200,000 miners, it hung by the slender chain of the men who made the iron. They were a much smaller group. It was their age and, above all, the age of the sweating puddlers, the men who raked and stirred the molten metal in rows of small glaring furnaces until it became fit for the hammer, pure malleable iron out of which rails and steam-engines and ships were made. Although Bessemer had announced his steel-making invention in 1856, and had made it what is called a business proposition during the next four years, the new cast steel was still on its trial during the early sixties, and the demand for wrought iron was growing faster than ever before. If the available figures are to be trusted, the 3,500 puddling furnaces in the country in 1860 had grown to 6,400 in 1865. (They grew to a maximum of 7,600 in 1875, after which date decline set in.) Each furnace, when at work, had its puddler and his 'underhand'. There were perhaps 10,000 of these key-men in the early sixties. Associated with them were the blast-furnace men who 'made' the impure cast iron from its ore, with the aid of coke fuel and the steam-driven hot-air blast, and the hammer-men and rolling-mill men who took the incandescent masses that came from the puddler's rake, 'shingled' them under the hammer to get rid of the ashy 'scale' and give them preliminary shape, and dragged them with tongs, white-hot, to the rollers from which they emerged as bar, or rod, or plate.

The essentials of this technique were pre-Victorian. Puddling had been perfected in south Wales between 1800 and 1810. The process had spread slowly northwards during the next twenty years. Coke-smelting and the rolling-mill were much older. But the final bit of equipment, Nasmyth's steam-hammer, was not invented until 1839, and was only installed gradually during the next decade. The seemingly limitless demand for railway material—in England, Europe, America, even Asia—gave it plenty of work; and in the fifties the chain of primary processes was turning out what seemed impossible quantities both of wrought iron, for all those uses which involved tensile strain, and of the much cheaper cast iron for those which did not. The workers at these processes during that decade numbered from 60,000 to 90,000 men and boys. A majority were employed by giant firms whose business usually included many things beside the mere making of the iron. In some districts small firms hardly existed. The average firm in Glamorgan and Monmouth employed something like 600 men in 1865. And although the survival of a great number of comparatively small businesses in the Black Country, the West Riding of Yorkshire and elsewhere, but especially in south Staffordshire, brought the national average down to about 200, that was high enough to put iron-making in the very forefront of the large-scale industries of England. The average coal-mining enterprise or cotton mill, whether for spinning or weaving, or both, was definitely smaller. And there were no women, and only a minority of lads, in the ironworks.

Men did jobs in them for the firm by the piece, and they worked in gangs, employing one another, so their exact earnings are even more obscure than those of the miners. There was sub-contract of this kind also in mining. Those 'butties' about whom Benjamin Disraeli learnt from the Blue Books of the forties—there is no record of his borrowing overalls to go down a mine; but it is easy to annotate *Sybil* from a well-known report on midland coal-mining—the 'butties' were sub-contractors, small master miners so to speak. Hence their harshness and their unpopularity; they had elbowed their way just out of the ranks, and had the ethics of most small conquerors. But the 'butty' system was confined to the midland coal-fields. In the average English coal-mine there was no regular hiring grade between the miner and the coal-owner, though above the miner there were overseers and managers, and below him lads whom he might hire. In the ironworks the grade system was exceedingly common. Puddlers were paid by the work done; they usually took on their underhands at a wage. There were gangs at the blast-furnace and the rolling-mill. Every great works, no doubt, would have a certain number of labourers working on time-rates for the firm. In the Manchester district the central level of their wage was about 15*s*. a week in 1850, very near to that of the miners. In south Wales it was rather less, approximating to the much lower local wage of the agricultural labourer. But the head puddler might be making his 5*s.* to 6*s.* a day, and the leading 'shingler', or roller, or shearer (of the iron plates when rolled) considerably more. Their takings fluctuated more violently than those of almost any other group in the world of labour, but were always relatively good. The whole organization was, however, so complex, and knowledge of exactly how much remained with the sub-contracting heads of ironworking gangs is obviously so hard to come by, that no precision can ever be aimed at. All that is certain is that these picked, masterful, and, as a rule, physically powerful men, were in at least as good a position as the foremen and overlookers in textile and other factories, whose place in the scheme of production was akin to theirs.

§ 6. ENGINEERING

About on the same wage level, and in much the same social grade as the puddlers, stood the fast-growing body of the engineers. Many of them were paid by the piece, but there was much less sub-contract in the 'shops' than in the ironworks. So knowledge of their earnings is more certain. The central level was 30*s.* a week for the skilled men of all the principal groups, which were specializing out as mechanical engineering developed—pattern-makers, fitters, turners, smiths, and so on. In 1837 the trade was still young and plastic. The very term engineer, as applied to the workers in it, was new. Millwrights, master and man, were the trained and apprenticed 'engineers' of the eighteenth and early nineteenth centuries. They were a close body who stood out for a uniform high time-rate of pay, and at first would have nothing to do with men brought in from all kinds of skilled occupations—cabinet-making, clock-making, instrument-making—to fill leading places in the new and small engineering firms. At one time the millwrights had refused to work with an engineer. They used to 'scoff and spurn at the name', one of the early employers said in 1824.[1] That phase was over by 1840; but the fight of the millwrights, which the engineers took up after them, for a standard time-wage in place of those piece-rates, that payment by results,

[1] Alexander Galloway before the *Committee on Artisans and Machinery*, p. 30.

which the leading employers favoured and had dubbed 'the engineers' economy', was never altogether abandoned.

Still mostly small during the twenties and thirties, when only a handful of leading firms employed so many as a hundred men, the engineering businesses were growing fast, both in numbers and size, during the forties and fifties. In 1844 Joseph Whitworth, perhaps the greatest name in the second engineering generation, employed 172 men in Manchester, where he had then been in business for eleven years. In 1854 he had 636 names on his pay-roll. Three years earlier 677 firms, described as engine- and machine-makers, had sent in employment returns to the census officers. They must have covered a considerable part of the trade, and certainly they furnish an excellent sample of it. More than two-thirds of them (457) employed fewer than 10 men, but 34 firms reported 100 or more, and of the 34, 14 reported 350 and upwards. These were the Whitworths, Platts, Kitsons, Fairbairns, Hawthorns, Stephensons, and the like—men who stood before kings, were even knighted, like Andrew Fairbairn of Leeds, whom Victoria, who saw him in his mayoral robes in 1858, thought 'the personification of a Venetian doge'.[1] From the Queen to the millwright there was no one left to scoff and spurn at the name of the engineer; though the poets had not yet learnt to sing it.

Small engineering firms never disappeared, but the smallest did; and the great ones grew so great that by the end of the early Victorian age the average firm employed nearly as many men as had been employed by the few, picked, leading firms forty years earlier. Engineering had taken its place finally beside spinning and ironworking as a large-scale, a 'factory' industry. And, thanks largely to Whitworth's leadership, there was an improvement in mechanism and a precision of workmanship which, far as they were behind what a later age came to regard as normal and necessary, were equally far ahead of the practice of the early nineteenth-century pioneers.

To the end of the age the men who made knives or files or nails, the locksmiths, brass-workers, chain-makers, gunmakers, and workmen in the innumerable light metal trades whose head-quarters were in and about Birmingham, were nearly all more likely to be working in small shops, or in some

[1] *Life of the Prince Consort*, iv. 304.

wretched 'home', than in true factories. Even a few years later (1870–1) when the factory inspectors were required to deal with, or at least to collect information about, this group of trades, they found themselves faced with between 10,000 and 11,000 separate places in which work was carried on, and in which the average number of workpeople was not much above ten. Fifteen or twenty years earlier the average would have been very much less; for the factory system had been making headway rather rapidly in some of these trades since the early fifties. Many men who had been small masters were becoming 'overlookers or foremen in large establishments', as Joseph Chamberlain wrote in 1866.[1] Even as things were in 1870–1, the contrast between this figure of 10 or 11 and the corresponding figure of 85 for engineering, 177 for the cotton industry, or 219 for the ironworks, is conspicuous.

Though small masters were to be found in factories, they were by no means all foremen or factory 'hands'. In the Sheffield trades especially, the 'little mesters' always retained a rough independence; and there were traces of independence among masters become factory-workers in the Birmingham trades. The hiring of power, originally of water-power, was an old story in Sheffield neighbourhood. It had begun among the grinders, who hired the 'troughs' in which their grindstones ran. It continued when steam came in, and it spread among the cutlers and all their various specialized subdivisions and associated trades. A man whose job needed power would rent a little and work with a few men and lads under him. When the inspectors set out, after 1867, to find 'factory owners' in Sheffield their task was far from easy. Familiar as they were with the hiring of power in the textile mills, where more than one 'business' might sometimes be found in the same mill running machinery off the same engine, they had no previous experience in the extreme variety and subdivision which they met at Sheffield. In a single building might be men working in the ordinary way for an employer; other men hiring power from the proprietor and doing work for him on commission; others hiring the power and working on their own account, or for a different employer. Besides all this, most, even of the greater master cutlers, had a good deal of work done 'out' by 'little mesters',

[1] In *Birmingham and the Midland Hardware District*, p. 605.

in workshops where power was neither available nor required. Last, came similar men working in similar places and disposing of their knives and what not through a factor; or sometimes taking the road and hawking them themselves; or sometimes, when luck was against them, becoming jobbing workers for luckier people.

By the late sixties the traditional Sheffield trades could show more factories, in the strict sense, than many of the light metal trades of Birmingham; but, even so, the average number of workpeople per 'works'—the term which the inspector used to cover both workshops without power and power-using factories—in cutlery and the associated trades of making saws, files, and tools, was only 21·5. Thirty years earlier, though many of the small men might be economically something very like employees of the factors who marketed their goods, and often made advances to them of cash, raw materials, or tools, factories were a very recent innovation in the cutlery trade. The first in which all the processes, from making the steel up to hafting the knife, were performed under one roof was only started in 1823. That particular type remained exceptional. Steel-making for cutlery was usually a distinct trade, the steel-makers being a small capitalistic group whose raw materials were fine Swedish iron, which was turned into steel by the slow elaborate process of 'cementation', or scrap-steel melted and cast from the crucible.

It was amongst this complicated, changeable, rough, democratic industrial society that Henry Bessemer started to make steel by his new quick patent process in 1858. The first man to roll rails out of his steel was John Brown, one of the steel-making group. He had made his money first as a cutlery-factor, but had taken up steel-making in 1844. A lifelong pioneer, he was rolling armour-plates experimentally at the same time that he was rolling the steel rails. Sheffield of the armament firms was rising amid the old Sheffield of the cutlers. But that did not get rid of the 'little mesters'. Working in their tenement factories, they were said to be gaining ground again at the end of the first quarter of the twentieth century, when armaments were under a cloud.

The semi-independence of the 'little mesters' had its parallel among the Birmingham and Black Country trades, before the factory invaded them. A Frenchman who visited

Birmingham in the early years of Victoria's reign compared its industry to French agriculture. It had got, he said, 'into a state of parcellation. You meet hardly any big establishments.'[1] As power came in, which it did very slowly, it was often hired in small doses by employers who took rooms in houses where engines had been installed. With their journeymen and apprentices, such people were nearer to the old-style handicraftsman than to the Victorian factory owner. Into many of the trades power never came at all until the new-style factories began to rise. These sometimes housed labour-saving machinery invented in America, where labour was scarcer and dearer than in the English midlands. In the older system, locks, chains, and nails, and many other things, were wrought by hand in the locksmiths' and nailers' living-rooms, or in little lean-to forges attached to them. It was in industries of this class, with their squalid, filthy, workshops in unswept alleys and back-yards, that the commissioners on child labour of the forties found every kind of exploitation and abuse, for dealing with which they made no proposal of any kind, because it was all so widespread and inaccessible. The early Victorian age was over before the simple cure was adopted of obliging all the children to be at school.

There was every degree of economic dependence and independence among the masters of the midland trades. The power-hiring masters of Birmingham might be completely independent, buying their material and themselves disposing of their goods. But, as the trades were highly specialized, selling was usually in the hands of factors who had opportunity to study the market. The weaker working-masters became, the nearer they sank into mere out-workers for the factor, who might make advances to them or supply them with material. At the bottom of all came the half-barbarous domestic nailers of Cradley Heath, Dudley, and Sedgeley, whose trade, although it declined latterly before the factory, employed 19,000 men and 10,000 women in 1851, and was believed to be still employing about 20,000 of both sexes in 1865. These were all entirely dependent on an employer, or middle-man, who gave out the 'nail rod' and collected the nails. A 'fogger' the middle-man was called. His reputation was of the worst, and he constantly broke the Truck Acts, forcing his subject nailers to take out their pay in 'goods'

[1] Faucher, L., *Études sur l'Angleterre* (1845), ii. 147.

which he supplied. Foggers were specialists. One gave out light rod which the girls and women, working half naked, turned into 'brads' and small nails at a thousand a day; another, heavy rod, from which the men made ten-penny nails or other strong stuff. The French visitor said that the men married early, had huge families, and retired early from work, letting their families keep them. It was, no doubt, a hasty generalization. He went about that country, and about Willenhall and Wolverhampton, in horror, feeling himself 'a thousand leagues from the civilized world'. Things bettered a little among the nailers during the next twenty years, but only a little. Civilization was not yet very near.

Among workers such as these there was no defensive organization, nor any possibility of one, any more than there had been among the factory children and women whose defence was taken over by the State. Those few defensive measures to which the State had for a long time been committed, like the Truck Acts, or the beginnings made with sanitary and housing legislation about 1850, did little for scattered cottage workers, many of whom lived in areas which had most of the defects, but none of the self-governing machinery, of industrial towns. Only very gradually were 'urban sanitary districts', with local Boards of Health, carved out of them during the fifties; and Truck Acts were never successfully enforced where social and industrial conditions connived at their breach. Even among the men of skilled and concentrated urban industries, the defensive barriers which trade-unionism tried to erect were weak and full of gaps. They were always falling down, or being shot down, to be rebuilt slowly and with inadequate tools.

§ 7. THE ORGANIZATION OF LABOUR

There was a tradition of union and self-defence in all the older crafts, and as new trades developed there had almost invariably been an effort to transplant the tradition to them. Clubs among cotton-spinners are heard of a few years after spinning first became a man's job. Engineers' clubs and societies, similar to the old ones among the millwrights, appear almost as early as the engineers themselves. Illegal at eighteenth-century law, such trade clubs had secured the bare legal right to exist, and to bargain about hours and conditions of work, a dozen years before Victoria's accession.

But the common-law doctrine of conspiracy and the statutory inequality of the law of master and servant might be invoked against them. More dangerous, and much more regularly used, was the natural strength of informally associated employers, who resented all attempts at 'dictation' and set out, again and again, to break trade-union power and frustrate trade-union policies by the lock-out or by the hated 'document', an extorted promise to abstain from union membership; or by the simpler, and often most effective, device of merely refusing to employ known unionists. The 'document' roused just passion, because the State had recognized the bare right of combination: it generally led to an industrial struggle, and so was relatively ineffective. The less formal and less obviously inequitable devices were more useful to the employer, especially when trade was bad and there was a local, or even a national, 'reserve army of labour' to be drawn upon. So they were most often adopted.

Between 1837 and 1850 there was not much need to adopt any of them against formal trade-unionism because in most trades it was at that time so weak; but they were, of course, employed in local industrial disputes and against the spasmodic 'turn-outs' by which unorganized workers tried to defend their claims. It is doubtful whether during the forties there were ever more than about 150,000 enrolled and subscribing trade-unionists in the whole country. For the early forties the number has been estimated at less than 100,000. The easy association of factory or coal-pit might take the place of regular organization in a struggle for limited objectives; but a workers' force which had no more secure base than this was easily defeated in detail. Most of the enrolled unionists were scattered and more occupied with friendly-society activities—insurance against sickness, burial, or loss of tools—than with considered plans for industrial aggression, or even defence. There had been great ambitions in the early thirties, an attempted consolidated union of all trades for the broadest, and most vaguely conceived, interests of the wage-earners, and the first talk of a general strike—though that was not what it was called—which should bring the new governing class created by the Reform Bill to reason, perhaps to its knees. But these ambitions had been dissipated and were, in any event, not quite natural to the ordinary member of a trade club. Whatever individuals may have done, as organizations the unions of the forties kept aloof from the Chartist movement to which dreamers and demagogues gravitated. Most of their members at that time were skilled men—compositors, masons, shipwrights, hatters, engineers, wool-combers—economically stronger and safer than most of those who filled the ranks of Chartism. If such men became active Chartists, as many did, work and enthusiasm for the Charter were likely to swamp their interest in what might well seem the narrow local ends and interests of the typical trade club. If trade-club members sympathized with Chartist aims, which they could scarcely fail to do, they might well distrust the methods of those demagogue middle-class leaders who gained control of the movement.

The 100,000 to 150,000 trade-unionists of the early forties may have grown—all figures are highly speculative—to 200,000 or 300,000 by the early sixties. (Population had grown by a quarter meanwhile.) Unions were constantly coming to the birth, but the rate of infant mortality among them was exceedingly high. There had been three 'sets of unions' in the ironworks before 1867. Unionism among coal-miners had fluctuated with the fluctuations of the industry and with the success or failure of local strikes. By 1855, according to Alexander Macdonald, the man who did more than any one to revive it during the next decade, it had almost died out in the whole country. Some crafts in which the old club tradition was strong, like that of the masons, were not very expansive. In some, which were expansive, there were many local clubs but no effective attempts at joint action; the Amalgamated Carpenters and Joiners was only started in 1861, though it had a predecessor. In others where unionism was powerful locally, as among the London compositors, it was nationally weak. The 'provincial' Typographical Association was not founded until 1849. Its first head-quarters were in Sheffield, a town rich in small, locally minded trade clubs; and it made slow progress for many years. Trades in decay, or undergoing transformation, were not fit soil for the growth of unionism. Weavers had their gilds in King John's day and their, prohibited, clubs in the eighteenth century; but the Victorian hand-loom weavers were mostly too weak for combination, and the power-loom weavers, being predominantly women and girls, had not generally taken to it, though mixed power-loom weavers' societies were being founded in Lancashire during the fifties, and rather aristocratic little unions were growing up among the male overlookers. Wool-combers had once been organized in strong and masterful clubs; but the machine came and ground them to powder. Organized shipwrights had led turbulent strike movements in the twenties. Their trade was still far from death in 1860; but the boiler-makers, whose club had been founded in Lancashire during the thirties, were learning the business, and would soon take the name of boiler-makers and iron ship-builders; and the shipwrights would be thrown on the defensive—less against employers than against these plate-riveting rivals. However, there were only a very few thousand boiler-makers 'in union' by 1865.

The representative union of the age was the Amalgamated Society of Engineers. The trade club had been transplanted early from among the millwrights to that engineering ground which they had affected to despise. Steam-engine makers had their society in 1824. Many organizations followed, some local, some general, among turners and fitters and other skilled men. Then, in 1851, these masters of the new era brought together more than a hundred of their societies and started the Amalgamated with a membership of 12,000. Not every society came in: that was inevitable; but the Amalgamated stood far above all the rest, though its organization was loose and in many ways ineffective. A fight began at once rather accidentally—against piece-work, that 'engineers' economy' which employers favoured; against the employment of unapprenticed men; and against overtime working. Employers countered with an effective lock-out, which the society survived. From that time forward its leader, William Allan, made the least possible use of the strike weapon. He kept subscriptions high—never less than a shilling a week—and so recruited only among picked men; he arranged for generous sick, funeral, and other benefit payments to make the Amalgamated attractive to solid people; and by 1865 he was at the head of about 300 branches and some 30,000 members. They were still only a minority of his constituency, for there were more than 70,000 'engine- and machine-makers' in the country; but no other trade-union leader of the day could show such a high recruitment figure or so strong a force, though his critics said truly that its fighting power was not proportionate to its size. But Allan was not out to fight. He was the safe, self-help, Victorian type who made trade-unionism a reality. He thought little of Utopia or revolution, and has been condemned for it by more ardent root-and-branch people.

It is certain that trade club and trade-union action, in the building trades for example, helped that shortening of the week's work which set in after 1850;[1] possible, but far less certain, that it had a hand in the gradual contemporary rise of wages. But as only a fraction of the wage-earners was in union at all; as no amount of union action did, or could, raise wages in trades marked down for decline; as the rise occurred in organized and unorganized trades alike, provided the demand for labour in them was active; and as few early Victorian employers were prepared to deal with the unions, their influence must have been limited and mainly indirect. Probably, however, as Friedrich Engels argued in the forties, they had sometimes helped to start 'a more rapid rise of wages after a crisis'[2] than the unstimulated working of economic law (or force) would have permitted, in a world in which the bargaining powers of employer and employed were often singularly unequal. Besides that, and vastly more important, they were bringing a new security, dignity, and self-confidence into the estate of the wage-earners; although it was still usual in other estates to view them with suspicion, or hostility, or uneasy contempt.

That concentration of industry into factories, and of factories and works into towns, which was going on all through the age, was a great help to trade-union organizers. It goes far to explain the progress of the movement. Among out-workers, even in towns, and still more in rural or half-rural areas, and among those who worked in the detached water-driven valley mills which were still common in the thirties, co-operation was never easy. In 1834–5 a quarter of the power used in cotton-spinning, and more than a third of that used in the various wool-working processes, was still water-power. Although some of these textile water-mills were in real towns—in Stockport for instance—most were not. Very often, as at Dale and Owen's New Lanark mills, a factory townlet had been laid out or allowed to spring up about them. The townlet might grow in time into a town, if

[1] See p. 46 above. [2] In his *Condition of the Working Classes*, p. 145.

more factories followed the first; but often the first remained dominant. Place-names like New Mills in Derbyshire or Saltaire, where Titus Salt built his model worsted factory by the river in 1851, tell something of the story. Salt used both water and steam and went there, no doubt, partly for the water's sake; but his buildings and their site are a reminder that early Victorians could plan towns and appreciate a rural environment for industry.

Yet those who did either were a small minority. The town where workpeople were easily got and houses for them need not be specially provided, where coal came automatically in bulk along the main railway lines, was the natural place for big steam factories. Agriculturists remained 'the great central productive class of the country'[1] and the rural population, as a whole, had not begun to decline; but the urban population was nearly 50 per cent. greater than the rural in 1865, and more than one person in England out of every four, and in Scotland one in five, now lived and worked in a city of 100,000 inhabitants and upwards. There had been five such cities in England, besides London, in 1831; still only five in 1841. By 1861 there were eleven, though all the eleven together had fewer people than London. What London was to England, Glasgow was to Scotland, and more. By the early sixties its 395,000 people formed a slightly larger part of the Scottish population than London's 2,800,000 did of the English. And, unlike London, it had an industrial society and industrial sub-towns all about it. Economically speaking, Clydeside was a blend of London and south Lancashire with a strong dash of the Black Country.

North and west of it lay the only part of the island where as yet there had been any rural depopulation. Back in the eighteenth century the Highland 'clearances' had begun, small-holders and crofters being moved by the lairds from the glens to the sea-coasts, or encouraged to emigrate. The lairds of the early nineteenth century had supposed that they were showing public spirit by 'drawing the people into villages' or encouraging them to become colonists; but the clearances, some of which in the early days had been carried out callously, all left an evil memory. Yet the danger of over-population had been real since Highland and Hebridean life had become safe and free of the small-pox. There had been

[1] See p. 3 above.

13,000 people in Skye in 1772: there were 23,000 in 1841. If the census can be trusted, the little island of Tiree held 1,200 in 1801 and 4,400 in 1841. There had been similar increases in some sea-board mainland parishes, where men brought down from the glens lived like the islanders by fishing and the precarious trade of 'kelping'—gathering seaweed to be burnt for potash. But they could not have lived at all without the potato which there, as in Ireland, was carrying a population that a grain or meat diet will not tolerate. By the forties potatoes 'furnished about two-sevenths of the food consumed by the population of Scotland', a dangerously high proportion.[1] It was far higher in the north-west and the Isles.

In Glasgow and on all Clydeside 'redundant' Highlanders competed with 'redundant' Irishmen, during the thirties and forties, for the heavy unskilled work. Together they helped to make the Glasgow wynds, where they lived side by side in 'squalid misery', perhaps the most detestable human dwelling-places in Britain. Some Scotsmen thought that squalor and 'addiction to the use of ardent spirits' were worse among the Irish, and some among the Highlanders.[2] When in 1845–7 the potato crop failed in the Highlands and Isles, much as it failed in Ireland, more destitute cottars and kelpers were driven to Clydeside—or overseas. Public spirit among the Scottish landlords and the intelligent charity of comfortable Scotland averted the worst evils of famine. In August 1847, when the bottom was about reached, the Scottish Poor Relief Board was able to report that its inquiries 'had proved no case of death entirely from starvation'. No one could have said that of Ireland, nor of any important part of it; but the cautious phrase itself implies a world of misery. The misery meant a yet harsher struggle for life in the Glasgow wynds; for starved-out Irishmen also were landing there, in much greater numbers relatively than in England. In 1851 it appeared that one person in every fourteen living in Scotland had been born in Ireland.

Glasgow's population grew by more than a quarter in the decade which ended in that year; but the population of the county of Argyll, which contained some of the most ravaged glens and islands, fell from 97,000 to 89,000. By 1861 it was

[1] From the Report of the Scottish Poor Law Relief Board for 1847.

[2] See Dr. Cowan's report from Glasgow quoted in Edwin Chadwick's *Report on the Sanitary Condition of the Labouring Population*, p. 132.

below 84,000, and Skye, with under 19,000, was slipping back towards its eighteenth-century figure.

§ 8. THE ECONOMIC RHYTHM

The early Victorians were increasingly and uncomfortably conscious of the rhythmic wave-moment of the economic life and work of the country; but very few, even of the most inquisitive and acute minds, had begun to think about it systematically. Thomas Tooke, whose *History of Prices* was appearing in instalments between 1838 and 1857, had all the facts, but he had a queer horror of averages and scales. He never drew a diagram and 'had no general picture in his mind of the trend of prices'.[1] He knew well enough, no one better, how wars affect trade (he was born in 1774 and was in business all his life) and how all particular events immediately affect it, especially bad harvests; but he spent his time pricking other men's generalizations and had no taste, or gift, for making them. John Stuart Mill, whose *Principles of Political Economy* of 1848 became at once the text-book of his generation, had no clear view even of the facts. When young Stanley Jevons, who made later the heroic attempt to correlate trade fluctuations with harvest fluctuations and harvest fluctuations with the sun-spot cycle, first discussed the matter before the British Association in 1862, he noted how very little had yet been done to investigate the ups and downs of commerce 'according to the same scientific methods with which we are familiar in other complicated sciences'.[2] He made a beginning there and then with diagrams of wheat prices, prices of consols, discount rates, and bankruptcies. Next year he applied the method of index-numbers to establish 'a serious fall in the value of gold'—the result of the Californian and Australian discoveries—and in 1865 he was examining price-variations during the preceding seventy years, feeling his way towards his ultimate, and exceedingly controversial, theory.

Whatever the fate of his theory, he was right to begin with harvests, for, as has been seen,[3] the harvests and the harvest cycle—if there be anything so regular as a cycle—were probably the most powerful factors in the very complex

[1] Gregory, T. E., 'Introduction' to the 1928 edition of Tooke's *History*, p. 21.
[2] *Investigations in Currency and Finance* (Jevons's collected papers, ed. Foxwell), p. 4. Jevons was born in 1835.
[3] Above, p. 4.

problems of prosperity and adversity. There had been a run of splendid harvests from 1830 to 1835. Harvests had nothing to do with the invention of the locomotive; but the accumulation in the banks of surplus purchasing power, to the creation of which good harvests contributed, had a great deal to do with the first little railway boom of 1836–7 during which the Victorian curtain was rung up. A large block of government war debt had been converted from 4 per cent. to 3½ per cent. since 1830, a natural and proper operation when purchasing power was abundant and 'money' cheap. 'The funds' had only become everybody's investment since Waterloo, and now their yield was dropping. People accustomed to the old rates on their savings wanted to retain them. Railway promoters said they could improve on them. During the ten years which ended on December 31, 1835, there had been just over five private Acts a year for the construction of railway lines, very short lines for the most part. In 1836–7 there were thirty-nine British Acts and several Irish. 'Railways were at once a fashion and a frenzy.'[1] Capital for the Stockton and Darlington, the Manchester and Liverpool, and the other early lines had been found mainly by business men of experience. It was now the turn of the general, and often profoundly ignorant, investor. A symbol of the new phase was the temporary existence of five distinct companies for making a line from London to Brighton. Even more symbolic is the fact that, at one time or another, the shares of all of them were at a premium. Yet there could hardly be more than one Brighton line. The general investor was being taught how to give capital value to an offchance, an old gambler's habit.

In the four years ending with 1841 there were only six more railway Acts. Bread was dear, the harvests being at best only average, that of 1838 definitely short. (The Anti-Corn-Law League was founded that year.) Foreign trade was relatively stagnant under the protective system which, by preventing the free purchase either of foreign food or foreign manufactures, set a limit to the expansion of British exports: he that will not buy neither shall he sell. It was a difficult time in domestic politics—Chartist competing with Anti-Corn-Law leaguer for the support of an unenfranchised, under-employed, and discontented people. But though much

[1] Francis, *A History of the English Railway* (1851), i. 290.

money raised for railway schemes was frittered away, railways were really being built, though with such financial strain that the Great Western once had its cheques dishonoured. The building gave employment and kept the iron-works busy; and in course of time the first set of railways began to pay dividends.

Peel, coming into power in 1841 and beginning at once to ease the tariff, was given by Heaven an excellent harvest in 1842 and fair harvests all the way to 1845. Bread in London was cheaper in 1843, and again in 1845, than it had been in any year of the nineteenth century except 1835.[1] Money, like bread, had been dear in 1839–41, following its dissipation in the first railway boom and the shortage of country surpluses available for investment which always accompanied spells of poor harvests. In 1843–4 money was quite abnormally cheap and 3 per cent. Consols rose to par for the first time for ninety years. The Treasury took the opportunity to convert no less than £250,000,000 of 3½ per cent. Consols into 3¼ per cents. Investors were again hungry for 5 per cent., and there was free capital available in the banks. The early railways were beginning to pay. Then the real Railway Mania began. Its predecessor, and the earlier isolated enterprises, had provided the country with about 2,000 miles of line. In four years (1844–7) 9,400 more miles of line were sanctioned by Act of Parliament. At the end of 1848 there were 5,000 miles open for traffic, including the original 2,000, and more than 7,000 authorized but unfinished, some of which never would be finished. This was much more than a financial and engineering feat; it carried with it social revolution.

The upper railway world was a strange jumble of ranks and personalities—George Stephenson educated at the pit-mouth, and his son Robert who had studied for a spell at Edinburgh University; Isambard Brunel, an accomplished engineer of the second generation, whose father had served for six years in the French Navy and had emigrated in 1793; the substantial business men from the midlands and the north—Quakers, Unitarians, or what not—Peases, Ellises, Booths,

[1] The notion that food was unusually dear in the forties has no foundation, except for the year 1847. Bread in London was a trifle cheaper in the six years 1841–6 than in 1831–6 or in 1821–6. In 1848–50 it was abnormally cheap, the Corn Law being repealed.

Croppers; Carr Glyn the banker, son of a Lord Mayor of London; Rowland Hill, who had kept a school and invented the penny post; ex-service men, a class often drawn on for railway managers in the early days, like Captain Laws of the Leeds and Manchester or Captain Mark Huish, that notable strategist, of the Grand Junction; Edmund Denison, M.P. for the West Riding, a gentleman of family, with as much fighting zest as Mark Huish, if not so much finesse; the great contractors, men completely self-made like Thomas Jackson, mainly self-made like Thomas Brassey, or sprung from families already experienced in contracting like Samuel Morton Peto; and George Hudson, the York linen-draper and Railway King, of whom the story goes that when asked about some current project by the Prince Consort, for he had worked his social way through the peerage to the steps of the throne, he said—'Yer Royal 'ighness, it's an 'umbug'. The Prince, so the story goes on, had to ask a gentleman in attendance to construe.

Through the working of the system of private bill legislation, all this posse of engineers, promoters, contractors, and directors, with the barristers whom they hired to plead for them at the parliamentary bar, came into the closest possible touch with Lords and Commons. That suspicion of railways which in the early days had made landlords object to the cutting-up of their property soon died away; though the railway had often to circumvent or tunnel under a park, or keep itself invisible from the terrace. Landowners now wanted new lines to come their way, if not too near the house; and as nearly every one with money to spare had railway shares, and as almost everybody in society was touched, directly or occasionally, by some railway or project of a railway, the failure or success of this or that Bill might disturb the air of drawing-rooms. Great ladies took sides in what was called 'the battle of the gauges', according as their interests or fancies inclined them towards lines projected by Isambard Brunel with his broad gauge or those of the Stephensons with their narrow one. In the servants' hall, if Thackeray is to be trusted, Jeames the footman might be making his fortune before his mistress upstairs had mastered stock-exchange slang.

England was finding the capital not only for her own railway projects, but for others in America and on the Continent.

Much of this capital went out in goods—railway metal and locomotives. (At the very end of the nineteenth century there was plying on a branch line in Baden a locomotive made at Manchester in 1847.) Returns on it were likely to be more remote than those on capital invested at home. *Per contra*, its expenditure meant a big 'make' of iron; while even some of the capital remitted abroad as cash was paid back to Brassey and the English navvies whom he used to take about with him.

Far into 1846 the pace was kept up without a check or a fall. There was anxiety late in 1845 lest the huge sums due as deposits and calls on the shares of new railways early in 1846 should not be procurable; but the burial of a number of still-born companies, and good management by the banks, solved the difficulty. There was an easing of pressure in the markets, even in the iron market, as the first rush of railway building passed; but railway Bills in thousands went on flowing through committee. Nature took a hand in the game with the short harvest of 1846. She had flown a danger signal a year earlier by arranging the first, partial, failure of the Irish potato crop. Peel had responded with the abandonment of the Corn Laws. The policy of an open market proved less satisfactory than might have been hoped, because the European harvests were even shorter than the English in 1846, and it was from Europe that emergency imports had generally been drawn in the past. Besides, Ireland now wanted food from abroad, which usually she did not. Yet, until some time after harvest, corn prices did not rise much, and the average price of bread in London for the whole year was reasonable.

In the autumn Nature played again. The Irish potato crop was far worse than in 1845; and the crop failed also in England, Scotland, and the Continent. Millions of Irishmen and thousands of Highlanders must be fed from overseas or die. Hundreds of thousands of the Irish died either of starvation or of disease, but a majority was fed. For such an undertaking the world's corn-markets were not organized. From December 1846 to June 1847 the price of wheat rushed up, to average 80*s*. 6*d*. a quarter for the three months ending May 29, and 94*s*. 10*d*. for the six weeks ending June 26. The foreign railways in which so much English money had been invested were calling it up month after month. This, combined with the abnormal demand for grain, deranged the English trade-balance for the time being. Normally a creditor nation, she became, momentarily, a debtor; for it was far too early for any yield to come from the railway investments overseas. Gold was flowing almost continuously from England to the Continent, and even to the United States, not yet a gold producer, between Christmas 1846 and May 1847. High prices for cotton, owing to a short crop, had further increased England's indebtedness to America. But the Bank of England carried on and, by refusing to lend and putting up its rate of discount, checked the outflow of treasure in May. For a moment it seemed that the risk of financial disaster was over.

It was hard that the very success of the efforts made to feed Europe should bring the risk back; but so it was. With the high corn prices of 1847, the whole world had been combed for grain. The Irish had been taught to eat maize—yellow maize flour, 'Peel's brimstone'—of which the world had plenty. Wheat contracts had been made everywhere, at prices no matter how high, in the sure conviction that the bread would be wanted and the prices paid. (In fact the average price of the four-pound loaf in London for the whole year 1847 was 11½*d.*, against 8½*d.* in 1846.) With sailing-ship transport and no international telegraph, the purchases had to be made many months ahead, the risks being carried by the merchants. By the end of June, when at Uxbridge market a parcel of wheat had recently changed hands at 124*s.*, the docks were crowded with grain-ships, and more were coming up Channel to call at Falmouth for final orders as to their destination. Already there was talk of reasonable harvest prospects, unless the weather went wrong in July.

It did not. The harvest was got in well. Prospects for the potato crop were very much better than in 1846. Continental harvests also were favourably reported on. And still the corn ships put into Falmouth to find out in which market of England or Europe their cargoes were most urgently needed. The result was wheat at 49*s.* 6*d.* by the middle of September. The price of maize had fallen lower still; for no one would eat it who could get anything else. There was a rise of wheat prices in October, but not nearly so great as was common after the first price-depressing effects of a good harvest were over; and for the six weeks which ended at Christmas the English average price was 52*s*. 10*d*. as against the 94*s*. 10*d*. of six months earlier. That was more than any group of merchants could stand.

The action of the Bank of England when it curtailed its advances to the commercial world in May had damaged a few firms; but this had been nothing serious. Real disaster began in August with the failure of London corn-dealing firms, including, unfortunately, that to which the Governor of the Bank of England belonged. From London the failures spread to Liverpool. As free trade in corn was a new thing, the number of specialized corn-importers in the country was small. General merchants, with connexions in different parts of the world, had all searched their trading areas for grain. The search had brought them profit and had been their public duty. Now, cargoes bought at spring prices must be sold at the prices of the autumn. Any firm that had put much of its resources into corn-dealing might be in danger.

Disaster spread from the merchants to the bill brokers who held their promises to pay and to banks who had financed them. After the long orgy of the railway mania the business of the country had plenty of weak, even rotten, patches. Railway companies whose works were still unfinished, and there were many of these, finding that shareholders could not pay their calls, borrowed at whatever rate they must to avoid a stoppage. Some were unable to borrow and left their new cuttings and embankments to grow green unused, or to be bought from them later at bankrupt prices. Meanwhile, the Bank of England had terrified the world of business on October 1 by refusing to make advances against Government securities; though it was using its resources freely and quietly at selected points of danger, lending to Liverpool banks and to other important firms in difficulties.

Its position was most delicate. Only three years earlier Peel's Bank Act had deprived it of its traditional free control of note-issue. Beyond a certain fixed point, it was now bound to have gold to cover every note printed. The state of the trade-balance had kept its stock of gold low all through the year. Cessation of abnormal food purchases in the autumn was easing the strain, and as, apart from that, England was the world's great creditor the future was not dark. But the present, in October, was full of anxiety. The Bank's 'banking reserve'—the notes and coin which it could lend—was under £2,000,000 on October 23. Two days later the Chancellor of the Exchequer suspended the new Bank Act. On certain conditions the Bank might increase its lendable notes, gold or no gold. The Governors of the Bank said the Chancellor's letter was not necessary. They believed they could have turned the corner without it; and, in fact, they did not exceed their legal issue. But the best City opinion was against them. It said that as soon as people knew that there was no rigid limit to the supply of notes they stopped clamouring for them or hoarding them.

However that may be, the mere monetary position righted itself very quickly. Corn remained cheap, and no new abnormal purchases were needed. England's creditor position told. The essential gold reserve came back. The speculative promotion of railways stopped. Comparatively few railway Bills were submitted in 1848, and most of them were for obviously useful links or extensions in the existing system. Free trade in corn left the farmers grumbling and the average price of bread in London falling, from the 11½*d.* of 1847 to 7½*d.* in 1848, and 6¾*d.* in 1850. Since the great French wars began it had never been so cheap.

Though bread was cheap, and remained cheap until 1853, it took some time for business to recover from the shock of 1847. There was no revolution in England in 1848; but since Russia was the only European country of importance in the same position, as the Tsar told Victoria, the year was not a good one for business with the Continent. France remained politically unsettled, and so economically rather inactive, until Napoleon's *coup d'état* of 1851 decided her form of government for the next twenty years. The German States were restless and quarrelsome. For two more years trade in England dragged; but loanable capital accumulated and the railways did their work and earned dividends. By about the end of 1850 a new force began to play on English trade—demand from the gold-diggings of California. Before 1851 was over the gold discoveries in Australia were announced. California had taught the business world what to expect. Freight rates to Australia rose at once; shipwrights' wages soon followed; and general prices turned sharply upwards before the year was over. It was natural—America was paying for imports with gold, and the first Australian gold was also reaching London. By the middle of 1852 there was more of it in the Bank of England than there had ever been before.

The consequence of this was that for a time business was exceedingly active while the rate of interest remained very low. No sooner had the Bank put gold into circulation, or sold it for shipment abroad, than more gold came in from the west or up from the south. But by the beginning of 1853 interest rates were following prices upwards. Men and companies and Governments made haste to borrow. Thomas Brassey took on railway contract after railway contract in Europe and America. Imperial France, and a group of Franco-Jewish financiers, became the focus for every variety of imaginative enterprise. The *Crédit foncier* was to lend money for all kinds of purposes connected with land; the *Crédit mobilier* for every other kind of purpose. These credit banks as they were called—they were very unlike the contemporary English notion of a bank—were imitated all over western Europe. They did a great deal of more than doubtful business; for all Europe had the gold fever. By the middle of 1853 gold was flowing out of London about as fast as it was coming in.

Then the harvest failed. In spite of free trade, the England of the fifties imported only about a quarter of her wheat, and very little of her oats and barley. Her imports were mainly either west European, and so subject, more often than not, to the same weather conditions as her own crops, or Russian, at the mercy of the policies of Nicholas the Tsar. Nicholas's armies were in the corn lands of what is now Rumania in June, and by October he was at war with the Sultan. The price of wheat, which had averaged little over 40*s*. from the harvest of 1849 to that of 1853, touched 80*s*. by Christmas; and for three years after that, two of them the years of the Crimean War, the four-pound loaf in London was always above 10*d*. But as the war was localized the general trade of the country was not interrupted. If Russian flax ran short, there was plenty of American cotton and Australian wool. Gold came in steadily with the wool. The munitions industries were busy. Even bread would not have been so dear had there not been another bad harvest in 1855. The cost of war was not heavy in proportion to the growing wealth of the country, so that there was capital available for investment both at home and abroad. Indeed, the high rate of interest which ruled almost without interruption from 1853 to 1857 was rightly traced by Thomas Tooke less to war than to the capital demands of 'new, distant, and costly enterprises'. These could not have been financed at all, another financial authority declared in 1857, but for the 'extraordinary amount of bullion . . . entirely beyond all calculation, coming from the bowels of the earth'.[1] So much of this bullion went out almost as soon as it came in that the Bank was working with a rather narrow margin when 'distant and costly enterprises' had no rival, after the signing of peace in March 1856.

Since the company promotions of 1852–3, the whole civilized world had been in speculative mood, America even more so than Europe, for she had had no war. The United States was the greatest buyer of English manufactures and the greatest borrower of English capital. England was troubled in 1857 with the news from Cawnpore and Lucknow; but the English harvest was good and Delhi fell in September. Before the good news came from the east, however, bad news had come from the west. A panic shattered American finance in September. Railways went bankrupt, and sixty-two banks stopped payment in New York. Glasgow and Liverpool felt the repercussion at once. Firms essentially sound could not pay their debts because Americans were not paying theirs. Banks began to suspend payment, and in Glasgow there was a rush of small depositors to get gold. The Bank of England sent more than £1,000,000 worth into Scotland. But panic swept up to London, and on October 12 a Chancellor's letter again came to the Governor of the Bank. This time he used it, issuing £2,000,000 of extra-legal notes, only a part of which, however, actually went into circulation.

The currency crisis was once more soon over. Gold came back from Scotland and, as always during the fifties, in from Australia. But the commercial crisis was world-wide, like the boom which had preceded it. England suffered least of any country. America, north Germany, France, and even central Europe were strewn with wreckage. America, with her characteristic elasticity of those days, recovered first. Her banks pulled their shutters down and mostly paid 20s. in the pound. Fresh railway kings took over the bankrupt lines. But her buying power could not recover at once.

[1] Chapman, the directing partner of Overend and Gurney, the 'bankers' bankers', before the *Committee on the Bank Acts*, 1857, Q. 5310.

England, though less hurt, got into her stride again more slowly; the Continent, much more hurt than England, more slowly still. English exports suffered, and 1858 was a year of very heavy unemployment. In 1859 there came a European war, though a short one. Before 1860 was over people were beginning to fear civil war in America. All this made recovery from the crises of 1857 slow and difficult. But bread was cheap in 1858–9 and so was money—the two cheapnesses which usually went together.

In a purely economic world the cheap money and cheap bread should have spelled a general revival not later than 1861, the more so as a commercial treaty with France had removed some impediments to trade in 1860. But by June 1861 the uneconomic armies of the American North and South were facing one another on the Potomac. Lancashire had been active in 1860, in speculative anticipation of the revival in demand which seemed due, at a time when work was still sluggish in many other places. Just before and just after the outbreak of war in 1861 cotton was rushed out of the Southern States, in anticipation of war or to pay for it. So when the famine of fresh cotton really began, manufacturers and dealers faced with equanimity a situation which they thought could not endure long and which, meanwhile, helped them to clear their stocks at good prices. Later, when, like the corn-dealers in 1846–7, they were scraping the world for supplies, they managed, on the average, to get about half their pre-war quantity of cotton, though most of it was of inferior quality. But as the cotton goods exported in normal times formed between 30 and 40 per cent. of the whole export trade of the United Kingdom, the years 1861–2 were the only years between 1850 and 1865 in which overseas trade did not expand at all.

If cotton working was slack in 1862–5 there were compensations. The heavy trades were full of work. There was active railway building in India. The South made effective use of the field-guns which Joseph Whitworth had invented but could not persuade the English War Office to try. It got Lairds of Birkenhead to build those rams for it which Lord John Russell would not permit to sail. North and South both wanted woollens for the armies and for civilians; so there was plenty of work in Yorkshire. Silks and linens to some extent replaced cottons, which meant fresh business in

Macclesfield, Belfast, and Dundee. And by 1863, after a moderate rise in 1860–2, bread was again cheap, cheaper than it had been in 1858–9. As money remained cheap, and as an Act of 1862 had codified the company legislation of the previous decade and made the creation of limited liability companies the easiest thing in the world, all available capital was absorbed into ventures of every kind, including a new sort of finance company, copied from the French *Crédit mobilier*, which was to direct British capital into selected enterprises at home and abroad—from the Millwall Docks to the Varna and Rustchuk Railway. By the end of 1863 money was no longer cheap, and throughout 1864 it was dear, at times very dear.

Towards the close of the year the pace slackened. The South was evidently losing and the restoration of peace in America would have results not fully calculable. In fact, when peace came, in April, America was not ready at once to resume her natural furious economic activity. There was a spell of quiet working in English industry for the first six or seven months of 1865. The Bank Rate slipped down to 3 per cent.; bread was still cheap; the home-trade demand was satisfactory, surpluses were again accumulating. And America, after only a brief halt in which to stretch her limbs, was at full work again by the autumn, farming and railway-building, buying and selling. Her demand, combined with the demands of the Empire, the Continent, and the Far East, set England working as furiously as the English temper permits. During the months January–April 1866, United Kingdom exports were 30 per cent. greater than they had been a year before—and in May, Overend, Gurney & Co. failed for over five millions. There was a panic in the City, and the breaking of the Bank Act was once more authorized by a Chancellor's letter. So the age throbbed out; but England was busier, when work was slack, and more comfortable at all times, than she had been when it began.

That the well-to-do and the middle classes were more comfortable was patent. The greater comfort of wage-earners, if less patent, was yet real. During Victoria's first decade wage-earning had been unusually intermittent and wage-rates about stationary. The cheap food of Peel's last years had been the first net gain. Early in the fifties all wage-rates had begun to move up. Railways, emigration, and the drift to the towns reduced the risks of village unemployment. Half-starved hand-loom weavers, typical members of a Chartist gathering in 1841, became more scarce year by year. By 1865 wages were, on the average, nearly 20 per cent. above the level of 1848, even for men who had not changed their trades. But as there was a steady movement from ill to better paid trades, from agriculture for example to railway work, the rise, viewed nationally, was more than that—probably about 25 per cent. The prices of necessaries had also risen, but certainly not so much. Bread in London, during the four years 1862–5, was less than 12 per cent. dearer than it had been in the four cheapest years of the century, 1849–52. Lowered taxes had cheapened the rare luxuries of the people. The beginnings of an intelligent sanitary policy, of urban parks and free libraries, were making town life more tolerable. Mine and factory laws had eased some of the worst pressures of the new industrialism. So old Chartists allowed that progress was not a rich man's catchword, though certainly it was much too slow. Plain men who had never seen visions found that they had a little more to spare for the Sunday dinner, the savings bank, the friendly or co-operative society, or perhaps for the King's Head or the Bricklayers' Arms. It was in this way that they became aware of what economists and statisticians called the wonderful growth and the rather better distribution of the national income.

Watch-cases, *c.* 1850

The Rich in Victorian England

- cost of living

II

HOMES AND HABITS

§ 1. THE HOUSE.

§ 2. THE DAY.

§ 3. COST OF LIVING.

§ 4. NURSERY AND SCHOOLROOM.

§ 5. MEALS AND PARTIES.

§ 6. KITCHEN, CHEFS, AND COOKERY BOOKS.

§ 7. THE POOR.

§ 8. THE DOMESTIC SERVANT.

II

HOMES AND HABITS

By MRS. C. S. PEEL

§ I. THE HOUSE

AT the time this chapter opens, the English aristocracy was at the height of its wealth and pride, and the union of comfort and magnificence in the great house was proverbial throughout Europe.

As we descend in the social scale, the homes of the lesser aristocracy, the gentry, and country clergy, still reproduce in their arrangements, service, and decoration, the model of the great house. But at that point we encounter another type also traditional: the house of the yeoman or substantial farmer, and parallel with it the town or suburban home of the commercial, clerical, and lesser professional classes. Still lower comes the cottage or the house in the humble street, and lowest of all the slum or warren, sometimes of almost medieval date, sometimes newly run up by speculative builders.

But all through our period and beyond it we can trace a definite tendency to standardize the home on the lines of the great house in miniature. 'Ideas', Bulwer said, 'travel upwards, manners downwards.' The merchant left his shop and moved into a square; it was not Berkeley Square, but it was rather like it. Or he went out to the suburbs; if he had not a park he had grounds, or at the very least a garden; there was no avenue, but there was a carriage sweep and a shrubbery. The farmer gave up the gabled, half-timbered, home of his father to his labourers and built himself something in red brick and slate. The working family ran into debt to buy a large gilt mirror and a carpet for Sundays. And this process, going on all over England, at a time when the aristocracy were still objects of intense interest, and the life of the gentry an ideal to which all aspired, diffused the ways of the gentry, the arrangement of their rooms, the sort of food they ate, downwards, just as the suburban or provincial dress-maker spread the fashion of their clothes.

This standardization, to which railways and illustrated

papers contributed about equally, proceeded with unequal speed in different counties and classes, a fact which makes it difficult to write of the Victorian home as a unit. In 1850 one might still have found in the Yorkshire dales, old squires leading an eighteenth-century life of coarse and jolly plenty, keeping to the old hours, old drinks, and old amusements and speaking broad dialect, while a neighbour, recently imported from Bradford, had risen to late dinner, hot baths, and the *Athenaeum* weekly. In the village one might have caught a glimpse—though rarely—of breeches and buckled shoes surviving amongst the town-made clothes, and on the road the riding-cloak of many capes still made a picturesque change from the all-encroaching mackintosh. It was an age of rapid and often destructive change, but in all changes the great house set the note and with it therefore we must begin.

Of the palaces of the aristocracy, Stowe, then the seat of the Duke of Buckingham and Chandos, may be chosen as an example.[1] This great house contained a chapel, a chaplain's room, a marble saloon 60 by 42 ft. and 56½ ft. high, four drawing-rooms, a music-room, two libraries, two dining-rooms, and three small rooms known as the Shakespeare, Jewel, and Japanese closets which were entered from the Duchess's drawing-room, the Duke's sitting-room, a billiard-room, armoury and gun-room, the State bedroom occupied by Queen Victoria and Prince Albert when they visited Stowe in January 1845, and a number of bedroom suites, some with accommodation for my Lady's woman, or dresser, or as by 1830 she was coming to be called, my Lady's maid, and some with a separate staircase leading to the servants' quarters.

On the estates of the aristocracy and the gentry, meat and poultry were home-killed, vegetables and fruit grown and preserved, butter churned, beer brewed, wines, cordials, and medicines concocted, eggs preserved, soap and candles made, vast quantities of linen washed, furniture made and repaired. Thus the service premises of such an establishment including stables and workshops, and the accommodation needed for grooms, gardeners, and other outside staff, constituted a settlement as large as a small village.

At Stowe, for example, the service premises consisted of

[1] See the Illustrated Catalogue prepared for the sale which took place on Oct. 11, 12, and 13, 1922. A previous sale was held on July 1921.

OLD GENTLEMAN, 1830

steward's room, housekeeper's room, tenants' hall and evidence room,[1] servants' hall, pantry and strong room, still room, kitchen and great kitchen including one for confectionery, sculleries, larders, cold room and general storeroom, six beer and wine cellars, coal bunker, brushing room, two sitting-rooms for housemaids, butler's room and bedroom adjoining, six footmen's rooms, pages' room and (upstairs) housekeeper's bedroom, cook's room, laundrymaids' room, ladies' maids' rooms, housemaids' dormitories, and accommodation for visitors' maids and men.

Laundry and dairy were outside the house, and while the laundry maids lived in, the dairy people generally had their quarters attached to the dairy. The head men had their cottages, but the under-gardeners lived in the bothy, which was cleaned and kept in order by a woman employed for the purpose. An ice pit was placed near the house, its contents making possible the ices which were an important item of Victorian menus.

Carrying coals, making up fires, and attending to the vast number of candles and lamps required in such houses necessitated the employment of several footmen. In the early part of our period colza lamps, which needed to be wound up from time to time and made a tiresome sucking noise, were used, to be replaced by paraffin lamps—those lamps with their opaque white shades which stood upon the centre table round which the Victorian family gathered. Although little attention was then paid to labour saving, it was the custom in some establishments to use a miniature railway by which coal was conveyed from the outside coal store into the house, where it was loaded into scuttles. The house accounts of a north country mansion show that over a ton of coal a day was consumed in winter in a house containing about thirty bedrooms, hall, dining-room, library, justice's room, boudoir, and the usual offices.

Each department in these great houses was under the control of the head servant belonging to it and under the general supervision, as regards the men, of the house steward, and of the women, the housekeeper. These personages were regarded by the under-servants, shut away in their own quarters and never permitted to be seen in the front part of

[1] The evidence room was required at a time when a Justice of the Peace might administer justice in his own house.

the house after the family and guests had left their bedrooms, almost as kings and queens. Only the head servants, body-servants, and those in attendance on the sitting-rooms, or dining-room, would be likely even to know their employers by sight.

Prince Pückler-Muskau, a Prussian gentleman who travelled extensively in England, Ireland, and Wales in 1828 and 1829 and described his experiences to a lady in his own country,[1] pays special attention to the servants' premises of the house which he inspects.

'The ground plan of the building', he writes of one of these, 'gave occasion to certain details, which I am glad to be able to communicate to you, because nearly all large country houses are constructed on the same plan; and because in this, as in many other things, the nice perception of the useful and commodious, the exquisite adaptation of means to ends which distinguishes the English, are conspicuous. The servants never wait in the ante-room—called the hall—which, like the overture of an opera, is designed to express the character of the whole; it is generally decorated with statues or pictures and, like the elegant staircase, and the various apartments, is appropriated to the use of the family and guests, who have the good taste to wait on themselves rather than have an attendant spirit always at their heels. The servants live in a large room in a remote part of the house, generally on the ground floor, where all, male and female, eat together, and where the bells of the whole house are placed. They are suspended in a row on the wall numbered so that it is immediately seen in what room any one has rung; a sort of pendulum is attached to each, which continues to vibrate for ten minutes after the sound has ceased to remind the sluggish of their duty. (This pendulum may be used by acute servants as a sort of thermometer or hygrometer of the patience of their respective masters and mistresses, remarks the Editor of these letters in a footnote.) The females of the establishment have also a large common room, in which, when they have nothing else to do, they sew, knit or spin. (Again the Editor intervenes; knitting is one of the conditions of female existence in Germany, which may account for this unwitting misrepresentation of the author, he explains, and might also have added that by 1830 spinning was not part of a maid-servant's duty.) Close to this is a closet for washing the glass and china, which comes within their province. Each of them, as well as each of the men servants, has her separate bedchamber in the highest story. Only the housekeeper and the butler have distinct apartments below. Immediately adjoining that of the housekeeper is a room where coffee is made and the store room containing every-

[1] His letters were published in four volumes in 1832 by Effingham Wilson, Royal Exchange.

YOUNG GENTLEMEN, 1834

thing required for breakfast, which important meal, in England, belongs specially to her department.'

The room where coffee was made, that is the still-room, was an important department of the household. Here all the valuable china was washed, the tea, coffee and chocolate, toast and fancy breads prepared, the dessert set out. Jam-making and preserving were done here and the home-made wines and cordials, so much used in early Victorian days, brewed, though for the home-brewed beer the butler was responsible.

But let our visiting Prince continue his tale:

'On the other side of this building is the washing establishment with a small courtyard attached; it consists of three rooms, the first for washing, the second for ironing, the third, which is considerably loftier and heated by steam, for drying the linen in bad weather. Near the butler's room is his pantry, a spacious fire-proof room, with closets on every side for the reception of plate, which he cleans here, and the glass and china used at dinner, which must be delivered back into his custody as soon as it is washed by the women. All these arrangements are executed with the greatest punctuality. A locked staircase leads from the pantry into the beer and wine cellar, which is likewise under the butler's jurisdiction.'

The Prince is not quite correct in all he says, for in the town houses of the great, a porter sat in the hall and was provided with a hooded porter's chair to protect him from draughts. At certain hours one or more footmen were stationed there also. Again, each servant certainly did not enjoy a separate bedroom either in the highest story or elsewhere; in many large houses the footmen and the under maids slept in dormitories. We know that this plan was followed in some of the royal palaces and it was not uncommon to expect servants to sleep two in a bed.

In London houses the menservants' accommodation was what we should now consider scandalous. Footmen slept two, or three or four, in a small pantry on truckle beds, and in some of the great houses the basements needed to be almost continuously lighted by artificial means. A Victorian town mansion lately vacated which had never been modernized had the kitchen, pantry, servants' hall, housekeeper's room, and butler's and footman's bedrooms in one such cellar. Two rooms looked out on to a deep basement, two others on to a deep back basement, all others were lighted and ventilated by panes of glass set high up against the ceiling.

In many households the sewing-room was upstairs, and needlework kept the women busy; every stitch had to be put in by hand, for the sewing-machine did not come into general use until the mid sixties. It was the invention of a French tailor named Barthélemy Thimmonier and was shown in the Exhibition of 1851, where it did not attract much attention. Its inventor died friendless and poor in 1857, after which date his invention was developed in America and then introduced into Europe. We find the Wheeler & Wilcox sewing-machine advertised in one of the early editions of Mrs. Beeton's *Book of Household Management.*

Prince Pückler-Muskau mentions in his letters that the dairy of an English country house is an important part of the premises. Although little attention was paid to the question of indoor sanitation, the arrangement of the dairy seems to have been in advance of the hygiene of the house. Queen Victoria and the Prince Consort took personal interest in the dairy at Frogmore which supplied the milk to the royal nursery at Windsor, and when Balmoral was built —that palace of pitch-pine and tartan—the Prince had the dairy constructed on the latest principle. To let in the maximum amount of light it was designed in octagonal form with two rows of windows. The topmost, about 18 inches square, could be opened by means of pulleys and cords and the lower ones on the sash principle, but these generally remained closed as fresh air was brought in through ventilating pipes under the marble floor, fitted with gauze to keep out the flies. The walls and floor could be hosed down, and marble shelves were provided for the milk pans to stand on. All utensils were sterilized daily in boiling water. But in spite of the fact that so much thought was given to the equipment of the royal dairy and the English liking for cleanliness, Prince Pückler-Muskau notes that in an aviary even the birds drank out of well-washed porcelain vessels, but little attention was paid to the purity of the water used in such places or in the house itself.

Sanitation as we know it was in its infancy, and so ignorant were those responsible for drainage systems that it is no wonder that in the novels and memoirs of the day 'the fever' plays a striking part. An inconvenient character in

YOUNG LADIES, 1830

fiction might always die of a fever which but few people seemed to connect with dirt or bad drainage. The idea that disease might be fly-borne and that the presence of these insects accounted for putrefaction of food and consequent illness was one which certainly had not penetrated the average mind. Lady Georgiana Russell (afterwards Lady Georgiana Peel), the daughter of Lord John Russell, mentions in her *Recollections* that her mother died of fever and that 'in those old careless days (1837) no one thought of bad drains. . . . Indeed . . . bad drains were considered rather a joke. If they smelt, people considered it a sign of bad weather approaching and were rather pleased to have the warning.' In other and primmer circles drains were not considered a nice subject for conversation, a fact which is noted by Miss Charlotte Yonge in her novel, *The Three Brides*, so, what with amused apathy, niceness, and ignorance, fevers thinned the ranks of the rich and of the poor.

Water closets with overhead tanks were in use in the eighteenth century. Mr. John Howard, the prison reformer, mentions that such closets had been provided in 1791 at Guy's Hospital, the flush being worked when the door opened, but it was not until about 1830 that they came into general use. Even then they were to be found only in better-class houses, a primitive earth closet being used by country people, and 'privies' set over a cesspool in the back yard by the poorer town folk.

The cesspools into which the closets drained were, in the country, placed in the garden or the stable yard, or even under the house. In some cases the pits were cleaned out regularly, in others they were not, and it was common for a new pit to be dug and the old one left unemptied. As late as 1844 no less than fifty-three overflowing cesspits were discovered under Windsor Castle, and later still at a north country mansion attention was drawn to an old cesspool by the ground giving way as a carriage pulled up to the 'second front door' which led from a back hall into the stable yard on to which the service premises looked. It is true that footmen who used the pantry sink often had sore throats, but it was not until the earth opened and partly engulfed the carriage that the cause of their illness was discovered.

The water closets, or 'necessaries' as they were often called, which were used during the period of which this book treats, frequently were defective, as the joints of the pipes were not sufficiently tight, and much illness was caused by the escape of foul air. Glazed pipes were introduced in 1842, and various patent pans and valves were experimented with. All of them, according to present-day ideas, were insanitary and the more so because the water closets were insufficiently, and in some cases entirely, unventilated.

The modern earth-closet was not known until 1860, when the Rev. Henry Moule took out a patent, but in the early part of our period a rough sort of earth-closet was used and occasionally such might be found in a small room, or even in a large unventilated cupboard adjacent to the dining-room, billiard-room, gun-room or, as it was called, the hunting parlour. Here too were kept the articles which gentlemen who drank deep and long might be expected to require. In some houses built in the eighteenth century, shelved cupboards were arranged behind the shutter recesses of the dining-room windows to house the chambers, or accommodation would be found for them in a cupboard, the door of which was made to balance that of the serving door at the opposite end of the side wall of the room.

One of the few luxuries not to be found in even the most luxurious houses was the bath-room. As early as 1812 it is said that the Common Council refused the Lord Mayor's request for a shower-bath on the time-honoured excuse that other Lord Mayors had done without a shower-bath, and if this one required such a luxury he should provide a temporary one at his own expense. By 1832, however, they had come to think that the Mansion House should contain a bath with a hot water supply, probably because Lord John Russell had a bath, an enormous dishpan affair, installed in his London house. Baths, however, did not escape the usual adverse criticism of what was new, and daily bathing, it was threatened, would produce an alarming increase in rheumatic fever, lung complaints, and other diseases. When in 1832 Sir Walter Scott stayed at 24 Sussex Place, Regent's Park, that house was much as it is to-day, but whereas there are now two bath-rooms, there were none then. The fitted bath as we know it only began to be at all common after the time at which this history ends.

The bath of our period was a tub into which hot or cold water was poured as required. In the days of the Georges

YOUNG LADY, 1835: CONCERT DRESS

it was not unfashionable to be dirty. One of the royal dukes is said to have remarked that it was sweat that kept a man clean, and Beau Brummel did at least one good deed in preaching the gospel of cleanliness rather than of highly-scented dirtiness. The Duke of Wellington, home from India, was considered peculiar in that he took a bath daily, a habit which the fastidious adopted and the fashion for which slowly spread amongst those who could afford the fuel required to heat the water and the labour to carry water either hot or cold. By 1865 the daily bath had become usual amongst the well-to-do, but in the middle classes the daily wash and the weekly bath sufficed.

A person still living describes the Saturday night's bathing of a middle-class family of ten children, all of whom except the baby and the ex-baby, who were washed in the nursery, descended to the stone-floored back kitchen, where kettles were boiled and where in a round high tub child after child was washed by the maid of all work.

At boarding schools, even of a superior order, the daily wash and the weekly bath sufficed. Hands and face washed twice a day, feet three times a week, and a bath once a week was considered a liberal amount of ablution. Servants washed each day and bathed once a week, as did the respectable better-off poor. Those who were neither respectable nor better-off washed when and how they could, or did not wash, about which more is said in the pages devoted to the life of the poor.

As the cult of the bath spread, the lives of delicate children were made a misery to them by the icy cold baths which many of them were required to endure, and certainly until the end of our period a young man who took his bath hot would have been regarded as effeminate.

But although there were no bath-rooms in the early Victorian home, the bedrooms were well supplied with washing apparatus. On the wash-hand-stand in rooms of any importance there would be a double toilet-set consisting of two large china basins and jugs, a small jug and basin, two tooth glasses and bottles, two china receptacles for the tooth brushes, two soap dishes, and two bowls with perforated trays for the sponges. Why these double sets of washing apparatus should have been provided in the bedrooms of married couples does not seem clear, for the husband had his dressing-room. It was only by the lower middle classes that a dressing-room was considered unnecessary.

Underneath the wash-hand-stand stood a foot-bath and a china slop-pail and on the shelves of the bed-table other indispensable china articles politely termed chambers. In addition there would probably be a *commode* which served two purposes for being made in the form of a short set of steps, those no longer active were enabled by its help to mount into the high feather-mattressed bed.

In the room or in some convenient place nearby there would be a Sitz or hip bath provided for each lady and for a gentleman a flat saucer-bath.

About an hour before breakfast-time one or two housemaids would knock and enter. The head housemaid would draw the curtains and blinds and if—which was then improbable, for a liking for fresh air was still unusual—the window was open, shut it and set the wash-hand-stand in order while the under-maid tidied the grate. ('Doing' the grate was a process which took place when the room was vacant, and when brass or steel fenders, fire-irons, and a sort of curved grid which stood upon the hearth and into which the ashes fell, needed daily polishing, it was a task which might take some time.) A bath sheet was then laid on the floor, the bath placed upon it, a can (generally painted to resemble grained wood) full of hot water placed in the bath and covered by a large towel. A jug of cold water, the soap and washing utensils were put ready together with smaller linen towels. If the lady did not employ a personal maid, the head housemaid put out the day's attire and put away the evening clothes and brought the early tea. Meanwhile the manservant, assisted by the valet, had attended to the gentleman's dressing-room.

In single rooms but a single set of wash-hand-stand ware was provided. By the time the mid-Victorian period was reached dressing-table 'sets' had come into general use. These consisted of a tray, a ring-stand, some bottles, covered bowls or jars all made in elegantly ornamented china. On the toilet-glass might hang a 'tidy', that is a receptacle for hair-combings. This, like pen-wipers, needle-books, and pin-cushions, was a gift which children, supervised by nurse or governess, would make for mamma, an embroidered case holding shaving-paper being suitable for papa.

DANDIES, 1838

'Tidies', however, were always a somewhat middle-class article and gradually sank in favour until patronized only by the working-class woman.

Before going down to breakfast, let us look at the homes of the lesser gentry. In a mansion such as might be inhabited by a well-to-do Squire there would be kitchen and scullery, still-room and store-room, a couple of larders, one for meat, the other for dairy stuff and sweet dishes, housekeeper's room, butler's pantry, servants' hall, and brushing-room; near the back door would hang a rope attached to the house-bell which rang to waken the staff and to warn the inmates of the house that meal-time approached.

In many such houses might be found on the wall near the back door a board with hooks on which hung mugs, and beneath it a cask of beer, for to refuse hospitality to any person coming to the house on business was not the custom amongst a hospitable people.

Anthony Trollope introduces us to the houses of the clergy in the middle of the century. Archdeacon Grantly considers a dining-room 16 by 15 ft. quite impossible. His companion, Mr. Arabin, suggests that it will do very well for a round table. A round table the Archdeacon considers is the most abominable article of furniture ever invented. He has always been accustomed to a goodly board . . . comfortably elongating itself according to the number of guests, nearly black with perpetual rubbing and as bright as a mirror. He connects round tables with oak, and the nasty newfangled method of leaving a cloth on a table with Dissenters and calico-printers who, he imagined, chiefly used them.

Mrs. Proudie, wife of the new Bishop of Barchester, complains that there is no gas in the house, 'there is no gas through the house, none whatever, but in the kitchen and passages. Surely the Palace should have been fitted through with pipes for gas, and hot water too. There is no hot water laid on anywhere above the ground floor; surely there should be means of getting hot water in the bedrooms without having it brought in jugs from the kitchen. . . . The Bishop had a decided opinion that there should be pipes for hot water. Hot water was very essential for the comfort of the palace. It was, indeed, a requisite in any decent gentleman's house.' If this was so, it was a requisite denied to many gentlemen until a far later date. Evidently Mrs. Proudie introduced gas into the palace, for on the occasion of the first evening party which she gave, there were huge gas chandeliers with twelve burners hanging from the ceiling.

We have a description of life in a country vicarage in 1850 preserved in a letter written when in her old age by the daughter of the Vicar;

'In 1847 we came to live in Hertfordshire. . . . The Vicarage was an attractive red-brick house, built by my father, who spent, I believe, far more than he could afford in extras not covered by the Church grant. There was a park-like field, a small flower garden and excellent kitchen garden, stables and piggery. We kept poultry but not cows. The house contained a tiled entrance lobby and oak-floored hall, dining-room, drawing-room and study, three best bedrooms and two dressing-rooms, two servants' rooms and two nurseries. These latter were in a wing approached by a baize-covered swing door, and back stairs led down to the kitchen, pantry and a small parish room, which were approached from the hall by another baize-covered swing door. . . . There were no bath rooms then, and all hot and cold water had to be carried from the kitchen and scullery. But we all had baths each day in spite of that. Oil lamps and candles were used for lighting. Our drawing-room was papered with a buff and gilt Fleur-de-Lys patterned paper. There were book shelves and pier glasses and wool-work ottomans and an upright grand piano with faded red silk fluted across the front and a very fine harp. The harp was a popular instrument in my mother's youth. The carpet was red with a buff pattern, and my mother had a davenport (a small writing-table) sacred to her own use. In the best bedrooms there were four-post beds with damask curtains, though brass beds were by then becoming fashionable. . . . After the nurse left, our household consisted of a cook, house-parlour-maid and a girl. Their wages were £18, £16, and £6. A widow who lived in a cottage near-by came in to bake and to help when required. She always wore her bonnet and clattered about the kitchen and scullery in pattens. The family then were my father and mother and myself and two brothers who came on visits, as did later grandchildren. Our income then, I think, was about £800 a year. We kept an open carriage, called a Stanhope, which had seats for two in front which might be protected by a hood, and a seat for the groom behind, one horse and a groom-gardener, who also pumped and looked after the fowls and pigs. Extra help for the garden could be procured when necessary.'

§ 2. THE DAY

And now let us go into breakfast.

In a great house, when an important party is entertained, breakfast is as late as ten o'clock. The guests, who are

MODEL OF 1842, WITH LATER ACCESSORIES—*'FLORENCE DOMBEY'*

expected to be punctual, assemble in the drawing-room, the gentlemen smartly dressed, arming the ladies, who wear elaborate toilettes and white gloves, into the dining-room, where a grand meal is served. If ladies were not present, the men might appear in fustian and hobnailed boots.

On less formal occasions breakfast may be at nine o'clock, and if guests are unpunctual what does it matter when footmen are ever at hand to attend to late comers?

After breakfast the men—or to use the correct term of the day, the gentlemen—might engage in some form of sport, attend to estate or county business, or, if so disposed, join the ladies in the practice of archery, croquet, boating, riding, or walking.

Walking and riding were popular forms of exercise, though for ladies to go out on a wet day was considered quite out of the question, as being likely to lead to serious illness, which, indeed, might have been the case when skirts were long, petticoats many, shoes thin, and galoshes and macintoshes found no place in the wardrobe. In 1820 both Macintosh and Handcock[1] were working on the problem of applying rubber to cloth, and were making, in keen competition, many kinds of rubber goods, such as diving-dresses, boots, air-beds, air-cushions, and hot-water bags, which at the breaking out of the cholera and during its prevalence were in great esteem.[2] Each firm held patents which were necessary to the other, with the result that in 1830, the two made a working agreement which ended in an amalgamation of the two firms under the name of Chas. Macintosh & Co.

The 'macintosh' as it was called did not, however, come into general use until later in the century. Galoshes were not introduced until about 1847, and then from America, though in one of her novels, *Hopes and Fears*, Miss Charlotte Yonge mentions that Phoebe wears clumsy home-made galoshes.

When riding, ladies wore habits, the full skirts of which almost touched the ground, a voluminous white petticoat, cloth trousers, a lace or lawn collar, a top hat, its masculine lines softened by a flowing lace veil, and gauntlet gloves, and carried a whip, the handle of which, probably, was adorned

[1] *Personal Narrative of the Origin and Progress of the Caoutchouc or India Rubber Manufacture in England.* Thomas Handcock, London, 1857.

[2] The outbreak referred to is that of 1831–2.

by a cap of gold or silver in which was set some semi-precious jewel. This style of dress, unsuitable as it may appear to us, did not prevent its wearer from riding far and performing feats of good horsemanship. The long and full-skirted riding habit was worn throughout our period, though in the sixties, when the hair was arranged in a chignon enclosed in a chenille net, a low hat with a feather[1] might be substituted for the top hat.

If left to their own society ladies had plenty of indoor occupation, for the upper-class women generally were well educated, readers of serious literature, and good linguists. Talk, reading, drawing, painting, the study of botany and of languages, music, music copying and needlework (Miss Emily Eden mentions that she had brought a piece of 'Company work'), and letter-writing, fill the hours until the luncheon bell rings, which, as she observes, 'is ever a cheerful sound'.

Writing letters was an occupation which took up a considerable amount of the time of ladies who, owing to the difficulties of transport by land and sea, might be separated from friends and relations for long periods.

Because of the cost of postage which was paid by the recipient of the letter and the severely restricted weight of letters, all of which had to be carried by horse-drawn mail-coaches, and the fact that a letter of more than one sheet was charged double, thin letter-paper was used and the lines of writing were crossed and recrossed, so that it was natural that much attention should be paid to the teaching of writing.

The cost of postage other than by local post varied according to distance from 4*d.* to 1*s.* 8*d.* Amongst those of the poor who could write, the habit prevailed of sending a letter which was refused by the addressee on account of the cost of postage, but as the handwriting of the sender had been recognized, it conveyed the news that he was alive. Another method of reducing the cost of postage was to give a small bribe to the guard of the coach to take the letter to its destination and there post it in the local box. Mention is made in Mrs. Gaskell's *Wives and Daughters* that Cynthia Kirkpatrick's cousin writes to her from London twice a

[1] See 'An incident in a hunt with the Quorn in the Merry Sixties'. *Chit Chat* by Lady Augusta Fane.

week, the postage on each letter being 11½*d.*, while Jane Austen in *Sense and Sensibility* makes Marianne send letters to the faithless Willoughby by the 2*d.* (local) post. The 2*d.* post continued until the inauguration of Penny Postage in 1840.

The pen then in use was the quill which needed frequent trimming, a task considered specially suitable for gentlemen, in whose pockets a penknife was ever to be found. Steel pens had been known and experimented with since 1748 and wooden penholders to hold the new pens had then made their appearance, but in 1830 a steel pen cost 1*s.* Not until 1850 was it in general use, and after then one with metal supports for the fingers was introduced, which ensured that children should hold their pens correctly. Ink during the first few years of our period was often home-made, the ingredients being powdered galls mixed with camphor and water, and directions for its concoction were included in cookery and household books. By 1832, however, Dr. Henry Stephens, who had been making ink for his own use and that of a few friends, began to manufacture it on a commercial scale and gradually ink-making ceased to be a domestic task. Letter writing was so favourite an occupation for leisured persons, that it followed that much attention was paid to the writing-table and its appointments.

Blotting-paper was in use in 1830 (Prince Pückler-Muskau mentions it), but although this paper was known as early as the fifteenth century, it does not seem to have been used until about 1820, when by the accidental omission of certain ingredients a batch of paper thought to be useless was produced. Some one trying to write a note on a piece of it found that the ink soaked in, and having a quick brain, saw the possibilities of the error and 'Slade's Original Hand-Made Blotting' was the result. This novelty took the popular fancy at once. In 1859 a Mr. Ford, who had married the niece of Mr. John Slade, commenced to manufacture machine-made blotting-paper. Prior to the use of this article, fine sand was dusted over letters in order to dry them quickly.

In 1830 and for some twenty years after letters were sealed or fastened by wafers, for envelopes were unknown. In 1839 Rowland Hill spoke of 'the little paper bags called envelopes', and Mr. Mulready, R.A., designed an envelope which was put on the market at the same time as the adhesive stamp, that is when Penny Postage was introduced. These envelopes, however, did not please the public fancy, and vast quantities of them were destroyed. The few which remain have become philatelic curiosities. The first machine for making envelopes was invented in 1844 by Messrs. de la Rue & Hill, but not until 1850 did the use of envelopes become common.

Two other articles which found a place on the writing-table were the seal and the wafer-box. These were generally of elegant shape and made of costly material. To effect a seal, heat was required, and a length of thin wax taper, coiled round and round, and imprisoned in a little china or silver urn with a hole in the lid through which the end of the taper protruded, was another common object on the writing-table, as also was a small silver candlestick holding a little coloured candle. To light the taper or candle, tinder ignited by flint and steel was generally employed until about 1834, when phosphorus matches came into fashion. Matches made with chlorate of potash had been invented by a druggist named Walker at Stockton-on-Tees in 1827, and imitations of these were made in London by Sam Jones and G. F. Watts, who sold them under the name of 'Lucifers'. They were ignited by drawing them through a piece of folded sand-paper.

Some form of penwiper was included in the writing outfit. Favourite designs were an object like a small beehive with strands of black wool inside or a flat embroidered or beaded cover with two or three thicknesses of flannel inside. As Victorian families were large and every young lady could not enjoy the use of a separate writing-table, portable writing-desks were in fashion, some of which were fitted in a costly manner.

To write interesting letters and elegantly worded short notes was part of a young lady's education. Notes were sent by hand and the sheets of paper might be formed into the shape of a cocked hat or folded into a strip with one end turned over. Did not the ladies of Cranford send such notes to each other on the occasion of a card-party? And did not Queen Victoria in the haste of her wedding preparations on the great day of February 16, 1840, pause to write her Albert a little note folded in *billet doux* form? 'Send one

YOUNG LADY AND MAID, 1844

word when you, my most dear, beloved bridegroom, will be ready,' it ran.

Halfpenny cards were not introduced until after our period, and the franking of letters, which was the privilege of Peers and Members of Parliament who franked their own and their friends' letters, ended in 1840.

Luncheon puts an end to the morning, and was served at any time from one until two o'clock. In some houses, especially in the early part of our period, this meal is a cold collation to which every one helps himself, punctuality not being enforced. The children of the rich do not eat their dinner with their elders; so seldom indeed do the inmates of the schoolroom eat at their parents' table that Ude complains in the preface to his cookery book that the ladies of England are unfavourably disposed to the culinary art because they are not introduced to their parents' table until their palates have been completely benumbed by the strict diet observed in the nursery and boarding schools. Coffee was not served after luncheon until the sixties and then the innovation was coldly received. In a private letter a lady of fashion mentions that it is feared that young men would stay on after luncheon—drinking coffee with their hostess—which would be a most improper procedure.

The next item in the day's programme was to take 'carriage exercise', and when in London to pay calls and to leave cards, a solemn social duty at a period when the rules of a complicated etiquette were followed with meticulous care. Visitors may be taken to gaze at some object of interest or neighbours are visited, who in the thirties and forties or even in the fifties offer to their guests wine and cake. Or there may be an archery or croquet party or a picnic, or my lady may visit the village school or some of the village people, who receive her with respectful awe. The men and boys touch the cap or pull the forelock, the younger boys express their respect by a sweep of the hand from the chin, which catches the tip of the nose and causes it to become, for the moment, an exaggerated example of the *nez retroussé*. Women and girls curtsy low, and should the Quality be so condescending as to enter the house there is a great dusting of chair seats. 'Poor peopling', as Miss Florence Nightingale expresses it, was already popular in 1830 and became more so throughout the years with which this volume deals.

Miss Hannah More, Miss Elizabeth Gurney of Earlham (afterwards the renowned Prison Reformer, Mrs. Fry) had set the example of organizing poor schools and a great lady might support an orphanage. Such a charitable institution is described by Mrs. Gaskell in *Wives and Daughters*. Lady Cumnor (the Countess, as she is known locally) expects the ladies of Hollingford to visit the orphanage and rewards them once a year by inviting them to spend the day at the Towers, to walk in the gardens, gaze at the flowers and fruit in the hothouses, to listen to Lady Agnes's lecture on orchids, to partake of a cold collation, to enjoy respectfully the society of the dear Countess and the Lady Harriet, to drink coffee at four o'clock, and to be trundled home in the 'charyot' or 'charrut'.

In this institution the little girls are taught 'to sew beautifully, to be capital housemaids, pretty fair cooks, and above all to dress neatly in a kind of Charity uniform . . . ready curtseys and "please, Ma'am" being *de rigueur*'.

In many of the great families a traditional good feeling for the poor on their estates was displayed, and the ladies themselves or their housekeepers, together with the clergyman's wife, distributed coals, blankets, joints of meat, and garments at Christmas, and soup, wine, and other comforts to those who fell sick. Almost all the cookery-books of the age include a chapter on cooking for the poor.

Miss Milbanke (afterwards Lady Byron) in one of her letters says that thanks to the example of her father and mother,

> 'it seemed to her a mere matter of course that the best horse should be sent many miles for the best doctor to attend on rustics who usually are consigned to the Parish Medical Officer; that the finest claret should be taken out of the cellar to be applied to the exhausted patients in a tenant's home. I did not think that property could be possessed by any other tenure than that of being at the services of those in need. . . . My Mother put a spirit into it—she did not leave it to the servants. She saw that the execution was as good as the intention.'

Some of the country physicians and surgeons enjoyed a very large practice and were greatly respected for their skill and fine character, but even so, in the houses of great people they were, if it was necessary to offer a meal, entertained in the steward's or housekeeper's room, though not, be it

THE CRINOLINE, 1855

understood, expected to eat with those worthies. Should a renowned physician be called in, he would dine with the family and probably the local medical man would be invited to meet him. To the apothecary still less respect was accorded; his task, generally, being to attend to the servants. An example of aristocratic hauteur to the medical man is given to us by a certain Countess of Carlisle,[1] who, being indisposed, sent for the local doctor. The lady felt it impossible to converse directly with so humble a person, therefore the conversation was carried on through my lady's woman, ending eventually in the statement: 'Inform the doctor that he may bleed the Countess of Carlisle.'

The local attorney was treated in the same manner, and the clergyman, unless, as might often be the case, a man of good family, only a little better, being permitted, accompanied by his wife, to 'dine at table' on the occasion of the visit of some dignitary of the Church and also on some other occasions to do honour to his cloth.

The pleasures or duties of the afternoon ended, ladies did not, in 1830, drink afternoon tea. That meal was not part of the social programme until the forties, when certain great ladies set the fashion for this refreshment. Though mammas and even papas might drink a cup of tea in the schoolroom or nursery, or an invalid might be pampered with a cup of tea, the rest of the world went tealess between breakfast and the time when the after-dinner tea-table was set out in the drawing-room.

Miss Fanny Kemble, the famous actress, writes that when staying at Belvoir (the seat of the Duke of Rutland) a co-guest, the Duchess of Bedford, used to invite her to private tea-drinkings. It was the Duchess who introduced afternoon tea at her country seat, Woburn, and at her town house in Belgrave Square. The Duchess of Sutherland (Harriet) and the Paget family liked their afternoon tea, although in the case of the Pagets the old Marquess of Anglesey, of Waterloo fame, forbade his daughters to indulge in it. They continued to do so, however, hiding the tray under the sofa if his footsteps were heard in the passage.

For a considerable time afternoon tea was adopted only in

[1] Squire Osbaldeston, his *Autobiography*. This incident occurred in 1807, but the hauteur of the aristocracy was not greatly diminished throughout the early part of the Victorian era.

fashionable houses, but by degrees as the dinner-hour became later, tea became more and more popular and took the place of cake and wine.

Although Queen Victoria, when she first came to the throne, dined as late as eight o'clock, the dinner-hour of ordinary people might be fixed at six to seven o'clock, or during the latter part of the period at half-past seven. Until the death of Lord Holland in 1840, he and Lady Holland dined at seven o'clock, as did Lord and Lady John Russell, while the Carlyles, following more middle-class modes, dined at six. Miss Fanny Kemble when staying at The Hoo with Lady Dacre in 1842 says that dinner was at half-past seven, while Miss Charlotte Yonge in *The Heir of Redclyffe* mentions seven o'clock as being the hour of a dinner-party given by the Edmondstones, county people of good standing.

After dinner the family settled down to their reading, writing, music copying, round games, or fancy work. Papa, if of a domesticated nature, might read aloud while the ladies worked at cross-stitch or, as it was also called, Berlin woolwork, producing rugs, carpets, chair seats, cushions, bell-pulls, and possibly curtain borders and pelmets. Did not the young Queen work at her cross-stitch while the Prince read aloud or played double chess 'very deep'? Some of the work was beautiful in colour, some harsh and glaring. A cushion with a spaniel's head worked in cross-stitch enriched with beads was a popular piece of fancy work. Slippers and smoking-caps—round stiffened caps with a centre tassel—were worked for the gentlemen, or long bag purses were netted, fire-screens painted, and fruit and flowers modelled in wax, coloured, and then imprisoned in a glass case. To press flowers and arrange them in an elegant album with their Latin names inscribed beneath them was also a fashionable practice.

Singing and playing upon the piano, and during the thirties and forties, upon the harp and the guitar, were approved feminine accomplishments. Gentlemen also sang and duets were in high favour, but play the piano gentlemen did not, that being considered a task only fit for ladies and professional musicians. Lord Chesterfield had been firm about this, holding that if a man loved music he should pay fiddlers to play for him but never make himself appear frivolous and contemptible by playing himself, and as it was in his day, so it was in the early Victorian era.

When guests were present there might be dancing or charades as well as music. At any time between nine and ten o'clock, the tea-table was set out, coffee having been served directly after dinner. Between ten and eleven o'clock good-nights were said, and the gentlemen lighted and handed to the ladies the bedroom candlesticks, complete with snuffers and extinguisher, ready assembled on a table in the hall. The ladies, if young, retired to the nocturnal hair-brushing conferences beloved of young females to the present day.

The frequency of references in literature of the earlier part of our period to warming-pans, which were long-handled copper pans in which live coals were placed, shows that the rubber hot-water bottle was not then generally employed, though in time it superseded the warming-pan. Those who could not afford such luxuries used stone bottles or a brick heated in the oven and wrapped in flannel.

The ladies having retired, the gentlemen donned their smoking-caps and jackets, or even complete and elaborate suits, smoked, played billiards, and drank brandy-and-water. Smoking-caps and jackets were designed to prevent the dress coats and hair of the wearers from becoming tainted by the smell of smoke. To smell of smoke would have been considered most ungentlemanly. The etiquette books of the period devote attention to the 'weed', as it is termed. In 1830 and for many years after we are told that 'a man must never smoke nor ask to smoke in the company of the "fair"'. He should never smoke in the street in daylight (Tom Hughes made himself conspicuous by smoking on the way home from the Temple about 1848), on a racecourse, or in a room frequented by ladies, and *never* must he offer a cigar to a clergyman above the rank of a curate. The 'dear creatures' are, however, warned that a little concession to the smoking habits of men is prudent for 'the pipe is the worst enemy of women'. If the cigar was also an enemy we are not told.

Cigarette—or, as the cigarette was first called, paper cigar smoking was not practised in England until after the Crimean War. It was introduced into this country by returned soldiers who had acquired the habit from the French soldiers, who in turn had acquired it from the Spaniards in the early nineteenth century.

Smoking-rooms did not come into fashion until the later part of our period. Men might smoke out of doors or in the stables or possibly in the gun-room, and in the evening when the servants had gone to bed they might smoke in the steward's room or the servants' hall, or, in modest establishments, in the kitchen. In Mr. Bradshaw's first plum-coloured railway guide, published in 1840, it is noted that smoking is not allowed either in the railway stations or railway carriages. But some enterprising companies ran a Divan.

Finally the members of our family seek their beds, both gentlemen and ladies having clothed their heads in night-caps, the men's being shaped like a cornucopia with a tasselled end, the ladies' caps varying according to taste. Victoria, roused in the early morning of June 1837 to be told that she had become Queen, appeared in a loose white night-gown, a shawl, and a nightcap which had all but fallen from her head. The typical feminine nightcap was made of fine muslin or cambric delicately embroidered or adorned with lace edged ruffles and tied under the chin. The ladies' night-dresses were made of cambric or fine linen, high to the neck and with long sleeves, prettily ruffed, while the gentlemen wore silk or linen night-shirts reaching to the ankles, with a short slit on either side, and indulged in dressing-gowns, rich both in colour and material, in which an idle bachelor would spend the whole morning.

Here is another transcript from the life of 1850, as lived by those who were gently born but not rich:

'Our meals consisted of nine o'clock breakfast, one o'clock luncheon and seven o'clock dinner. The walls of the dining-room were hung with a greyish buff paper. There was a Turkey carpet and mahogany furniture. The table-cloth was removed for dessert. We dined late on Sunday, for there was no evening church but an afternoon service was held to which women came who were kept at home by their domestic duties in the morning and at which christenings and churchings took place. The kitchen was brick-floored and had a closed range; the brick oven heated by means of wood and used for bread was in the washhouse. We had a number of visitors and we dined out at neighbouring houses, dinners being fixed when the moon was high . . . these parties were called "Moons" and at some houses "grapes", these being given at a time when the grapes were at their finest. Hot-

STATE BED, 1851

house fruit was a treat to people who had no green-houses, for, with the exception of oranges, one could not buy foreign fruit then. There were archery parties and in hay-time syllabub parties. Afternoon teas did not come in until later, but when visitors called cake and wine were offered. There were croquet and archery parties, and when tennis became fashionable I remember a local magnate playing tennis in a top-hat, but he, I dare say, was old-fashioned.

'There were balls and the neighbouring great houses—Hatfield and The Hoo—were very hospitable. . . . I visited a good deal amongst friends, and I remember that most people of any means had men-servants, or at all events a page-boy. . . . When I was a young girl (in 1850) we visited in the village, taught in the Sunday School and trained the choir. There was a Harvest Festival and a Sunday School treat and Mothers' Meetings, but there were not the ceaseless services and Guilds and to-dos that there seem to be now (1912). The servants wore bonnets on Sundays and went to church and sat in their own pew. There were boxed-in pews in those days where the quality sat in state and the poor people waited to leave the Church until the gentlefolk had made their way out. The men and women of the lesser order were separated, the men sitting on one side, the women on the other. The children were in charge of the Sunday School teachers and fidgetted and sniffed and shuffled their feet in spite of all efforts to keep them quiet. The women would carry a Prayer-book, a clean handkerchief and a posy of flowers, and before oil lamps were used there were tall iron candlesticks fastened to the end of each pew. When my father was old he went to sleep while reading family prayers and my mother had to wake him, and then sometimes he began all over again, so that prayers were very long or he skipped a page so that they were very short. The parlourmaid used to bring in the large Prayer-book on a salver and say, "Prayers are on the table, Sir". It amused my brothers and they would not let my mother tell her not to do this.

'It was usual to have family prayers in those days and the servants attended them. At one house where I stayed the parrot used to walk about the room while prayers were being read. He invariably turned his attention to the stout cook's ankles and chuckled obscenely when she endeavoured to kick him away. At last she refused to pray in public unless the parrot was confined to his cage. Well do I remember her white cotton stockings and elastic-sided paramatta boots with their black tabs sticking out at the back. My mother as an old lady wore a full-skirted dress, the bodice cut a little low and buttoned down the front. It had bell sleeves and lace under-sleeves and chemisette. Her cap had lappets on either side and covered all but just the front of her parted hair. I am not sure if she was old-fashioned; certainly she did not trouble much about fashions then. . . . I remember too that she told me that as a young girl she had a dress allowance of £100 a year and never could make it do. I was allowed £30 a year for my clothes and could not make *that* do. As a grown-up girl I wore a crinoline and a little pork-pie hat. When we went to balls our admirers (if we had any) gave us bouquets, prim and round, bordered by a paper frill. We wore yards and yards of tarlatan and our shoulders came right out of our low-cut silk or satin bodices. . . . I remember when hats were re-introduced—brown straw mushroom hats—somewhere about 1856, I think, and they were considered curiosities that only a few daring spirits ventured to wear. Everyone had worn bonnets for ages before that. . . .'

In *Wives and Daughters* vivid pictures of life in the home of a Country Squire and of a Country Doctor are presented. The drawing-room at Hamley, the home of Squire Hamley, is 40 feet long, has five high, long windows, and had been fitted with yellow satin at some distant period. There are spindle-legged chairs and Pembroke tables, cabinets full of old India china, and a threadbare carpet of the same period as the yellow satin. There are stands of plants—in the novels of Miss Yonge and in *Almacks*, a novel written by Miss Marianne Spencer-Stanhope and published anonymously in 1826, stands of flowers are mentioned—and great jars of flowers, and outside a garden with brilliantly coloured geometrically-shaped beds and a sun-dial. The ladies garden—snipping off the dead roses. . . . The dining-room is vast and the family dine at six o'clock at a small table and are waited upon by a butler and a footman. The white damask tablecloth is removed before dessert which is arranged on a table polished like a looking-glass. The Squire peels an orange . . . they play cribbage after dinner . . . there are family prayers; the cards are huddled away and the men and maids troop in. At breakfast the Squire reads the *Morning Chronicle*. There is a study and a library, and Molly Gibson, a guest, but not regarded as a suitable match for either of the Squire's sons, reads *The Bride of Lammermoor*.[1] Molly's father, Mr. Gibson, a surgeon with a good local practice, is able to afford to keep a wife and step-daughter, his own daughter, to employ two adult maids and a young girl. His second wife comes home to 'new paint, new paper, new colours; grim servants dressed in their best and objecting to any change—from the Master's marriage to the new oilcloth in the hall 'which tripped 'em up, and threw 'em down, and was cold to the feet, and smelt

[1] The first novel the Queen ever read.

just abominable', from which paragraph we learn that oil-cloth was a new-comer in the earlier years of our period and are reminded that the head of the house was then and throughout our period referred to as 'the Master', while the lady of the house was 'the Mistress'. The old servants dislike the new Mistress; there is murmuring and grumbling. They give notice and then there are floods of tears. Betty cannot leave Miss Molly, her erstwhile nursling, but the new Mrs. Gibson has all but engaged a certain Maria, 'such a genteel girl!—always brings in a letter on a salver . . . it's a pity we had not Maria before the County families began to call'.

Mr. Gibson is so greatly respected that his county patients call, though it is not recorded that their social efforts went any further. Their morning visits are paid at the hour of the Gibsons' early dinner, giving Mrs. Gibson an excuse for dining late—at six o'clock. The cook leaves. She dislikes the trouble of late dinner and being a Methodist objects on religious grounds to trying any of Mrs. Gibson's recipes for French dishes . . . 'if she is to be set to cook heathen dishes after the fashion of the Papists she'd sooner give it all up together'.

In 1830 the interior of the home is more Georgian than Victorian. It is not until after the Queen's marriage and especially after the Exhibition of 1851 that we find the typical mid-Victorian home with its striped or trellised wall-papers, crimson, royal blue, magenta, or green rep or brocade curtains, gilt or fringed pelmets, inner curtains of Nottingham lace, gaily patterned Brussels carpets, back to back settees, hour-glass ottomans, Berlin woolwork enriched with beads, wax flowers and fruits under glass cases, the round table and the paraffin lamp with its globe of white ground glass, the steel-mounted fire-place, the clock and mantle ornaments *en suite*, the woolwork bell-pulls. Sometimes the curtains have pelmets and borders of tartan, for the Queen and Prince Albert love tartan, and when Balmoral Castle is built and furnished there are tartan curtains and chair-covers and even tartan-patterned floor-coverings and pictures by Landseer, and therefore pictures by Landseer or engravings of pictures by Landseer with wide white margins in ornate gold frames find a place in the homes of the loyal subjects.

By 1865 the Victorian home is at the apex of its mode.

§ 3. COST OF LIVING

We learn something of the cost of living in the early part of our period from the *Cook's Oracle* and from a new edition dated 1824 of *A New System of Practical Domestic Economy founded on Modern Discoveries and from the Private Communications of Persons of Experience*, printed for Henry Colburn, New Burlington Street.

Both of these books were published before 1830, but the information they contain was applicable for a number of years after. The *Cook's Oracle* family consisted of three in the parlour, two maids, and a man, and allowance is made for a dinner-party once a month, the table of expenses being 'for people living in a small way' in a household 'where there is plenty of good provisions, but no affectation of profusion'.

	£
Meat	65
Fish and poultry	25
Bread	18
Butter and cheese	25
Milk	7
Vegetables and fruit	20
Tea, coffee, sugar	15
Table ale	25
Washing	20
Coals	30
Candles and soap	20
Sundries and forgets	50
	£320

Deducting coals, washing, and table ale—£75—that leaves £245, which is practically £4 15*s*. a week or roughly 16*s*. per head for food and cleaning materials.

The estimates of household expenses given in *A New System* are always planned for a man, his wife, and three children, and those in Part I are referred to in the pages devoted to the life of the poor.

In Part II, beginning with an income of £150 per annum, the man becomes a gentleman, and when his income rises to £250 per annum, his 'wife' becomes his 'Lady'. On £400 a year the family enjoy the services of two maidservants, one horse, and a groom. On £700 they keep one man and three maidservants and two horses. On £1,000 they blossom out into an establishment of three female servants, a coachman and footman, a chariot or coach, phaeton or other four-wheeled carriage and a pair of horses. On £5,000 a year the

DRESSING CASES, 1851

establishment has grown to thirteen male and nine female servants, ten horses, a coach, a curricle and a Tilbury, Chaise or gig. We give in full the estimate for incomes of £250 and £1,000 a year.

Income, £250 per Annum

Family—A Gentleman, his Lady, Three Children, and a Maid Servant.

Provisions and other Articles of Household Expense.	*Weekly.* £	s.	d.	*Annually.* £	s.	d.
Bread and Flour for six persons—1*s*. each . .		6	0			
Butter—3½ lb. at an average of 1*s*. per lb., 7*d*. each or 6*d*. a day		3	6			
Cheese—¼ lb. each, 1½ lb. at 10*d*.—2½*d*. each . .		1	3			
Milk—3*d*. each		1	6			
Tea, Coffee, &c.—5 oz. Tea at 8*s*. per lb. . .		2	6			
Sugar, &c.—4½ lb. at 8*d*.,—6*d*. each . . .		3	0			
Grocery—including Spices, Condiments, &c., 6*d*. each		3	0			
Butcher's Meat—18 lb. at 7*d*. per lb. . . . 10*s*. 6*d*.						
Fish, &c. (6*d*. per day) 3*s*. 6*d*. 2*s*. a day .		14	0			
Vegetables and Garden-Fruits—6*d*. each . .		3	0			
Beer and other Liquors—1*s*. a day		7	0			
Coals and Wood—3¾ chaldrons of coals a year at 48*s*. —91 and Wood, 15*s*.		3	9			
Candles, Oil, &c.—say 6½ dozen Candles a year, at 7*s*. per dozen—2 lb. a week		1	2			
Soap, Starch, &c. (8 dozen Soap a year at 7*s*. per dozen), nearly 2 lb. a week, and Starch, &c.—2*d*. a day .		1	2			
Sundries—for cleaning, scowering, &c. . . .			9			
Total for regular Household Expenses	2	11	7	134	2	4
Extra for Entertainments, Medicine, and other Incidents				7	11	2
Total for Household Expenses . . .				£141	13	4
Clothes—(Gent £15, Lady £12, Children £10)				36	0	0
Rent, Taxes, &c.				25	0	0
Education, Extra and Private Expenses . . .				10	10	0
Maid-Servant				16	0	0
Total Expense .				£229	3	4
Reserve, 1/12*th* .				20	16	8
Amount of Income				£250	0	0

The family consisting of a Gentleman, his Wife, and three children; with an establishment of three Female Servants, a Coachman and a Footman; in all *Ten Persons*—a Chariot or Coach, Phaeton, or other four-wheel Carriage, and a pair of Horses.

Expenses of the House, weekly.	£	s.	d.	£	s.	d.
Bread and Flour—for ten persons, at 1*s*. each					10	0
Butter—¾ lb. each—7½ lb. at an average of 1*s*. per lb. . .					7	6
Butcher's Meat—¾ lb. per day each, or 52½ lb. at 6*d*. per lb. (2*s*. 7½*d*. each)	£1	6	3			
Fish, Poultry, &c. (9*d*. a day)		5	3			
				1	11	6
Carried forward				£2	9	0

	s.	d.	£	s.	d.
Brought forward			2	9	0
Beer or ale—1 quart each per day or 17½ gallons at 8*d.* (1*s.* 2*d.* each)	11	8			
Other Liquors—1*s.* 4*d.* per day	9	4	1	1	0
Cheese—½ lb. each per week, or 5 lb. at 9*d.* (4½*d.* each)				3	9
Garden Fruits and Vegetables—(9*d.* each)				7	6
Grocery of all kinds (except Tea and Sugar), including Spices and Condiments (9*d.* each)				7	6
Sugar—¾ lb. each, per week or 7½ lb. average, 8*d.* per lb.—6*d.* each				5	0
Tea, Coffee, &c. (Servants finding their own Tea, &c.)				5	0
Milk and Eggs—(4½*d.* each)				3	9
Total for Provisions, weekly, being £266 10*s.* per annum			£5	2	6
Coals and Wood—Four fires—2½ chaldrons of Coals each fire, on an average all the year round, or 10 chaldrons, at 45*s.*—£22 10*s.*—Wood at the rate of 7*s.* to each chaldron of Coals, or 17*s.* 6*d.* to each fire, per annum, £3 10*s.*—2*s.* 6*d.* each fire per week				10	0
Candles, Gas, Oil, &c.—equal to 10 lb. Candles per week, on an average, all the year round—viz. 2 lb., moulds at 10*d.* and 8 lb. stores at 8*d.*—(1*s.* per day)				7	0
Soap, Starch, &c. for washing—6 lb. Soap, at 8*d.*—4*s.* Starch, Blue, Mangling, &c., 1*s.* 3*d.* (9*d.* per day)				5	3
Sundries for Cleaning, scowering, &c. (about 4*d.* per day)				2	3
			£6	7	0

Household Expenses, per week, £6 7*s.*	£330 per annum or	33 per cent.
Extra for Entertainments, per annum	20 ,, ,, ,,	2 ,, ,,
Medicine, Medical Attendance and other Incidental Expenses	10 ,, ,, ,,	1 ,, ,,
Carried forward	£360 ,, ,, ,,	36 ,, ,,

Distribution of Income.

			£ s. d.
1. Household Expenses (brought forward)—36 per cent.			360 0 0
2. Servants, Horses, and Carriages, 22 per cent., viz. Coach or Chariot (as per Appendix, Table II)		£40 0 0	
Two Horses (as per Appendix, Table I)		65 17 0	
Two Male Servants, viz.			
Coachman			
Wages	£24 0 0		
Livery	12 0 0		
Duty	1 11 0	37 11 0	
Footman and Groom			
Wages	22 0 0		
Livery	11 17 0		
Duty	1 11 0	35 8 0	
Three Female Servants, viz.:			
Cook	16 0 0		
House-Maid	14 14 0		
Nursery-Maid	10 10 0	41 4 0	220 0 0
3. Clothes, Haberdashery, &c. 12 per cent.—viz.:			
The Gentleman 4 per cent.		40 0 0	
Lady 5 ,, ,,		50 0 0	
Three children 2½ ,, ,,		25 0 0	
Haberdashery, &c. 0½ ,, ,,		5 0 0	120 0 0
Carried forward			£700 0 0

			£	s.	d.
		Brought forward	700	0	0
4. Rent, Taxes, and Repairs—12 per cent.			120	0	0
5. Extra Expenses—8 per cent.—viz.:					
Education	4 per cent.	£40 0 0			
Pocket Expenses	2 ,, ,,	20 0 0			
Private Expenses	2 ,, ,,	20 0 0	80	0	0
		Total Expense, per annum	900	0	0
6. Reserve, or Saving, for Contingencies, 10 per cent.			100	0	0
		Total Income	£1,000	0	0

Note.—Instead of a Coach or Chariot and a pair of Horses, with a Coachman, and another Man-Servant, as above-mentioned; a Curricle, Gig, or other two-wheeled Carriage with *three* Horses, a Groom, and a Footman, may be kept at about the same expense.

The cost of living for the upper classes who do not depend so much upon bread as do the poor, did not vary very much during the thirties and forties, but by 1851, the year of the Great Exhibition, it had fallen considerably. Beef and mutton were then 7½*d*. and 8½*d*. a lb., butter 1*s*. 2*d*. lb., oysters, the best natives, 7*d*. a dozen, and Mrs. Beeton, who gives the average prices of her dishes, notes that in 1861, soles were 1*s*. to 2*s*. the pair, pork 9*d*. lb., veal 8*d*. to 9½*d*., bacon 10*d*. to 1*s*. primest cuts, calves' heads 5*s*. 6*d*. to 7*s*. each, large fowls 2*s*. 6*d*., rabbits 1*s*. to 1*s*. 6*d*., wild duck 4*s*. to 5*s*. a couple, partridges 2*s*. to 4*s*. 6*d*. the brace, pheasants 2*s*. 6*d*. to 3*s*. 6*d*. each, quails 1*s*. 3*d*. to 2*s*. and snipe 1*s*. 6*d*. to 2*s*. 6*d*. each. On the other hand, the servant problem was beginning to make itself felt. The establishments of 1830 have begun to contract. Mrs. Beeton suggests that on an income of £1,000 a year a cook, two housemaids, and a man servant may be kept; on £750 a cook, housemaid, and boot-boy; on £500 a cook and housemaid; on £300 a maid of all work; and on £150 up to £200 a maid of all work or a girl for the rough work. A nursemaid may be added when the income exceeds £350 'or an elder daughter if old enough, good enough and careful enough may mind the young ones'.

We may put the matter thus. In early Victorian England a family in good society could live more or less comfortably on £800–£1,000 a year. About 1850 a lady with daughters writes: 'Young people of good position may marry comfortably on £500 a year and expectations, anything from £500 to £1,500 is considered a possible, sufficient or comfortable income.' Mrs. Eleanor Bold was thought to be left quite unnecessarily well off with one child and £1,200. A beneficed clergyman with house and garden free could do on £300 to £400. In the Line an officer might start married life on £200 to £400. But it would not have been a comfortable life, and the curate or poor parson who had to do with less must have been very uncomfortable. We shall see that on £100 a year it took some contrivance to keep a working family of five.

§ 4. NURSERY AND SCHOOLROOM

It will be noticed that family budgets assume three children. The natural rate of fertility was four or five to a marriage. In the poorer quarters the death-rate was appalling, but in the country, and the cleaner quarters of towns, the destruction of young life had been reduced to a more moderate figure. Victorian families were large, not because more children were born, but because more of those who were born, survived. But this advance in civilization imposed in its turn a new and heavy burden on the family budget and temper. The large family involved strict discipline and demanded much mutual helpfulness. In any growing family, not positively rich, there was always a mother to be nursed or helped, younger brothers or sisters to be cared for or taught, and a father to be attended to or amused. In the large family order was maintained by subordinating, possibly by sacrificing, the children to the father, the girls to the boys, the mother to them all. In the great house the problem was solved by keeping the children in a nursery quarter.

The nurseries in such households as these, where a head nurse and two or three under-nurses would be employed, and indeed, in those of lesser importance, were complete in themselves and, except for the service of footmen for tray and lamp carrying, were independent of the general staff. The schoolroom party had a housemaid, or as she came to be called later, a schoolroom maid, allotted to them, and a footman to wait at table and for 'carrying', which task might mean a journey of a quarter of a mile or so from the service premises.

But in spite of the fact that service was cheap and plentiful we find that servants disliked waiting on the nursery and that cooks were apt to be careless when cooking the nursery and schoolroom meals. In a private letter of the late forties, the writer notes that the fashion for allowing the elder children to dine at their parents' luncheon table may be attributed partly to the ill feeling which existed between Mrs. Nurse and Mrs. Cook. Mention is made of such domestic difficulties in books on household management, and Mrs. Beeton notes that it is usual in middle-class households to carve the joint in the dining-room and dispatch portions to the nursery, and suggests that it would be better that the children should dine downstairs as waiting on the nurse may be objected to.

In the main, the diet of children was monotonous. Boiled mutton, varied by chicken and sometimes by fish, plain boiled vegetables and milk-pudding, porridge, bread and butter, and bread and milk and a limited quantity of jam or cake were nursery foods. Fresh fruit was not in great favour, and it is not surprising that children looked forward eagerly to the hour at which, after a special toilet, Mrs. So-and-so, the head nurse, attired in a black silk dress, would escort them to the dining-room for dessert, where each child might be regaled with a taste of such dainties as he desired and a sip or two of wine.

Foods other than ordinary fare were treats, and children so greedy for them that the prim story-books of the day are often concerned with the child who, when occasion offers, eats until he is sick or even steals cakes and sugar. It is also worthy of note that in addition to wine at dessert, a glass of wine at eleven o'clock might be given to a delicate child and that in cases of sickness, wine was often ordered by the doctor for his young patients.

Mrs. Nurse also had her full share of intoxicants, a fact to which Thackeray bears witness. Beer, porter, and gin were her favourite beverages, and when nurse wished to enjoy them in peace, her infant charges might be stupefied by one of the draughts which chemists sold under harmless-sounding names, such as Godfrey's Cordial, a mixture of laudanum and treacle. This habit of drugging children is also mentioned by Miss Charlotte Yonge in *The Daisy Chain* when Flora Rivers' little daughter is doped to death by her nurse and Daffy's Elixir is recommended to young Mrs. Bold [1] together with a coral rubbed with carrot juice to ease the tooth-cutting pangs of her infant son.

In spite of a plain diet much dosing took place in the

[1] *Barchester Towers*, by Anthony Trollope.

Victorian nursery and little trouble was taken to make the doses palatable. Brimstone and treacle, castor oil, liquorice and Gregory's powder, found a place in the nursery medicine chest. That such drastic remedies were needed may be attributed to some extent to lack of fresh air and exercise. Closed windows were the order of the day and night, rooms being aired only when the children were absent and walks forbidden if the weather were cold or damp. During our period babies were carried out of doors until far older than is now the case, for the perambulator had not then developed into the luxurious baby-carriage in which the babe may sleep as comfortably as in a cot.

As regards the dress of the nursery folk, little boys had their own fashions, but those designed for little girls were mere replicas in miniature of their mothers' modes. Babies were clothed in tight stiff binders, linen shirts, a flannel and several other petticoats and very long and elaborately-trimmed robes, and for outdoor wear, heavy, elaborate pelisses. Some of the robes—of exquisitely hand-worked cambric or India muslin—measured as much as 72 inches from shoulder to hem and were invariably made with low necks and short sleeves. Even at that stage of their being boy-babies must not be dressed like girls. When they took the air they wore a trimmed-up cap, while their sisters wore an equally trimmed-up bonnet. Even when in the house the heads of babies were covered by embroidered or lace-trimmed cambric caps.

When the child left the nursery and entered the school-room, boys and girls might study together for a year or two before the boy went to school. Thereafter the girl might be educated entirely at home by the governess with the help of masters for certain subjects or after a year or two sent to a boarding school.

The education of girls is dealt with elsewhere. Here it will be enough to say that the education of a girl in a good home, where the parents took an interest in their children and the governess was well chosen and well treated, was probably as good as it has ever been. Otherwise it was a poor affair. In many fashionable households, the children rarely saw their elders: the governess was a poor down-trodden creature to whom her employers and her charges were often scandalously rude; and the most esteemed text-books, Blair's *Preceptor*, Pinnock's *Catechisms* (9*d*. each), Butler's *Guide*, and Mangnall's *Questions*, if they gave (to quote Mrs. Barbauld[1]) 'a general tincture of knowledge', were hardly calculated to make their victims 'agreeable companions to a man' or to awaken in them a desire for 'rational entertainment'. In such a home the schoolroom was often a dreary apartment behind baize doors, sunless and airless. The young ladies had their 'walking exercise' at regular hours and if long hours in semi-darkness and bad air produced 'poking' heads, rounded shoulders, anaemia, and constipation, the shoulder yoke, the backboard—an unpadded plank tilted upwards with a hollow cut to accommodate the head—and Dr. Dose were always there to put things right.

§ 5. MEALS AND PARTIES

Any one passing from one of the exquisitely simple and well-proportioned eighteenth-century rooms preserved in the Victoria and Albert Museum to an average Victorian room is at once struck by the fact that everything seems to be heavy, overloaded, and crowded. Every space has to be filled, every surface covered. *Bare* is a term of severe disapproval. In this we see two tendencies symbolized: on the one side competitive expenditure, which some economists say is the driving force in bourgeois life; on the other side, imitation of the surroundings of the great. At its best Victorian decoration achieves a certain naïve and homely charm; we feel that the inhabitants must have enjoyed it so much that we can sympathize when we cannot admire. At its worst it is a mass of shop-made extravagance without selection or meaning. And it was at its heaviest on the dinner-table, because the dinner was the great occasion for the display of wealth and dignity. The plate matched the fare and both had to be on the baronial scale.

Large families and the dinners of twenty-four, so popular, required large dishes. There were huge silver or plated soup tureens, great dishes to hold a whole salmon or a turbot garnished with fried smelts, a saddle of mutton or gargantuan sirloin of beef, and by the side of the dish might be a silver utensil full of hot water in which the gravy-spoon

[1] Mrs. Anna Letitia Barbauld often visited at Norwich and was a friend of Mrs. John Taylor, to whose *salon* she added a new grace by her charming manners and learning.

was warmed. Extra gravy might be handed from a closed utensil with a spout. The *épergne* was a feature of every table; there were vast salvers, tea and coffee 'equipages' as was the term in use, urns, bread-baskets, wine-coolers, and cruets. The table glass used during our period might be lavishly cut or a mixture of plain and coloured, certain wine glasses being made in red or green glass with white stems. Table-napkins were folded into intricate patterns and, at one time, placed in one of the wineglasses required for the service of four or five wines, but were not generally provided at luncheon until after 1865.

The service of dessert—plate, d'oiley and finger-bowl (which might be of white or coloured glass), dessert knives and forks with handles of silver or mother-o'-pearl—differed little from that of to-day except that in the dessert services a special dish for the pineapple was included, that fruit being an expensive and highly prized delicacy. It is said that it cost a gentleman who grew pines in his own hot-house at least £2 to produce each fruit.

The housewife prided herself upon her double damask table-cloths and napkins to match, and more than ever when, as in Mrs. Beeton's day, the habit of removing the table-cloth before dessert was less frequently observed. The china—Crown Derby, Chelsea, Rockingham, Worcester, Spode, Copeland, Wedgwood—then used was for the most part far better in design than the glass and silver. In small households the best china generally was washed and put away by the housewife, who wore, during the morning, a little apron to protect her dress and carried the keys of the store cupboard, linen-press, sideboards, and tea-caddies about with her in a little basket.

The day began with an elaborate breakfast with tea and coffee, toast and fancy bread, butter and preserves, hot and cold dishes and an ample number of boiled eggs. As an example of an admirable breakfast Prince Pückler-Muskau describes the meal set before him at a Welsh Inn: 'Smoking coffee, fresh Guinea-fowls eggs, deep yellow mountain butter, thick cream, toasted muffins and two red spotted trout just caught, all placed on a snow-white table-cloth of Irish damask.' At another inn he notes that on the breakfast-table there are a tea urn, silver tea cannisters, a slop basin, milk jug, Wedgwood plates, plenty of knives and forks, a

TABLE LAMPS AND CHANDELIER, 1851

plate of boiled eggs, muffins on a hot-water plate, cold ham, bread, toast, butter, and a choice of green or black tea, for all of which he is charged 2*s*. A Holland House breakfast consisted of 'very good coffee, very good tea, very good eggs, butter kept in the midst of ice, and hot rolls'. In the eighteen-thirties country gentlemen sometimes adhered to an earlier fashion, and drank beer and ate cold beef at breakfast, but the practice soon became the peculiarity of the old-fashioned.

In spite of a lavish breakfast, ladies regaled themselves with a glass of wine and a biscuit in the middle of the morning.

The midday meal developed between 1830 and 1865 from a cold collation into a hot meal, and in the fifties and sixties it began to be fashionable to allow children and governess to make their dinner at the parents' luncheon table.

The next refreshment in the day's list was the cake and wine served to afternoon callers, which was superseded by afternoon tea.

Then came dinner, which, as luncheons became more solid and afternoon tea general, was served later. The Royal Victorian dinner had always taken place at a later hour than that of ordinary folk, who, if they dined late, generally ate the meal at 6 o'clock, and as the years went on at 6.30, 7, or 7.30, Royalties and the *haut ton* often dining as late as 8 o'clock. Coffee was served after dinner to the gentlemen in the dining-room, to the ladies in the drawing-room, and tea was dispensed from a tea-table set out in the drawing-room after the gentlemen had joined the ladies at 9, 9.30, or even 10 o'clock. At bedtime there might be some sort of 'night cap', brandy-and-water being the favourite masculine drink.

In middle-class and lower middle-class houses dinner was served at hours varying from noon until two o'clock, a hot supper being provided for such husbands and fathers as could not return to the mid-day meal. Two o'clock was the favourite hour for Sunday dinner, which in such families was ever a specially elaborate meal. The rich dined late on Sundays as on weekdays.

In 1830 dinner was served in two vast courses. Hayward in his *Art of Dining* objects to the bad waiting; the servants, of whom a large number were needed, dodging about and often colliding with one another in order to offer the dishes first to the ladies and then to the gentlemen. He considered that they should proceed straight round the table, as became the fashion towards the fourth quarter of the nineteenth century. Guests brought their own footmen to wait at table, and in houses where the number of footmen was insufficient, coachmen and even grooms were employed and all were provided with white cotton gloves. The stable people apparently did not, like Mr. Jorrocks's Benjamin, object to performing double duty. When required to carry the urn Benjamin remonstrated, being of the opinion that 'If I'm a grum, I'm a grum, if I'm a butler, I'm a butler, but it's out of all conscience and calkilation expecting a man to be both grum and butler'. Carving took place upon the table, and to carve well was one of the gentlemanly arts. Almost every writer of a cookery-book devoted some pages to this subject, or to use the words of the author of *The Housekeeper's Instructor or Universal Family Cook,* a book still in use in 1830, 'The instructions here laid down by words, are materially enlivened by the representations of the respective articles described, so that the young and inexperienced may, by proper attention to the description, and reference to the plates, soon make themselves proficient in this useful and polite subject.'

Ladies, too, were expected to be able to carve, though at dinner-parties only the helping of the soup and of the sweet dishes, sometimes extremely ornamental, fell to their share. In very grand establishments the meat and the game were carved off the table by the butler.

A dinner for twelve to fourteen persons might be arranged thus:

FIRST COURSE

Two Potages.

Good Woman's Soup, dite flamande, white and thick.
Soup à la beauveau, brown and clear.

Two Fishes.

Turbot with lobster sauce.
Slices of crimped salmon, boiled, with same sauce.

Two Removes.

Turkey à la perigeux, purée of chestnut.
Leg of mutton roasted.

TABLE GLASS, 1851

Six Entrées.

Cutlets of mutton braised with soubise sauce.
Salmi of young partridges à la Espagnole.
Vol au vent of salt fish à la maître d'hôtel.
Casserole of rice with purée of game.
Saute of fillets of fowl à la Lucullus, with truffles.
Fillets of young rabbits à la orlies, white sharp sauce.

SECOND COURSE

Two Roasts.

Three partridges roasted.
Three woodcocks.

Six Entremets.

Spinach with consommé, garnished with fried bread.
Whole truffles with champaign.
Lobster salad à l'Italienne.
Jelly of marasquino.
Buisson of gâteau à la Polonaise.
Charlotte of apples with apricot.

Two Removes of the Roast.

Biscuit à la crême.
Fondus.

For sixteen or twenty persons eight entrées must be provided, and if one would entertain twenty-four guests there seems to be no end to the number of dishes and kinds of food which must be served. Ude is kind enough to suggest that 'if you have eaten too much, doubtless you will feel inconvenienced. In that case have immediate recourse to some weak tea which will speedily liberate your stomach from the superfluities which encumber and oppress it.' Almost all Victorian dinners, except in the houses of very great people, were provided entirely or in part by a professional caterer, and according to Lady Dorothy Nevill[1] it was Mr. Disraeli who set the fashion of employing a caterer to provide his dinners at a fixed price.

Prince Pückler-Muskau gives us a detailed description for the service of a dinner in 1828 or 1829. The table modes he describes survived in fashionable houses with but few changes up to the sixties and long after the sixties in old-fashioned houses.

'The gentlemen lead the ladies into the dining-room, not as in

[1] *Life and Letters of Lady Dorothy Nevill*, by Ralph Nevill.

France, by the hand, but by the arm; and here, as there, are emancipated from the necessity of those antiquated bows, which even in some of the best society in Germany are exchanged every time one hands out a lady. On the other hand, there is a most anxious regard to rank, in the midst of all of which the strangest blunders are made as to that of foreigners.

'After the soup is removed, and the covers are taken off, every man helps the dish before him, and offers some of it to his neighbour. If he wishes for anything else, he must ask across the table or send a servant for it;—a very troublesome custom in place of which, some of the most elegant travelled gentlemen have adopted the more convenient German fashion of sending the servants round with the dishes.

'It is not usual to take wine without drinking to another person. When you raise your glass, you look fixedly at the one with whom you are drinking, bow your head, and then drink with great gravity. . . . It is esteemed a civility to challenge anybody in this way to drink; and a messenger is often sent from one end of the table to the other to announce to B— that A— wishes to take wine with him; whereupon each, sometimes with considerable trouble, catches the other's eye, and goes through the ceremony of the prescribed nod with great formality, looking at the moment very like a Chinese mandarin.

'At the conclusion of the second course comes a sort of intermediate dessert of cheese, butter, salad, raw celery, and the like; after which ale, sometimes thirty or forty years old, and so strong that when thrown on the fire it blazes like a spirit, is handed about. The table-cloth is then removed; under it, at the best tables, is a finer, upon which the dessert is set. At the inferior ones it is placed on the bare polished table. It consists of all sorts of hot-house fruits, which are here of the finest quality, Indian and native preserved, stomatic ginger, confitures, and the like. Clean glasses are set before every guest, and, with the dessert plates and knives and forks, small fringed napkins are laid. Three decanters are usually placed before the master of the house, generally containing claret, port, and sherry or madeira. The host pushes these in stands, or in a little silver waggon on wheels, to his neighbour on the left. Every man pours out his own wine, and if a lady sits next him, also helps her; and so on until the circuit is made when the same process begins again. Glass jugs filled with water happily enable foreigners to temper the brandy which forms so large a component part of English wines. After the dessert is set on, all the servants leave the room; if more wine is wanted the bell is rung, and the butler alone brings it in. The ladies sit a quarter of an hour longer, during which time sweet wines are sometimes served, and then rise from the table. The men rise at the same time, one opens the door for them, and as soon as they are gone, draw

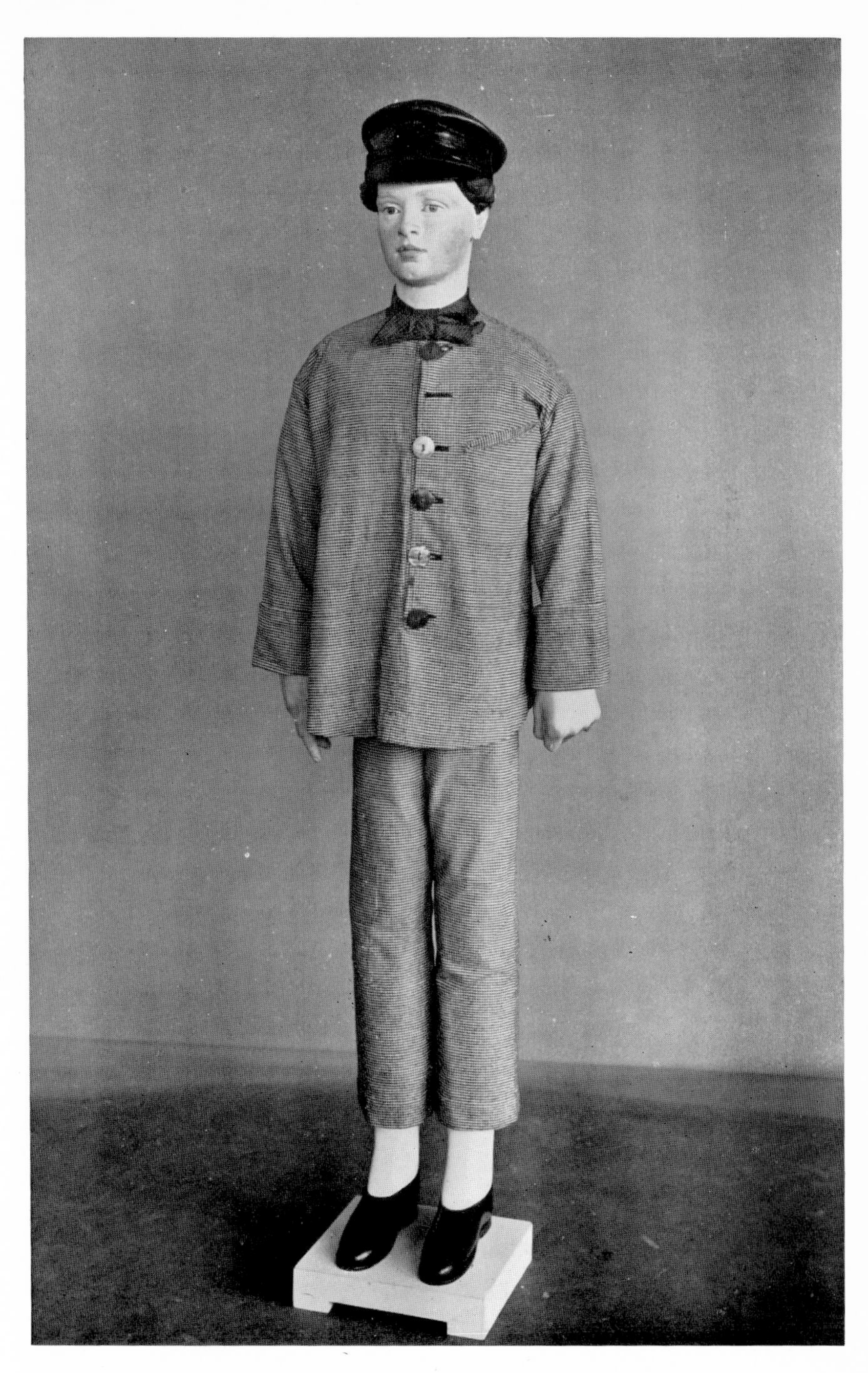

BOY OF 1856: '*ERIC, OR LITTLE BY LITTLE*'

Victoria and Albert Museum

closer together; the host takes the place of the hostess, and the conversation turns upon subjects of local and everyday interest. . . . Every man is, however, at liberty to follow the ladies . . . who received us in a "salon" grouped around a large table on which are tea and coffee.'

In 1830 and on into the forties men drank deep after dinner. If a gentleman was not in a fit state to join the ladies, his servant loosened his neckcloth and if necessary put him to bed, or if he was a dinner guest got him into his carriage and when arrived at home into his bed, and wives were so well used to this state of affairs that they accepted it as a matter of course. Queen Victoria, however, aimed a blow at heavy after-dinner drinking when she required her gentlemen to join her in the drawing-room shortly after the ladies left the dining-room.

The tea-table which welcomed the gentlemen on their arrival in the drawing-room was presided over by the hostess or by her daughters if they had been 'introduced' or as the later expression was 'brought out', though occasionally those not yet 'out' were permitted to assist.

An important article of the tea equipage was the urn. The boiling water, with which it was filled, was kept hot by means of an iron heater, made red hot and dropped into a holder fixed in the centre of the urn or by a lamp filled with spirits of wine. We find that housewives complained of water which was not boiling, as in the case of the lady described by Mrs. Carlyle, 'John, John, how is this? Water in the urn not boiling.' To which John, finding the time-honoured excuse that it *has* boiled unavailing, admits that if not boiling it is at least 'hotter than you can drink it'.

Mrs. Beeton tells us of dinner fashions in the early sixties, mentioning amongst other items that fancy name cards were introduced in 1863. Dinner guests were now expected to arrive about half an hour before dinner, and photograph albums, crest albums and new music helped to pass the time.

> How sad it is to sit and pine
> The long half-hour before we dine!
> Upon our watches oft we look
> Then wonder at the clock and cook,
> And strive to laugh in spite of fate,

she quotes. But it was not always the cook who was to blame. A guest might be late in spite of the fact that to be late for dinner was regarded as a social crime. It is spoken of in the *Cook's Oracle* as 'the impertinent affectation of opulent upstarts and commercial mushrooms—the newly rich of the Napoleonic Wars', and no more liking for late guests was evinced in the sixties than at a previous date.

But in the sixties the fashion was turning towards greater simplicity, as some menus arranged by Mrs. Beeton bear witness.

DINNER OF TWELVE PERSONS

First Course.

Soup à la Reine. Julienne Soup. Turbot and Lobster Sauce. Slices of Salmon à la Genevese.

Entrées.

Croquettes of Leveret. Fricandeau de Veau. Vol-au-Vent. Stewed Mushrooms.

Second Course.

Forequarter of Lamb. Guinea Fowls. Charlotte à la Parisienne. Orange Jelly. Meringues. Ratafia Ice Pudding. Lobster Salad. Sea Kale.

Dessert and Ices.

DINNER OF SIX PERSONS

First Course.

Tapioca Soup. Boiled Salmon and Lobster Sauce.

Entrées.

Sweetbreads. Oyster Patties.

Second Course.

Haunch of Mutton. Boiled Capon and White Sauce. Tongue. Vegetables.

Third Course.

Soufflé of Rice. Lemon Cream. Charlotte à la Parisienne. Rhubarb Tart.

Dinners like these would be served in the old style, for although *Service à la Russe* was making its way in the fifties, when it was introduced into some important houses, it did not become general until the seventies. It resulted in still further reducing the number of dishes served, and shortening the function by accelerating the service.

The standard family meal may be disposed of in simple terms: soup or fish, meat and vegetables, pudding, cheese.

THREE GENERATIONS, 1857

It was not dainty, which mattered little to a middle-class who despised what they termed 'kickshaws', but it was wholesome and it was contrived to make things go as far as possible.

Here is a week of Mrs. Beeton's menus; the shortage of fresh fruit and salads is noticeable, and this, together with lack of exercise and fresh air, probably accounts for the quantity of aperients taken by the English of all classes, which surprised such foreigners as became acquainted with their domestic habits. Where their stomachs were concerned the Victorians were anything but reticent. Revalenta Arabica cured the Countess of Castlestuart of nervousness, indigestion, bile, and irritability. Perhaps the advertisement was inserted by a grateful family. Maria Jolly furnishes an even more comprehensive testimony to its virtues as her symptoms include dyspepsia, nervousness, cough, constipation, flatulence, spasms, sickness at the stomach, and vomiting. It is significant that these testimonials appear in the *Athenaeum*, a paper with a decidedly upper-class circulation.

PLAIN FAMILY DINNERS

Sunday.

Clear Gravy Soup. Roast Haunch of Mutton. Sea Kale. Potatoes. Rhubarb Tart. Custard in Glasses.

Monday.

Crimped Skate and Caper Sauce. Boiled Knuckle of Veal and Rice. Cold Mutton. Stewed Rhubarb and Baked Custard Pudding.

Tuesday.

Vegetable Soup. Toad in the Hole, made from the remains of cold mutton. Stewed Rhubarb and Baked Plum Pudding.

Wednesday.

Fried Soles. Dutch Sauce. Boiled Beef, carrots, suet dumplings. Lemon Pudding.

Thursday.

Pea Soup made from liquor that beef was boiled in. Cold Beef. Mashed Potatoes. Mutton Cutlets and Tomato Sauce. Macaroni.

Friday.

Bubble and Squeak, made with remains of cold beef. Roast Shoulder of Veal, stuffed, and spinach and potatoes. Boiled Batter Pudding and Sweet Sauce.

Saturday.

Stewed Veal and Vegetables, made from remains of the shoulder. Broiled rumpsteaks and oyster sauce. Yeast Dumplings.

Lower middle-class and working-folk and artisans had their favourite dishes, such as boiled leg of mutton and trimmings (carrots, turnips, and dumplings), black puddings, pig's and sheep's trotters, sheep's head, tripe, and faggots (finely minced and highly seasoned meat formed into cakes, fried, and generally eaten with boiled peas or pease pudding), and then as now, certain localities were famed for certain dishes, such as Lancashire Hot Pot, Cornish Pasties, Yorkshire Pudding, Norfolk Dumplings, Banbury Cakes, Cornish Clotted Cream, and many others. Another favourite food, especially of men who could not return to dinner or afford an eating-house meal, was the Mutton Pie hawked about London by a man known as the Flying Pieman.

Other social opportunities for eating and drinking were the Ball and Ball Supper, the Rout, the Breakfast, the Wedding, the Christening, and the Funeral.

It was at Almack's—*the* fashionable dance club of its day—that the waltz was introduced by Princess Lieven in 1815 or 1816, a dance which remained in favour throughout Victoria's reign. It was at first considered shocking, although 'practiced of a morning in private houses with unparalleled assiduity', and that in spite of the verdict of a gentleman who objected to it because it 'disordered the stomach and made people look ridiculous'.

About the same time Lady Jersey sponsored the quadrille, while the polka was introduced in the early forties, one of the first houses at which it was danced being that of Lady Elizabeth Spencer-Stanhope, where people stood up on the rout seats to watch the performance. Refreshments offered at Routs, Crushes, Drums, or Assemblies, and Soirées, as evening parties were termed at various times, might be more or less elaborate according to the taste and purse of the host and hostess. The ball-suppers were even more elaborate than dinners, as we see from the menus of well-known *chefs*. Mrs. Beeton considers that for sixty dancers there should be sixty-two dishes on the table and three separate épergnes with fruit. Ices, wafers, biscuits, tea, coffee, wine, liqueurs, and if possible *Punch à la Romaine* should be served in addition. She does not suggest floral decorations, but fresh flowers and also artificial flowers and fruit were used more or less throughout the period. Jeaffreson in his *Book about the Table* notes that under the Regency, and after the Regent's example, fashionable folk called the gardener to the aid of the cook and brightened their tables with the choicest flowers from the conservatory.

At the evening parties of the small folk dancing might take place, interrupted at intervals when some young lady could be persuaded to sing, meantime the elders played cards and snuffed the candles between the deals. Evening gatherings for cards and other games, such as Commerce, Speculation, Vingt-et-un, Pope Joan, and Limited Loo, when counters of bone or mother-of-pearl might take the place of money or represent it until the time for settlement arrived, were also popular. At even smaller gatherings what was termed the Supper Tray—gracefully shaped dishes which fitted on to a wooden tray generally circular in shape—was brought into the drawing-room at 8.30 or 9 o'clock. At all such entertainments a popular beverage was negus, which was made of port or sherry and hot water, sweetened and spiced.

The breakfast might range from the simple meals given by Lady Holland or Rogers, where the talk was the chief attraction, to the elaborate functions, half breakfast, half lunch, given by D'Orsay and Lady Blessington at Kensington Gore. The wedding breakfast was a special variety of these entertainments. To be married in church was now the rule and the party returned to drink champagne, consume solid refreshments, including the iced cake decorated with artificial flowers and silver leaves, and listen to speeches. A christening furnished an equally good occasion for food, oratory, sentiment, and display.

In one direction the universal imitation of the Great assumed a really horrible form. The Victorian funeral derives from the pageantry of Tudor times, when the mourners were marshalled by the Heralds and the banner was borne by a squire. The herald was now the undertaker. His prices were high: £60 to £100 for an upper tradesman, £250 for a gentleman, £1,000 to £1,500 for a nobleman. Four black horses with black plumes drew the hearse enriched with gilded skulls and lacquered cherubs: the family provided carriage accommodation for the funeral party, whose empty coaches trailed behind: mutes and mourners, hired from the same establishment, walked at the side. Undertakers' men were commonly of the lowest class and character: sometimes they returned in the hearse because they could no longer walk beside it. The procession dragged its way along crowded streets to one of the new cemeteries, Kensal Green, Highgate, or Abney Park, where portentous monuments advertised the grief of the family and the wealth of the deceased. Some of the companies kept a clergyman, Episcopal or other: sometimes an attendant would slip on a surplice and read whatever service was required, and the rite not uncommonly ended with the grave-digger, half drunk already, pursuing the mourners to the gate with demands for more. In humbler circles the funeral carriage had a boot under the driver for the coffin and the party tumbled in behind. An official estimate reckoned that £5,000,000 a year was spent on funerals, of which £4,000,000 went on 'silk scarves and brass nails, feathers for the horses, gin for the mutes, and satin for the worms'.

§ 6. KITCHEN, CHEFS, AND COOKERY BOOKS

In spite of Soyer's gas kitchen at the Reform Club, which was one of the sights of the thirties, the Victorian cook would have none of such newfangled notions. She cooked by means of coal and roasted her prime English joints before an open fire in front of which stood the meat screen, and did a great deal of basting with the help of a long-handled ladle. She had a hot plate for boiling and ovens for baking, though she might bake bread in a brick oven in the scullery or outhouse.

In some houses a closed roaster introduced by Count Rumford in the late years of the previous century was to be found. This gentlemen objected to the enormous waste of fuel in the kitchens of this country, and had ideas on the subject of cooking ranges and utensils much in advance of his day.[1] By the early sixties the closed range was in common use and is advertised in the early editions of Mrs. Beeton's book.

The pots and pans of our period were large and heavy, and those made of copper, with an inner lining of tin, were the pride of the cook and the detestation of the kitchen maid, whose duty it was to keep them clean and shining.

[1] Those readers specially interested in the subject should study the four volumes of the *Life and Works of Count Rumford*, published by Macmillan & Co., Ltd.

YOUNG LADIES, 1860

Among the implements needed by her were the sugar-clippers and pestle and mortar, for loaf sugar was then sold in cones, wrapped in blue paper, and had to be cut into cubes, or when powdered sugar was required, pounded with a pestle in a mortar. Ready prepared foods in packets and containers were uncommon, and suet was shredded, almonds pounded, and coffee ground (as indeed it still is where coffee-making is an art) at home, though by Mrs. Beeton's day Goodall is already advertising his Blancmange Powder and Egg Powder, 'a penny packet of which will go as far as four eggs'.

In the beginning of our period the cook must work by the light of tallow dips or moulded candles and colza oil-lamps, later by the light of paraffin oil, and then, in town houses, by gas.

The kitchen in well-to-do houses is large, the floors paved with stone or brick or made of well-scrubbed boards. There is a scullery and in it a copper. The sink is of stone or of wood lined with zinc, and although it is impossible that all cooks should have been fat, the typical domestic cook of the Victorian home *is* fat. Her face is red, she wears a cap and a print dress, turns back her sleeves, and is inclined to be tempersome with intervals of jollity. In 'good' houses she is addressed and referred to as Mrs. So-and-so, while in middle-class circles, although housemaids have names, one finds that the cook is 'Cook' plain and simple.

Famous chefs of the period were Felix, Carême, Ude, Francatelli, and Soyer. Felix left Lord Seaford to take service with *the* Duke. His new employer is said to have had a passion for rice but otherwise was rather indifferent as to what he ate. 'I serve him a dinner which would make Ude or Francatelli burst with envy and he says nothing. I serve him a dinner badly dressed by the cook-maid and he says nothing. I cannot live with such a master were he a hundred times a hero.' The wounded feelings of an artist caused Felix to seek service elsewhere. Carême, who wrote *Maître d'Hotel Français*, was at one time chef to the Regent at a salary of £1,000 and perquisites which included *pâtés* which, having left the Regent's table untouched, were bought for large prices by snobbish persons.

But by far the most illustrious name on the roll is that of Alexis Soyer, the only chef recorded in the *Dictionary of*

National Biography. At twenty-one the Revolution of 1830 caused him to leave France. After serving in various great houses, he became in 1837 chef to the Reform Club, which had just begun to rear its Radical front against the Tory Carlton and the Whig Brooks's. The engagement of Soyer was a master-stroke of the management; his Coronation breakfast to 2,000 members and friends made him a national celebrity. In 1847 the Government asked him to take charge of the soup-kitchens established in Dublin. His skill, combined with the natural frugality of the French peasant, made them a complete success. Later he invented a small cooking range on which he demonstrated before crowds of distinguished clients. His Symposium at Gore House, Kensington, opened to cater for the visitors to the Great Exhibition, was for some reason not a success, but the Crimean War brought him great opportunities. He went to the East at the request of the Government, organized the victualling and dietry of the hospitals, and became the leading authority on military and naval cooking. His books became classics, and his example was one of the principal forces which made for economy and simplicity in the waste and elaboration of the Victorian cuisine.

Charles Elme Francatelli was *maître d'hôtel* to Queen Victoria and the Prince Consort, a pupil of the great Carême, and at one time presided over the kitchens of that famous gambling club, Crockford's, following the celebrated Louis Eustache Ude, who was an engraver, a printer, a haberdasher, an *agent de change, maître d'hôtel* to Madame Letitia Bonaparte, chef to Lord Sefton and to Crockford's. The writings of these gastronomic celebrities were in use throughout the years with which we deal, as indeed they are to-day.[1]

Of cookery-books written by women, the *Cookery Book* of Margaret Dodd published in 1830, and those of Mrs. Rundell, Miss Acton, and Mrs. Beeton were the domestic Bibles of 1830–65. Long titles were the fashion in the earlier part of the nineteenth century and Mrs. Rundell's book appeared as a *New System of Domestic Cookery, formed upon Principles of*

[1] Other books on food and its service which we have already mentioned were the *Cook's Oracle* and the *Housekeeper's Oracle* by Dr. Kitchiner, which were published in 1821 and 1822 and were much in vogue at the beginning of our period, as was Hayward's *Art of Dining*.

YOUNG LADY, 1860

Economy and adapted to the Use of Private Families. In the advertisement the author says:

'The following directions were intended for the conduct of the families of the Author's own daughters, and for the arrangement of their table, so as to unite a good figure with proper economy. She has avoided all excessive luxury, such as essence of ham, and that wasteful expenditure of large quantities of meat for gravy, which so greatly contributes to keep up the prices, and is no less injurious to those who eat, than to those whose penury obliges them to abstain.'

The author of this admirable book complains of the general ignorance of the domestic arts, pointing out that there is no opportunity of obtaining a knowledge of family management at school, and during the vacations all subjects that might interfere with amusement are avoided. She also hopes that as she will receive no emolument for her book it will escape without censure. Why Mrs. Rundell should have made this statement is not clear, for up to 1823 she received about £200 in royalties and then Messrs. John Murray bought the copyright for 2,000 guineas. It would appear that this book was first published in 1819, but it was undoubtedly still *the* cookery-book of the English household in 1830 and for some years later.

In the forties Miss Eliza Acton's *Modern Cookery in all its Branches* appeared. Miss Acton wrote Byronic poetry when younger, and ultimately, when on the threshold of middle-age, asked for an interview with Mr. Longman, the publisher, to whom she said that she had written a book that was little wanted. 'Give me the subject of a book for which the world has a need and I will write it for you. I am a poet but I shall write no more poems. The world does not want poems.'

Mr. Longman said to the lady who was ready to write prose on any subject: 'Well, Miss Acton, we want a really good cookery book, and if you write me a really good one, I shall be happy to publish it for you.' Miss Acton took years over the preparation of her book, and it was said that before long there was neither epicure nor chef in England who had not addressed to her highly flattering letters.

In the mid-fifties Mrs. Beeton came upon the scene. Her famous work was first published in sixpenny monthly parts. Then in 1861 a one-volume edition was published, which in its turn, like the works of Mrs. Rundell and Miss Acton, became *the* book on domestic cookery and household management of its day, and in revised editions is still a best seller. Those who study her book now probably think of Mrs. Beeton as an elderly lady in flowing bombazine skirts and a cap, akin to the mythical Mrs. Grundy, goddess of Victorian convention. In reality, Mrs. Isabella Mary Beeton was a pretty young thing and a clever young thing, too. She went to her wedding with Mr. Samuel Orchart Beeton, the publisher, in flounces and a white bonnet, was a clever journalist, produced her masterpiece, gave birth to four little boys, and died in her late twenties. One might wish that she had lived longer to enjoy the success resulting from 'four years of incessant labour'.

§ 7. THE POOR

The same difficulty that we had in dealing with the middle classes recurs with double force when we come to the poor—rapid change and local variation. On the same wage, and in the same trade, one man might be comfortably housed and well fed, another wretchedly housed and half-starved. A street which was putting money by in 1830 might be existing on poor relief in 1840, bursting with prosperity in 1850, and kept alive by charity in the Cotton Famine. On the whole, for the town worker, things had decidedly improved between 1830 and 1865; for the rural worker, not. But both in town and country between 1830 and 1865 lay the deep trough of the later thirties and the hungry forties.

To fill in this outline is the problem. The people themselves, except when their voices cry to us direct as witnesses before Royal Commissions, are for the most part inarticulate. What we know of them is conveyed at second hand, mostly by reformers and novelists. Reformers must prove their point: novelists must interest their public. We have domestic budgets, but unfortunately with the exception of Le Play's in 1855 they are almost invariably made not *by* the poor but *for* the poor. And, as every social student knows, a family budget tells only half the tale. Yet, such as they are, with the family budget we must begin.

As a datum we will take from *A System of Practical Domestic Economy* (1824) the family budget of a household living on

OLD LADY AND CHILD, 1860

48*s*. a week. The family, as usual, consists of man, wife, and three children.

	£	s.	d.
Bread and Flour for five persons, 24 lb. at 2¼*d*. per lb.		4	6
Butter—2 lb. at 1*s*.		2	0
Cheese—¾ lb. at 10*d*.			7½
Milk—1½*d*. per day			10½
Tea or Coffee—say ¼ lb. Tea, at 7*s*.		1	9
Sugar—3 lb. at 8*d*.		2	0
Grocery, including Fruits, Spices, Condiments, &c.		1	0
Butcher's meat, Fish, &c., say 12 lb., at 6*d*.		6	0
Vegetables and garden-fruits—say 3*d*. a day		1	9
Beer, Ale, &c.—6*d*. per day		3	6
Coals—2½ Chaldrons of Coals a year, say 48*s*. per chaldron, £6 and Wood 10*s*. a year		2	6
Candles—1 lb. a week on an average			7
Soap, Starch, &c. for washing			7
Sundries, for scowering and cleaning—1*d*. a day			7
Total for Household Expenses	£1	8	3
Clothes (Man, 3*s*. 6*d*., Wife, 2*s*. 6*d*., Children, 2*s*.)		8	0
Rent		6	0
Extra (including Schooling)		1	9
Total Expense	£2	4	0
Saving, 1-12th		4	0
Amount of Income	£2	8	0

'This man and wife arrange their affairs thus: he rents a neat little house, of six rooms, in the vicinity of London, the rent of which, with the taxes &c. costs him about £35 10*s*. a year; out of which he receives £20 a year for the first floor and the occasional use of the kitchen; he consequently stands at about £15 10*s*. a year, or 6*s*. a week for rent. His wife, knowing that *a small income will not admit of any irregularity or inadvertency*, purchases all the unperishable articles of necessary consumption, in quantities, at wholesale prices, and as she knows how long they ought to last, she manages them accordingly. Candles and soap are laid in for the year, in summer time, when cheapest; and these articles, when kept in a dry place, become harder, fitter for use, and go further. By getting a neighbour to join in the purchase of coals, they lay in a year's stock, that is, five chaldrons, about August, when they are cheapest; and thus they get the ingain, or three sacks over, upon that quantity. Half a ton of potatoes laid in in October, and kept in a dry place, properly secured from the frost, serves the family come next year. Traces of onions are bought in October, and hung up in a dry place serve the winter. A firkin of good table beer at 7*s*. serves the family, as their beverage at meals for about a month, besides the parents occasionally drink porter. All the lesser branches of domestic arrangement are managed with the same steady view to regularity and economy; thus they live happily and are well respected.'

We begin with this, not because it is typical, but because it is ideal. This man is in regular employment, in a responsible position. He is a Ten-pound householder with a vote. The children will probably go to an Endowed school or a British Day. There will be occasional jaunts to Gravesend or Margate: sound boots, Sunday best. The inner suburbs are ringed with the homes of these people, little houses with little gardens. 'They live happily, and are well respected.' Incidentally, they are much better off than the average curate or schoolmaster. They keep themselves to themselves: at an election it is their votes that tell: they are not at all Radical, and they have not much sympathy with the class below. They are the solid substratum of the middle classes. To a working man, success means a life like theirs. They are the lowest class which feels the attractive power of gentility.

Our next stopping-place shall be the skilled mechanic in good work at 33*s*. a week. He manages his affairs thus:

	£	*s.*	*d.*
Bread and flour for five persons—24 lb.		3	9
Butter—3 lb. at 9*d*.		1	6
Cheese—½ lb. at 10*d*.			5
Milk			8
Tea—¼ lb. at 5*s*. 4*d*.		1	4
Sugar—2¾ lb. at 6*d*.		1	4½
Grocery, &c., as before			9½
Meat, fish, &c., say Meat 7 lb. at 6*d*.		3	6
Vegetables—including 35 lb. Potatoes		1	4
Beer, or Table Ale		2	3
Coals, &c.—nearly 1½ Bushel on an average, at 1*s*. 4*d*. per bushel and wood		2	1
Candles			4½
Soap, &c.—for washing			4½
Sundries—for cleaning, scowering, &c.			3
Total of Household Expenses	£1	0	0
Clothes, Haberdashery, &c.		5	6
Rent		3	6
Incidents		1	3
Total Expense	£1	10	3
Saving, 1/12th		2	9
Amount of Income, weekly	£1	13	0

But in 1841 hard times are shown by the restricted diet and inferior clothing. This is Bosanquet's budget for the same family that year:

YOUNG LADIES, 1861: OUTDOOR STYLE

30*s*. per week for man, wife, and three children (London).	*s.*	*d.*
5 4-lb. loaves, at 8½*d.*; 1 quartern flour, 9½*d.*	4	4
14 lb. meat, at 6*d.*	7	0
7 quarts porter, at 4*d.*	2	4
1 cwt. coals	1	7
28 lb. potatoes	1	3
¼ lb. tea at 5*s.*; 1½ lb. sugar, at 7*d.*	2	1½
1½ lb. butter, at 1*s.*	1	6
1 lb. candles, 6½*d.*; 1 lb. soap, 6½*d.*	1	1
Rent, 4*s.*; schooling, 6*d.*	4	6
Clothes and sundries	4	3½
	30	0

Then we come to the guinea a week family. When he was forming the London police, Sir Robert Peel found that a guinea brought him all the recruits he wanted. It may therefore be taken as being, in London, an attractive wage for a single man and especially one who might have other sources of gain, but the family must have been very poorly off indeed.

	£	*s.*	*d.*
Bread and Flour, for five persons—24 lb. at 1¾*d.*		3	6
Butter, Cheese, and Milk		1	9
Sugar and Treacle			9
Rice, Oatmeal, Salt, &c.			6
Butcher's-Meat, or Fish—say Meat, 6 lb. at 4½*d.*		2	3
Vegetables—(including a ¼ cwt. of Potatoes, or 4 lb. a day, at 3*s.* 6*d.* per cwt.)—2*d.* a day		1	2
Table beer—1 quart a day, at 2*d.*		1	2
Coals—1¼ bushel per week, on an average all the year round, at 1*s.* 4*d.*—1*s.* 8*d.* and Wood, 1*d.*		1	9
Candles—on an average all the year round, ½ lb. per week, at 7*d.*			3½
Soap, Starch, Blue, &c.—for washing			3½
Sundries—for cleaning, scouring, &c.			1
Total for Household Expenses		13	6
Clothes, Haberdashery, &c.		3	6
Rent		2	3
Total Expense		19	3
Saving, 1/12th		1	9
Amount of Income	£1	1	0

'We give this and other low Estimates because we are aware that there are many families in the country, and in retired situations whose incomes are even less than is here premised, to whose circumstances these statements may be applied. They may also serve for a numerous class of industrious mechanics and others, in manufacturing towns and districts, to whom it may be as advantageous to know how to *save*, as how to *get* money; which knowledge, when habitually practised, must infallibly tend to the improvement of their morals, as well as to their future advancement in life. We understand that *this* Estimate is considered as too low, and it may appear to be so to the majority of that class of the community into whose hands this work is most likely to come; but we are anxious to be of use to all, particularly to those whose means are small, and who wish to live honestly independent, and *must live within bounds*.

'We are now, however, in possession of several documents which prove the practicability of this Estimate, of these we shall mention two; one of them is from a mechanic in Bristol, who follows our plan literally, but as coals are cheap here, they use them unsparingly, it affords the family some little extra aids, and "now and then a Dobbin of Ale for himself"; the other is from a servant in a brewhouse at Norwich who has a wife and three young children, whose account corresponds almost *verbatim* with our own items, and out of twenty shillings, he contrives to save something, because, as he says, he is determined to save.

'Respecting *Bread*, which is the principal article of consumption, we have founded our calculation on the price of sound household bread in *London*—namely, from seven farthings to two-pence halfpenny per pound, which is a trifle higher than the price given in our last edition; but this is more than the average price in the country; there, too, barley, rye, or oaten bread, is generally eaten in such families, many of whom, also, bake their own bread, which is a considerable saving; so that our Estimates may be too high for the country, which, however, is an error on the right side. But respecting this and other articles of food, we have made it a point to be as correct, and as generally applicable, as it is possible to be. As to the *quantity* of bread stated, we consider it as correct. The two adults will eat six pounds each, per week, and we consider the three children as consuming as much as their two parents—that is, twelve pounds more; but this, we are told, is too much for the children: yet, as bread and flour for puddings, &c., constitute the chief part of children's food, and present appearances indicate no immediate reduction in the price, we conceive that we cannot with propriety, reduce the quantity. Should not this in any case be enough—as the income will not afford more—recourse must be had to potatoes, rice, oatmeal, and other wholesome and nutritive articles of food for the children, which will save bread, and should be constantly given to them, as proper and economical substitutes for this and other expensive articles of diet.

'It is better to buy large loaves than small ones; and bread should not be eaten till it is one day old.

'The quantity of butcher's meat given here is very low, and it is necessarily so; but at all places on or near the sea-coast, fish may be bought at a cheap rate, to supply its place; even in London, very frequently, mackerel, herrings, cod, flounders, and other kinds of fish, may be had cheaper than butcher's-meat. The price of good beef and mutton is now from five-pence to seven-pence per pound;—for common joints, the average is about six-pence. But much may be saved by the mode of cooking: meat roasted, baked, or broiled loses fully one-third of its nutritive qualities; if boiled *fast*, it loses nearly as much, but *stewed gently*, it loses least, and what it does lose the liquor acquires, and this is thickened with a little meal, ground rice, Scotch barley or pease, and vegetables, affords a most wholesome food, and the family gets nourishment of the whole meat at the least possible expense.

'The prices of coals vary much, according to local situation, and other circumstances. Generally, where coals are dear, coke, wood, turf, or peat, is reasonable; and for six months in the year, but little will be required for either coals or candles. To save expense, oil is frequently used instead of candles in families of this description.

'Nothing is given in this Estimate for tea and sugar; and if these must be had, when the income is so small, the amount must be saved out of more necessary articles.

'We have, in this Estimate, taken the expense of each child at one shilling and nine-pence per week; and though a child in arms will not cost so much, yet the expense of lying-in will be fully equivalent. After the third child, the wife will naturally cause the oldest to attend to the youngest, and by that means gain time for other purposes; and the mind that is bent on frugality and economy will learn to surmount little difficulties. Besides, in manufacturing neighbourhoods, children are taught at an early age to earn something towards their own support. These, and similar circumstances, will tend to counterbalance such dilemmas as may arise, that would otherwise be disheartening.'

Very disheartening, indeed.

This seems to have struck Mr. James Lubbock, whose *Hints for Practical Economy* appeared in 1834. He will only allow a family of four, and even so he seems doubtful whether it can be done.

Another suggested budget for the 21*s*. family.

		s.	*d.*
Rent, per week		2	0
Eatables, 4*d*. per day each		9	4
Beer		1	2
Clothing, Man, including shoes		1	9
Ditto, Woman, ditto		1	3
Ditto, Children, 9*d*. each		1	6
Coals		1	9
Washing		1	0
Wear and tear		1	3
	£1	1	0

'It would appear a very ungracious task to attempt to exhibit a lower scale; for, though every reader must be conscious that thousands or millions are compelled to live on a very much reduced rate, yet he will be utterly at a loss to know how it is accomplished.'

We are not at a loss to know how it was accomplished, because the thousands or millions lived in a state of serious malnutrition.

What happens if the family wage is only 15*s.*? Bosanquet (*Rights of the Poor*, 1841) will answer.

	s.	*d.*
5 4-lb. loaves, at 8½*d.*	3	6½
5 lb. meat, at 5*d.*	2	1
7 pints porter, at 2*d.*	1	2
½ cwt. coals		9½
40 lb. potatoes	1	4
3 oz. tea, at 5*s.*; 1 lb. sugar, at 7*d.*	1	6
1 lb. butter		9
½ lb. soap; ½ lb. candles		6½
Rent, 2*s.* 6*d.*; schooling, 4*d.*	2	10
Sundries		5½
	15	0

This family is apparently clothed by charity.

Or if there are more than the standard five-in-family? Again Bosanquet answers the question—or shows that it is unanswerable—with a budget for man, wife, and five children.

	£	*s.*	*d.*
2 oz. tea			8
7 oz. coffee			10½
3 lb. sugar		1	9
1 cwt. coals		1	8
½ bushel coke and wood			7
12 loaves, at 8*d.*		8	0
18 lb. potatoes			9
1½ lb. butter		1	6
1 lb. soap, ½ lb. soda			7
Blue and starch			2
Candles			7
Bacon		2	6
Greens or turnips, onions, &c.			6
Pepper, salt, and mustard			3
Herrings			9
Snuff			6
	£1	1	7½
To this ought to be added about 6*d.* a day for butcher's meat		3	6
And rent		4	0
	£1	9	1½

As the author points out:

'The wages of a man earning 30*s.* a week are wholly expended, leaving 10½*d.* for clothes, beer, medicine, tools and other accidents and contingencies.'

Here it will be observed that the bread ration has been cut down and clothes must be found at the expense of other food.

With these data in mind let us examine some of the actual budgets collected by Le Play in 1855. Our first is a working cutler living in Whitefriars Street. The house, which has one room on each floor, is less insanitary than most, but damp and sunless. It has water laid on in the cellar and 'latrines'. The four children play in the street or in Temple Gardens. Grandmother helps in the house and the wife carries her husband's work to and from the master's shop in Oxford Street. They live thus:

	£	s.	d.
Rent		7	9
Food	1	0	0
Coal and Light . .		2	10
Cleaning . . .		1	0
School			10
Clothes		3	2
Sundries . . .		1	2
	£1	16	9

	£	s.	d.
Furniture . . .	26	10	0
Other effects . .	3	5	0

There are two umbrellas, a wardrobe (£5), a mirror (£2), a carpet (£1), put down on Sunday. The family are in debt.

But the Londoner is worse off than other townsmen because rent and prices are higher, and he rarely has a garden. A working cutler in Sheffield has five children, one of whom supports herself as a dressmaker. For 3*s*. 4*d*. he has a small house with parlour, kitchen and two bedrooms, with a garden where he keeps fowls, pigs, pigeons, and canaries, and his wife dispenses ginger-pop made of water, sugar, cream of tartar, barm, white of egg, lemon and pepper.

Their expenses are:

		s.	d.
Rent		2	4
Bought Food . .		11	4
Coal and candles . .		1	5
Cleaning . . .			6
School			5
Clothes		3	7
Sundries . . .		1	7
	£1	1	2

	£	s.	d.
Furniture . . .	9	10	0
Clothes	7	15	0

This family are less pretentious than the Londoners, but far more comfortable. Indeed, with the canaries and the ginger-pop, the fowls and the potatoes, they contrive to live very well, with a meat meal every day. Another Sheffield budget is available:

	s.	d.
Rent	2	9
Food	14	0
Coal and light . .	1	6
Clothes	4	10

	£	s.	d.
Furniture . . .	31	8	0
Clothes	11	10	0

Here the earnings are only 28*s*. a week. But the man is ambitious. He puts a shilling a week in the offertory: he has saved £40 through a Building Society, and is making much of his own furniture. The explanation is simple: he has only one child.

A foundryman in Derbyshire with four children, with 27*s*. 8*d*. a week and garden, also enjoys some comfort. They spend 14*s*. a week on their food and they live thus:

Breakfast at 7: Parents, tea or coffee, with milk and sugar; bread and butter and cold meat. Children, bread and milk.

Dinner at noon: Meat, bread, potatoes, vegetables: fruit or cheese.

Tea at 4: tea, sugar, bread and butter.

Supper at 8: remains of dinner.

He works twelve hours a day for 355 days a year at 4*s*. a day, for a good employer who supports the sick club and the school.

Finally, let us compare an actual budget of 1859 from Manchester, with the estimated budget of the 33*s*. mechanic of 1834.

	1834			1859		
		s.	*d*.		*s*.	*d*.
Food		16	11		18	6½
Coal and light		2	5½		1	6
Clothes		5	6		3	0
Rent		3	6		4	0
Sundries		1	10½		2	11½
	£1	10	3	£1	10	0

The differences are not very great. The most important is that the cheapness of coal and clothing enables the 1859 family to eat more. In '34 the bread ration was 24 lb.; in '59 it was 32 lb., besides half a peck of meal.

This brings us to the vital point in the domestic economy of our period. What made all the difference, what gave significance to the Chartist and free-trade movements, was the price of bread. The cost of the 24-lb. bread ration in London was:

	s.	*d*.
in 1830	5	3
in 1835	3	6
in 1840	5	0
in 1845	3	9
in 1850	3	5
in 1855	5	5
in 1860	4	5
in 1865	3	6

THE GREAT OF 1865: INCLUDING TENNYSON, BROWNING, SWINBURNE, AND LONGFELLOW

The high prices of 1855 are war figures. Allowing for this, the variations reflect, and explain, an undoubted increase of well-being. The life of the town worker was much more precarious than it is now: he was, even when employed, much nearer the margin, and he was always in danger of being swept across it. And even these figures, being for the year, do not tell the whole truth: the fluctuations within the twelve months were equally steep. Any one who asks about the state of the poor, therefore, is confronted with the baffling question: Do you mean the man in good work, with a garden, with the loaf at *7d.*, or the same man a few months later, in a slum cellar, out of work, with the loaf at 1*s.*[1] It is possible to paint one picture, too painful to contemplate; and another of considerable comfort, and to find that the same family has sat for both. But if we want a central type by which to adjust our ideas, a workman who is not as Macaulay bluntly said 'a blackguard' and who has no aspirations to bourgeois gentility, I think we shall find it, in real life, somewhere about 30*s.*, like the Derbyshire founder and the Sheffield cutler, and, in fiction, in the families of Mr. Peggotty, Mr. Toodle, and Inspector Bucket.

Cobbett laid it down that on 10*s.* a week a labourer who avoided tea and the beer house, had a garden and a good wife who could bake, need never see his children crying for bread. If we accept his ruling we must conclude that in the most-favoured counties (Kent, Stafford, Lincoln, Notts., Derby, Cheshire, the North) the labourer was doing well: the average wage was 12*s.* In the bad counties (Wilts., Dorset, Devon, Somerset, Wales) he was doing badly on 7*s.* 6*d.* or 8*s.* How badly we know from the experience of the recruiting sergeants: they observed that the young men from the south-west were habitually underfed. But on the whole we have less information about the rural workers than any other class. No one tried to budget for an 8*s.* family. Perhaps it was too 'disheartening'. In fact after going through the town budgets with their minute allocation of resources we ask how was it possible to keep body and soul together on a Dorset labourer's pay.

In default of figures we must fall back on personal experiences and again I will begin at the top of the scale. Here

[1] It must be remembered that the prices given above are annual averages and in the year the price of the 4-lb. loaf might fluctuate considerably.

are the recollections of a Derbyshire woman and her mother, going back to about 1855.

'The cottage was on the outskirts of Buxton and what grandfather earned mother did not know. May be 28*s.* to 30*s.* a week, for he was a wheelwright. There was a good garden, and grandfather was a grand man at gardens, so there was a plenty of green stuff and some over, and the best of it was sold. There were two pigs, bees and chickens. Mother said often she wished they could eat the things instead of selling them, but they didn't do badly, plenty of plain food, but the children weren't allowed to eat for the sake of eating. There were thirteen of them, all girls but one, so you may fancy what they made of that boy. Meals were breakfast with bread and milk or porridge, sometimes dripping toast or fried bread, and always something extra for grandfather. Tea for the elder ones. The school children took their dinner along, bread and butter, a bit of lardy cake, sometimes cold bacon, or a pasty, or cheese, or bread and dripping, and maybe an apple. Grandfather came home for his dinner, a stew or boiled bacon, vegetables, dumplings, or a rabbit and roast for Sunday. Grandma was a proper cook and would make something out of nothing, and she'd a light hand with puddings and cakes. Grandfather drank beer, but all the girls was brought up teetotal. There was tea and bread and butter, and a cake of some sort, and milk for the little ones and something extra for Grandfather, and a bit of supper for grandfather and grandma before bedtime. The girls went out to service near about when they were thirteen or fourteen and some of them married. My mother was eighteen when she married, and she wore the same dress as her elder sister. On a Sunday afternoon it was a sight, all the children, and the married ones with their children, and the boys that was courting the girls and the little ones all gathered together sitting how they could, and tea and cake for all. The married girls would bring a cake, or maybe an egg or a pat of butter, and the ones that was in service would save some of their tea and sugar for Sundays, and perhaps buy something too. Grandfather wouldn't take much notice of any of them, but he would miss any that didn't come, directly. He was a strict man, took the strap to Grandma once, and mother said they would all have killed him if they had dared, for that. Grandma was a reader and could say poetry. When they was sitting sewing, she'd say poetry to them, and that made it pleasant, for the girls had to sew, like it or not, till half an hour before bedtime. They were not allowed out after dark, except for something special, and then an older and a younger together, and young men that came courting had to be out of the house by 9 o'clock sharp. "Your mother will want you home to shut up and go to bed herself" she used to say, and they had to go, but they loved her, all the lads did. Clothes were plain and home-made but Grandma took a pride in her girls. She'd a sister married well who used to send things, and what a big one grew out of, a little one would wear, and then every bit was made up for a rag carpet, or a cushion for grandfather's chair, and patch-work there was, bed covers, curtains, and a fine frill for the mantel shelf with china dogs and funeral cards and brass candlesticks and a warming pan. Pot plants in the window and lace curtains. There was a tall clock as had been grandma's mother's, and some furniture like you see people giving Lord knows what for nowadays. And when grandfather died there was a bit put by and one way and another grandma managed nicely, and said that the Lord had blessed her that she had thirteen good children.'

This might be set against the respectable person living on 48*s.* a week in a London suburb. Nearer to the average is a Berkshire man's recollections of life about the same time. His father was a shepherd in regular employ at 12*s.*, and made a bit by cow doctoring: he was therefore above the run of the ordinary labourer at 10*s.*

'Seven on us there were. Father a shepherd. There weren't what there be today, but I don't know as people did the worse for it. Baked . . . had a bit o' garden, milk from the farm—t'was easier to get then than now. For breakfast, porridge or bread and milk and bread and lard and p'raps a bit o' sugar to it. There weren't jam and marmalade and such when I was a boy. Cocoa . . . herb tea . . . Dinner time were noon, father'd take his wi'en—bacon and bread and may be a bit o' pudden or bread and cheese and onion. Mother'd put it on a plate and tie it up in a spotted hankercher. Dinner'd be vegetables and dumplin, suet pudden and treacle. Rice pudden, Dunch dumplins. What be they? Why suet dumplen wi' apple chopped up in 'em. I don't recall as there were cake. Bread were what folks ate, tho' mother'd make a lardy cake if t'was anything special like a weddin' or a christenin' or may be a buryin'. Bacon and a bit o' butcher's meat Sundays and potatoes most always. Milk ½ skim, 3*d.* the quart new. Beer . . . The women would drink tea when they could 'ford it. In my father's time t'was too dear. They'd drink herb tea . . . or they'd drink mint tea. They'd give away tea leaves up to the House and that with a pinch o' fresh tea were'ny zo bad. Wages 9*s.*, 10*s.*, 12*s.* Father earned 12*s.*, and never were out o' work, and made a bit cow and horse doctoring. Garden stuff and a bit extra at harvest and what Squire give come Christmas and rabbits now and agen. Women went gleanin, men mended boots . . . wi' one thing and another they'd make do.'

A little lower down comes this report of life in Northamptonshire in the fifties:

'The principal course at the morning meal would be a small basin of bread soaked in water, and seasoned with salt, occasionally a little skimmed milk added, and a small piece of bread tinged with lard in the winter. During the summer season we might at rare intervals get some dripping from the Hall. For dinner we might get plain pudding —flour and water—or pork dumpling, sometimes both, with potatoes or onions added to fill the crust. . . . "Tea" such we called it, bread and potted butter. I never remember grumbling about this being sparingly spread, it was at times so rancid. "Supper?" I might get something very much like a small piece of bread and a little piece of pork rubbed over it. Sunday was a high day, of course. We might get a penny black pudding (one between 4 or 5 of us, with a small piece of fried pork) for breakfast, suet pudding and a pig's foot for five of us to feast thereon. Beef? Yes, we might get a small piece at our feast and a bullock's heart at Xmas. We did occasionally get a pennyworth of bullock's liver. . . . To illuminate our cottage in winter we would get half a pound of candles (10*d.*) and a rushlight for father to retire and rise with, as it did not consume so rapidly. As an additional drink we had mint tea for summer, and we might get toast and water, especially in winter.'

Which is the typical picture? The truth is that the observer can see anything he wishes to see, because everything is there. But on the whole, the verdict must be that, whether we consider wages or what wages can buy, conditions of labour or housing, the golden age of agriculture left the rural worker rarely better off, usually worse off, at the end than at the beginning. We must think of village life in some such terms as these:

The money wage, which varied according to locality and season, whether the men were married or unmarried, head men or underlings, was not the only source of income. Some men were given one or more meals a day, others an allowance of beer, firewood, or skim milk, others again an allotment. The men also earned harvest money and the women and children went gleaning. In some counties the church bell was rung to tell them that they might enter the fields, in others they came at the sound of a horn. Sometimes fuel, in the shape of wood or furze, might be obtained, lawfully or otherwise, and dung might be collected and dried. Women also worked in the fields when they could get such work, and obtained other odd jobs. In an old housekeeping book there is mention that in the fifties the Housekeeper at The Hall paid women for extra cleaning at the rate of 2½*d.* an hour and their 'elevenses' (bread and cheese, beer or tea), and one

WALKING DRESS, 1866–67

or two aged women recall that 1*s*. a day and meals was the sum paid for charring, while others give it as 1*s*. 6*d*. and sometimes 'a bit o' something to take 'ome'. A woman with no more knowledge than she had acquired by hearsay and experience, might earn a little by attending a neighbour in illness or a woman in her confinement, by laying out the dead and acting as a 'watcher', by church and school cleaning, by 'doing' for some bachelor or widower, looking after some one's unwanted child, or an old woman would earn perhaps 3*d*. a day by tending the children of women out at work.

Children, too, could earn a trifle. Toddling babies were sent out into the lonely fields to earn sixpence a week scaring birds, and older boys and girls would make a penny or two in one way and another. Girls went into service young—as early as nine years old in 1830 and at a rather later age at the end of our period, and were extraordinarily generous to their families. As prospective employers would not take them without decent clothes, which few parents could provide, it was a favourite form of charity and occupation for kind ladies to prepare a little maid's outfit, or to make warm, homely garments for the aged or respectable poor. Kind ladies also did a certain amount of mild doctoring, providing salves, potions, and bandages. When a baby was expected a 'maternity bag' might be borrowed, and was there a death, the squire's or parson's lady would doubtless provide 'a bit o' black'.

Another recognized method of obtaining help in cases where the death of a horse, donkey, or cow might bring starvation within sight of the owner was to obtain the signature of some respectable person to a statement of the facts. The horse or cow 'paper' was then taken round the neighbourhood, first to persons of importance whose names were affixed to it to encourage the others. A man might add to his wages by acting as a cow or horse doctor. A woman might brew medicines from herbs and other less pleasant ingredients, such as mice, snails, worms, toads, hairs from horses' tails, and even nail parings, or they might even indulge in a little witchcraft. Such doctoring and witching were often employed to obtain abortion, a not uncommon practice both in country and in town.

Poaching, too, helped to keep the pot boiling. Many

poachers were the employees of town game dealers who organized poaching gangs or sent pimps to persuade local men to poach. In the last resort, an easing of hunger pangs might be achieved by the pilfering of turnips, and pig, cattle, and fowl food.

The poor benefited, too, by the charity of better-off folk, especially the wives of squires and clergy, though many of the latter, especially while their husbands were still curates, were themselves painfully poor. Most of the cookery-books of the period contain recipes for food for the poor. In addition to occasional gifts of 'nourishing broth' which the poor disliked but ate for lack of anything better, it was usual to give away used tea-leaves and coffee-grounds, the 'boilings' (water in which meat had been cooked) and broken meats, and even cinders to 'the poor'. With the 'boilings' referred to the women would make a dinner of 'Brewis' consisting of bread crusts or oatmeal, seasoned and soaked in the liquid. Substantial gifts of food, blankets, and clothes were made at Christmas, and in some houses it was the custom to have jars placed on the sideboard into which food was served from the table and taken to invalids and old people. A lady now recalls how, in the sixties, the governess and children would set out, each with a gallipot full of food for the 'respectable poor'. At one ducal establishment, mutton chops were thrown out of the windows to those whose poverty or lack of self-respect made such alms-receiving endurable.[1]

When all else failed there was Parish Relief or the dreaded Workhouse, not only for the slacker, the malingerer, and the drunkard, but for those who had lived decent hard-working lives, and whose only crime was the poverty which unemployment, sickness, or old age, made them powerless to avert. This coming to the Workhouse, Poorhouse, or Bastille, as it was known, was a cruel thing to decent people, who exchanged liberty and all that they knew of home and of loving companionship, for a harsh discipline, or worse, a brutal tyranny, squalor, and maybe semi-starvation, for although the diet when set out on paper may seem an improvement on anything that the lower-paid labourer could afford, it would appear that the paper diet and the real diet differed widely. At Andover, one of the tasks imposed on male paupers was

[1] The quantity and nature of the charity is an indication of the volume of the poverty.

to crush bones, and so hungry were they that they fought among themselves for the stinking gristle and marrow.

One decided advantage the rural worker had was air and sunlight. Cottages were often damp and dark: fever brooded over undrained hamlets: the drinking water was polluted: whole counties were underfed. But there is no denying the figures of child mortality. In 1831 the death-rate under five in England as a whole was 348 per 1,000. But this meant 250 in the North Riding, 390 in the West, 320 in Devon, 440 in Plymouth, 240 in Herefordshire, and 480 in Nottingham.

In the later years of the seventeen hundreds and throughout our period large numbers of country folk had moved into the towns and crowded into the already crowded and insanitary dwellings. Other buildings which had seen better days fell vacant as the richer people moved into pleasanter surroundings, and were taken possession of by the poor, whole families, or may be two or three families, living in one room, such rooms becoming known in the slang of the twenties as 'slums', a term which later was used to describe a debased neighbourhood. Then the jerry-builder seized his opportunity and as there were few, if any, building regulations, he was quick to avail himself of it. The jerry-builder built to make money, not to make homes, and his activities, and the neglect of the town authorities to guide and restrict them, brought with them death and disease, discomfort and the sadness which comes of living in ugly, squalid surroundings. The authorities were indeed right when they admitted that amongst the town poor there was now 'a low and grovelling style of living'. True, the new houses did not have cellars, in which poor families could live rat-like, as many did in the old houses, but neither did they have foundations. The walls were but half a brick thick, the houses built back to back without ventilation or drainage. Double rows of these closely packed brick boxes formed courts with, perhaps for twenty houses containing as many persons as could be packed into them, a pump at one end and a privy at the other.

The window tax (repealed in 1851) was a curse to dwellers in tenement houses. To escape the tax, houses were built with as few openings as possible, and closets, privies, passages, cellars, and roofs were left unventilated. More often than not their few windows looked on to the close-set wall of another building or over a street into which refuse was thrown, or in some cases, into the yard of a slaughter-house.

Another hardship was the lack of water. In the slums of Drury Lane, for example, water was only turned on for about an hour or even less a day. The people fought for it when running and went begging for it when it was turned off. At the week-end, water was turned off on Saturday at 6 o'clock and no more was to be had until Monday.[1] If the pump was some distance away water must be bought from carriers or water-carts.

Mr. Thomas Ashton of Hyde, a cotton magnate, found that his workpeople often paid as much as one shilling a week to the water-carrier, and that some families paid two shillings a week for carted water, so he then built two hundred and thirty houses for his workpeople, and laid water on at a charge of 3*d*. a week. No wonder the poor were dirty; the wonder was that they went on trying to be clean, washing in the costly water clothes which when hung out to dry were quickly covered with smuts.

The foul atmosphere of industrial towns was another hardship to the housewife and also a health-reducing factor. It is a sad little item in a tale of miseries that Faucher, a French visitor, said that one of the evils of which the poor were most conscious in Leeds was the smoke that destroyed their little window gardens. In some towns there were wash-houses, but generally the prices charged were too high for the poor to pay.

The filth amongst which many working-folk were obliged to live caused the courts and yards to swarm with flies. It was not then generally realized that disease may be fly-borne, or that their presence accounted for the fact that food became putrid almost at once.

The working-classes were helpless. But reformers had come to see that all their plans were likely to be shipwrecked on the housing difficulty. They took advantage of the humanitarian and profit-making instinct together and launched the model dwelling at economic rents. Wise employers had shown the way. As Mr. Edmund Ashworth, an employer with enlightened views, pointed out, 'whatever the weekly income, the housewife could never make such a house comfortable. . . . It might readily be supposed that the

[1] Pamphlet by George Godwin, F.R.S., editor of *The Builder*, 1865.

husband would not find the comfort he wished . . . the public-house would be his only resort.'

The Ashworths started an experimental housing scheme, led to do so by the outbreak of that dread bogy 'the fever', which was due to filth. They began a system of health visiting, to learn that habits of life were in most cases caused by conditions of life, so they built bigger and better cottages, the tenants of which soon showed 'better habits and a more respectable feeling in society'.[1]

The best-sized houses for general use were, they found, those with a living-room 15 by 9 feet, a back kitchen the same size, and three bedrooms.

The Metropolitan Association for Improving the Dwellings of the Industrial Poor was founded in 1842, and the tenement for which Prince Albert received the Gold Medal Class VII at the Great Exhibition represents the highest point reached by housing science in our period. There are four flats in a block, with external staircase. Each has a lobby, a living-room with heating cupboard (150 sq. ft.); scullery with sink, rack, dustshaft and ventilator, meatsafe, and coal-bin; three bedrooms with external ventilation (one of 100 sq. ft., two of 50); a water-closet flushed from a cistern. They cost about £450 a flat and could be let at 3*s.* 6*d.* to 4*s.* Wherever these Model Dwellings rose, fever disappeared as by magic. But they could not rise fast enough. A rent of 4*s.* was only within the reach of a mechanic in good and regular work, and the slums which were one of the unsolved problems of early Victorian England remain an unsolved problem still.

§ 8. THE DOMESTIC SERVANT

In any history of domestic life the servant must be an important figure, and perhaps especially so at a time when amongst moneyed people life shaded from magnificence to solid comfort, but time and effort-saving machinery was almost unknown. In 1830 to go into service was, outside the great industrial areas, the natural destiny of the working-class girl and not uncommonly the ambition of the working-class boy. This was partly because agricultural wages and unskilled industrial wages were low, conditions hard, and unemployment rife, and because owing to the difficulties and

[1] *The Age of the Chartists*, by J. L. and Barbara Hammond.

cost of transport, persons needing employment could not go so far afield to seek it as is now possible. Lack of education also limited the kind of work which working-class children could be put to. In the early part of our period country servants of the lesser order were hired at the annual mop or fair, a cook wearing a red and a housemaid a blue ribbon and carrying the emblem of her profession, the cook a basting ladle, the housemaid a broom, the milkmaid a pail, but by its end this custom as regards house servants had died out, though farm workers continued to present themselves for hire at fairs.

In good houses there was little need for the services of a registry office or a newspaper, for the supply of local boys and girls seldom failed, and employers, housekeepers, and stewards if they had no post to offer, might place the applicant with some member of the family living elsewhere.

In towns, tradesmen often acted as registry office keepers, the Chelsea baker mentioned in one of her letters by Mrs. Carlyle for example. There was also a 'London Society for the Encouragement of Faithful Servants' at 10 Hatton Gardens. The servants applying for situations were not charged a fee, but none were accepted who had not been two years in one place or who were applying for a first place.

Housewives needing servants also advertised in *The Times* and not always with success, as Mrs. Carlyle found, noting that 'the only applicant as yet resulting from it is not to be thought of'.

Mrs. Carlyle's maids gave her considerable trouble; she suffered from 'a half-dead cook with a shocking temper' and had a maid who left 'to be made a sort of lady' by a rich uncle who had amassed a fortune by making upholstery fringes and guimps, then needed to trim the seats of the new railway carriages. She pays another girl £8 a year, this young person having a grandfather who gave £5 for a couple of pineapples! A certain Helen she describes as being 'the strangest mixture of philosopher and perfect idiot I have ever met in my life'. If this was the servant who slept in the kitchen, kept her box in the back kitchen, and found 200 bugs in her bed, she must have needed all the philosophy she could bring to her aid.

A very old lady describing the home of her girlhood (about 1848) says that the house staff consisted of a man cook and

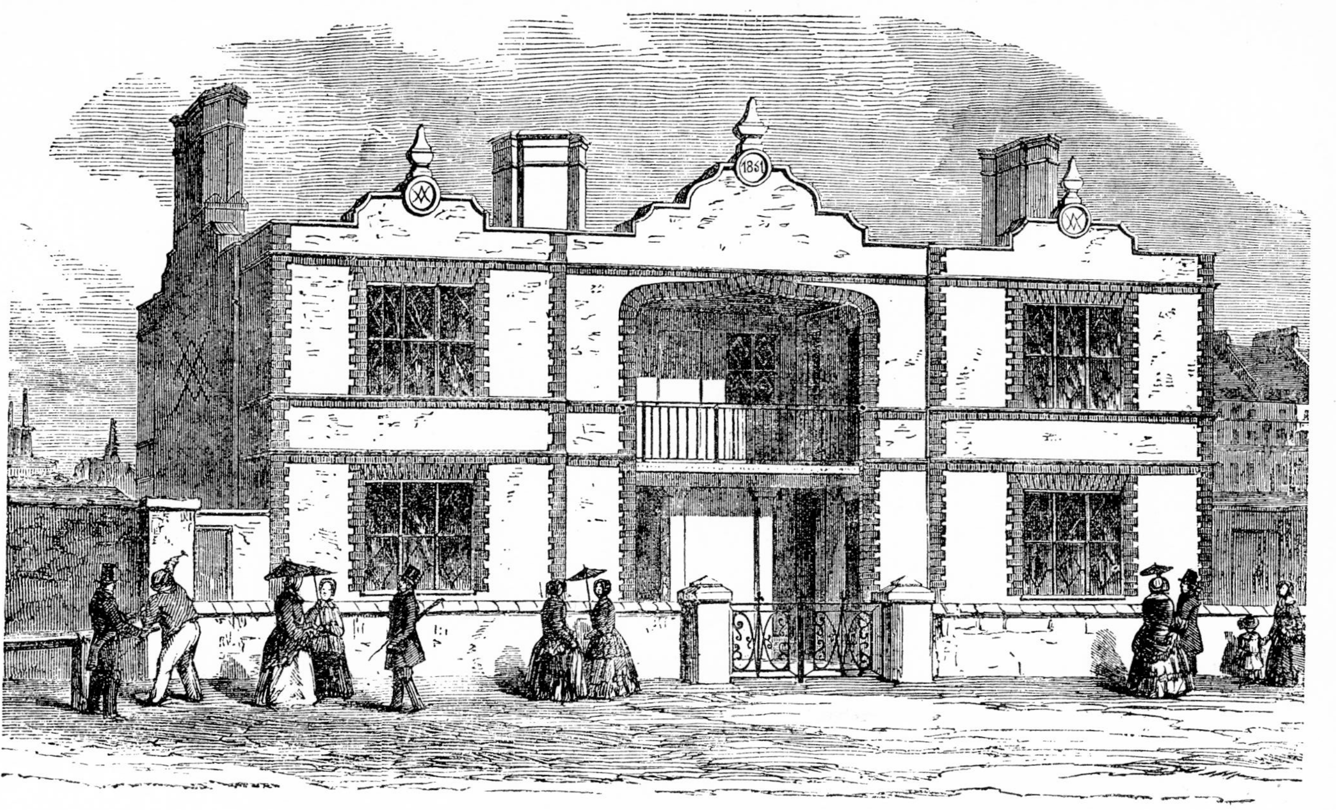

PRINCE ALBERT'S MODEL DWELLINGS, 1851

about six helpers male and female in the kitchen, a still-room maid and two helpers, six women in the laundry, eight housemaids, a housekeeper, house steward, valet, butler, four footmen and four ladies'-maids. The mother and three daughters each had her maid, and each grown-up son had a footman in special attendance upon him. There was an usher in livery who waited on the steward's room, and one of the younger housemaids waited on the housekeeper. The maid was often known as My Lady's woman. Occasionally the maid was called the 'dresser', the term now used for the maids of Royal Ladies, and was provided with an assistant who did the brushing, pressing, and cleaning and less important work, and who was not accorded a seat at the housekeeper's table.

In another large household the staff consisted of a chef, a pastry-cook, two or three kitchen-maids, a couple of scullery-maids, and a male scullion. There were fourteen housemaids and three still-room maids. The laundry staff lived in the laundry and were in charge of the head laundry-maid. There was a nursery staff of nurse, French *bonne*, and two nursery-maids; a schoolroom staff of an English and a French governess, a schoolroom maid, and a footman for carrying. My Lady had a dresser and a maid, and My Lord a valet, the other male staff being Groom of the Chambers, butler, five footmen, an usher, and a hall-boy.

The strictest etiquette was observed by the staff. The upper servants, although they ate in 'the hall', departed after the meat course had been consumed to eat their pudding and drink their wine in the housekeeper's room (an apartment known to the understaff as Pugs Parlour), where they also supped. After their departure from the hall, the first footman took the place of the butler and the cook that of the housekeeper. In some households the cook and the kitchen-maids dined in a room off the kitchen, and then the head laundry-maid or, if the laundry people lived and ate in the laundry, the head housemaid took the place of the housekeeper. The underlings were not permitted to speak at meals in the presence of their superiors.

In the houses of the lesser gentry the staff might consist of butler, one or two footmen, and a hall-boy, a cook-housekeeper, kitchen and scullery-maids, one or two housemaids, a nurse and under-nurse, while the governess and her party might be waited upon by an under-housemaid. Madam's maid might be a maid-housekeeper or maid proper.

Descending the social scale, in town and country we may find a household of cook and kitchen-girl, footman, housemaid, and single-handed nurse, or if the family is of the usual numerous Victorian order, a nurse and a young nursery maid.

Finally, by way of the £700 a year family with one man and three maids and the £400 a year family with two maids, we reach the one-maid house of which we learn much from Mrs. Gaskell (*Cranford*) and from Mrs. Carlyle (*The Memorials of Jane Welsh Carlyle*). At Cranford the disagreeable and Hon. Mrs. Jamieson's equally disagreeable butler, Mr. Mulliner, tyrannized over his mistress and the meek ladies who came to her house to be 'called for' later by little maid-servants in demure shawls and bonnets, who escorted their elderly employers home and carried their cap boxes.

In the early part of our period persons who aspired to make any show of gentility kept a male servant. We note that directly Mr. Kirkpatrick[1] became a Q.C. he keeps footmen, and when a butler or footmen could not be afforded the foot-boy, teaboy, or page, as he came to be known later, supported the social standard of the family.

We remember that Mrs. Captain Budge, Mrs. Hobson's mother, thought it necessary that her daughter should keep a manservant: 'It is proper; it is decent. . . . In Captain Budge's lifetime we were never without our groom, and our tea-boy.'[2] So Peter Gundsell the knife-boy becomes foot-boy or page and changes his name from Peter to Philip as being more genteel, and wears a 'hat with a gold cord and a knob on the top like a gilt Brussels sprout and a dark green suit with a bushel of buttons on the jacket'.

The menservants of the Victorian era were noted for their insolence to inferiors, for their insobriety and for their large appetites. In fact they copied the ways of their masters, but by the sixties the parlourmaid, a more amenable creature, was beginning to penetrate even into 'good houses' of lesser size.

£12 a year was regarded as a good wage for an experienced woman servant. When, soon after their marriage, the Prince Consort reorganized Queen Victoria's establishments at

[1] *Wives and Daughters*, Mrs. Gaskell. [2] *Hobson's Choice*, W. M. Thackeray.

THE PASTRY-COOK

Buckingham Palace and at Windsor, he fixed the wages of the housemaids at £12 to rise to £18, beyond which a housemaid could not go. Little girls, who often went out to service when about nine years old—their mothers being thankful to get them into a household where they would be secure of a sufficiency of warmth and food, neither of which might be available at home—might earn from £2 to £6 a year, while girls of twelve or fourteen began at £6 to £8 and worked up to £15, which about 1850 was considered by one well-known registry office as the dividing line between the wage of an upper and an under servant.

In the thirties the cost of an experienced manservant, including wages, tax, board, lodging, livery, and all other expenses, was reckoned at £60 to £70 a year. The tax on menservants was first imposed in 1777 and was 1 guinea per head. In 1812 it was raised to £2 8*s*. for one servant and a larger sum per head when several men were kept. In 1823 the rate was halved, and in 1840 again increased by 10 per cent. Ten years later it was reduced to 1 guinea for men over eighteen and 10*s*. 6*d*. for those under, and in 1869 it became 15*s*. for all males irrespective of age. Registry office records show that by 1860 wages in houses of good class were as follows: butler £45 to £50, cooks from £20, head laundry-maid about £25, still-room maid £16 to £20, housemaids £16 to £18, kitchen-maids never more than £20, scullery-maids £10, a wage of £6 to £8 for young girls taking first place in the kitchen or house and for young boys who were trained as tea-boys, pages, or hall-boys and worked their way up to become footmen and butlers.

The wages of chefs, stewards, grooms of the chambers, and housekeepers were, of course, higher, though a chef in a private house might not be paid more than £50 to £100 a year. Carême was paid, it is said, as much as £1,000 a year by George IV when Regent. Lord Sefton paid Ude £300 a year and left him £100 a year for life. Such cooks were great artists, and their scale of payment had no connexion with that of the rank and file. In London wages might be a trifle higher than in the country.

The wages-book of a vicar's wife living about thirty miles from London records the wages paid from 1849 until 1866. The maids were paid quarterly and their mistress encourages them to save, keeping at the end of the book a note of the sum which they return to her for safe keeping and on which she pays the same interest allowed by the Savings Bank until the sum is large enough to invest. A certain E. Jackson put by 5*s*. a quarter.

The wages paid by this lady to her cooks vary from £10 to £18 a year, to housemaids she gives £10 to £14 a year. In the fifties she gives parlourmaids from £16 to as much as £24 a year, the highest wage mentioned. In several cases travelling expenses are paid.

The maids sign for their wages, and their handwriting is, as a rule, illiterate, one Emma Haliday being sadly uncertain with regard to the number of M's in Emma and L's in Haliday. The Christian names of these girls are of the order considered suitable to their station in life; Ann, Emma, Eliza, Sarah, Martha, Mary, Elizabeth, Mary Anne. Only one young woman is named Adelaide, and one, by a strange flight of fancy, is Jessaline. Notes are made of reasons for leaving: 'Eliza Jackson gave me warning; Emma Ricket had fits; A. Baidmore discharged for being a bad cook, careless and dirty; E. K. married; S. M. bad health.' Then comes a short and tragic entry: 'H. D. sent to Gaol. M. Tyler sent away because she is dirty; E. J. for inefficiency; Ann C. idle and no cook; Our dear Clements married; M. S. gave me warning a week after arrival.' 'E. C.' is obliged to depart, being 'very strange'.

What these young women thought about their employer is not, unfortunately, recorded, but as many of the girls remained until they married, conditions evidently were not unusual.

The daughter of this lady when recalling the manners and customs of her youth notes that wages were all found and beer or beer-money was given.

> 'I think', she writes, 'that the Blue Ribbon movement killed that; at all events as regards young girls, and money wages rose a little in consequence. Maids had no regular days out, but could go when they wanted, always being back before dark. They had no difficulty in finding husbands, and at one time three of our cooks were married and living in the village, so matrimonial projects did not suffer from the non-weekly day out.'

In the early part of our period female servants were expected to buy their own tea and sugar, but gradually it became customary for the employer to make an allowance of

Will you forgive, will you receive,
The simple lay I send you!
It is an honest one, believe,
So let it not offend you.
Indeed my fancy you bewitch,
My heart says, (though I chid it).
That you and I might claim the flitch,
If ever couple did it.
Then let my flame not burn to waste,
My heart has long been thine Love,
I know your worth, your truth, your taste,
Then be my Valentine, Love.

THE COOKMAID

2 oz. of tea and ½ lb. of sugar per week. Later again, as tea became cheaper, the tea allowance was increased to 4 oz. Tea and sugar were expensive items in the domestic budget and not to be used extravagantly, hence the locked tea-poy with its compartments for sugar, black and green teas.

Servants were allowed beer or beer-money, and in good-class houses a washing allowance was granted, or their washing was done in the laundry attached to the house or in the smaller establishments in the back kitchen or washhouse, which almost invariably contained a copper for boiling clothes. To wash at home was then considered part of a maid-servant's ordinary duty except in establishments where laundry-maids were kept.

An estimate of a maid-servant's expenses is given in the *Cook's Oracle* of 1821. By 1830 neither the cost nor the style of the articles varied to any appreciable extent.

	£	s.	d.	
½ lb. of tea per *month*	3	10	0	(11*s.* 8*d.* per lb.)
½ lb. of sugar per week		17	4	(8*d.* per lb.)
4 prs. shoes		18	0	
2 prs. black worsted stockings		4	0	
2 prs. white cotton		5	0	
2 gowns	1	10	0	
6 aprons		10	0	
6 caps		10	0	
Bonnet, shawl, pattens, ribands, &c.	2	0	0	
	£10	5	4	

Boots were not then worn, stout shoes taking their place, and the pattens mentioned were wooden soles with straps mounted on a ring of iron and were used for many a year after the end of our period.

Pattens were more generally worn in the south of England and clogs—that is wooden shoes—in the north. The latter might be worn in place of shoes, but pattens were designed to keep the wearer's shoes out of the mud and damp.

The dresses were made of print, a stuff dress as a rule being too expensive for any but upper servants earning what were then considered to be high wages. A housekeeper or a head nurse might wear stuff, and on occasions, silk.

Servants of lesser importance were content with print—often of a lilac colour—and charming a pretty girl must have looked in a clean print frock, white cap with its gay ribbon, white cotton stockings, and black shoes.

The outdoor dress consisted of a shawl and a straw bonnet

tied with a ribbon. Cap and bonnet-ribbons were almost the only pieces of finery to which the young servant might aspire. Writing of an establishment in a small way in 1842, Thackeray causes Mr. Hobson[1] to say of his female servants, 'I like to be waited on by a neat-handed Phillis of a girl in her nice fitting gown, and a pink ribbon in her cap', and an old woman now in her nineties tells how she left service to be married, and wore at her wedding a bonnet with quillings of ribbon inside the brim and tied with ribbon, and a dress of check silk made from material brought home by a sailor-brother, and which had been worn by her elder sister at *her* wedding.

We hear of these cap ribbons in *Handley Cross*[2] (1854) when Mr. Jorrocks went to visit Sir Archibald Depecarde of Pluckwelle's Park. Sir Archy was away when his guests arrived, so the footman returns with 'a smiling comely-looking personage, dressed in black silk, with sky-blue ribbons in her jaunty little cap and collar'.

Later in the century when stuffs became cheaper, the black afternoon dress came into fashion. Some old housekeeping records show that in 1850 lilac prints, white aprons and caps were the morning uniform of the maids in a large country house, these dresses being replaced in the afternoon by black stuff dresses, white caps and aprons, all of which, until the advent of the sewing-machine, were made by hand.

The fashion of a maid-servant's working dress varied little throughout the years with which we deal. The skirt to some extent followed the mode as regards width, though even in the crinoline and bustle period these articles of dress were not worn under the worker's print. They were kept for wear under the Sunday dress and if not available, the girl would do her best by other means to attain a fashionable appearance. Mrs. Carlyle notes the fact that 'the very servant girls wear bustles . . . a maid went out one Sunday with three kitchen dusters pinned on as a substitute'.[3] Housekeepers, head nurses and ladies'-maids, however, followed the fashions more closely.

Footmen were required to be tall and of good appearance

[1] *Hobson's Choice, or the Tribulations of a Gentleman in search of a man-servant*, by W. M. Thackeray. [2] *Handley Cross*, by R. S. Surtees.

[3] Bustles were worn before crinolines came into fashion, and again after the crinoline period.

and were matched like carriage horses as to height and build, and when the 'charyot' or 'charrut' was used two were required to stand at the back, the coachman sitting in lonely state on the box, which was covered by an elaborately trimmed hammer-cloth. As the century grew older but one footman or carriage groom attended the more ordinary-looking carriages which took the place of chariots. To this day, however, a few State 'charyots' or coaches exist and make an appearance on occasions of great ceremony.

When My Lord or My Lady drove out there must be two footmen, but if the governess or nurse with her charges was permitted to use the great carriage one footman sufficed. Footmen were supplied with livery and silk stockings and were expected to have well-developed calves; if nature was unkind the calves were improved by padding. It was a favourite trick of street boys to throw mud at the white silk-clad legs of footmen, and a favourite trick of footmen to 'sit square', that is, to rest themselves by sitting with their legs dangling over the wheels on either side of the coachman when their employers had been set down and the servant could become a human being rather than an automaton.

In the early part of our period traffic was practically unregulated and on occasions of large parties much confusion resulted, and the service of the footmen might be required to disentangle the horses and bring them and the carriage to the appointed place. A footman, or in families of lesser importance, a page, was required to attend fashionable ladies when walking in town and to carry the family prayer books when they went to church.

III

TOWN LIFE

§ 1. A LOCAL AUTHORITY IN AN EMERGENCY.

§ 2. THE PROBLEM OF TOWN LIFE.

§ 3. LONDON:

Area and population.
Communications.
The City and the new town type.
The West End.
The Spectacle.
The leisure of the Middle Classes.
The Underworld.
Public Health.

§ 4. THE DECLINE OF THE PROVINCIAL TOWNS: NORWICH.

§ 5. THE GREAT EXHIBITION.

III

TOWN LIFE

By R. H. MOTTRAM

§ I. A LOCAL AUTHORITY IN AN EMERGENCY

DOES any one escape the feeling of kindliness and plenty that belongs perhaps more intimately to Devon than to any of the other English counties? Exeter is a pleasant place to-day. A hundred years ago its inhabitants must have had every excuse for believing they were safe from most ill fortune. The river Exe, in sufficient body to constitute the place then a port for sea-going vessels, here runs in a south-easterly direction, making a wide sweep round the south-western side, one of the shorter sides of the, roughly speaking, oblong town enclosed in the walls that had survived from the Parliamentary Wars. This oblong is quartered by four main streets, North and South Streets running parallel to the river from north-west to south-east, High Street and Fore Street from north-east to south-west. These had in 1831 already been prolonged by suburbs, Saint Sidwells to the north-east, Magdalen to south-east, the bridges over the Exe, and over many small fulling-mill 'leats' leading to St. Thomas's on the south-west, and St. David's on the north-west. Within the walls, the northern quarter had good frontages with squalid yards behind and was dominated by the Castle, at the northern extremity. The eastern was almost filled by the Cathedral and Close. The western quarter was largely filled by Bartholomew Yard burying-ground and narrow lanes on the site of the old Friary. But the southern quarter, where Butcher-row and Stepcote Hill led precipitately down to the port, below the bridge, was the danger-point. Nor can we, a hundred years later, be surprised. The quarters containing the Castle, Close, and Bartholomew's Yard, if largely medieval, had space and air. But in the Butcher-row, the old over-hanging houses, so built to keep the rain out, had shop fronts which were still unglazed; while the confusingly named west quarter, really the south-west suburb, where old-fashioned manual industries and hovels crowded on the walls above the bridge, was full of accumulated offal, pigsties, chicken runs, and manure heaps so valuable that their removal was strongly resisted.

The good people of Exeter may well be excused if they felt their troubles were behind them. They had suffered considerably from the plagues of medieval days. But these seemed far enough away in 1831, no doubt; much nearer was the establishment, by the Chamber of Exeter, under Act of Parliament, in 1694, of a water works. A 'stream wheel' pumped water from the Exe at a spot just outside the west angle of the walls, and it was distributed in wooden pipes to such as would pay for it.

The lease of 200 years of this privilege had 80 years still to run in 1808 when a Mr. James Golsworthy bought it, and 'applied his ingenious mind to their (the pipes') improvement'. He invented a cast-iron pipe (going to Chesterfield on purpose) with funnel-shaped joints, so 'practicable' that it was copied by the New River Company in London. Very few of the inhabitants, however, purchased his water, and all the poorer classes fetched it in buckets or small carts from wells or pumps (either belonging to individuals, or one or another of the twenty-two vestries or cognate bodies, or to the Commissioners of Improvements), or by far the most often from the river Exe, wherever it was least trouble, below or above the town. A large number of persons drove this trade, the usual charge being a halfpenny per bucket.

The population of 28,242 persons is described as 'dense', inhabiting the older houses, with numerous courts, lanes, and alleys within the walls. 'The pavement consisted of rounded pebbles, locally known as "pitching", so arranged as to secure a fall from the sides to the centre of the road, which thus formed the gutter; this, in very nearly all the streets, was the only means whereby the sewage and nuisances of the City were removed.' The 'soil' thus obtained was removed by contractors who paid £63 annual rent for it. We are told they 'look at the business as a matter of profit, and never remove dirt where the quantity to be collected is insufficient to remunerate them for the labour bestowed'.

In some of the principal thoroughfares and districts occupied by the more wealthy inhabitants, sewers had been recently constructed, but upon no general or very perfect principle. The infrequent stop-cocks were sometimes turned on for a limited period, while men in jack-boots blocked up the gutter with a piece of tarpaulin and others splashed the water thus collected over the roadway with malt scoops. This appears to have been the extent of street cleansing and was paid for by subscription of those traders who desired to have the portion of the street before their doors so washed.

The place throve; on good market days the old streets were impassable, and 3,000 persons would come through the western turnpike alone. They kept Christmas and the 5th of November liberally, but the great social event was the Assizes, when the theatre opened. The popular entertainment was, however, a good hanging, which drew much more attention than boxing, wrestling, or the Sunday parades of the militia. The inhabitants of neighbouring parishes inside the walls felt each other to be foreigners and apprentices fought in this cause. There was plenty of bacon, eggs, and cider; a whole Cathedral and a strong body of Dissent ministered to spiritual needs.

When it became known that the 'Asiatic Cholera', which had appeared on the Ganges in 1817, had, after a steady progress west, reached Europe, many people in Exeter, as elsewhere, regarded the rumour as humbug, designed to disturb business. By June 21, 1831, however, the appearance of the disease at Hamburg and subsequently at Gateshead, Musselburgh, and Sunderland, was sufficiently menacing to cause the Privy Council to issue an order setting up a Board of Health at the Royal College of Physicians. On this body 'broadcasting' its rules and observations to the chief magistrates and citizens of England in October, Exeter suddenly remembered the plague, the Mayor called a meeting and feeling became tense.

Dr. Thomas Shapter was not then practising in Exeter. His arrival coincided with the dark days of the following July. His narrative is all the more convincing because his own immediate offer of his services seems to have been in keeping with the magnificent conduct of his profession as a whole during the crisis. Much that occurred varies from broad comedy to tragic irony. But the medical profession, however insufficient their knowledge and incorrect some of their views may now appear, worked night and day for months, in face not merely of the danger of infection, but of personal injury by riot, under insult and defamation. And one curious fact emerges from this. The exact causes and communication of the cholera may be now understood (Dr. Shapter and his senior colleagues certainly did not pretend to understand them), but the chart of mortality tells us that while poverty and bad conditions seemed to have favoured the disease, one certain cause of it was panic and excitement. All those who took fright at, all those who ridiculed, the cholera were seized by it, and died. The medical profession, their assistants the apothecaries and dispensers, and most of the staff employed in tending patients and burying bodies, and in disinfecting premises and destroying clothing, &c., escaped. Dr. Shapter's interest was of course professional and his account is arranged from this point of view. Rearranged chronologically the story appears to run as follows:

Oct. 27. Meeting of Mayor, Magistrates, and Physicians formed Local Board of Health, as recommended by Central Board of Health in London.

Nov. 1. At the instance of the above, Public Meeting attended by Local Board, Cathedral Authorities, Clergy, Poor Law Corporation, and Citizens. As a result:

Nov. 5. Medical Committee of the Board drew up a report, subsequently issued as a handbill, which recommended that the Commissioners of Public Improvements take steps to see to cleanliness of premises, repairs to water system (such as existed), scavenging and whitewashing of premises, and more generally, to the public, alertness in watching the advent of the disease, first aid, removal of possible cases, and opening of public subscription list. The city was also divided into districts, each with a District Board, for efficient mobilization of resources.

Nov. 9. Local Board of Health applied to military authorities for use of the empty barracks as a hospital if and when required. This was refused. Further, it recommended that 4,000 flannel belts, expected to cost 7½*d.* each for work and materials, be made and distributed by clergy and parish officers, and that the Mayor open a subscription for this. Further, that it be ascertained if the supply of water of the (unique) conduit in South Street could be increased, that the Dean make public the pump in the Close.

As a result the Commissioners of Improvements decided that they could repair, but could not sink or erect new pumps or wells. They applied to Mr. Golsworthy, lessee of the waterworks, to know how much he would charge to water the south and south-west quarters of the city. He replied that he usually charged £24 to water High Street daily for one hour all the summer. The Commissioners requested him to water the parts designated at the same rate for a fortnight.

Nov. 12. The clergy exhorted the population to repentance for their sins.

Nov. 14. The Central Board of Health, London, issued a more hopeful circular, deprecating any coercive measures.

On the same day, Mr. Golsworthy wrote lengthily to the Commissioners, protesting against the rumours that he was withholding water for his own purposes, and offering a free service of water, 300 days per annum, after it had served his customers. The Commissioners made no reply to this, but requested him to turn it on in Milk Lane and Mary Arches Street and sent their surveyor to rectify levels and lay a main.

Nov. 19. The Corporation of the Poor decided to appoint eight additional medical officers when required.

On the same day, the Local Board of Health made further inquiries for a hospital. The Corporation of the Poor refused to allow a site near the workhouse to be used. A Mr. Cornish proposed building one in a brickyard near by, but the Corporation refused to sanction this.

Nov. 28. The Committee of the Commissioners of Improvements reported to that body that Mr. Golsworthy was supplying water gratis and would extend this facility to Lady Day. He proposed that a contract be made on the basis of the terms on which he supplied the gaol and Bridewell. He was thanked but no arrangement was made.

Dec. 6. The Corporation of the Poor appointed its eight extra doctors, and eight apothecaries.

Dec. 14. The Commissioners of Improvements took notice of the condition of the churchyards, and the city burying grounds adjacent the walls.

Dec. 16. It now transpired that the Commissioners of Improvements were busy on an Act of Parliament for erecting a waterworks of their own. A long correspondence ensued. Mr. Golsworthy regarded the proposed Act of Parliament as an injustice, and said so. The Commissioners were so doubtful of their success that they received various propositions for wholly or partially hiring from him, and he got as far as offering 1,200 hogsheads per week for £3 15*s.* 6*d.* weekly, they to supply new tanks at specified places.

While these negotiations had been dragging on a stricter tone had appeared in the circulars sent by the Central Board of Health in London. But more important still, on December 15 it was discovered that the Local Board of Health was not, and could not be, legally constituted, and even the efforts of Mr. Buck, one of the members for the city, could not get this body made legal. A clash occurred with the Corporation of the Poor in March, when it was pointed out that Exeter, not being a parish but a corporation of parishes, could not legally have such a Board. The Central Board of Health wrote voluminously, referred the Local Board to the Norwich Act, sent sheaves of forms. The Local Board did not blench. It induced the Corporation of the Poor to undertake the distribution of flannel belts to persons in receipt of relief (the Corporation on November 26 authorized its Treasurer to spend £40 on this), the Commissioners to order a second hearse (Dec. 14) and circularize (on Dec. 17) the citizens for further subscriptions.

Possibly the outbreak of cholera in London, February 13, 1832, expedited matters, for on February 18 the Local Board had £467 2*s*. in subscriptions and had spent enough to distribute 7,440 flannel belts to persons *not* in receipt of Poor relief.

Finally, on April 23 the Privy Council by special order legally set up the Exeter Board of Health. The members had not waited. On March 16 they had again been in active negotiation for a large house outside the walls on St. David's Hill for a hospital.

'The application gave much offence and was indignantly refused; for such was the feeling that, while all, whether public bodies or private individuals, were loud and clamorous on the necessity of procuring such accommodation, they each shrunk from being parties in any way to harbour on their own grounds or property, the dreaded pestilence. Thus matters continued, now the Board of Health negotiating with those who met them with refusals, now entertaining plans which fell to the ground.'

Meanwhile Lady Day arrived and Mr. Golsworthy's free supply of water ceased. The Commissioners did nothing until June 30, when they again applied to Mr. Golsworthy to know his terms for certain specified watering of the streets.

Mr. Golsworthy replied that the gratuitous supply he had

given during the spring had greatly inconvenienced him and that he regretted the Commissioners had not pursued some arrangement by which these difficulties might be overcome. He 'met the necessities of the inhabitants in fear of the Cholera' by a limited periodic supply at five shillings per hour, but declined to supply the water-cart, for lack of piping and reservoir accommodation.

By this time (July 13) cholera had appeared in Plymouth. On the 19th the Commissioners met and once more approached Mr. Golsworthy. Complicated negotiations were put in hand involving argument and much correspondence. But it was already too late. The cholera had come. That night it was known that two cases had occurred, and Mr. Gidley, the indefatigable Secretary of the Local Board, at last had a use for the forms sent him from London, as follows:

No. 3

CHOLERA.—*Daily Numerical Report of Cases for the District of Exeter.*

To be furnished to the Central Board of Health.

Date.	*Remaining at last Report.*	*New Cases.*	*Dead.*	*Recovered.*	*Remaining this Day at 10 a.m.*
1832 July 21	0	3	1	0	2

From the Commencement of the Disease, on the 19th July, 1832.

Cases.	DIED.
3	1

JOHN GIDLEY,
Secretary.

The blow fell with a sinister impact quite perceptible to us across a century crowded with change. For nine months all sorts of individuals and institutions had been preparing for this moment within their limited scope. Most of them had done little but confirm their own limitations. The Local Board of Health, extemporary and mainly powerless, had at least raised money and energized the older, more precisely constituted bodies. But the pestilence came just as surely as if they had sat still. It is as fitting as if it had been planned by a dramatist, that the Board, after renewing the application to the Corporation of the Poor for leave to build a hospital in the brickfield (the plan of the architect was before them) and being refused, had tried to adapt a bleaching factory, an infant school, both withdrawn, and had then besought Lord Melbourne to intervene with the Ordnance authority and obtain the use of the barracks; that they had again applied to the Corporation for a burial-ground, and been advised to consider a site in Barrack Lane. On the 17th they had actually applied to the Central Board in London for extended powers. It was all of no avail. On the fatal day all they could do was to repair three pumps out of their own funds, while the Commissioners required the vestry of the parish of Trinity to reopen the pump in Magdalen Street.

The negotiations with Mr. Golsworthy, after another week, broke down altogether. It was no longer a question of argument. He wrote:

> 'The Committee are, I fear, impressed with the belief that it is practicable for me, in the existing state of my establishment, to furnish these large and sudden supplies of water without inconvenience or loss. This impression, however, is altogether erroneous, which will be readily believed when I inform you, that the unexpected demand on Saturday night placed it entirely out of my power to furnish my numerous private customers with their regular Monday's supply, limited the watering the streets around the London Inns to once instead of twice in the day, and prevented me from filling the cisterns at the baths, the hospital, and the jails. Your resolutions proceed to give directions for fixing stop-cocks in certain other streets and lanes which are enumerated. I have before repeatedly stated, and now again beg most distinctly to assure you, that fixing cocks will not enable me to water all or any of those streets. It is wholly useless to provide for the discharge of extra water which my mains cannot carry. It is extremely painful to my feelings in the present state of excitement and alarm, to have the odium of a deficiency of water thrown upon me; I feel it to be wholly undeserved. I have done, and will continue to do, all in my power for my fellow-citizens, but it is unjust and cruel to condemn me because I cannot effect impossibilities.'

Nothing in fact was done, except that the Local Board of Health authorized doctors, clergy, and others to issue tickets entitling the poor and needy to have two buckets of water

HAS
DEATH
(IN A RAGE)

Been invited by the Commissioners of Common Sewers to take up his abode in Lambeth? or, from what other villanous cause proceeds the frightful Mortality by which we are surrounded?

In this Pest-House of the Metropolis, and disgrace to the Nation, the main thoroughfares are still without Common Sewers, although the Inhabitants have paid exorbitant Rates from time immemorial!!!

" O Heaven! that such companions thou'dst unfold,
" And put in every honest hand, a whip,
" To lash the rascals naked through the world."

Unless something be speedily done to allay the growing discontent of the people, retributive justice in her salutary vengeance will commence her operations with the *Lamp-Iron* and the *Halter*.

SALUS POPULI.

***Lambeth, August,* 1832.**

J. W. PEEL, Printer, 9, New Cut, Lambeth.

delivered to them. Mr. Golsworthy appears to have dealt generously with such. (On September 19, the day on which the cholera ceased, the Commissioners offered a reward for a plan for a better supply of water to the city. A Bill was passed by the House of Commons in 1833.)

In face of the danger, the Custom House Authorities declared a state of quarantine in the port, and the Corporation of the Poor made a parallel regulation regarding their premises. The latter body also set up a Station House, in Mary Arches Street, hired twenty-four nurses at half a crown per day to attend the extra medical men and dispensers now set in motion, and remonstrated strongly with the Local Board of Health which had advertised for nurses with promise of an increased scale of remuneration. The eventual expense was £265 by the Corporation, £5 8*s*. 6*d*. by the Board. It was, in fact, already too late.

By July 25 (i.e. in less than a week) the burials in Bartholomew Ground were 'creating alarm'. A deputation of residents of the quarter waited on the Local Board with a view to stopping these, and the Board so energized the Corporation that that body voted £200 for a cemetery for cholera burials in Little Bury Meadow, out by St. David's suburb. The first burial here, however, on July 26, was the occasion of a riot in which the undertaker's men were assaulted, their tools destroyed, their work totally prevented, and the warden of the parish, with a posse of parishioners, remained on guard all night to see that it was not resumed. The body therefore was conveyed to Bartholomew Ground, where further riot arose. On the other side of the city very violent scenes were witnessed at an interment in Southernhay cemetery for quite other reasons. It was rumoured that the medical profession were making off with alleged cholera patients for purposes of dissection. The task of clergy and ministers was difficult and even dangerous, undertakers' men had to be bribed with extra pay and brandy, and even then the crowd forced them to produce pieces cut from the tarred antiseptic covers of the previously interred coffins, to prove they were still there. A further difficulty arose for strict ecclesiastics from the fact that the Bury Meadow had not been consecrated. (By August 10, however, the Bishop had given his licence.)

In this state of affairs on July 31 the Assizes, the chief

event of the year, fell due. The Mayor wrote to the Recorder, describing the condition of the town, but reply was made that His Majesty's Judges would hold their Court, and so they did, with all the usual pomp and procession. The theatre even opened, though Miss Martin, who 'warbled sweetly' throughout *William Tell* was rewarded by but 'a beggarly array of empty boxes' until the High Sheriff attended on the Friday. The Bishop proceeded undaunted with the Consecration of Bedford Chapel. The Judge addressed the Jury in measured terms and promised to 'repress sternly any persons, high or low, who did not assist, or who attempted to offer obstruction to the endeavours to eradicate the pestilence'.

But neither the Bishop nor the Recorder nor the Judge lived in the city. The Local Board of Health mostly did. Ill-equipped with water, refused camp equipage (bedding, &c.) by the Master of Ordnance at Plymouth, refused any place for tending the sick or burying the dead, they struggled on, under the splendid leadership of Mark Kennaway, the Mayor, and all the doctors, and by means of the exertions of Mr. Gidley, the secretary. The crucial week was that between August 13 and 20. Perhaps the figures on the daily returns impressed the Central Board in London. At length when the visitation was just passing its zenith the Privy Council granted the extra powers needed, military stores were made available, the joint weight of the Bishop and the Commissioners controlling the Expenditure of the Corporation of the Poor forced through the laying out of Little Bury Meadow and finally of another burying-ground at Pester-Houses. The Bishop refused to entertain the petition of the inhabitants of St. David's against it.

It is comforting to note that the turning-point was reached about August 22, the day appointed by all the religious bodies for humiliation and prayer. We may as well attribute the conquest of the epidemic to this cause, as it was clearly not due to the Local Board of Health, which had been impeded at every step, nor to the constituted authorities that moved so slowly and were still jealous of any invasion of their privileges. Just sufficient procrastination had taken place to cost the lives of some 400, mainly poor, persons. One woman wandered about the streets, deranged, with her hair about her face, bemoaning her child. A man who returned from his work to find his children dead 'became permanently disordered; for twelve years he lived a homeless wanderer and died in a hay-loft in the adjoining county'. It was necessary to indemnify the clergy for the risk they ran (further rioting took place in Rackclose Lane on August 13, when the 'police' had to effect removal of a body), and the individuals whose relatives, dying of the pestilence, were left without bed-furniture (for all such was destroyed) by order of the Local Board of Health.

Even so, the scenes of drunkenness, demoralization, and riot were sufficiently shocking. An attempt was made to induce employers of labour to alter pay-day from Saturday to Thursday, so that wages might be spent in purchase of necessaries, instead of laying in a stock of brandy, that Sunday might be spent drinking. Tracts appeared advocating every nostrum, even such as the firing of cannon to clear away the contagion. More efficacious, perhaps, was the distribution of 8 hundredweight of chloride of lime among 500 persons, so that many streets were white with it, while others were impassable owing to fumigation by tar barrels.

By August 24 the rivalry of the Corporation of the Poor with the Local Board seems to have subsided, for that body then began admitting necessitous cases to its infirmary, and even provided a 'bed on wheels' for transport. The parish of St. Sidwells, which had set up a Board of Health of its own, allowed it to disappear. Best of all, two soup kitchens had been established, and by September 1 a house for the reception of the friends of the dying had been procured and furnished, in spite of the protests of the south quarter, in which it was situate. It was used by only one family. The daily figures of infection and death were falling rapidly. By September 19 there were no new cases, and though twenty-one more occurred before October 27, and eight deaths, the cholera was gone, and one has an uncomfortable feeling that it went of its own accord. On October 10 a General Thanksgiving was held. Shops and taverns were shut and the Bishop preached. On the 22nd a 'numerous and respectable' public meeting was held when steps were taken to show appreciation of the services of the Medical Profession, who had already been thanked by the Corporation of the Poor, on September 25. Even before that, on September 20, the Commissioners of Improvements had shelved the question of pumps.

The final statistics are as follows:

	Population 1831.	*Cases.*	*Deaths.*	*Cases per cent. to Population.*	*Deaths per cent.*	
					to Cases.	*to Population.*
Exeter . .	28,285	1,135	402	4·0	36·3	1·4
St. Thomas .	4,176	275	38	6·5	14·1	.0·9

The expenses were:

	£ s. d.
Board of Health	2,929 2 0
Corporation of the Poor . . .	2,034 9 0
Commissioners of Improvements .	Unknown, but two sums, £1,000 and £2,000, voted.

Such was the fight of Exeter against the Asiatic cholera. As Dr. Shapter sagely remarks, it differed but little from the usual struggle of corporate bodies of humanity against plagues. But it had direct and lasting result in the pulling down of rookeries, establishment of an ample water distributing system, removal of markets to new sites outside the walls, and the laying of thirteen miles of sewers. 'A Pleasure Park occupies the ground first devoted to the burial of those dying of the Cholera; a spacious cemetery without the walls has relieved the former overcrowded grounds which are closed and planted. A Church stands over the grave of the last Cholera patient.'

§ 2. THE PROBLEM OF TOWN LIFE

This story has been told at some length because it brings out two aspects of early Victorian town life which we are apt to forget. It was almost wholly unorganized: the physical basis of it was perilously unsound. There was little or no local government, and there were no drains. And this in an age when year by year more and more of the population were living in urban agglomerations. If Exeter, a favoured city with an old tradition of civic life, could thus be reduced in a month to panic, rioting, and dismay, what might have happened in those great industrial territories which were not cities at all, but casual accumulations of factories and slums? And what was happening between these occasional outbreaks of pestilence?

Let us look at some of them as they appear in the curt statistical abstracts of the thirties.

In Bristol, the condition of nearly 6,000 families, or 20,000 inhabitants, was investigated. Of 3,000 houses, 1,300 had no water. Of 6,000 children, 2,500 escaped school. Of the better class of labourers, half paid £7 a year for their lodging, half paid £12. The lowest house rent was £3. A room was let for 1*s.* 3*d.* a week unfurnished, 2*s.* furnished. But three-quarters of the houses were drained. Of the 6,000, three-quarters professed to go to church: 500 were Catholics; the rest went elsewhere or nowhere. Bristol is a favourable case. Let us try Leeds: it is more typical.

Five hundred and sixty-eight streets were taken for examination: 68 were paved; 96 were neither paved, drained, nor cleaned; one of them, with 176 families, had not been touched for fifteen years. Whole streets were floating with sewage; 200 were crossed with clothes-lines. Over 500 cellars were in occupation. One hundred and fifty-six rudimentary schools provided for 7,000 children; the Sunday-schools took in 11,000; 15,000 went altogether untaught. Finally we learn there were 451 public-houses, 98 brothels, 2 churches, and 39 meeting-houses. The death-rate in the clean streets was 1 in 36; in the dirty streets 1 in 23.

This last figure might have been anticipated. But it is ominous. Town life as it was lived in the slums was gradually destroying the race. In Manchester the difference was even greater. In Ancoats, out of 100 children born, only 40 or sometimes 35, reached their fifth year: in the healthy quarter of Market Street, 60 survived. But in Manchester, where a sixth of the labouring population was Irish, one working family in ten lived in a cellar. In Liverpool, incredible as it sounds, the figure was one in five. And Liverpool was only maintained by immigration: the homebred population was actually shrinking from the excess of deaths over births.

Statistics like these go far to explain the constant apprehension which hangs over early Victorian England until it disappeared in the general good will and prosperity of the fifties—the fear of what would happen if cholera broke out, or the mob broke loose. But they only begin to shape themselves as a picture when we follow them into details and realize that Tom All Alone's and Jacob's Island are not declamation or propaganda but plain statements of fact, which can be supported from the account of scientific men. Our first impression is that England was helpless in face of the problem which the new industry and the new finance together had created. Then gradually we become aware of an array of half-forgotten figures, each in his own line fighting manfully to redeem some small sector from barbarism. Officials: the truculent and indomitable Chadwick, Kay-Shuttleworth, whose stately reports never allow us to forget that he was the father of Sir Willoughby Patterne, Mr. Inspector Tremenheere, Mr. Inspector Horner. Doctors: with the great name of John Simon, medical officer to the Corporation of London, at the head, and Walker, whose *Gatherings from Graveyards* can hardly be read without bodily discomfort. Public benefactors of all ranks and professions: from the Duke of Devonshire, who set an example by giving Sheffield land for a park, to Captain McHardy, who made the Essex police force a model which all England copied. And behind them an unnumbered host, clergymen, temperance workers, ragged-school teachers, city missioners, chairmen of benevolent organizations, secretaries, committee men. There are times, in the thirties and forties, when it seems to us, as Macaulay told his Edinburgh constituents, that civilization might have been destroyed by the barbarism it had engendered. It would be true to say that unrestricted private enterprise had created a problem which was only soluble by the intervention of the State; and private enterprise kept it manageable until the State was ready to act.

These things, the struggle of reformers with ignorant or corrupt vestries, the rise in the standard of municipal government, the simultaneous development, not always harmonious, of local patriotism and central authority, the Permissive Act, the Obligatory Act, the Inspector, the Grant in Aid, belong to political history and have often been recounted. We are concerned with Town Life and not its legal or administrative framework. But there are two characteristics of early Victorian life which are involved in them. One is that the townsman was hardly ever really well. Late in our period it was calculated that over half a million people were dying every year from preventible causes, mostly from the conditions under which they lived. The fever, the sore throat, the headache, the flushed skin and irritable temper, were constant visitors even to the better houses, as they were constant inmates of the worse. The other is that town life, which to the Southerner comes natural and into which

JACOB'S ISLAND

FLEET PRISON, 1848

the Dutch or German burgher fits so comfortably, was to the Englishman at best a necessary evil, at worst a horror to escape from. Necessity created the town, but strong preference and an instinct of self-preservation drove the townsman out into the suburbs, if he could get no farther, into the country if he could. And of the two processes, agglomeration and expansion, London was the chief example.

§ 3. LONDON

Area and Population.

Eighty-five years of internal peace, the partial and sometimes ruthless improvement in the use of land, had rendered possible the feeding of an increased population in what was then Greater London, an increase amounting to 222 per cent. during the eighteenth century. Yet London was actually, in our period, slightly declining from the excessive relative importance as compared with the rest of the country, where the increase in population over the same period was no less than 254 per cent. Between 1801 and 1831 Manchester had risen from 95,000 to 238,000, Glasgow from 77,000 to 200,000, Birmingham had doubled, and Liverpool was two and a half times its earlier size. The case of London is special, partly because we have more detail, partly because it was already so big, so that it illustrates the process that goes on beyond mere increase, the emptying of the centre, which in many a northern town, and particularly in the old provincial capitals such as Norwich was hardly noticeable at the end of the nineteenth century.

Between 1801 and 1831 Greater London had increased from 865,000 to 1,500,000. But the increase consisted in the addition of 33 per cent. to the borough of Southwark (swollen so that it ran southward from half-way between Blackfriars and Waterloo Bridge, down to the site of Bethlehem Hospital, east to Elephant and Castle, back to Borough High Street, over a mile down the Old Kent Road, and behind Long Lane to St. Saviour's Docks), 25 per cent. to what was still Westminster (especially from Oxford Street down to Millbank), fifty per cent. to the parishes within the bills of mortality (from Stepney up to Hackney, and west across Islington, and south the river, Lambeth, that followed the Camberwell Road to Denmark Hill, and Rotherhithe, that began at Bermondsey and ended at New Cross). Beyond these again, was an increase of 115 per cent. in St. Pancras, Camden Town, Paddington, Kensington, and Chelsea. While these areas were thus being thronged, the City within the walls, with slight additions along Liverpool Street, and westward to Chancery Lane, was actually diminishing. The City proper was 30 per cent. less populous in 1831 than in 1801, and the narrow borderland just without the walls 20 per cent. By 1850 the process had so far advanced that Cunningham remarked that no one any longer lived in the City. And figuratively this was true even then.

The early Victorian Londoner, therefore, was less and less a man descending, as did Pepys or any other of his predecessors, from a bedroom above, to a shop or office below, to pursue his avocation. He was increasingly a person who had to come some distance to get to his work. Here the vague nature of the statistics fails us. Of the totals we have for Greater London in 1831 already more than half relate to women, who mostly worked where they lived. So did the 169,000 domestic servants enumerated in the Metropolis at the following census. At that time, however, there were 20,000 clerks and 13,000 messengers, most of whom had to get from the Greater London without, into the administrative area known as the City, plus the strip east of Chancery Lane and along the northern wall. Many of them had some distance to go. For it is one of the distinctive traits of London, as distinct from Paris or any continental town, even as distinct from Edinburgh and Glasgow, that she never developed upwards, has in fact only recently begun to do so. Even Bath and Newcastle have a taller air.

When she increased, therefore, the additional population was housed by overcrowding, and by lateral expansion in houses, mainly two-storied, built on estates it was desired to develop, and ribboned along roads. This is why, in the *Pickwick Papers*, Mr. Wicks, of Dodson and Fogg's, found it was 'half-past four before he got to Somers Town' after a convivial evening, and why Lowten, Mr. Perker's chief clerk, was horrified to see the hour, as he came through the Polygon (now Clarendon Square), on his way from Camden Town to engage in the Gray's Inn Road, and thus attain his master's office, and Mr. Wemmick cultivated the family affections behind a ditch in Walworth. In fact since that crowning disaster—the failure after the Great Fire of 1666 to

THE HUB OF THE CITY, 1851

implement Wren's plan for a London that would have been the architectural wonder of the world—the financial and accounting circles of the City had packed themselves, for their day's work, tighter and tighter into the area confined within the streets that mark the site of the Roman walls. Beginning at the Tower these ran northward up the Minories to Aldgate, north-west along Houndsditch to Bishopsgate, and followed the street called London Wall past Moorgate, and turning then south-west to Newgate, and so by Ludgate to the river. And the law was faithful to the Temple.

The area, however, which in 1831 is marked as closely built upon, begins, in the east, upon the river, at Regent's Canal docks. Shadwell and Wapping were already solid, but Commercial Road had a few houses on its northern side, Stepney Green and Bethnal Green were still green, and Limehouse and the Isle of Dogs were not built up, until the forties. Hackney was a straggling street, and Shoreditch marked the north-eastern limit of what the French would call the 'agglomeration'. West of this point houses only lined the City Road and Pentonville Road. Euston Road, the New Road, had dense Somers Town to its north, but Regent's Park stood isolated and only scattered buildings filled the angle between the Marylebone and Edgware Roads.

Nash once told a Committee of the House of Commons that speculative building would be the death of English architecture. The healthy suburb of Marylebone was its first large field of operation, and the area west of Bloomsbury, between Oxford Street and the Regent's Park, was becoming the real capital of the new, middle-class England. A wail over these improvements and the loss of 'our old happy fields' reached Canning from an unknown correspondent. But the 'almost oriental magnificence' of the Park seems to have dazzled contemporaries. 'That interminable succession of streets and squares, all consisting of well-built and well-furnished houses—the brilliancy of the shops—the crowd of well-appointed equipages—that magnificent circle of palaces which surround the Regent's Park' displayed the prosperity of a class which 'was probably superior in opulence, intelligence, and respectability to any city in the world'. Gradually the space between the Parks was absorbed. In 1830 the houses north of Hyde Park had their backs open to Paddington. In the forties the Westbourne area had filled up, and in filling up had created a ghastly problem for its southern neighbours. It drained into the Serpentine and as late as 1850 an evening stroll by the waters sometimes ended in sudden fever, collapse, and death. The parks closed the fully built area to the west. Kensington was rural and the mossy palings and secluded gardens of Campden Hill are the last surviving fragment of the country belt that ran round Victorian London from Clapham and Battersea to Notting Hill and St. John's Wood. Brompton Road was not entirely lined with houses and in 1849 was still considered 'a place where actors and singers lived'. Below them Vauxhall Bridge Road and Millbank Penitentiary stood open to the river, though behind them in 1825 Belgrave Square had taken shape, and houses straggled along Fulham Road, Sloane Street, and King's Road to Chelsea village, whose Bun House was removed in 1839. South of the river, Kennington Lane and Albany Road marked the extreme limits, while Bermondsey and Rotherhithe were but narrow strips near the river, and confined of course by the docks.

Communications.

The problem, therefore, was how that portion of the population that lived at the extremities of this new and larger area was to cover the distance of three or four miles to get to its place of business, within the walls of the City.

One answer is, they walked. The walking powers of the Cockney are conspicuous in history and fiction. They were always in training: an eight-mile tramp to Hampstead and back after work was nothing: Macaulay constantly went from the Albany to Clapham and so to Greenwich on foot. And when we find that a young officer had a choice of two routes to Woolwich and the quicker—steamer to Greenwich and then bus—took three hours, we realize that over many routes walking saved time.

For conveyance inside the bounds of this Greater London there was in 1830 little or none. We are still before the era of railways, the Thames is not so situated as to provide a thoroughfare, except east and west, where it was least required even then, or for those engaged with the shipping. There were, we know, stage coaches running to and from such neighbouring places as Hampstead on the north, while contemporary prints show how considerable was the wheeled traffic passing through the Elephant and Castle cross-roads on the south. But of actual inter-suburb facilities we know only of Shillibeer's unique omnibus plying from the Yorkshire Stingo in Lisson Grove to the Bank. Bob Cratchit and others of his kind whose mufflers were substitutes for overcoats, could not have afforded to use omnibuses had they existed. What better evidence of the pressure to get to the City of a morning could there be than that between 1830 and 1837 no less than 400 omnibuses were put into use? The 600 hackney coaches of the latter date were spoken of, even then, as cumbrous affairs and cannot have done much to solve the city man's daily problem.

Even in 1837 there were only 1,200 'cabs', a species of hooded gig, the driver of which sat in a tiny seat above and beside his fare. The hansom with its seat behind, and more commodious plan, did not come in until 1850.

But almost at the moment when the outward movement of the population was taking place, London was assuming its modern shape by means of a vast and surprisingly rapid displacement of activity. The immense new populations that in a decade or two overran the face of the earth from Hackney Down to the Isle of Dogs never went near the City at all. Cunningham laments that, in 1849, Bethnal Green parish contained 80,000 souls and only three clergymen to look after them. By 1845 the docks were able to accommodate 2,000 vessels, and the population living upon the trades connected with them remained east and increasingly farther east of the Tower. In fact there began to be noticeable, far more on this side of the City than the other, that segregation of different classes of the population according to the rents they could pay which is the key to the geography of modern London, if we add to it, for the twentieth century, the discrimination demanded by the season ticket.

The same influence was observable less markedly in the west. The inhabitants of Mayfair and the more recent Belgravia had no long journey to their clubs, and the legislative and administrative centres of Westminster and Whitehall, and if they went farther afield commanded their own means of conveyance. Around them, too, was growing up a population that never needed to come east of Charing Cross. Kate Nickleby and her fellow apprentices may have lived as far as Pentonville or Islington and walked to Cavendish Square and its neighbourhood, where trade dribbled in to a remarkable extent among the habitations of the highly connected. The Pantechnicon was set up in Belgrave Square in 1834, and many of the 70,000 persons engaged in the making of clothes and footwear must have been centred anywhere westwards and northwards from Regent Street.

Furthermore, that portion of Greater London which, while outside the City limits, was on the very inside of the enlarged metropolis was most desperately crowded, more particularly towards the west. No doubt Wapping and Shadwell and the opposite riverside parishes suffered the disadvantages of a great port, but, long before, Defoe remarked that Whitechapel escaped the Plague. The early inhabitants of Bethnal Green were highly respectable French weavers. At length, no doubt, the immense influx of cheap alien labour, the worsening conditions, and the forsaking of the district by all people in comfortable circumstances brought about such reality as lies behind the legend of the East End. Yet Besant, writing in 1901, compares its slums favourably with those of the west. The source of the western slums was very ancient and had its root in the right of sanctuary which lingered into the days of William III, 250 years after the abolition of the religious houses that gave it birth, and accounts, according to Thornbury, for perhaps the most persistent and notorious district, that of Whitefriars, roughly bounded by the Temple, Fleet Street, Bridge Street, and the river. But another prolific cause of bad conditions and low standards, inevitable concomitants of low rents and overcrowding, was to be found in the presence of the great houses that once stood between the City and St. James's and even in Westminster itself. As these changed hands, always for the worse, they became rookeries such as Whetstone Park and Hatton Garden, significant names. The presence of prisons and equally of theatres seems, in early days, to have been a cause of the depreciation of property, the positive degradation of the former being little or no worse than the shifty insecurity of the latter—that 'lifetime of draughty waiting' as Galsworthy has called it. All these conditions were present in Whitefriars, where the house of the Earls of Dorset had become a theatre and was close to Newgate and the Fleet. Bankside with its three prisons is another instance, and we recollect that Little Dorrit could see but small difference

TEMPLE BAR, 1846

between the hangers-on of her sister's rehearsals and her own companions in the Marshalsea.

The overcrowding outside Temple Bar seems probably traceable to that edifice being the limit of the activity of the more or less efficient City watch. The street-walkers' parade was then not Piccadilly but from Temple Bar along the Strand to Westminster Hall. As one by one the rookeries succumbed (the demolition of property for the approaches alone to New London Bridge in 1830 cost a million and a half) the inhabitants went—where? The answer is familiar enough to modern students of housing. Unless they were lucky enough to find room in one of the new Improved Dwellings—to the next rookery! That is why, in 1849, at Calmel Buildings, Orchard Street, Portman Square, Cunningham found a court 22 feet wide surrounded by 26 three-story houses, down which ran a common sewer, the effluvium of which was sickening. These houses contained 426 male, 518 female persons, of whom 178 were under seven years old, 200 between that age and twenty years, and such congeries were let at £20 to £30 each; nor were the rookeries of Westminster much better.

One chronic cause runs through the condition to which circle after outer circle of ever-growing London passed. From the days when Cripplegate, just outside the walls became the first slum, down to the hasty jerry building that more or less housed the armies of 'navigators' who dug the railways, there was no compelling authority, military or other, to insist on some rudimentary town-planning. Once, therefore, Wren had failed to control the renascent city, only a few individuals such as Lord Southampton, in dealing with Bloomsbury Square, and less effectively Cubitt and other creators of West End squares, can be said to have planned anything, and the Metropolis grew under the impulse of small owners exploiting such areas as they could handle. No boulevard restricted and no other consideration than that of investment guided them. Rickman includes in his Comparative Account of 1831 a most instructive contemporary map of Paris and its four-mile radius, corresponding to the four-mile radius from St. Paul's that he treated as the Metropolis of his day. Actual Paris is a small patch in the centre and outside it are fields. The area of Greater Paris equivalent to Greater London contained roughly only two-thirds of London's population, because the French excess population was housed in *sou-sols*, *entre-sols*, *mansards*, anywhere, in fact, except in widely and irregularly spread two-story houses. This one feels to be the final and most striking difference between London and any other capital, and especially Edinburgh. And this contrast goes much farther than mere housing, and it has helped to determine the easy-going, amorphous anonymity of the greatest city in the world. Men speak proudly of having been born in Paris or Aberdeen. No one boasts of being a Londoner. And in such matters as diet, and the little pathetic patch of 'garden' that surrounds the nineteenth-century Londoner's home (still seldom an apartment on a common stair), we see the emergence of a type that was not merely sharply divided from the citizen of other big cities, but just as much from the previous citizen of the old Close City, such as Sir John Houblon or Samuel Richardson, Dr. Johnson, or Sir Christopher Wren. We see the type that, however poor and helpless, and from however remote a hopelessness, stares steadily up at the hardly visible star of an imaginary gentility. London created the black-coated proletarian. And the Cockney, at Gravesend or Epsom, or farther afield in Boolong or Paree, is the same figure in his house of ease, escaped from the restraints of business and not yet sobered by domestic cares.

But to return to our Londoner as he engages in his day's work. After allowing for most of that half of the population that was composed of women and was more or less anchored to the home, for all the leisured and wealthy who had no business and did it in St. James's or Westminster, for all the industrious of the nascent East End of manufacture and transport, for all the poor and destitute in their warrens, there must have been 100,000 persons passing down these main thoroughfares, mainly on foot. Nor can this estimate be very remote, for 90,000 people 'crossed London Bridge' (i.e. in two directions) daily in 1837. That is to say, if they had been drilled to march ten abreast and a yard apart, they would have made a solid column two miles in length, in each of the principal entrances to the City, a procession that must have taken at least forty minutes to pass any given spot. And we know that the mere jostling crowd they were did not achieve the journey with anything like this expeditiousness.

There is of course only very flimsy foundation for such a calculation, but there is no doubt as to the efforts that were made about this time to improve the means of communication. The well-meaning and accessible monarch, William IV, opened new London Bridge with a carriage way of 31 feet, considered ample, and soon found to be insufficient. Under him began that great reorganization of Trafalgar Square that embraced the destruction of the Royal Mews and of the unsavoury rookery known as Porridge Island before St. Martin's Church (though twenty years later Cunningham says that Hemming's Row in St. Martin's Lane used to be called Dirty Lane and still deserved the name), the opening of the Lowther Arcade, the rebuilding of Hungerford Market, the building of the National Gallery, the setting up of the Nelson statue in 1843, and the final opening of the Square in 1844. In the east, Liverpool Street was remodelled, in the west New Oxford Street was driven through a tangle of slums, and with the opening of Hungerford Bridge in 1845 early Victorian London achieved a system of communications which sufficed till a second wave of improvement set in with the establishment of the Metropolitan Board of Works in 1854. The lighting of London was famous: gas had been in use since the beginning of the century and the last oil lamps disappeared from Grosvenor Square in 1846. The paving was less satisfactory. The noise and vibration of early Victorian London must have been terrific. Wood blocks were laid in Oxford Street in 1838, but the substitution of wood was slow, of macadam (which a rainy day converted into a sheet of yellow slime) piecemeal. We must think of Central London in those days as an endless roar of traffic, under an opaque sky and a steady drift of smuts, sending up, according to season, fountains of mud or whirlwinds of dust, straw, and paper.

The City and the new town type.

Where did this army that invaded the City every day go to? We can account for some of them. The staff of the Bank of England was reduced on the resumption of cash payments in 1821, and remained all the rest of the century between 700 and 800, to which may be added 100 porters and watchmen.

This establishment had crowned a most chequered career by absorbing the whole block of buildings that we associate with it to-day, suppressing the Church of St. Christopher le Stocks, turning its churchyard into 'garden court' and diverting the line of Princes Street which used to run into Lothbury opposite St. Margaret's Church. The staff hours of work were from 9 a.m. to 3.30 p.m. or 5 p.m. if the clerks took the allotted 1½ hours for dinner. Actually they had to stay until their work was finished, and this hour must have varied considerably. Employment there had not the status it has since achieved, and particularly at the opening of our period there was much discontent. Some of the Bank's clerks resigned, one to keep an inn, and one to become governor of a gaol. Few of the salaries exceeded £300 a year, though there were certain 'miscellaneous payments' for special work and overtime, and a general disposition to take tips from the public. In addition to the increasing strictness that was the mark of this post-War period, the lodging the clerks found had changed in twenty years from 'Pope's Head Alley, Tokenhouse Yard, Bishopsgate and Cheapside' to Pentonville, Islington, Hoxton, Bethnal Green, Walworth, Newington, and Camberwell, thus confirming our view of the shifting of the Londoner's domicile. Many of them tried various ways of supplementing their salaries. One kept an eating-house, one was a coal-dealer; a bookseller, tea-dealer, and butcher also figured in the list, which descends to an oil shop and a small shop for the sale of snuff and tobacco, all of which were failures and caused either imprisonment for debt, or at the least, absence from, or preoccupation while engaged in their duties.

But these were not the extreme troubles with which the directors had to deal. Besides a tendency to take part, professionally, in theatrical enterprise, there were, in so large a staff (it never fell below 650 at the extreme limit of the 'economy stunt' of the eighteen-twenties) men who did stock jobbing on their own account, those who 'consorted with John Thurtell, an uncertified bankrupt and bad character from 6.30 p.m. on Saturday to 5.0 a.m. on a Sunday, at the Saloon at the top of the Haymarket' (this was the Thurtell who was hanged for the murder of Weare), and finally there were those who merely threw inkstands at clerks from private banks who came to the Bank of England on duty.

The Bank of England clerk is interesting because he forms

an almost central national type. He represented the highest type of executive the City could produce. Above him was a different class, administrative or professional. The insurance, Stock Exchange, and mercantile and law clerks were below him in condition and were then all the private servants of their masters. His work was then far more highly specialized than theirs, his responsibilities, in time of stress or riot, greater. More than once detachments of his kind were summoned to do semi-military duty as supplement to or substitute for the guard, and there was always a certain provision of arms and ammunition about the place. During the eighteenth century he had enjoyed forty-seven holidays a year. By 1830 these had diminished to forty-two, and on the fifth of August 1830 a notice was posted that only eighteen would be kept. These included the Conversion of St. Paul, St. Matthias, and St. Philip and St. James.

The observance of these even then half-forgotten feasts of course affected the daily work of the private Banks and other offices, all of which depended more and more closely on the Bank of England. And in 1834 the number of days on which the Stock Offices were closed was reduced to Good Friday, Christmas Day, May 1, and November 1, the two former being (to this day) holidays by Act of Parliament, the two latter to enable the Annual Election of Clerks (whose appointments, in theory and occasionally in fact, only continued at the discretion of the Directors) and for the balancing of the ledgers. Upon which a member of the staff, a Mr. Burrows, wrote a set of verses lamenting that it would no longer be possible for the clerks to see the cornfields or the sea, or to breathe other than the 'smoky London air'. In fact, the less scrupulous members of the staff then began to take the now historic course of massacring imaginary relatives in order to attend races, meetings, or to visit the seaside, or the British Museum with what now seems extraordinary frequency. On the whole they were leniently dealt with when discovered. Early closing on Saturdays did not come in until 1863, and Bank Holidays as we understand them do not affect our period.

These are, of course, domestic details of the Bank of England. But they have a far wider importance. They set a kind of unconscious maximum standard not only to the other Banks, but to other large financial—i.e. credit—houses.

Institutions such as the East India Company, the Stock Exchange, and Lloyds tended to synchronize with Bank habits. It is not very wonderful when we reflect that the Bank of England was the reserve Banker of all the other Banks, and the current Banker of the institutions grouped about it, and also the authority controlling the oldest, in all senses the largest, and up to our period almost the only group of Stock Exchange securities open to investment of the public's surplus, in a country which, long before all others, began to prefer this type of accumulated wealth to ownership of land or hoarding of specie. As in all things English, the gradual building up of a system of office discipline was slow, and maintained by a series of mild shocks. When abuses made themselves undeniably manifest, they were legislated for and not until then. Thus the gentle stream of regulation deprived the clerks of the licence to import strong drink into the office, to smoke cigars while at work, to take tips, even to wear moustaches (and these restrictions can be exactly paralleled in Cox's Bank and Lloyd's Building), but it assured them regular hours, holidays, pensions, and other provision. And we may be sure that the other clerks employed in the neighbouring institutions were not, on the whole, better off, as they shaded down through private banking, stockbroking, insurance, and mercantile accountancy, to the legal profession in which, as individual clerks often worked alone, the differentiation of individual employment makes generalization impossible. For instance, in *Pickwick*, Sergeant Snubbin's Mr. Mallard was probably as well off as the head of a department in the Bank of England, though he did nothing but make appointments for his master. But he had of course to provide for his own old age and sickness, and those of his dependants. In this body of clerical activity, poured daily into the City, drained from it at night, we have the central distinctive type of our period. The classes above it, Royal, noble, or propertied, legislators, merchants, members of learned professions, had existed before, but for the first time they became dependent on the, so to say, negative virtues of a body of men who made nothing with their hands, except figures in books of account, and whose great quality was not manual skill, but probity as regards other people's affairs entrusted to them. Below them again were shop assistants, like the pitiable 'hero' of *Ten Thousand a Year* living in a slum behind Oxford Street, where he worked, skilled workmen, a growing number of mechanics, then labourers and the very poor. All these classes had existed, if under different conditions and classifications, from the beginnings of civilization, but now became dependent on accountancy as never before.

Above it, but equally dependent, were the City merchants who made the Victorian age a world-wide instead of an insular phenomenon, Dombeys and Sedleys, Cheerybles and Clennams, East and West India merchants, exporters, shippers, dealers on commission, and correspondents of foreign houses.

All these now lived well without the City, at a greater distance than their clerks, and were not, naturally, dependent on omnibuses, or the lack of them. They drove into their offices in gigs, traps, cabriolets, or even carriages and pairs, and some few perhaps still rode, like Dombey's Mr. Carker, though he was only a manager, a new type called into being by the very fact that Bloomsbury had now ceased to suffice for the directing and owning class. Their houses had spread all along the north of Oxford Street, and they came from as far afield as Norwood and Highgate, Westcombe Park and Sydenham. The class then that was 'making money' in the exact sense of creating fresh credit, and not merely inheriting land with a rental value, was becoming detached from the scene of the operation, as surely as it was becoming dependent on hypothetical wealth, whose token was a figure in a banker's book, instead of living solidly next a warehouse crammed with goods, as Hogarth's City merchants had done. And with the rise of this class came the expansion and elevation of the Stock Exchange. The figure indicated by Dr. Johnson's definition of a stockbroker, 'a low wretch who lives by buying and selling the funds', had given place to that of Wilkins Flasher, Esquire (in *Pickwick*), who just as our period opens was recovering from the first post-War boom, in which the list of available investments had suddenly swollen from 30 entries, by 624 newly promoted companies, more than half of which were doomed to immediate total extinction. The extension of joint-stock share-owning in the thirties saw the downfall of many a dubious foreign loan, but the introduction of Bank shares strengthened the list, while the forties was the period of the great Railway boom. The City had fallen into a habit of crises recurring so nearly every ten years that there was some idea that such events were inevitable. Boom and depression certainly alternated during the whole of our period with a regularity that gave grounds for that impression. But it now strikes the observer, from a longer perspective, that although the top-hat had crowned the respectability of business, and the umbrella had replaced the sword as part of the daily wear, there still lurked an omnipresent and perpetual precariousness.

It is hardly surprising, therefore, that Mayfair, solidly based on landed values, still looked down on the City, much as the County Magnate shoo'd the railway line from his park walls. The attitude is well expressed by the consternation of the Swell in *Punch*, at the subsequent threat of the demolition of Temple Bar:

'What? . . . why, it's the only Bawwier between us and the howwid city!'

The West End.

Clubland, which earlier, in Brummell's time, had been a compact district from which one could not depart, was, in fact, expanding. The *Monthly Magazine* volume for 1837 gives the following list: Albion, Alfred's, Arthur's, Athenaeum, just built in Pall Mall and representing a new element, Boodle's, Brooks's, Carlton, founded by Wellington, Clarence, Cocoa Tree, Dilettanti, Garrick (away in Covent Garden), Graham's, Guard's, Oriental, Oxford and Cambridge, Portland, Royal Naval, Travellers, Union, United Service, Junior United Service, University, West India, White's, Wyndham's. Crockford's swell gaming-house still existed until 1845, and Almack's exclusive Assembly Rooms until 1835 was controlled by the survivors of the clique of titled people who had kept it select. But the age of deep play was over.

This body of twenty-five semi-residential associations, many of them even then half a century old, and most of them extant together with their palatial premises to this day, at the time of the Queen's Accession was spreading from St. James's Street along Pall Mall. They present a phenomenon unique in history. For they cannot be dismissed as mere idling places of the rich. They contained many of the

SMITHFIELD, 1850

best brains in the country as well as some of the nastiest characters. It was with the support of the public they represented that the *Edinburgh Review* went crusading for political reform, the *Quarterly Review* for social reform. The Conservative revival of the thirties was organized from the Carlton; the foundation of the Reform to be a Radical counterweight to the pure Whiggery of Brooks's involved as much agitation as a Cabinet shuffle.

Tacked on to them was a phenomenon difficult for us to-day to comprehend. The Dandy was still paramount. There is no historical reason for regarding Brummell as an excitingly wicked man. Shallow, pert, and cowardly he certainly was, and was abundantly punished for his gambling habits. Too little justice is done to the fact that his influence, gone before our time, has bequeathed to us one remarkable legacy. He established the trouser sooner and more firmly than mere undirected public taste was ever likely to have done, and thus performed a great and unintentional service for the new, poor, but obligatorily respectable clerk population of London and the towns. It was a great step towards comparatively sensible if not rational dress in an age still thoroughly horsy, in which fashion otherwise clung to Wellington boots and the corresponding uncomfortable and useless knee-tight garments. It was only a first step, but perhaps the one that counted. After it, we approach the time when *Punch*, infallible barometer, began to picture the retired tradesman, or clerk, who had horsy pretensions, as 'Old Briggs' or 'Little Tomnoddy' in satiric vein.

The dandy of our epoch was Count D'Orsay, who was a far more worthy figure than Brummell, an athlete, horseman, artist, connoisseur, as well as magnificent in clothes. It was one of the fundamental misfortunes of Disraeli that he could only imitate his model in the last respect. D'Orsay scintillated on the fringe of Clubland, but during his partnership with Lady Blessington made Gore House (where now the Albert Hall stands) a Salon as splendid and far more reputable than the fabulous ones of eighteenth-century Paris. Politically, Lansdowne House and Stafford House were of far greater consequence. Holland House was more solid in contemporary influence and more select. But it was at Gore House that one met Dickens and Thackeray, Sydney Smith and Rogers, L. E. L. and Monckton Milnes, Disraeli, Moore,

Landor, and Wellington. It came to an end in 1849 from sheer lack of cash, having outlived its more heavily-metalled rival by nine years.

Unfortunately, the fringe of Clubland (which may be taken as the male half of the more amorphous 'Society') was not entirely composed of D'Orsays. There remained in the shadow that George IV continued to cast long after he had disappeared from mortal view, something he had never deliberately created, a body known as the 'Swell Mob', of whom Sir Mulberry Hawk, Montagu Tigg, Captain Costigan, and others are the best-known representatives in fiction. The vague national progressive movement that began with our period soon expressed itself in police raids on some dozens of obscure noisome dens that surrounded and faintly imitated Crockford's and the great clubs without achieving their standards, perhaps without seriously desiring to, for these lower places were the gathering ground of all those who were refused admission to authentic privileged circles. The compactness and family spirit of this gang of blackguards and unfortunates are not now easily credible. But if one thing more than another mobilized them with almost military precision, it was a public execution. All readers of the *Ingoldsby Legends* know how 'McFooze and Lieutenant Tregooze, and also Sir Carnaby Jenks of the Blues' had hired for them 'the whole first floor of the Magpie and Stump' (opposite Newgate) to see a man hanged, a form of entertainment suggested to them by Tiger Tim, who shared their tastes, and how they got too drunk, and only awoke when the corpse had been cut down. That is generally regarded as fiction. It is a fact, however, that on the occasion of the execution at Norwich of Rush for the Stanfield Hall murder in 1849, the Swell Mob chartered a special train, and set out for that city, much as a learned society, a philanthropic conference, or the supporters of a big football team would to-day. The Norwich Police, however, feeling that they had enough trouble on their hands (among the thousands who thronged the Castle Hill was a woman who had just been confined, but who had walked eleven miles to see that defective farm bailiff 'turned off'), met the special train at Attleborough and transferred its occupants to the next 'up' train. A few evaded this precaution, but were caught the same night and lodged in Norwich gaol. No warrant was

NEWGATE, BEFORE AN EXECUTION

necessary. They were all sufficiently well known not to risk an action for false imprisonment.

The Spectacle.

It is on the other side of the 'bawwier', however, that we shall find that attitude that is more distinctive of nineteenth-century England than her island position or mercantile pre-eminence, that almost divine snobbery of very strong motive power, that keeps the Englishman from being content ever to be classed a workman or labourer, a priest or soldier or scholar, as men of other civilizations are, and makes him always desire to be a gentleman, a word without equivalent in any other language. Very instructive on this point is the *Manners and Customs of the English*, a burlesque diary of a nineteenth-century 'Pips' (Pepys) written by Percival Leigh and illustrated by Doyle that appeared in 1849, collected from *Punch*. Here we have the social scene as the merchant of, but no longer resident in, the City, looked at, enjoyed, and estimated it.

This seems to give an excellent cross-section, from the newly-enfranchised-from-the-City merchant upwards. As a mere spectator, he looked on at the events of the real exclusive West End that centred round the Court. He was all agog at the toilettes and uniforms that passed him up St. James's to the Drawing Room, of which four or five were held in the Season, hardly less so at the well-dressed crowd that attended the playing of quadrilles by the military band in Kensington Gardens, and the equipages and riders in the Row at a fashionable hour. (The younger smarter men portrayed wore the D'Orsay throat whisker, the elders were clean shaven and tightly stocked. Doyle does not omit to place in the foreground a figure to-day scarcely credible—a nearly naked, hardly human thing, nursing its bare feet under loathly rags, in full sight of the crowd.) He attends also the imposing Guard mounting, at St. James's. He becomes a participant in the pleasures of the *beau monde*, however, when he (urged by his wife) mixes with the throng round the new expensive shops in Regent Street, and the equally new cheap ones in Oxford Street, both furnished with new plate glass windows; he patronizes the Arts, that is, he gets a stiff neck at the Academy, a crumpled shirt in the rush to hear Jenny Lind (the police plus a picket of the Guards being totally unable then, or even as late as the marriage of Edward, subsequently the Seventh, and Alexandra, to control a crowd), but he is best pleased perhaps with Jullien's Promenade Concert at Drury Lane.

He also looks in on the Commons in their temporary House and finds them obstructed by the Irish and dominated by 'Pam' and Lord John Russell; and on the Lords and finds their Chamber empty but for two or three sleepy individuals engaged in hearing (or failing to hear) appeals, until roused by Brougham's witticisms. His further contact with the law is to attend the State Opening of Term at Westminster Hall. But another busy centre of the Law lay then between Doctors' Commons next St. Paul's, with its extraordinary medley of ecclesiastical (thence able to license the marriage of Alfred Jingle and Rachael Wardle) and admiralty courts (known and feared by every port in the world) and Old Bailey, where Mr. Pips attends, with a gusto left over from old Tyburn days, a murder trial.

This brings us to his own preferred amusements as distinct from those he merely aspires to, because they belong to circles he has hardly left off describing as 'the gentry'. We find him visiting that mass of filth and cruelty at Smithfield, from which his daily joint comes, and indulging his wife at Madame Tussaud's Waxworks, and finding there Stanfield Hall, where Rush committed his celebrated murder 'as famous as Waterloo'. He has private amusements too, an evening's classical music which he makes portentous efforts to enjoy, a *soirée* at 'Lord Wilkinson's' who professes himself glad to see him and wife, though he knows he is only on the invitation list because he had his name put down in the Court Guide; and a modest dance, at which the polka is performed so vigorously that on the way home he and his wife stop at a tavern and drink a pint of beer each. But he is, in the main, as he always was before or since, an outdoor man, a dim urbanized attempt at a country gentleman, accepts invitations to shooting-parties, attends races and steeple-chases, fishes solemnly at Richmond, sees the Thames Regatta rowed at Hammersmith, and cricket played at Lord's (one bowler is worn, and one cap, in a field otherwise surmounted by toppers). He takes his wife to the Horticultural Society's Flower Show at Chiswick, which held its Exhibitions in May, June, and July, and to the Zoo, with

CHAMBER
OF
HORRORS.

MADAME

TUSSAUD & SONS,

Anxious to gratify the Public, respectfully announce that they have added a

PORTRAIT MODEL
OF

RUSH

TAKEN FROM LIFE

AT NORWICH,

DURING THE TRIAL.

It represents him as he appeared dressed in black, &c. and conveys a good idea of probably the Greatest Criminal that has been brought to justice for several years.

EXHIBITION,

BAZAAR, BAKER STREET,

Portman Square.

ADMITTANCE - ONE SHILLING.

CHAMBER of HORRORS, 6d.

Open from 11 in the Morning till 10 o'clock at Night.

J. W. PEEL's Steam Machine, 74, New Cut, Lambeth

a true Londoner's pathetic interest in flora and fauna. He most emphatically does not take his wife with him by steamer to guzzle whitebait at Blackwall nor to roister at Greenwich Fair. Finally we catch him sneaking off with a party to visit the vaults at the docks, and taste the wines, and lowest of all, to descend into the Cyder Cellars, in Maiden Lane, where a half-shaven blackguard lugubriously mouths the loathsome 'Ballad of Sam Hall', his murderous act and hanging. The writer has had the advantage of hearing an old *habitué* attempt as many stanzas of this 'turn' as he could remember. For dreary objectionableness nothing can be imagined equal to it, even indecency is lacking.

The leisure of the Middle Classes.

This is probably the lowest point touched by 'Mr. Pips', whom we may take to be a City merchant of fifty, comfortably married, possibly retired, but at least in full command of his time, and the means to spend it as he wishes. He is a predominantly English type, who existed (and exists) in England in greater proportion to the 'fonctionnaire' continental type than anywhere in the world. On his level as regards income, the civil servant, doctor, and lawyer were raised above him by education and far more tied by rule, even if the hours of the first were not very long, and those of the last limited by lengthy vacations. But immediately below these classes we come to masses of which the Bank of England clerk whose condition we have examined must have been substantially the most fortunate, and the shop assistant 'like a hedgehog, rolling and unrolling for twelve hours a day' the most unlucky. The best shops closed at 7; the rest when they liked. Saturday early closing comes late in our period, and Sunday being still a day of almost fanatic gloom, their evenings were the only time at which they could be said to have any leisure.

They reached it at varying hours. The classes' adoption of the continental late dinner-hour never affected the masses. They dined at midday in the innumerable small chop houses, taverns, and eating places pictured in Dickens, of which the names, often the sites, and occasionally the fittings can still be found. The Cheshire Cheese is a classic example that has been preserved, and also the Cock in the Strand, though contemporary accounts make it seem that the Rainbow was equally valued for the quality of its beer. In the City such were very numerous, fitted with seats of the 'horse-box' type, and served that national repast of joints, steaks and chops, potatoes, greens, cheese, and limited sweets, washed down by considerable potations of malt liquor and followed by hot spirits and water.

Here are two bills of fare:

Liver and Bacon	10*d*.	Veal and Ham	8*d*.
Potatoes	1*d*.	Welsh rabbit	7*d*.
Bread	1*d*.	2 poached eggs	8*d*.
Pint of Stout	4½*d*.	Gooseberry pie	5*d*.
Cheese	2*d*.		
Celery	2*d*.		

With these may be compared the meal of which Messrs. Guppy and Jobling partook under the direction of Chick Smallweed in *Bleak House*. Here the papers were to be seen, and were bespoken, many readers deep. The waiter was an influential character, rising in type from the slipshod 'gal' to a potentate who could and did materially influence the customer's comfort, though there is little evidence that he ever received a tip in metal finer than copper. As in the case of the Bank of England, the very favoured, capable of forgoing this meal, may have been free to go home between 3 and 4, but the general assumption in the fiction of the time (backed by such actual figures as we have for the Bank and its immediate neighbourhood) makes 6 o'clock the usual hour for the closing of City offices, a considerable reduction, due to changed habits and domicile, for the eighteenth-century denizens of Lloyds had been with difficulty dislodged at 9 o'clock at night.

The volatile population of the City, then, left the scene of its daily labours to watchmen and porters, and their families, about 6 p.m. (There were a few charwomen, some employed at the Bank from 1849 washed it once a month.) Some of the clerks thus set free spent their time in the taverns and entertainments close at hand. For the more serious there were the Polytechnic and the Mechanics' Institute. These would be mainly single men. (There were no business women in the City of course, and as late as the seventies it was extremely difficult for any unattended female with the appearance of a lady, or pretensions to good looks, to obtain any food when there on the most pressing business except at a pastry cook's

ST. JAMES'S STREET, 1840

shop. For the wealthy, there was Gunter's in Berkeley Square for ices; and for buns, Birch's, of which the front alone remains —in the Victoria and Albert Museum. Otherwise a wife or sister could only be entertained in the coffee-room of a good hotel, and we know from *Great Expectations* how meagre the entertainment could be.)

The married clerks made their way home to their (mainly distant) suburban abodes, from which it seems unlikely that they could return to partake of most of the entertainments situated in London proper.

In 1850, we know by Leech's drawings for *Punch* that the clerk who lived at Brook Green, Hammersmith, had become a recognized type. If, however, they did, either alone, or with wife and family, join the unattached in the search of amusement, they had the choice, as regards theatres proper, of the Old House in the Haymarket, or the newer one, also devoted to Italian Opera, in Covent Garden, opened in 1847, and Drury Lane, closed by Macready in 1843 and later used by Jullien. (Drury Lane seats cost 7*s.* in the Stalls, 3*s.* 6*d.* in the Pit, 2*s.* Upper Boxes, 1*s.* in its celebrated Gallery, but in the palmy days of the Haymarket, its Boxes are said to have let at a rental of £8,000!) There were also the Haymarket Theatre, Adelphi, Lyceum, Sadler's Wells, Princess's, Queen's, Olympic, Strand, Coburg, Royal Pavilion, and Garrick, and one in Norton Folgate. But many must have preferred to the regular theatres such amusements as were provided for them at the Panorama in Leicester Square, Diorama in Regent's Park, Cosmorama in Regent Street, the Hall of Commerce in Threadneedle Street, the Freemasons' Tavern in Great Queen Street, the Egyptian Hall, where Tom Thumb was long the leading attraction, and kept people away from poor Haydon's paintings. Madame Tussaud's has already been mentioned. There were open to them, nearer their own doors, two kinds of entertainment, one passed and one passing, to our great disservice, from English life: the Tea-garden and the Circus. Fortunately the memory of the former is carefully preserved in the important work of Mr. Wroth, who collected every available detail concerning them, and justifies us in classing them, with the single exception of the Circus, as the usual evening entertainment of the lesser clerks and suburban family parties. No amount of historical research can create their atmosphere as well as this is preserved for us in *Sketches by Boz* and *Vanity Fair*, but Mr. Wroth, if he disillusions, comforts us with the facts and figures. After all, Dickens disillusioned us in the sketch entitled 'Vauxhall Gardens by Day'.

It is clear that none of these establishments bear any comparison with the eighteenth-century Ranelagh (closed in 1803) and Vauxhall, which struggled on until 1859, although reduced prices, and rumours of impending fate had been lowering its prestige all the forties. Mr. Wroth lists fifteen establishments that had a certain vogue north of the river, and five to the south, and pleads eloquently (his preface is dated 1907) for the many social and hygienic advantages that might have been secured had it anyhow been possible to maintain these places. Alas, they were displaced by the one of our island institutions that strikes more dismay into the breast of the foreigner (or equally, of the social reformer) than any other, except the already passing Victorian Sabbath, of which indeed it is the ally —the English stand-up drinking bar, for the rapid consumption of stereotyped gulps of beer or whisky. Since *Cremorne and the later London Gardens* was written, changing habit, the ubiquity of the cycle and motor-car, above all the revolt of the Englishwoman against the nineteenth-century purdah, have wrought a wonderful transformation. Yet one can but share Mr. Wroth's dismay at the eclipse, not merely of the twenty more important gardens, but the further seventy minor ones that he lists, mainly pleasant little enclosures behind public houses. For in spite of climate, of touchy English morals, and the more powerful attraction, steadily growing, of the English home, with its garden plot, however small, the Gardens did preserve an amenity that connected us with continental life, on most of which we have increasingly turned our backs since A.D. 1500. It was certainly possible, all the thirties, and even into the fifties, to take a family party to such places as these, on a summer evening, to find a not unpleasing 'rustic' shelter, where a choice of viands was obtainable, as well as a wide selection of beverage far beyond beer or whisky (even brandy and gin were not obligatory, though usual), and to have music, dancing, and fireworks, and sometimes balloon ascents. But it could not last. Besides English climate, English morals, and the English home, the growing conception of English business

HYDE PARK, NEAR GROSVENOR GATE, 1842

was a fatal objection to such places. No one was willing to lay out capital and to work for long hours for the meagre reward on which most European cafétiers would have founded a fortune. Nearly all were in considerable financial difficulty most of the time, and the undoubted decline in the quality and behaviour of their frequenters does not entirely account for the opposition to them, founded on the fact that they were places of entertainment, and cheap entertainment at that. And when new conceptions of leisure and recreation eventually triumphed it was in the form of organized games, or of great 'exhibitions', and finally we became a nation on wheels. But as early as 1839 Dickens had seen through the factitious glamour of Vauxhall, the dreary appearance of spangles and 'cascades' by daylight, and how the fine point of catering was to give as little for the money as possible.

Cremorne was by far the largest, longest lived, and best known. In the King's Road, Chelsea, on a site now enclosed in Uverdale Road, Dartrey Street, and Lot's Road, stood once Cremorne House, belonging to Lady Huntingdon, founder of the sect that bears her name. In 1830 it was bought by Baron Charles Random de Berenger, a French-speaking Prussian, mixed up in the Stock Exchange adventures of Lord Cochrane, and wearing a uniform that had survived from the Napoleonic Wars. He was certainly a good shot, and as such opened a Stadium here in 1830, for 'manly exercises' with a 'Ladies' Links' attached. It chiefly flourished by the aid of galas and 'fêtes champêtres' and balloon ascents, fireworks, music, and dancing. The famous bogus 'Baron Nicholson', who held scandalous 'comic' trials full of obscenity and wit, at the Cyder Cellars, the Coal Hole, and such places succeeded him. He put in some good variety entertainment, including Tom Matthews (who sang 'Hot Codlings'), Fanny Matthews, and Green's balloon. In 1849 Simpson, ex-head waiter at the Albion opposite Drury Lane, bought the Cremorne from a proprietor who failed for £16,000 (execution was levied in Cremorne for £8,000). He added the grounds of Ashburnham House (now Ashburnham Street) to the existing 12 acres, and G. A. Sala described the lay-out and timbering as 'magnificent'.

If principally a caterer, Simpson built a monster pagoda (illuminated), two theatres, and provided 'side-shows innumerable fortune-telling, 'Salamanders', Circuses, a tight-rope crossing of the river, a miniature naval engagement, a medieval tournament in costume, and increasingly, dancing for ordinary couples said to be possible for 4,000 dancers, down to the days of the 'Crystal Platform'. Simpson retired in 1861 and said he made £100,000. In 1857 the Chelsea Vestry presented a petition against the renewal of the licence. (Simpson had already been fined for allowing a balloonist to take up a heifer with him.) The company was deteriorating. Occasionally fashionable or titled people presided, but more often, one did not take one's wife. The place fell into increasing disrepute until it was closed in 1877.

Lesser known places were Batty's Hippodrome and Soyer's Symposium, where Soyer, ex-chef of the Reform Club, at Gore House (its site lies 150 yards east of the Albert Hall), hoped to make a fortune, and lost £7,000; the Hippodrome, Notting Hill (now covered by Ladbroke Grove and adjoining streets), a small race-course, strongly objected to by neighbours. Chalk Farm, once the White Horse Inn, now 89 Regent's Park Road, was more entirely a tea-drinking and athletic establishment, where duels had been fought. There were many gardens in Hackney and Hoxton, the Panarmonion (Reggiori's, 1 and 2 Euston Road), the celebrated 'Eagle' at Islington (corner of City Road and Shepherdess Walk) made famous by the song, 'Pop goes the Weasel'. The Music and Spirit Licence here is said to have damaged the lesser theatres. There was the Globe Tavern, 359 Mile End Road. The Red House, Battersea, was the scene of cricket matches and pigeon shooting, and was replaced, to the never-ending credit of the public opinion of the forties, by Battersea Park. The Flora Gardens, Camberwell, had, in 1854, a Lady Godiva in a torchlight procession, the rôles in which were sustained by 'Artists from the Royal Academy'! The Montpelier Tea-Gardens, Walworth, were the scene of a game of cricket played between eleven one-legged and eleven one-armed pensioners of Greenwich Hospital, for a thousand guineas wager between two noble lords.

It is strange and significant that already, in those days, *tea*-gardens were a national institution, coffee-gardens unheard of; tea, the name of a daily meal, coffee never penetrating below the level of the leisured and cultured classes and certain professional castes. Even for them, coffee had had its

MAKING A CLUB MEMBER, 1840

day. Jonathan's, the Jamaica, and the Jerusalem Coffee-houses were less heard of, as regards the City, for Lloyds and the Stock Exchange no longer depended on doing their business there. In the west were still the Grecian (closed 1843), Peele's, 177 Fleet Street, where the Foreign newspapers might be seen, and the Coffee and Cigar Divan, 102 Strand. The cigar habit had been brought back by the troops from the Peninsula, and figures oftener in *Punch* than the coffee-house. But then coffee could be taken at home. Cigars often could not. The small coffee-house became a general restaurant.

The connexion in our minds between tea-garden and circus is fitly symbolized by the Surrey Zoo, which the able Mr. Cross, the proprietor, had moved from Exeter, Change (condemned because it obstructed the Strand) to the Royal Mews. When this was demolished to make Trafalgar Square, Mr. Cross was able to obtain the grounds of the Manor House at Walworth, which were 15 acres in extent and had a 'lake' of 3 acres; he altered and arranged the gardens, erected aviaries, and installed his lions (one of which cost £800) and tigers in a great circular conservatory of glass 300 feet wide. A similar octagon housed the zebras, emus, and kangaroos. There was a gigantic tortoise on which children rode. The prospectus announces (1831) that the Queen, the Duchess of Kent, and the Princess Victoria and a long list of the nobility were patrons, the season tickets were a guinea, admission one shilling.

By 1837 'Panoramas' began here, in which the lake was utilized, with canvas scenery, and grand firework effects. Seventeen annual repetitions, with varying subjects followed, one, 'The Great Fire of London', moving Cruikshank to a comic picture of stage-hands 'stirring it up'. Balloon ascents, tight-rope feats, and orchestral concerts (not vocal) supported the programme. When Cross retired in 1844, an orchestra was erected for Jullien's band of 300 performers, and in 1855 the menagerie was sold and the Surrey Music Hall Company took over the premises (with a working capital of £30,000 and a yearly rent of £346). Jullien was interested in the new building, which cost £18,200, held 12,000 people and an orchestra of 1,000 performers. It opened on July 15, 1856, with the *Messiah*, the principals being Clara Novello, Sims Reeves, Miss Dolby, and Piatti.

That autumn C. H. Spurgeon preached there, when his own Chapel and Exeter Hall were too small, at a rental of £15 a Sunday. On October 19, during the service, a cry of fire being raised, there was a rush for the doors, seven people being killed and fifty injured. Spurgeon remained calm.

The new Company was not successful, and when, in 1861, the Music Hall was burnt, St. Thomas's Hospital, then rebuilding, was glad to use the grounds, and there our period ends.

This leads us back to the circus proper, the largest and best known of which was Astley's. So long-lived and so famous was it, that in *Sketches by Boz* we find two separate periods of it in the memory of the young Charles Dickens. The best-known home of this entertainment was in Westminster Bridge Road, but it was three times burnt out. Yet for the first half of our period it was the standard English entertainment, enjoying a European reputation, the school for clowns, and putting on, besides the usual 'turns', a melodrama.

Such were typical occupations of the leisure of the time, of all those below the level of the propertied and titled, professional and directing classes. Gradually habits changed. The tea-gardens and circus united all the aspirations of this class, the social event with the feast, the open-air excursion with the theatrical-acrobatic-wonder show. The component parts split up under the increasing complication of life and the command over material obstacles of space and time—or the bus, railway, and steamboat took people farther afield, and early closing, Bank, and finally annual holidays rendered folk less dependent on the garden or ring behind the public house at the country end of the street.

The social event was relegated to the home, and became the party. The feast came to be held in the restaurant. For open air, in the fifties, we have the cheap ticket and the excursion train, and Leech began to draw comic pictures of the 'Husband's Boat' arriving at Margate, a sure sign of contemporary feeling, and this element was partly side-tracked later by organized sport. The tavern or circus entertainment merged in the music-hall, or was forsaken for the hobby, as money and leisure became more plentiful and education, with the serious purpose that the mid-Victorian saw in life, more general. The passing of the tea-garden particularly touches our sentiment. It was so innocent, so

AL-FRESCO PAINTING OF MOUNT HECLA, SURREY ZOOLOGICAL GARDENS.

'familiale'. If there were frail creatures 'loitering', as it is now called, at such places, it was less sordid than their doing so in the streets, or herded into a 'promenade'. On the other hand, it was usual to do every discourtesy to the waiters, from practical jokes to bodily violence. We hope they were rewarded, and we may draw some slight comfort from the fact that the decay of the gardens coincides (perhaps accidentally) with the disappearance of the 'Funny man' with his egregious horseplay.

The Underworld.

Below the person who had a surplus in an assured income, however small, and certain stated leisure and could thus afford entertainment, below the clerk in fact, what masses of want and servitude hung on all the daylight hours, as best they could, to occupations that were subject all the time to wholesale displacement that they could control as little as they could foresee?

The waterman was going out. During the eighteenth century he had numbered perhaps 40,000, and at the opening of Blackfriars Bridge his company had been compensated by £13,600—3 per cent. Consols—for the loss of ferry. But by our date his numbers had shrunk to a few thousands, scavenging the river, as in *Our Mutual Friend*, and waiting on the shipping. The town had widened and there were too many bridges higher up. The waterman we meet in Dickens was a different person; he attended at cab-ranks, watered the horses, and called 'Next Cab' when a fare approached.

The railwayman was coming in. Market-gardening was increasing, armies of navvies and brickmakers, and all connected with the constructional trades, worked at the great new improvements of streets and public utilities. On the other hand, the convulsions that had stirred the whole agricultural population, however inevitable and eventually beneficial, had the immediate effect of increasing the mass of loafers and beggars, poor and sometimes honestly unfortunate persons. In the fifties the vagrant population was reckoned at 25,000 and sooner or later most of them found their way to London. Mayhew's *Life and Labour in London* (1850) reveals a vast underworld living by its muscles, its wits, or its misfortunes. This was the scene from which Dickens drew his unclassable types, and this was the field into which the Christian Socialist and the City Missioners went down and worked.

Unfortunately, human nature, being what it is, and faced with the threat of armed disturbances that was never absent from 1830 to 1848, was rather likely to find itself preoccupied by repressive measures. As such, certainly, Peel's uniformed Police, instituted 1829, were largely regarded. In 1833 a London jury sitting on the death of three peelers killed in a riot, found it justifiable homicide. They were, however, unarmed and too few, and partly on this account, partly, one hopes, from certain English characteristics, too restrained in their action to bear any semblance to continental gendarmeries—the very name is significant; and it must not be forgotten that before their advent St. James's Park was patrolled by Household Cavalry and that until 1836 Jerry Abershaw the highwayman's cottage still stood near Chelsea Water Works to remind people. Charged with the maintenance of order over an area of five miles' radius from Charing Cross, the Police soon made their presence felt in the removal of many persons of no fixed abode (like Mr. Jobling in *Bleak House*) to 'the market gardens round Deptford'. Though occasionally discomforted by the armed assassin (as in the time of the garrotters) they gradually learned the handling of traffic and tactful dealing with crowds by which they are best known. By the end of our period the Metropolitan force had grown to 8,000 men. Plain-clothes men were introduced by Graham, when Home Secretary to Peel's administration. The detective enters English fiction with Inspector Bucket. And we hear no more of that sinister figure that the cabman mistook for good Mr. Pickwick, when he set out on his travels, and that Noah Claypole, in *Oliver Twist*, is described as becoming—the Informer.

It is a significant fact that, resented as the policemen were, the organization of them synchronizes with a softening of the Penal Code. The last man to stand in the pillory did so at Newgate on June 22, 1830, for perjury. By the Act of 1834 the Central Criminal Court at Old Bailey was set up, hanging in chains abolished, and dissection of murderers' bodies made optional for the judge. (It was abolished in 1861.) For years juries had been bringing in increasingly verdicts adjusted so that the value stolen fell below the limit at which the law imposed the death and other extreme penalties, and the decline in hanging and transportation was rapid. It is not easy now to disentangle how much this movement had owed to Howard, the eighteenth-century prison reformer, and such characters as Elizabeth Fry and J. J. Gurney, who toured the country and threw floods of light upon dark noisome places and practices—how much mere reform was in the air—and how much the cessation of the menace of foreign invasion left the public mind free to consider such matters. The sheer overcrowding of prisons was sufficiently impressive, but it had impressed James the First and Edward the Sixth. At first the reformer was perpetually overtaken by the increase in the criminal class, due, one must believe, to increased police efficiency. Coldbath Fields Prison, which James had instituted because Edward's 'new' prison of the Bridewell was crammed to overflowing, was rebuilt in 1794 according to Howard's ideas of what a model prison should be, at a cost of £65,650. Although a further ward for 130 vagrants was added by 1850, the place was by then in a hopeless state of congestion, and the female prisoners were removed to Westminster. Yet by 1861 the cell accommodation for 550 prisoners was chock-full, and between seven and eight hundred had to be housed how and where possible. One shrinks from the thought of the sanitary conditions and ventilation. It was staffed by 141 persons, consisting of Governor, two chaplains, who must have worked hard, one surgeon, who must have worked harder, three trade instructors, 134 officers. The annual cost per prisoner was £20 19*s*. 4*d*.

It was obviously a progressive institution of the first rank, the prisoners were visited morally and medically, taught something, and kept in order! Yet how irony clings to the whole system, even of enlightened 'preventive' punishment. Here the treadmill (with a journey of 12,000 feet, reduced subsequently to 1,200 feet) had replaced the stocks. Here the Silent System was introduced, as an improvement of course, that which seems a devilish torture in our day being then a bright idea to stop the wholesale manufacture of criminals by the intercourse of comparatively innocent first offenders and young people with the hardened 'lag'. Even proper names were discarded and the prisoner reduced to complete anonymity. And this was obviously an almost incredible improvement on the 'farming', peculation, and corrupt practices for which Newgate was famous. That place, so notorious as to have a sort of diabolic glamour, must have been, well into our period, quite beyond control, like some burst sewer of human depravity and misfortune. Burnt again and again, rebuilt, reformed, the noisome infection that had soaked into the soil continually proved as fatal to the health as to the morals, not only of its victims, but of those who administered, or even visited it. Howard escaped both, and made his serious careful report, eighteenth-century foretaste of the great wave of humanitarianism that was to inspire so much of the nineteenth century. At his visit in 1779 it appears the gaol was 'clean and free from offensive scents', but the condemned cells struck terror into the most hardened cases, and at Sunday service a large black coffin stood before the condemned pew.

The building he saw was burnt by the Gordon rioters in 1780, and rebuilt on the same site, with no accommodation for separate confinement.

In 1817 Elizabeth Fry had already begun her work among prisoners. What were the conditions confronting her in her day may be judged by the fact that from 1831 to 1850 the yearly average of hangings was eighteen, and again and again serious and even fatal injury to sightseers occurred as the result of the unwieldy crowds that gathered to witness these scenes.

Yet by 1836 the Inspectors found the mass of humanity in Newgate drunken and gambling and making prison-breaking instruments. In 1840 they reported: 'It has been our painful duty to point attention again and again to the serious evils resulting from gaol association and the consequent necessary contamination of the Prisoner.'

In 1845 2,581 persons passed through it, of whom 1,960 were convicted. Perhaps Newgate was hopeless. As late as 1864 every window within sight was let to its fullest extent for the witnessing of an execution. Public execution was not abolished until 1868.

But if it was the most spectacular, Newgate was by no means the only prison within the City walls. The ancient Bridewell, though for long it had tended increasingly to be a receptacle for vagrants who were put to hard labour in it and 'contumacious apprentices', contained in 1843

1,324 persons, of whom 233 were under sentence and 466 well-known or reputed thieves. 'Solitary confinement' was prescribed for some, but was impracticable amid such overcrowding. The treadmill was the fate of five-sixths of the shiftless, unmanageable crowd. But public opinion was moving. The Seventh Report of the Inspectors of Prisons thus blasted the entire institution housed in this ancient (and as late as our period still handsome and ornate) building, which had seen the progress of Henry VIII's amours: '. . . it answers no object save that of custody . . . does not correct, alter, nor reform . . . associations counteract any efforts that can be made for moral and religious improvement of the prisoner.'

In 1863 it was pulled down and its prisoners sent to Holloway. The old 'Compters' in Wood Street and Poultry (just north of St. Mildred's church) were moved, and the noisome Clink on Bankside, relic of the jurisdiction of the Bishops of Winchester, between Deadman's Dock and St. Mary Overy, was abolished. In 1842 the Model Pentonville began its career, and in 1845 earned £1,150 by work prisoners were allowed to do, instead of rotting in idleness. Its accommodation of 1,000 cells and female side had cost £90,000. Giltspur Street 'Compter' lingered, and Clerkenwell House of Correction by Whitecross Street was only closed in 1854.

Thus far the criminal, for already some attempt was being made to separate him from the debtor. This is not merely a sign of the advance of intelligence, but is also in conformity with sentiment. The felon had done something, a line must be drawn and order kept, however vague may be the sense of justice on which it acts. We have only to look at the ordinary crowd on any race-course to-day to realize how necessary was the rough-and-ready promiscuous incarceration of a century ago. But the debtor had been, at worst, silly or weak. In the poignant tale of 'The Chancery Prisoner', in the *Pickwick Papers*, he was merely an innocent victim of an archaic corner of the legal system.

There is no trace of the imminent end of the Fleet in Dickens's narrative, but its course was nearly run. Many times destroyed and rebuilt, it had housed those who had fallen under displeasure of the law since the days of Richard II, had contained victims of the Star Chamber, and in 1776, when Howard visited it, was crowded with 475 persons, including the wives and children of the debtors. A quaint system of licence, dating from Richard's day, allowed the prisoners to roam the surrounding streets within certain 'rules' or boundaries, which in 1824 had been enlarged to include St. Bride's and St. Martin's churches, New Bridge Street to the river, Dorset Street, Salisbury Square, part of Fleet Street, Ludgate Hill to the entrance to St. Paul's Churchyard, Old Bailey, and the lanes surrounding. In the same way, the Marshalsea, an anachronism dependent on the Court of the King's Marshal in Scotland Yard, but indistinguishable in our time from other debtors' prisons, had 'rules' embracing a small area east of Borough High Street about Snow Fields, while the Queen's Bench (named from the Court under which it had originally been instituted), a little farther south on the other side of the Borough High Street, had even wider privileges. The Fleet was pulled down in 1843–6, and the Congregational Hall built on its site. The Queen's Bench prison survived our period, but not by much. With them went the practice of farming out a prison to a warden, source of continual oppression, and often of the lowest blackguardism.

Of the great mass of London's population we can only get the vaguest idea, within the limits thus drawn. Landed, titled, professional, and even regularly employed people, we can trace in statistics or fiction. The criminal classes are at least sparsely enumerated. In between all these existed in the then new Greater London alone over a million and a half people only visible to us as a vague crowd. We read of the crowd of women in Kingsgate Street when Mr. Pecksniff fetched Mrs. Gamp, of the teeming population of Little Britain or Bleeding Heart Yard, but once the magic of Dickens has ceased to touch them, they relapse into a grey opaque wall like London fog. Stagg's Gardens (in *Dombey and Son*) were destroyed to make a railway. The inhabitants went farther afield. The brickfields (in *Bleak House*) shifted. The brickmakers and their dependants tramped elsewhere. Although the Combination Acts had been repealed, these dim multitudes bear little resemblance to Organized Labour in the twentieth century.

In 1837 40 per cent. of the men and 65 per cent. of the women were known to be illiterate. Any number of them did odd jobs, ran errands, held horses. They were fed, for instance in the year 1846, by 210,757 cattle, 151,850 sheep, 250,000 pigs that passed through Smithfield during that twelvemonth, amid scenes of revolting cruelty and damage to life and limb. There were other markets of course, but making the widest allowances for them, the poor Londoner of those days did not consume half an animal in a twelvemonth. In the background loomed the workhouse. Indeed one may well ask how it was that no serious revolutionary movement came to a head between 1830 and 1850. And the answer is manifold. The railways gave the new mechanic, even before he began to combine, a status working men had never had. A better example was set by the Court. The rising moneyed class, led by the Quakers, were demanding a new standard of religious and philanthropic endeavour, of which their black coats were the merest external symbol, if that. And the steady march of parliamentary reform made possible legislative advances that were impracticable before 1830, and might have been later, had the country lain in the shadow of European war. Looking back on it, one catches one's breath to see the risk that we ran during a period untouched by general education, stated leisure, and the rising tide of prosperity that changed the complexion of affairs after the half-century.

Public Health.

To all this the cynic may add the strong motive power behind reform, of sheer fright. Politics were disturbed, recurrent financial crises bewildering, but the cholera could neither be ignored nor even studied dispassionately. Something had to be done. The memory of the plague had never been entirely obscured in London. The dignified pages of the *Quarterly Review* bear witness to the state of mind of perhaps the least vulnerable and most influential section of the nation. In the number dated September 1850 are marshalled the Reports and Evidence on Water Supply 1821–40, those on the Health of Towns 1844, 1845, on the Metropolitan Sanitary Commission 1847, the General Board of Health on the supply of Water 1850, Remarks on the same, on the Air and Water of Towns, on the absorptive Power of Soils, but above all, the monumental Report on the Sanitary Condition of the City of London, for the years 1848–9, by John Simon,

F.R.S., Medical Officer of Health for the City, and one of the Surgical Staff of St. Thomas's Hospital. Under the title 'Metropolitan Water Supply—The New Sources' and with the motto 'Tales sunt aquae, quales sunt terrae per quas fluunt' the *Quarterly* discussed the above documents. Its tone is amazing, for its readers were no coterie of cranks. It trounced the water authorities for irresponsible monopoly, for distribution of the primal necessity of life in a state of noisome impurity, at an exorbitant price, and for squandering in a greedy struggle for lucrative territory sums that should have been laid out in piping poorer districts of the town, and for combining in close confederacy against the public. There follows an elaborate exposition of the qualities of water and the dangers of its contamination in the gathering, distribution, and storing of it. All the northern towns were better situated than London as regards natural catchment areas, while the Thames and the Lea were noisome with 'guano, stable dung, rotten sprats, and other top dressings of the market garden, and finally the discharge of all the London sewers'. New catchment areas in 'the Surrey and Hampshire moors' are the practical conclusion.

In the next number inevitably this was followed by a review of the Report on the execution of the Nuisance Removal Act to July 1849, more water reports, one on the Subterranean Condition of Westminster, more of the imposing Medical Officer Simon, Toulmin Smith's Laws of England relating to Public Health, and, most important of all, the Report of the Select Committee on Private Bills. This article was entitled 'Sanitary Consolidation—Centralization—Local Self-Government'. The 'body politic' was envisaged under the figure of a human body and readers' attention was directed to the Conservative Development of Order, as being true progress. Nor was this so academic as it now sounds. The sewers of London pumped into the Thames in the year 1849 7,045,120 cubic feet of sludge on the northern (or left) bank, 2,457,600 cubic feet on the south (or right) bank. The fine waterworks of the northern bank may have had sources such as the New River Head from which to find its part of the total annual supply of 35,000,000 gallons, but one, at least, of the three authorities of the southern side pumped 'puddle' from opposite the outfall of the Ranelagh sewer. Over

Smithfield, first denounced as a nuisance in A.D. 1320, the writer fell into the Homeric vein:

'Like another Troy, this citadel of filth has stood a ten years' siege: and its sturdy garrison, led by their chieftains in Common Council—the Hectors and Memnons of intramural muck—so far from thinking of surrender are engaged at this moment in fortifying their defences. The bolts of the Thunderer, terrible to cabinets, have fallen quenched amid the mud of the Corporation sheep-pens. Vainly as yet have the serpents of Apollo wreathed themselves around the body of Mr. Lowman Taylor; and vainly have they hissed into the ears of Hicks their dreadful denunciations. The modern Cassandra, robed in Broad Street, has clamoured without avail at the gates of St. Bartholomew; and her iron lips, still glowing with the kisses of the God, have filled the seething Market Place with unheeded prophecy of pestilence and death.

'In those dismal vaticinations ourselves have timely joined. . . . The Defenders of Filth, corporate and parochial, have ruled London long enough. . . .'

The fact was, that the whole subsoil of London was sodden with 'seventeen million cubic feet of decaying residuum . . . Belgrave and Eaton Square, as well as the whole splendid neighbourhood of Hyde Park Gardens, stand over sewers abounding in the foulest deposits, in many cases stopping up the house drains and emitting the most disgusting effluvium', and that 'the more ancient sewers of Cavendish, Bryanstone, Manchester, and Portman Squares are in such a state of rottenness and decay that there is no security for their standing from day to day', and that 'even the attempt to evacuate them by flushing might bring some down altogether'. Curiously, the only satisfactory sewers were in Seven Dials. We may wonder if it was because the inhabitants didn't use them much. But worse, at Buckingham Palace, Her Majesty's apartments were ventilated through the common sewer, and were less salubrious than King Alfred's primitive abode, where the horn lantern had to be invented to protect the candles from the wind that blew through the chinks in the walls, but it was clean wind, not sewer draught, a thousand years earlier.

In Hanway Yard, Oxford Street, there were cesspools occupying 8,500 square feet, for 282 houses, on 9 acres of ground, owing to the piecemeal way individual enterprise had planned and constructed the property. The Rookery in St. Giles' contained 95 small houses into which 2,850 people crowded, and was flooded by its own sewage, while an outbreak of fever in the cloisters of Westminster Abbey led to the discovery that there lay beneath a network of old cesspools, barrel drains and brick sewers, crammed with 500 cartloads of stagnant filth. Nor was this merely a sanitary matter, nor was it confined to the reports mustered by the *Quarterly*. In 1836 the Directors of the Bank of England received an anonymous communication stating that the writer had access to their bullion room, and would meet them there when they pleased. They made an appointment, and at the stated time saw a man emerge from the middle of the floor of the place where the bar gold was housed. He had walked up the old sewer from Dowgate. The survival of these medieval rat-runs, some of them 16 feet in diameter (who does not know of a castle or abbey said to have a 'secret passage' to the nearest stream—the old sewer of course), was perpetuated by the extraordinary local government situation.

Greater London, outside the City, was administered by 300 bodies, mainly 'vestries' consisting of 10,448 persons, many self-elected, or elected for life, under 250 Acts, at fantastic cost, particularly in tavern bills and dinners; one sewage division alone, in twenty years, had spent £7,935 on the entertainment of its Commissioners. Small wonder that the streets were ill paved (St. Pancras parish had 16 paving boards, acting under 29 Acts of Parliament), that houses were burnt down before the appropriate authority could be discovered to quench the conflagration, and that, during the cholera, a number of poor wretches were found dead without medical aid. Added to all this was 'that black gruel-like compound, known as London mud', composed of soot, dust, and street sweepings. Many main thoroughfares, especially near markets, were ankle-deep in horse-dung. The pollution of the air can be judged from the fact that in 1849 a large tulip-grower had to remove from Walworth, as it ruined his bulbs. The Londoner of 1830 to 1850 was never really well. He was driven forward by native energy, a flood of strong drink, and insensitiveness, but when pestilence gained on him, he had to think.

The statuesque periods of the *Quarterly* are in the style of Burke—almost of that of Henry V: 'Once more unto the breach . . .' The signal mark of the period is that, for the first time, such sentences were directed, not against political revolution, or to the brightening of martial ardour, but to the maintenance of the decencies of everyday life. The solid statistics and stomach-turning descriptions account for the continual recurrence of hoarse voices, bleary eyes, and the various mannerisms found in the fiction of the time. To meet the chronic ill-health and constant casualties of the day Charing Cross Hospital 'relieved 7,000 persons and received 1,100 in-patients in 1849', while St. George's Hospital at Hyde Park Corner coped with 'Sick and Lame'. Infant orphans were received by yearly election at the newly formed Asylum at Wanstead to the number of 400, below the age of seven and a half years. St. Katherine's Hospital, moved from the neighbourhood of the Tower to Regent's Park, is described as 'residential'. Jews had their own Lazaretto in Mile End Road. King's College Hospital relieved 20,000 persons, and 363 confinements took place there in 1849. The Middlesex Hospital increased its accommodation to 250 beds in 1845. In Drury Lane since 1839 was a foundation for general treatment. In 1845 St. Thomas's had 3,552 In-patients and 46,733 Out. Bart's figures were 5,419 In, and 17,808 Out, 22,088 casualties for the same year.

These figures are open to correction and addition. They are deliberately taken from contemporary records, to show what medical mobilization had impressed itself on current consciousness at the time of cholera scares, frequent typhus cases, and perpetual reference to 'febrile influenza'. Everything, for instance, concerning Guy's is quoted, except its number of cases. When we reflect on the usually unjustified dread of hospitals, and the material difficulties in obtaining conveyance to them, both factors tending to reduce the number of patients, these figures can only indicate the desperate, the helpless, and the willing cases. What must have been the total incidence of illness and accident in the population?

The battle in which the *Quarterly* took so dignified a part was won. Already the Building Act of 1844 and the Sewers Act of 1848 had set things in motion. In 1855 the Metropolitan Board of Works was instituted. From that day, until it was superseded by the London County Council in 1888, it spent six and a half millions on main drains, maintained 2,603 acres of Parks, controlled half a million buildings. Its major effort, the embankment of the Thames, does not come within our period, but its street improvements, without which London is now unimaginable, such as Queen Victoria Street and Shaftesbury Avenue, are evidence of its energies. And London was saved from strangulation above ground and below.

§ 4. THE DECLINE OF THE PROVINCIAL TOWNS: NORWICH

While the growth of industry in the north threatened the ascendency of London, the development of finance confirmed it, and the improvement of communications made London more metropolitan than it had ever been before. Gradually the variety of county and provincial life was levelled by London fashions. It is seldom realized now how brief was the period of really fast efficient coaching. It certainly followed, rather than preceded, the earlier railway development. Crabb Robinson remarked on the marvellous speed at which he was carried by coach to Manchester in 1835, an average of twelve miles an hour. On August 23, 1836, the Exeter Mail Coach, which had been used to taking twenty hours, was speeded up to sixteen and a half. This was a remarkable effort, bearing comparison with Palmer's fast coaches on the favourite London–Bath road that took as long, but many overseas mails went via Exeter to Falmouth.

These coaches were painted red, weighed a ton, and carried but four inside and four out. Most Exeter passengers had to be content with the more usual thirty-hour journey, by vehicles carrying six inside and fourteen out.

But now the main lines of rail began to stretch out from the London termini. In 1838 the Great Western reached Maidenhead, and the London to Birmingham line was opened. In 1840 Southampton was a terminus. In the following year the Great Western broad-gauge line was pushed on to Bristol, and the Brighton railway opened. In 1844 the line to Dover was completed, and in 1848 the London and North-Eastern Counties Company ran from 'Shoreditch' to Ipswich, Colchester, Cambridge, and Norwich. The Birmingham line was perhaps the most important, as it gave access to the Birmingham and Liverpool (opened 1837), and thus to the Manchester and Liverpool (opened 1829). The Stockton and Darlington had preceded the latter by five years. By 1866, in spite of the misdeeds of Hudson, the capital embarked in railway undertakings equalled three-quarters of the National Debt, and the population of England indulged, on the average, in eleven rail journeys per head per annum.

Other means of communication accompanied the railway development. The old London Penny Post, instituted in 1685, had been raised to twopence in 1794, and coaches had been utilized for the carriage of such letters as went beyond the City a little earlier. In 1840 Rowland Hill's scheme for Penny Post, prepaid by adhesive stamps, was introduced. The electric telegraph had been working since 1838; it became available for the general public in the fifties, but in very piecemeal fashion.

Science, in the proud phrase of the day, had annihilated time and space, and progress had to be paid for. Local seats of culture no longer set the tone to their neighbourhood but only transmitted it. At the beginning of the century, for example, Norwich had an intellectual character as strongly marked as Edinburgh. At the beginning of our period it still had hopes of a Royal Charter incorporating its school of painters. But it was in the wrong place on the new map—too near London and too far from coal. Its decline illustrates the process which was remoulding the old social structure everywhere.

At the time our period opens, Norwich, a byword for corruption, was about to become a reformed municipality, but already the ancient antagonism between it and its more immediate, indeed overlapping, administrations was dying away. For centuries the citizens had been prone to attack the Cathedral Close in any quarrel in which their rival jurisdictions had clashed. But by our period, although the civil government of the precincts is still described as 'entirely distinct from that of the City or the County of Norfolk, the Dean and Chapter being in Commission of the Peace', that body had begun to send their prisoners to the county jail, and their workhouse had been demolished. Though the gates of the Close were (and are still) shut at 9.45 p.m. each night, distinctions began to disappear. On the other hand, the Norwich Close, lying aside from the main stream of traffic, never became a thoroughfare like that of Exeter, or of York. Like Salisbury it tended rather to withdraw itself within the beauty and dignity of its buildings and the select nature of its social standards, preserved by the common outlook and education of its inhabitants. In fact, at the end of our period, the Grammar School within the precinct was less a school for the sons of citizens than it was at the beginning, turning more and more towards the growing prestige of the public schools and ancient Universities.

In our period the Castle had ceased legally, as it had long ceased in fact, to be a royal stronghold. The garrison was now housed in what were known as the Cavalry Barracks, outside the north-eastern gate of the city, and divided from the centre of the town by the river and the Close.

The attitude of the military authority to the civil was rendered more intimate by the frequent calls the latter was obliged to make on the former for aid, in its police-less days (the Norwich Police Force was instituted in 1836, the constables being eighteen in number) and even later, during the 'hungry forties', and the nascent attempts at industrial organization. Norwich was the last place of its size to possess anything that could be described as a factory, its considerable weaving and other trades being conducted in dwellings or small workshops attached, and the change was bitterly resented. Its electioneering habits also demanded military control at times, and there lay below all this the immemorial tradition of defiance of authority which had made Norwich the centre of so much heresy and rebellion. Taken together, there are plenty of reasons for the banquets to officers of the garrison and presents to the rank and file that were given between 1830 and 1850. The change, however, was very gradual, and until 1914 the private soldier was always likely to rescue any of his comrades apprehended by the police, and at times this necessitated the addition of a picket to the civil arm.

Another change observable already in progress in 1830 was the abandonment of their town houses by the county nobility. As late as the end of the eighteenth century, Astleys, Wyndhams, and others kept residences in the city, though the palace of the ducal family of Norfolk was already forsaken. This coincides with a similar influence arising from an entirely different cause, the outward movement of successful merchant or property owner, to residences without the walls. Yet both were so slow that, at the end of our period, there was no district of offices and warehouses, empty at night, such as grew up in London, or naturally

COWGATE, NORWICH, *c.* 1830—*HENRY NINHAM*

existed in newer towns. As the Custances and the Harveys, the Gurneys and the Springfields moved from the fine old houses of which the ground floor front, and seldom more, had been adapted to the needs of their business, their places were taken by their clerks or managers. Those who had not reached the stage of success or age which invited removal still lived along the main streets, as did perforce retailers, however dignified, and the professions of Law and Medicine, Clerks in Holy Orders and Ministers of the numerous and powerful dissenting 'Meetings'. These may have looked down on the inhabitants of the 750 courts and yards (largely built on the gardens and stabling of the older great houses or inns, or great houses that had become inns) but they had not to look very far. There was nothing like the segregation of the classes that had already taken place in London. Tiny imitations of 'industrial' and 'residential' districts had sprung up, the former across the river, at the foot of Mousehold, called Spitalfields, and outside the wall at Peafields, in the south; the latter in Catton, Thorpe, and hamlets to the south. But the bulk of the working population lived within the walls, of which long stretches remained (and remain) though the gates had been removed in 1781. For the ample curves of the river, which passes through and around the city in a great S, permitted water to be used as sufficient defence over nearly a third of the total circumvallation of nearly four miles. Space within the enclosure was ample, the peculiar habits of the place preserved these.

Even to-day, when Norwich is surveyed from the heights of Mousehold, tree-tops and grass plots appear to cover as much space as roofs and chimneys. The name City of Gardens was not given it in sarcasm. When our period opens the city was still larger than Newcastle or any town south of itself except London and Bristol and Plymouth. But it had the appearance of a prosperous village, in spite of patches of desperate overcrowding, owing to its receiving the vagrants of three counties at a time of wholesale displacement of the population; by this means, in spite of the tremendous upheaval caused by the introduction of steam-power in the north, the population continued to increase.

It had, however, to adapt itself, and to pay the price. A hundred miles from any coal-field, it could not, in the long run, continue as a textile town.

About 1830 Norwich was, in fact, staggering under a blow as serious as any it had suffered since the Black Death cut off a third of its population in 1348. Only this time it was not the population, but their means of livelihood that disappeared. The closing of foreign markets to its heavy woollen cloths by the war, and the introduction of machine-spun yarns from Yorkshire had been bad enough. But following these, the East India Company ceased to export the Norwich Camlet cloth. Disastrous unemployment, semi-employment, and rioting followed.

Jacquard looms were introduced in 1833, and the leading masters (the almost total lack of factories made these consist of a class of capitalist merchants who gave out materials and took in finished, or partly finished products) strained every nerve to invent new materials. For centuries there had been a good deal of making of mixed fabrics. In 1841 Crapes, Challis, plain and figured Poplins, Mousseline-de-laine (all wool), Cotton-de-laine (mixed wool and cotton), a new fabric called Paramatta cloth, which began to supersede Bombazine, Gros-de-Naples, and Bandana handkerchiefs, an imitation of a French article 'Palestine' (cotton and worsted figured), and 'Lunetta' were made. The celebrated Norwich shawl was perhaps the best known, and enabled a man and wife to earn as much as fifteen pounds a week. This was undercut by Scottish competition. In 1839 the condition of the weaving industry was the subject of a report to the Royal Commission, which showed that of 5,000 looms, mainly single ones established in the dwellings of the work-people, only four-fifths were employed. Two large factories were built to try to supply yarn locally. But it was impossible to compete with the great industrial centres. By the end of our period the looms were reduced to 1,000. Norwich was no longer a textile centre in any noteworthy sense. A few looms survive as curiosities, and in many an old street, the thorough-light windows can be seen running along the second story of the old houses. Certain individual silk businesses survived, as did the dressing of cloth of various sorts (including Suffolk hempen cloth), but Norwich became the centre of the Colman mustard and milling business, of the boot and shoe trade (then still an affair of small masters jobbing weekly, with a few hands, in old converted dwelling-houses, for the large assembling and marketing firms), and of a vast number of packing trades, attracted by low rates for wages and land, and dexterous manual labour of the descendants of generations of weavers, in whose veins ran a large admixture of French and Flemish blood.

It would appear superficially that prosperity was unabated, much of the precariousness of the old individual domestic trades eliminated, far better conditions gradually being obtained by a larger, better-fed and circumstanced population. But the industrial changes had another side. London was brought within a few hours' journey, and Norwich, while not able to assume the independence of the great northern towns with their new specialized key industries, had lost her old position, being less self-supporting, and deprived of the tribute of the old village yarn spinning.

It is not certain that this caused the decline in her social and cultural pre-eminence which began about 1830.

It is quite possible that the death of Crome the painter, and the dispersal of the circles of Gurneys and Martineaus, Opies and others who had gathered round the Close and the Quaker and Presbyterian meetings, would anyhow have produced this result. But these facts do not account for the neglect of the Assembly Rooms, the cessation of sporting and social events, and the decline of the stock company at the theatre. The fate of this last may indicate what was happening. For a hundred years a resident company had occupied the House in Theatre Street and conducted the circuit embracing Lynn, Cambridge, Colchester, Ipswich, and Yarmouth.

As 'the King's Servants from the Theatre Royal, Norwich', under patent, like Drury Lane and Covent Garden, they were permitted to play dramatic pieces without disguising these as concerts, as was necessary elsewhere for all such until 1843. Norwich had sufficient reputation to attract Mrs. Siddons and Macready. But Elizabeth Brunton, the Fishers, and bearers of other names that may be found in many a list, beside famous ones covering the whole period from Edmund Kean to Irving, were natives of the town or district, as was Ball, who wrote the libretto of *Maritana*. However, by 1852 the stock companies were disbanded, and from thence onward touring companies from London were increasingly inclined to list Norwich after the larger-paying houses of greater towns.

The Theatre Royal ('chaste in appearance' as a contemporary described it) was doing well when it held £200 a night. How typical the place had been of a phase of life of those days is shown by the fact that Dickens drew Vincent Crummles from Davenport, lessee from 1844 to 1846. The Annals of the Triennial Musical Festival tell the same tale. Local talent ceased to be brilliant enough, though Dr. Buck's reputation was national, and principals and orchestra were brought increasingly from London, while at the same time local gentry were more and more inclined to go there for entertainment.

§ 5. THE GREAT EXHIBITION

This unification of England was symbolized and cemented by the Great Exhibition of 1851, the one event which in an age of progress, independent, spasmodic, and often blind, stands out as clearly willed and ably directed. To understand the early Victorian Age it is necessary to enter into the emotions of 1851. Something unusual is required to make English people shake hands with strangers and weep in public places. What was it?

In part, no doubt, the pure magnificence of the spectacle which the Crystal Palace presented: even in its diminished state to-day few buildings give the visitor the same impression of magnitude, and we must imagine it blazing with colour in the unbroken summer light. Nothing struck contemporary fancy more than the sight of the elm trees which had been spared and rose high up toward the galleries. In part also it expressed the final disappearance of that cloud of alarm and rancour which had hung over the relations of the classes for a whole generation. The great event brought to London thousands who perhaps had never seen a train before, people speaking the strange tongues of Lancashire and Durham, and the official reports of their behaviour as they flocked through museums and gardens are full of unconcealed pride. Not a flower was picked, not a picture smashed. And ten years before, the Londoners who now welcomed them had stood silent in the streets to watch the guns going north to Lancashire.

For those who knew how the Great Exhibition had come about, it was a spectacle of deeper interest, an achievement of executive efficiency unmatched in history. It owed, in

OPENING OF THE GREAT EXHIBITION, 1851

fact, its execution, if not its inception, to the foreign, especially to the German, education of Albert, Prince Consort. The idea was no novelty in France, where four such exhibitions had been held during Napoleon's tenure of power, and five under the restored Bourbons. In England, Manchester and Birmingham had organized local exhibitions, and the Great Free Trade Bazaar at Covent Garden Theatre, in 1845, had been run on the same lines. The Society of Arts had always favoured the idea. It was at a meeting of this Society held at Buckingham Palace on June 30, 1849, that Albert produced the plan which he had drawn up the previous day. His main proposals were the setting up of a Royal Commission, of which he would be president, and the use of the Society of Arts to form the nucleus of a Committee, and to organize the accumulation of funds; these projects were to be submitted to the Government privately.

From the Minutes of the Society's next meeting at Osborne on July 14, it is evident that Albert himself had done this, and had received little encouragement from Sir Robert Peel. But he had induced the President of the Board of Trade, Labouchere, to be present at the meeting, and this official required the proposals to be fully set out in writing. Prince Albert had already suggested the site and date, but, perhaps because Labouchere was so non-committal, we next find him, on July 31, writing to the Home Secretary, Sir George Grey, speaking of a Quinquennial Exhibition of the Industry of all Nations. He received a formal acknowledgement, which he read at the Society's next meeting at Balmoral, in August. Parliament was in recess. The Prince, however, was able to induce the Lord Mayor of London to give a banquet at the Mansion House on the 17th of October, to further the matter. This focused influential support, but even more progress was made by visits which members of the Society paid to sixty-five places in the manufacturing districts, which resulted in some 5,000 persons enrolling themselves as promoters. The general scheme had now crystallized into an exhibition of four classes, (1) raw materials, (2) machinery and mechanical inventions, (3) manufactures, (4) sculpture and plastic art.

At last on January 3, 1850, the Royal Commission was duly appointed. The list of names is interesting, if only because it shows which have impressed themselves on the public memory. Peel, Cobden, and Russell were already famous,

Gladstone destined perhaps to be even more so; Westmacott, Gibson, Barry, and Eastlake represented art; Lord Rosse and Sir Charles Lyell, science; Philip Pusey, the country gentleman, agriculture; and S. Jones Loyd, one of the three who drafted the Bank Act of 1844, and was to become Lord Overstone, finance and the City. Robert Stephenson was apparently the Contractors' nominee.

The prospectus was now issued in detail. In the first three divisions (raw materials, machinery and inventions, manufactures) it was enacted that no perishable articles, no wines, spirits, or fermented liquors, unless derived from unusual sources, and no oils or spirits unless in well-secured vessels would be received, and no highly inflammable or explosive articles, or live stock, unless specially excepted. In the fourth class (Fine Arts) only the work of artists living, or those less than three years dead, might be exhibited, no oil or water-colours, or portraits, and not more than three works from one hand. Exhibitors had to deliver their exhibits at their own expense but were charged no rent. The 1st of May 1851 was fixed for the opening, and apparently delivery was permissible up to the last moment, for J. M. Ellis, who compiled the catalogue, was quite unable to complete the portion dealing with foreign exhibits, and had to rectify it later. Although only the barest suggestions as to the extent of the site to be utilized existed, some 16 acres along the southern limit of Hyde Park opposite Kensington Gore, were enclosed; liberal allotment was made to foreign countries, amounting to 213,000 square feet in all, more than half the total area of the proposed building, and more than the whole extent of the French exhibitions of 1844 and 1849. Some of the allotments, notably that for France, were subsequently increased. British Colonies were allowed 51,000 square feet. When the 330 local Committees at work in the United Kingdom reported their demands for space, these exceeded, on the floor alone, 417,000 square feet, or 210,000 square feet more than available, and vertical wall space of 200,000 square feet was also requisitioned. There were 8,200 intending British exhibitors. Drastic revision was necessary and this side of the necessary organization was by no means complete by the end of 1850.

Meanwhile a Building Committee had been set up (January 1850) consisting of the Duke of Buccleuch, Earl of Ellesmere, Messrs. Barry, R.A., and Cockerell, R.A., Mr. Cubitt (President C.E.), Messrs. Brunel and Donaldson. The site was approved and the 16 acres temporarily covered in. Plans were invited and 245 were received, 38 being from abroad and 60 from the provinces; 7 were anonymous. This took until June, when the Committee announced that none of these were 'accordant with the peculiar objects in view', and submitted a plan of their own, involving a structure principally of brick with a dome 200 feet in diameter. The lowest tender submitted for this was £120,000. This seemed to mobilize the considerable, if latent feeling of opposition, that, if not vocal, was solid and went far beyond the usual parliamentary desire for procrastination. The choice of the site came now before both Houses, and was confirmed, after acrimonious debate, by sufficient majorities, on July 4. It consisted of a rectangular strip of Hyde Park between Queen's Drive and Rotten Row, 2,300 feet east to west, 500 feet deep, contained over 26 acres and sloped down, 1 in 250, eastwards.

On the 6th there appeared in the *Illustrated London News* an original design by Mr. Joseph Paxton, who in 1837 had constructed the great conservatory at Chatsworth. This ingenious essay in publicity, or perhaps the weight and venom of opposition encountered, hastened decision to an extraordinary degree. The next thing we hear is that by July 26 a tender was accepted from Messrs. Fox Henderson & Company for £79,800. When the actual deed (with a covenant to remove the building before June 1, 1852) was signed in November, the first iron column was already in position (fixed on September 26). With certain modifications, Paxton's plan was adopted. There was no time to lose. The number of men employed was 30 up to September 6, 419 to October 4, 1,476 on November 1, 2,260 on December 6, 2,112 on January 3, 1851. They handled 2,300 cast-iron girders resting on 3,300 columns, 358 wrought-iron trusses carried the galleries and roof; 30 miles of gutters conveyed the rain water to the columns from 900,000 square feet of glass held in position by 202 miles of wooden sash bars. The floor was of 1½-inch boards laid ½ inch apart, so that the dust might be swept between them, lying upon 13-inch by 3½-inch sleepers every 8 feet. Special drains conveyed the rain water as it descended the columns to the main sewer in Kensington

High Street. The major portion of the roof was shaded by a series of canvas blinds. The most ingenious devices were employed in the raising of the 72-feet trusses of the roof, for no steam derricks were available. Glaziers worked in little covered carriages that travelled along the gutters, enabling 80 men to place 62,600 square feet of glass in position in a week. Five hundred painters followed them. The total capacity of the building was 33,000,000 cubic feet, the area of the floor being 772,784 square feet and the galleries 217,100. The structure included 4,000 tons of iron, 400 of glass, and 600,000 cubic feet of wood. It is not wonderful, therefore, that elaborate calculations were made as to the pressure of the wind on its surfaces, while the marching, running, and jumping of troops, and the dragging of quantities of heavy round shot over the floors tested their solidity. 'Considering the difficulties of construction, the necessary perils to which the workmen were exposed, and their habitual imprudence, arising partly from real indifference to danger, partly from bravado, it has been a source of congratulation that in the performance of this contract, but very few accidents have occurred, and those, with two or three exceptions, of a slight nature,' said Mr. Wyatt in concluding his description.

As the day of opening approached, a good many gloomy forebodings and ill-natured predictions found vent. The Committees working under the Commission seem, however, to have done their best undismayed. The printing and issue of the immense, though necessarily incomplete catalogue was entrusted to Spicer Brothers and Clowes and Son, who tendered £3,200 for the privilege. They were allowed to fix the price of the larger (or full) edition and to publish a small one at 1*s.* Messrs. Schweppe paid £5,500 for the refreshment contract, to be carried out at certain specified counters. The bill of fare embraced patties, sandwiches, jellies, ices, &c., tea, coffee, ginger beer, and spruce beer.

£5,043 19*s.* 4*d.* was paid for the services of extra police outside the building, while within it, supervision was left to the discretion of the Commissioner of Metropolitan Police, and the Head of the Metropolitan Fire Brigade. The railways advertised extensive reductions in fares and freights, mainly to about half, but Clubs were accorded special rates. A register of lodgings suitable for artisans coming up from the provinces or farther was opened. Admission was by season

SCENE—EXHIBITION REFRESHMENT ROOM.

Visitor. "Pint o' Beer, Miss, Please."
Miss. "Don't keep it. You can have a Strawberry Ice and a Wafer."

ticket, three guineas for gentlemen, two for ladies, which carried the privilege of exclusive entry on the opening day. On the second day and third, ordinary admission was £1; on the fourth, 5*s.*; on and after the twenty-second, 1*s.* on Mondays, Tuesdays, Wednesdays, and Thursdays; 2*s.* 6*d.* on Fridays; 5*s.* on Saturdays. No change was given at the door. The personnel, servants of Foreign Correspondents and Exhibitors, the Press and Members of the Juries who allotted prizes, were provided with passes.

On the whole, these arrangements appear to have been judicious. The Treasury had washed its hands of all liability. When the final contract was signed, only £35,000 of the promised subscriptions had been paid. It is true that the Commissioners had a guarantee fund, largely subscribed among themselves, of £230,000, of which one individual had put down his name for £50,000. Still the fact remains that on April 22, when inescapably committed to the project the Commissioners were actually working on an overdraft at the Bank of England. The statement of income and expenditure on that date was as follows:

Receipts.	£	*Expenditure and Liabilities.*	£
Subscriptions paid . . .	64,344	Building	79,800
For Catalogue Rights . .	3,200	Extra galleries and fittings, estimate	35,000
,, Refreshment ,, . .	5,500	Prize Fund	20,000
,, Season tickets . .	40,000	Management, including Printing and incidental expenses	20,943
	113,044		155,743

Even the Prize Fund, the least binding, we might think, of all their undertakings, had involved a complicated system of Juries to make the awards, while the choice, design, and especially the Latin inscriptions of the bronze medals that, in three classes, were granted independently of money prizes, had demanded the care of two Committees including W. E. Gladstone and the Head Master of Westminster School, Lord Lyttelton, Macaulay, and the Dean of St. Paul's.

The four original Departments of Exhibits had become subdivided into thirty classes, the list of the Juries occupied four pages of the Catalogue. But the actual Management had demanded eleven Committees embracing 150 distinguished persons, while the Foreign Exhibitors' Committee fill six pages of the Catalogue. It would be most appropriate had we a record of Palmerston summing up the responsibilities of the Commissioners, with a jocular 'Well, they're in for it, by God!' But we haven't. These responsibilities were great. Parliament had been obstructionist. The number of mechanical exhibits was diminished by the lack of protection afforded inventions. Foreign exhibits were late. Behind much gloomy prognostication lay that attitude, not so much of ill will as of ill ease, which characterized the British Public when faced by anything Albert initiated.

However, the day of opening came. Carriage parties camped out and took their breakfasts in Berkeley Square. The attendants mustered in their places between 8 and 9 a.m. The season-ticket holders made their way into the building between 9 and 11 a.m. and were marshalled behind barriers. The Commissioners took post in the south transept at 11.30.

Shortly after, a discharge of artillery was heard muffled by the walls of the building. The Royal Party was approaching across the Park.

The building which they saw before them on that May morning was a gigantic glass house, 1,848 feet in length from east to west, and 408 feet in width from north to south. The ground floor was 24 feet high. Next, a first story of 20 feet ran the whole length, but was not so wide, as it contained only the nave and main aisles, 264 feet broad, of the ground floor. (Thus it embraced the galleries, but 72 feet of ground on each outer side remained a one-story portion.) Above this first story rose a second floor of a further 20 feet—the roof of the lengthwise nave, in fact. The most striking feature, and best remembered, at right angles across this from south to north, ran a transept 120 feet wide, at the same height. This was roofed by a semicircular vault that stretched a further 36 feet, making 100 feet to the topmost pane of glass. To emphasize the effect of distance, the frame-work was painted light blue, picked out with orange and bands of scarlet, on the choice of which colours Mr. Jones, the contractors' manager, lectured at length when opportunity offered. The parapets of the successive stories were adorned with flags. A gleam of sun broke through about noon, as the Royal Party entered the building, and reflected from all that glass, must have made a dazzling scene.

HER MAJESTY'S BOUDOIR, GREAT EXHIBITION, 1851

A robing-room had been provided, and when ready, the Queen ascended the throne which had been erected for her at the northern end of the transept, and her attendants to the number of about fifty grouped themselves about her, under the great elm tree. The enthusiasm of the 25,000 spectators knew no bounds. Albert now left her side, ranged himself with the Commissioners, and on their behalf reported formally to her the main lines, the gradual achievement and the actual state of the Exhibition, and handed her the Catalogue.

The Queen replied. The Archbishop of Canterbury offered up a prayer. Then the united choirs of the Chapel Royal, St. Paul's Cathedral, Westminster Abbey, and St. George's Chapel, Windsor, burst into the Hallelujah Chorus, assisted by the pupils of the Royal Academy of Music, the Band of the Sacred Harmonic Society, and many well-known public singers, foreign and English. Mr. Charles Tomlinson, who edited the *Cyclopaedia of Useful Arts* which was founded on the Exhibition, describes the result thus:

> 'The sublime effect of this sacred chorus was in some respects peculiar. The vast size of the building afforded such ample space for the floods of sound thus poured out, that their intensity was lost before they had reached the extreme ends. Here the effect is described as being similar to that of a musical snuff-box. On approaching the Transept the beautiful sound became magnified, but in the Transept itself, that loud and overpowering effect produced by a full band and chorus in an ordinary building, was completely absent. Everything was subdued and softened by the enclosed space, of the vastness of which the mind was thus accurately informed through the medium of the ear, as it had before been by that of the eye.'

A procession was then formed behind the herald, headed by the architect, contractors, finance Committee and Treasurers and Executive, who were followed by the Foreign, and then the British Commissioners; then came the Duke of Wellington, as Commander-in-Chief, Ambassadors, Ministers, Clerics, Officials of the Royal Household and State servants. Then Albert leading the Princess Royal, and Victoria leading the little Prince of Wales. The relatives of both followed, and the cortège closed with more of those royal attendants whose quaint archaic offices have survived so many centuries. The procession moved westwards along the north of the nave, turned between the Great Mirror and the model of Liverpool

Docks, as the gallery organ opened its mighty voice of greeting. Passing back by the south side of the nave, the procession 'glided into the (eastern or)Foreign portion'. Here the French organ welcomed it, and was followed by the Erfurt organ as the procession rounded the eastern end and passed along the north side of this portion of the nave, cheered by the foreigners. The Queen thus returned to her place in the transept, when the Marquis of Breadalbane announced that she declared the Exhibition open. A flourish of trumpets followed, the choirs broke into the National Anthem; the Royal Family attended by the Court withdrew; the barriers were removed and the visitors poured over every part of the building.

Mr. Tomlinson continues:

'The state of the Metropolis throughout the whole period of the Great Exhibition will be remembered with wonder and admiration by all. . . . Instead of confusion, disorder, and demoralization, if not actual revolution, which were foretold by some gloomy minds, instead of famine and pestilence confidently predicted by others, London exhibited a wonderful degree of order, good-humoured accommodation of her crowds, and power to provide for their wants. . . . Enormous excursion trains daily poured their thousands. . . . Throughout the season there was more of unrestrained and genuine friendship, and less of formality and ceremonial than has ever been known. It was like . . . a gigantic picnic . . . large numbers of work-people received holidays for the purpose . . . 800 agricultural labourers in their peasant's attire from Surrey and Sussex, conducted by their clergy, at a cost of two and twopence each person—numerous firms in the North sent their people, who must have been gratified by the sight of their own handiwork—an agricultural implement-maker in Suffolk sent his people in two hired vessels, provided with sleeping berths, cooking apparatus, and every comfort, . . . which were drawn up to a wharf in Westminster, and furnished houses to the excursionists—a foreman was there to enforce the rules.'

To sum up, the 19,000 numbered exhibits of the 17,000 exhibitors were seen by 6,009,948 visitors between May 1 and October 11. The mean daily average attendance was 43,311. They consumed nearly 2 million buns and over a million bottles of mineral waters. Forty-four thousand school children were taken there, 2,700 on September 18 alone; 900 persons were officially employed there, of whom 200 were sappers and 400 police, plus 264 attendants at refreshment rooms and 1,000 at the exhibits. The temperature gave some

The Original Statue of the Greek Slave, by Hiram Power. 1859

MR. PHILLIPS respectfully announces that he has received instructions from the Proprietor of this exquisite Statue (for whom it was expressly executed), to **SELL** by **AUCTION**, at his Gallery, 73, New Bond-street, on Thursday, the 14th of July, at 2 o'clock, this lovely **FIGURE**, representing an historical fact—the exposure of a young and beautiful Greek girl for sale in a Turkish bazaar. The expression is intended to be that of extreme dejection, mingled with shame and disgust. The chaste and beautiful pose of this figure has won the admiration of the first artists of the day, and lecturers on anatomy have added their testimony to its marvellous correctness and beautiful representation of feminine beauty. It was exhibited at the Great Exhibition of 1851, where it gained such universal admiration that it would be superfluous to enlarge upon its merits. The statue is now at the Kensington Museum, where it may be viewed, but it will be removed to Mr. Phillips's rooms for inspection six days prior to the sale. It has been engraved on steel by the late celebrated Mr. Thompson.

trouble in July, when the glass ends of the building were removed. It did not afterwards exceed 73·4°, which was surely enough! The ceremonial closing took place on October 18, when Lord Canning reported the awards to Prince Albert. These consisted in 2,918 prize medals, 170 council medals, while the grand total of awards including 'Honourable Mention' was 5,084 (3,045 foreign, 2,039 British). The Bishop of London offered up a prayer, and the Hallelujah Chorus closed the proceedings.

A revised statement of Receipts and Expenses to September 11, is as follows:

Receipts.	£	*Expenditure.*	£
Subscriptions	67,157	Building	124,452
Right to print Catalogue. .	3,200	Prize Fund	20,000
,, sell refreshments .	5,500	Management, including Printing and incidental expenses (37,000 letters were dealt with), and part payment to Police and award to Messrs. Munday	55,943
Season tickets	67,597		
Admission of the public .	274,521		
	417,975		200,395

There were certainly further expenses, for the subsequent criticism of the use to which the Commissioners put their surplus—and it was severe—never estimated it higher than £170,000 at this time. They purchased Gore House (for which no one had found any satisfactory use since Lady Blessington and D'Orsay left it) with 21½ acres of land for £65,000, and a further 48 acres for which Parliament voted them £150,000.

In 1856 the building of South Kensington Museum was begun here, and the result was long known as 'Brompton Boilers' until the less edifying portion of the structure was removed to Bethnal Green, to afford similar facilities. The new building was opened on June 20, 1857, without formality, and it was ascertained in 1860 that £167,805 had been spent. The final use of the Fund goes far beyond our period.

The Crystal Palace itself was removed from Hyde Park on August 5, 1852, and re-erected where it now stands by a Company with a capital of £500,000.

In 1853 the Lord Mayor of London opened a Mansion

House Fund to commemorate the edifice, the occasion, and Albert's part as a prime mover in it. Five thousand pounds was collected with the object of erecting a statue in Hyde Park, but the project languished unaccountably. Albert himself desired that the money should be utilized for professorships. At length in 1860 the choice of the selection committee fell upon the design of a Mr. Durham, which was not unlike the subsequent Albert Memorial in plan, the central figure being a Britannia holding a shield on which Albert's face was delineated. By the time it was ready the Prince was dead, and a site for the erection in Hyde Park having been refused, the memorial was erected in the grounds of the Royal Horticultural Society, by the Prince of Wales and his three months' bride, Alexandra, in 1863, a figure of his father having been substituted for that of Britannia, at the Prince's expense. The fund for the Albert Memorial we know was opened in 1862, and £60,000 was subscribed by the public. Parliament voted £50,000 to complete it in 1866, but the execution was delayed a further ten years. It stands symbolically at the point where the axis of the Albert Hall cuts the axis of the Exhibition.

These details, trifling in themselves, serve to expose the change of temper that supervened upon the triumphant effort, the genuine enthusiasm, and the high hopes of 1851.

It summed up an age of pacifism, industry, and useful knowledge. By an extraordinary irony it opened an age of scientific warfare and aestheticism. Our next industrial triumph was Armstrong's guns: our next pageant the departure of the Fleet for the Baltic: in a few years we are in the thick of pre-Raphaelite controversy, Ruskin's economics, Darwin's assault on the Victorian creed, Matthew Arnold's exposures of its culture. The statue of the Prince holding the Catalogue of the Great Exhibition was the memorial of an age which had passed into oblivion and almost into contempt. By 1865 we are far away from the naïve faith in progress, production, and machinery of which 1851 was the festival. The Exhibition of 1862 was a great show. The Exhibition of 1851 had been a great event. It had swept away the atmosphere of suspicion and distrust which had so long hung over the generation bred in the great war and the early years of industrial servitude. It inaugurated a new relationship between the Court, the manufacturing and moneyed classes and, most important, the new mechanic class. It symbolized the solid gains of early Victorian enterprise, cheap production, and easy communication, and a visitor looking back over the alarms of 1848, the misery of the early forties, the sack of Bristol in 1831, the fearful disasters of 1825, might well see in it also the realization of hopes which a few years before would have seemed too visionary for sober men to contemplate.

IV

LIFE IN THE NEW TOWNS

IV

LIFE IN THE NEW TOWNS

By J. H. CLAPHAM *and* M. M. CLAPHAM

THE new towns were big and ugly and were growing like toadstools; but they were still not too big to be walked out of by any one who had some energy and a couple of hours to spare, or even less; though in the earliest Victorian age the combination of energy and hours came seldom. From the foulest corner of the greatest of them, that corner in Manchester–Salford at the junction of the Irwell and the Irk where Engels in 1844 saw 'the most horrible dwellings which he had ever yet beheld', two and a half miles up a gentle hill brought you to the sand and heather of Kersal Moor, where there was horse-racing at Whitsuntide until 1846, and Chartist mass-meetings later. (Next year the race-course was moved nearer in.) Not more than a mile and a half upstream from the foul corner, the little bourgeois of the forties thought that the river bathing was excellent: they knew 'a stretch of clean, nice, yellow sand, in which after our dip we could roll and dry ourselves in the hot summer sun'. There or thereabouts, the first Manchester and Salford regatta was rowed in September 1842.

Liverpool had its long water front and an easy crossing to open country on the Cheshire side, that crossing on which Nathaniel Hawthorne in 1853 saw a 'labouring man' eating oysters 'which he took one by one from his pocket in interminable succession and opened with his jack-knife'. A mile and a half at most would get you clear of the central pit of Leeds or Sheffield on any side; less from that of Bradford; no more from the central height of Birmingham, though Birmingham was much the biggest of this group and its edges the least clearly defined.[1] And the moors within easy reach of Sheffield and Bradford were better than Kersal Moor.

It was as well that you could get out of town by walking, or at Liverpool by a cheap ferry-boat; for there was no other way of getting out often except for really well-to-do people.

[1] Population in 1851: Manchester-Salford, 401,000; Liverpool, 376,000; Birmingham, 233,000; Leeds, 173,000; Sheffield, 135,000; Bradford, 104,000.

True, there were popular excursions by canal, and in course of time by the new railways; but these were not for every day, though excursion days recurred more often in the prosperous fifties and sixties. Already in '53 Hawthorne, on another of his Mersey crossings, travelled with 'a multitude of factory people. They had bands of music and banners inscribed with the names of the mills they belong to . . . pale-looking people, but not looking exactly as if they were underfed. . . . These were from Preston', and they were going to Rock Ferry. But no labouring man went to his work, or to anything else regularly, except on foot. Nor did the average middle-class man before the fifties. There was no cab-stand in Manchester until 1839 and the few omnibuses of the forties were crude and cramped, 'with wisps of straw underneath the feet in wet weather'. It was only from about 1840 that the shopkeepers, smaller manufacturers, and miscellaneous commercial people had begun to move out from the very heart of the towns, and then only to the inner suburban belt within easy walking range of their places of business.

The commercial and industrial magnates, though they were becoming 'carriage folk'—there were 1,009 private carriages in Manchester–Salford by 1851—could usually walk to business if they wished. When their mill or their works was not in the great town itself but in some satellite town, mill village up a Pennine valley, or open country site where space and sweet water were needed for bleaching, the house was usually only a stone's throw away. There was just a yard between Green Bank, Rochdale, where John Bright grew up, and his father's mill. That arrangement, or some slight variant of it, was the rule in all those outlying places. Even on the edge of the great town men like Mrs. Gaskell's Mr. Thornton—drawn, they say, from James Nasmyth of the steam hammer—might be pictured as living in a big formal house in the mill yard. Of those who had left the yard, few lived much more than a mile or two from works, warehouse, or office, until after 1850–5. Sir Edward Thomason, inventor and medal-maker, died at his house in St. Philip's Square, Birmingham, in 1849. 'Fashionable Liverpool still dwelt in the large Georgian houses fringing Everton Hill',[1] little over a mile from the river front, in 1840. Most of the principal merchants, mill-owners, and engineers of Leeds,

[1] Forwood, Sir W. B., *Recollections of a Busy Life*.

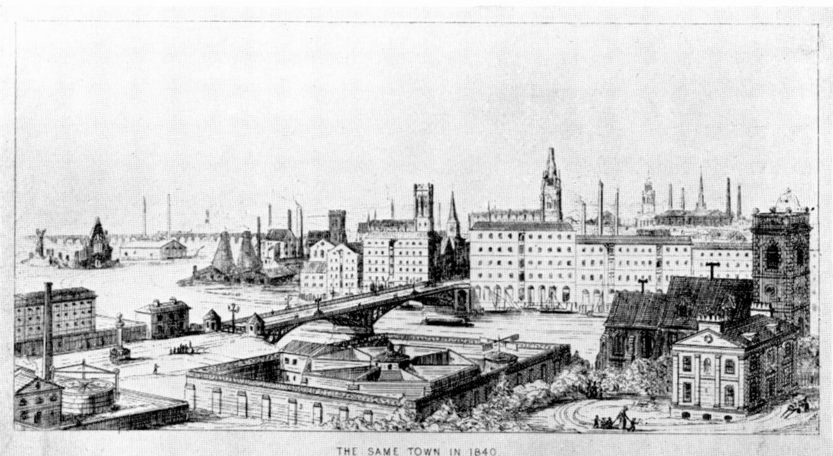

THE SAME TOWN IN 1840.

1. St Michaels Tower rebuilt in 1750. 2. New Parsonage House & Pleasure Grounds. 3. The New Jail. 4. Gas Works. 5. Lunatic Asylum. 6. Iron Works & Ruins of St Maries Abbey. 7. Mr Evans Chapel. 8. Baptist Chapel. 9. Unitarian Chapel. 10. New Church. 11. New Town Hall & Concert Room. 12. Wesleyan Centenary Chapel. 13. New Christian Society. 14. Quakers Meeting. 15. Socialist Hall of Science.

Catholic town in 1440.

1. St Michaels on the Hill. 2. Queens Crofs. 3. St Thomas's Chapel. 4. St Maries Abbey. 5. All Saints. 6. St Johns. 7. St Peters. 8. St Alkmunds. 9. St Maries. 10. St Edmunds. 11. Grey Friars. 12. St Cuthberts. 13. Guild hall. 14. Trinity. 15. St Olaves. 16. St Botolphs.

PUGIN'S CONTRASTS

though they were moving up out of the bottom of Airedale, where the heavy work was done, could get to Leeds Bridge or the Cloth Halls on foot in twenty minutes. But the very great, like the Drinkwaters and the Phillips of Manchester, had moved early, well beyond walking range. These two families had made themselves parks. They gave them geographical names, but Manchester knew better and the family names stuck. From the Park, Prestwich—'Phillips's Park'—the head of the Phillips family, having breakfasted at 8 a.m., rode some three miles to Kersal Toll Bar, by the Moor. There a shaky four-wheel cab met him and took him to his warehouse in the heart of the town. At night, being active, it was his habit to walk the stretch which in the morning he had ridden.

The really rich man whose business was in a warehouse or an office could plan his day like this. But the manufacturer had not the time. The greatest manufacturers, men such as the Gotts of Leeds, acknowledged leaders of the woollen industry, were in the mill at 6 a.m. 'The daughters often rode there at 8 a.m. to bring their father back to breakfast.' The more strictly commercial a town was, the more easily could its leaders adopt the late and spacious life. That lay at the root of the familiar Lancashire distinction, cherished in Manchester with an inferior-superior tenacity, between Liverpool gentlemen and Manchester men. Even in the sixties, many merchants 'still wore evening dress coats and not a few white cravats' on 'change at Liverpool. In Manchester they did not. A journalist of the fifties explained that these Liverpool merchant princes had 'their suburban villas, their marine villas, and their town mansions on a princely scale'. The 'marine villa' had come in approximately with the Victorian age, first at what was described in 1841 as 'the newly established colony of Waterloo', just clear of the Mersey estuary. Even before you got to Waterloo, there had sprung up recently along the shore 'a number of elegant and painfully constructed white cottages' and a charming hotel 'on the crest of a sandhill'. At Waterloo were 'upwards of a hundred cottages', laid out in a crescent and an esplanade, 'with a superb and spacious hotel in the centre'.

These cottages were regularly occupied a few years later (1847–50) by merchants' families, 'for in those times a cottage at the sea-side was the usual method of spending the summer', as Sir William Forwood wrote in his reminiscences sixty years later. You could get there by a four-horse 'bus or, more pleasantly, by express boats on the Leeds and Liverpool Canal, which, behind Waterloo, runs only a mile from the shore. 'Riding on horseback on the sea-shore was a very favourite pastime'; and from their 'marine villas' many business men rode into town, keeping to the shore so far as was practicable.

Eight was the standard breakfast hour, whether you went to the mill first or not. Phillips of the Park, Prestwich, took a light lunch at his club and dressed for dinner at seven o'clock. But the Gotts of Leeds dined at 4.0 or 5.0; Mr. Aitkin, 'a wealthy merchant of Liverpool', received Hawthorne at 6.0; and immediately below this thin upper stratum every one dined at 1.0. 'Rich, Poor—the mass, yes the mass, all dine at 1.0', a social explorer of Manchester wrote to *Blackwood's* in 1839: 'in a vast many houses of business, not even one solitary clerk is to be found at the counting office from 1.0 to 2.0 and not in one out of fifty is the principal to be seen from 1.0 to 3.0 p.m.' Inquiry showed him that after the sound eight o'clock breakfast many people took bread and cheese, with 'a glass of sherry and a thimble-full of brandy', at eleven; every one the square dinner at one; every one tea, and perhaps muffins and cakes and tarts, at five or six; every one supper, often with hot meat, at nine. 'I do beg the aristocracy at least of this Northern capital—to begin with dinner at five, suppress luncheons altogether, abolish suppers, and not let each day be consumed in the devouring of four meals, at the horrible hours of 8.0, 1.0, 5.0, and 9.0.' His article is called *A Week in Manchester* and his bills of fare are not infallible. In serious households 'at 9.30, with evening prayers, sandwiches were brought', instead of the hot meat. But his times at least are approximately correct.

When home was more than a mile from business, one o'clock dinner would be taken at the club or eating-house; but the economical habit of taking this meal also at home no doubt helps to explain the long dinner spell of the critics' 'principals'. In 1839 most of them still lived very near their places of business, if not actually at them. The club and eating-house habit grew with the radius of the towns.

Until the forties, neither the man of business nor the clerks or operatives who worked for him had much leisure in the factory towns. Things were rather different in places like Sheffield and Birmingham, where so much work was done by small handicraft masters and out-workers, who could more or less regulate their own hours, though not always to their own advantage. A slack Monday was balanced by rush work from Thursday to Saturday. Still, leisure there was, if irregular. Birmingham people were proud of the independence which ensured it, and of their relative equality as compared with the Lancashire towns; 'there is a more equal and general diffusion of wealth among the master manufacturers, and between them and the work-people, who as a class are independent and self-relying', their guide-book said. Irregular leisure in the cotton country had been cut into by the wheels of iron, until the State stopped their turning at 2 o'clock on Saturday afternoons by the Factory Act of 1850. Some years earlier, the general business community of Manchester had decided to shorten office hours on Saturday. There was a soirée—alien word for a favourite form of early Victorian celebration—held in the Town Hall in honour of the decision.

Before the Saturday half-holiday became general, and in those places and trades where it only came late, there was Sunday and there were the evenings. All labour began early, and as the ten-and-a-half-hour working day was much the commonest, most people were free for a few hours after 6 p.m. except publicans, poor men's shopkeepers, and the army of hawkers and street sellers. What was there to do? In winter it was dark. From the bigger towns, even in summer, few of those who had done a day's manual work were likely to walk beyond the houses, possible though it always was. That was why the Saturday halt was such a boon. Hawthorne found Saturday 'a kind of gala day' at Liverpool in 1853. 'I think I have never seen a populace before coming to England; but this crowd afforded a specimen of one.' By 1850 the cheap Saturday excursion trains from Manchester were crowded 'by thousands who have thus devoted their half-holiday to the rational delight of a ramble about the adjacent country, or who having friends . . . within railway distance . . . spend Sunday with them and yet . . . resume their avocations early on the Monday morning.' The week-end habit—the very word comes from the North—was creeping into English life.

Then, for summer evenings, there were the brand-new

urban parks, though not everywhere and not in Victoria's earliest years. Manchester opened three of them, naming one after the man who had just repealed the Corn Laws, on August 22, 1846. They were bought by public subscription. There was a great procession and there were festivities. Coming down to sample these 'now somewhat famous parks of Manchester', a few months later, the journalist 'learned from eyesight that even during the rain these parks are resorted to by the workmen. . . . It is certainly something to know that mechanics, glad of recreation, will play at nine-pins, under an ungenial sky, in preference to indulging in the more seasonable attractions of the tap.' Besides the nine-pins, there were bowls and gymnastic appliances, with swings and seesaws for the children. Twelve years later another explorer noted that 'a secluded portion of the grounds' in Peel Park was 'set apart for girls to allow them also some small chance of proper muscular development'. This Manchester of the fifties was a hardy pioneering place: 'even swimming baths for females have begun to make some progress', the explorer reports.

A few years after the public parks (in 1850–1) came the first free libraries. They were crowded on dark evenings from the start; but however crowded, they attracted and held only a tiny fraction of the people. Judging by the books most often taken out by these studious working men 'their great delight and refreshment appears to consist in an escape from routine life to dreams of romance and peril'. In romance, *The Arabian Nights* was their favourite, followed by *Ivanhoe*, *Robinson Crusoe*, and *Moll Flanders*: a good list. But 'histories of Napoleon have been somewhat more in demand than even the *Arabian Nights*'; and lives of Wellington and Nelson competed with *Moll Flanders*.

Long before the opening of the free libraries, all considerable towns had their Mechanics' Institutes. But every one agreed, in early Victorian times, that you saw few mechanics there, except perhaps in Newcastle and in the Scottish towns. The Institute at Liverpool was admirable, but already in 1842 its advantages were 'embraced almost exclusively by the middle classes'. 'A college for young merchants' some one called it five years later. It was the same clientèle at Manchester in 1842—'merchants, manufacturers, clerks, shopkeepers, tradesmen, artists'. Rather more democratic because cheaper, though their name hardly suggests it, were the three Lyceums of Manchester–Salford. The subscription was only 2*s*. a quarter; and besides libraries and evening schools they had news-rooms and provision for music, gymnastics, and dancing. 'Females are admitted . . . there are separate classes for teaching them reading, writing, grammar, sewing and knitting. The greatest care is exercised to guard against any species of impropriety.' In the classes for females at the Ancoats Lyceum the average attendance in 1841 was from 32 to 44—'some from the factories'. The teachers gave their services free. For the tea parties, soirées, and concerts there was a charge of 6*d*.; and when there was dancing from 600 to 700 people were usually present.

The Newcastle Mechanics' Institute was reckoned one of the best in the kingdom in 1840. Apparently it had not ceased to deserve its name, and at the Saturday popular lectures and concerts held in connexion with it there would be an audience of about 700, 'chiefly workmen and some young men from shops and warehouses'. Newcastle's reputation for serious thought stood high: 'no other town of its size is so ready a patron of the fine arts, or spends so much of its gains annually on literature', as tested by London booksellers' Newcastle sales.

Literacy seems to have increased as you got nearer to Scotland, where every one could read and write, except some of the immigrant English and Irish. But in the raw towns of the English Midlands and North, in spite of the work of National Schools and Sunday Schools and night schools and of the resolute self-education of picked wage-earners, a high percentage of illiteracy limited the influence of the free libraries and the popular press. According to the Registrar-General of births, deaths, and marriages, 60 per cent. of the people of Manchester–Salford in 1840–1 could not sign their own names. At Huddersfield in 1847, however, 60 per cent. of the women married made shift to sign. Difficulty with reading no doubt helps to explain the almost unbelievable tolerance of the endlessly spoken word. Methodist preachers seldom gave less than an hour to the sermon alone. Bronterre O'Brien the Chartist spoke as a rule for three hours and, at his best, could hold an audience for four or five—just like Gladstone on Budget night.

Week-night service, Methodist class meeting, or Chartist meeting; Mechanics' Institute, Lyceum, or free library—these drew the serious and those with more than ordinary mental hunger. For the majority there was the doorstep, the street, and the taps—the taps and music. The new towns were terribly drunken; there was no doubt of that. But the most patronizing journalist explorers were astonished at the musical zest of Yorkshire, Lancashire, and Cheshire, though they usually deplored the publican's exploitation of it, and shuddered at the 'singing saloon and similar haunts of vice and depravity'. In Manchester alone, excluding Salford, in 1850, there were 475 public-houses and 1,143 beer-houses—one for every eighty men and women of twenty years old and upwards. Of the public-houses forty-nine, and of the beer-houses forty-one, had regular musical entertainments.

Some years earlier it had been noted that 'the Manchester publicans . . . do not in their advertisements vaunt the goodness or cheapness of their spirits, but provide a good evening's entertainment . . . many of them have organs . . . or possess pianofortes; they employ musicians; they take care to publish that on such-and-such a night, Mr. So-and-so, the celebrated comic singer will oblige the company with his celebrated vocal drolleries.' Follows the reflection: 'in drawing an auditory of uninformed operatives, the comic singer offers incalculable odds against the scientific lecturer.' His humour no doubt was plebeian, too plebeian even for 'well-informed operatives' we are told.

Lower down the scale were the beer-shops, 'haunted' by 'the young of both sexes among the factory folk, the majority with faces unwashed and hair uncombed, dancing in their wooden clogs to the music of an organ, violin or seraphine' [an early form of harmonium]. Higher up were 'the most innocent of the favourite haunts of the people, the casinos or music saloons'. They were mostly open six nights a week but were specially thronged on Saturdays. 'I was never in the place myself,' a bourgeois memoir-writer notes of one of them, 'but to judge of those I saw going in and coming out there would probably be a strong flavour of corduroy and tobacco', for the place was 'liberally supported by the working classes'. On going in you bought a check for *2d.* or *3d.* The value was returned in refreshments, 'apples, oranges, cakes, ginger-beer, ale, porter and cigars'. If the supply seems excessive at the price, it is to be remembered that oranges were four a penny in the Manchester streets; and no doubt one could duplicate the check. Two witnesses affirm that, in the leading Manchester casino, ginger-beer was the favourite drink. It all sounds definitely innocent. Settled in and drinking, you had an entertainment of band-playing, 'songs in costume, acting, tumbling and dancing'. Some casinos 'aimed at giving short theatrical entertainments, 'or what were called—how did Manchester pronounce it?—'poses plastiques'. Yet singing was the main business. 'As it was usually found expedient to keep the windows open', the bourgeois who shirked a casino atmosphere could 'often hear the chorus or refrain of the last Music Hall ditty . . . wafted along on the breeze' down Deansgate to Manchester Old Church. When the singing was over, the man in corduroys could sup in the street on tripe and trotters with vinegar. Your north-country operative had his distractions—innocent and less innocent—from work, corn laws, Chartism, and factory agitation, even in the ten years between 1843 and 1853 from which these notes and descriptions come.

Besides, he was cultivating his musical talent in other ways—ways of which even the most comfortable people did not disapprove. There were singing classes, choral societies, factory bands—successors of that pioneer band which Robert Owen had ordered at New Lanark. It was some of these, not hired musicians, whom Nathaniel Hawthorne met at Rock Ferry in '53. One does not hear of the purchase of pianos quite so early, though it may have begun; for even in 1844 in the cottages of the more comfortable cotton operatives 'some of the parlours were carpeted and all contained chairs, tables, pictures, and generally a clock in the corner'. But when the cotton-famine came in the sixties, many pianos were pawned or sold: 'there is no part of England where, until lately, there have been so many . . . purchased by a long course of careful saving from the workman's wages. . . . The great works of Handel, Haydn, Beethoven and Mozart have solaced the toil of thousands of the poorest working people of Lancashire.'[1]

Another solace for many of them, though not for those who were literally the poorest, a solace specially common in Lancashire but available everywhere, was the Friendly

[1] Waugh, E., *Home Life of the Lancashire Cotton Folk during the Cotton Famine.*

Society Meeting. It was held at a public-house, unless it was a meeting of the teetotal Rechabites, who 'pitched their tents' in schools and chapels. There were the keen pleasures of secret signs and of ritual, at which, when they heard of them, members of Parliament and other educated people, most of whom took free-masonry and the trooping of the colour seriously, had often the impertinence to scoff. There were the pleasures of good fellowship: some of the societies were exclusively convivial. And there was the business connected with the still very unsystematic and actuarially unsound provision made by subscription for the sicknesses and funerals of members. One single society, though the greatest, the Manchester Unity of Oddfellows, had 252,000 members in 1845. They were by no means all in Lancashire, but there was a separate 'Unity' in Bolton and another in Nottingham. Besides, there were Druids, Hearts of Oak, Foresters, Shepherds, very convivial Buffaloes, and innumerable small local sick and burial clubs. These last, however useful, had no social life worth mentioning; but, in Lancashire at any rate, the figures collected by the Registrar of Friendly Societies before 1850 suggest that at least one man in every three, and a much higher proportion of the skilled men, may have belonged to societies which had some. There were middle-class elements in all, or nearly all, the societies—in the Oddfellows amounting to 15 or 20 per cent.—but, as the numbers show, the mass was made up of what contemporaries liked to call 'hard working sons of toil'.

On the face of them, the new towns were poor places for sport. Moreover, the early Victorian age fell between two sporting epochs. Bull-baiting is heard of as late as 1840, but at Wells, not in industrial England. Cock-fights, dog-fights, cock-shies, and the like survived, as time went on, less as recognized sports than as occasional brutalities like the ill treatment of cats or climbing boys, or the public executions. There was some prize-fighting and a good deal of fighting without prizes. But regular sport, whether brutal—like the Lancashire 'purring' matches: kicking fights in clogs—or not brutal, like whippet-racing and pigeon-flying, was more likely to be found in mining villages, among navvies on the railway works, or the half-rural industrial population, than in the big town itself. You could not run the dogs in Deansgate or in Peel Park, though you might on Kersal Moor; and

THE PLYMOUTH ATHENAEUM

there were of course the Manchester Races. It was in the smaller places, too, that the few days of annual 'wakes' or 'feasts'—when even the mills slackened off—were important. With them came round the ordinary distractions and dissipations of a fair, and a chance to organize excursions to Rock Ferry or Blackpool. In the great towns it was the sodden abuse of vacant leisure, rather than the abuses of sport, which oppressed humane and religious people.

But few of these people did anything to relieve the non-church-or-chapel-goer's Sunday. 'A Sunday's holiday is looked upon as a heinous sin by so many respectable people that it cannot be indulged in with impunity,' *Household Words* wrote in 1853. 'We have hardly a real holiday in England; executions and races make the nearest approach to one.' The writer went on to contrast the amusements and gaiety on Sundays and Fête days in France. Three years later, 'bands of music' were started in the new parks of Manchester and Salford on Sundays: 'the opposition on the part of the sabbatarian public was so strongly expressed that the experiment was soon abandoned.' So the only Manchester Sunday music, except that of Church organ or harmonium, was to be found in the thirty-six of those entertainment providing public-houses which refused to suspend their entertainments on the first day of the week. The religious, if not always the humane, were playing into the hands of sodden leisure.

But the new epoch in urban sport was opening out. The middle classes started it. They were not working men who rowed in that first Manchester regatta of 1842; though there may have been some working-class members in the Bradford cricket club founded in 1836. It met at the 'Hope and Anchor' and had a practising-ground opposite Horton Road. By 1850 there were at least two cricket clubs in Birmingham. The Birmingham club, which 'assembled every Monday and Friday', had one of the best grounds in England and hired a professional bowler. The Victoria Club—it met at Mrs. Smith's, 'The Fountain', Cheapside—kept its ground open daily during the season, 'but Tuesday was the principal play day'. Ten or twelve years later George Cadbury, who was at business by 7 a.m. and in summer used to play football and hockey before business, is found organizing a 'works' cricket team. It must have been among the earliest.

Manchester had several suburban clubs in the forties. One founded about 1845 by the Manchester Athenaeum—not to be confused with the Lyceum—combined cricket, its main object, with archery, quoits, fencing, boxing, and singlestick. The membership was entirely middle-class—'it was chiefly used by young men engaged in commercial pursuits'—and the cricket-scorer was an elderly Quaker. Manchester Quakers at that time, at least on ceremonial occasions, still wore broad-brimmed hats, grey or mulberry coats, frilled shirts and knee breeches. This old gentleman played an excellent game of quoits, which somehow seems more fitting than the later hockey of the young Cadburys.

At Liverpool, cricket and subsequently croquet are the only outdoor games of which much is heard. But besides being horsemen many of the Liverpool merchants, in the fifties and presumably earlier, were keen boat sailors and yachtsmen. Macgregor Laird of Birkenhead had set an example on the grand scale before Victoria's accession, when he explored the Niger in the iron steamer *Alburkah*, built for the purpose by his father's firm.

Indoors, the middle classes, greatly helped in several towns by an influx of music-loving Germans, showed nearly as much musical eagerness as the working men. Here was a field on which all could meet. Many leading citizens would have nothing to do with the theatre or with card-parties, and avoided both public and private balls. Middle, and some High Church men, common worldlings, and Unitarians were on the laxer side; Evangelical Churchmen, Quakers, Methodists, and Scotch Presbyterians on the more strict. There was a grand ball at Liverpool, organized by the Mayor for upwards of a thousand guests on the occasion of the Queen's marriage in '39; but when ten years later a different Mayor, eager 'to enliven the ordinary routine of municipal hospitality', gave a soirée at the Town Hall, dancing was forbidden, 'to the disappointment of many', though card-playing was allowed. However, when the Queen and her consort came to Liverpool in person in '51, loyalty and dancing prevailed and 2,500 tickets were issued for another grand ball.

Liverpool at that time had ten or a dozen public halls all of which were used intermittently, and some principally, for concerts. The Philharmonic Hall 'had gas lights arranged along the ceiling in an ingenious manner, producing a charming effect'. The concert hall in Lord Nelson Street, which could hold nearly 3,000 people, had a slightly unusual history. It was 'originally built for the use of a deluded body of men calling themselves Socialists. . . . Young ladies dressed in the Bloomer costume, tripped it on the light fantastic toe with young gentlemen who thought the laws of matrimony unnatural and tyrannical. The Directors lost much money in vain attempts to overthrow the Bible and reform the marriage customs of civilized society, wherefore the buildings had to be sold'—for music which takes no sides.

At Birmingham the old-established Choral Society began its subscription concerts in 1841; and a few years later the Birmingham Musical Festival was started. There were private subscription concerts also; for the musical life of the town was reasonably vigorous. All the familiar London names of the time recur there—Grisi, Mario, Jenny Lind, Sims Reeves.

During the early forties, middle-class music seems to have been hardly so well organized or so successful in Manchester as in Liverpool or Birmingham. The Choral Society only dated from 1833. Another Socialist Hall of Science was diverted from its original use; but it became a free library, not a concert hall. Sir Oswald Mosley bought it for £1,200 and gave it to the city. But the opening of the Free Trade Hall in 1842 had given Manchester its future musical head-quarters. (So early as 1843 the first great meeting of the Lancashire and Cheshire Workmen's Singing Classes was held there; when 1,500 people came to sing.) In 1848 Carl Hallé settled in Manchester, as conductor of a small theatre orchestra. The *Liedertafel* of the German residents, whose members had serenaded Jenny Lind on her visit the year before, gave him a fulcrum. The Lancashire natives were not too difficult to move. By the late fifties Hallé's concerts with Hallé's orchestra in the Free Trade Hall were the centre of the musical life of the North. 'All Manchester' attended, travelling in by suburban trains or driving in its broughams, sometimes for five miles or more, over streets paved with granite 'setts'.

Various well-meaning attempts had been made to draw the working men from their casinos and public-house music to something more refined. Cheap Saturday evening concerts at Mechanics' Institutes in the forties had not been able to stand the competition in Manchester; though they had done better at Liverpool. A cheap Manchester Monday evening in the Free Trade Hall had been more of a success. But on the whole the classes took their music apart, in those and in other towns; although the steadily increasing musical cultivation of the working men was tending to close the gap by the sixties.

Compared with music the drama took a poor, late, and patchy part in the life of the new towns. There were remnants of old popular drama on their fringes: Peace Eggers, playing a confused story of St. George, the Prince of Paradise, the King of Egypt and the Devil,[1] made their way even into the Manchester of the forties at Easter; and in the autumn Morris dancers came round with their rushcart. There was Punch and Judy, of course; and there were travelling dramatic companies which played where they could. Most of the bigger towns, however, had at least one permanent theatre by 1840; but its life was often difficult. 'There is an extraordinary apathy prevailing in Birmingham, with respect to theatrical amusements,' a guide-book of 1849 complains; 'the career of the manager of the Theatre Royal has generally been far other than a gainful one.' Yet great names had played in it. Macready in a six-night visit in 1841 accounted for nearly £1,000 of takings. Kean came. Taglioni came for the Ballet, and in 1847 Rachel herself, 'with the entire French company from St. James' Theatre', appeared for a single night. In the fifties the management would seem to have done better, especially with pantomime. There had never been Christmas pantomime in Birmingham before 1841. In the fifties the thing was so much prized that the pantomimes often ran on till March. The struggles of the theatre in a new town of the second rank are well seen at Bradford. After several theatrical ventures, one in a great wooden shed and one in Oddfellows' Building, a Theatre Royal (they were mostly royal) was built in 1841. But audiences were hard to get and small. The middle classes seem to have kept aloof—on principle no doubt. The chief patrons were the 'gallery'—'sons of toil . . . who liked good

[1] Singing— 'ere come I Beelzebub.
On me shoulder I carry me club;
in me 'and a drippin' pan,
an' see if I'm not a jolly old man.

acting and plenty of it'. In '46 pantomime came to Bradford and seems to have been as popular there as in Birmingham. Some of the best players also came in their turn, but it was not by them that the theatre lived.

Manchester down to 1860 managed with two theatres, or perhaps two and a half. There was the Royal, burnt out in 1844 but rebuilt, which kept its own Stock Company and received the greater visiting actors. Such of the middle class as were theatre-goers were to be seen there—sixty years later one of them was still arguing, in defence of his youth, with 'the good people who are shocked, almost horrified, at the bare thought of entering the door of a theatre'. Then there was the younger Queen's, actor-managed by an Irishman with personality named Egan, who stood six foot four and gave the galleries on which he relied full-blooded melodrama to their taste. Even fewer of the middle class were to be seen at Egan's. At one time there was also a City theatre, but it was short lived and of no account.

Liverpool, more cultivated, more worldly, carried four theatres; but the prices at the two smaller ones—boxes 1*s.*; pit 6*d.*; gallery 3*d.*—suggest a level not much above that of Egan's Manchester Queen's. The inevitable Royal, where all the best drama and opera which early Victorian England could supply came in proper rotation, charged regularly what at the Birmingham Royal was only charged for the visits of actors like Macready—boxes 4*s.*; upper boxes 3*s.*; pit 2*s.*; gallery 1*s.* These prices, comparable with those charged in London, were not for 'the sons of toil'.

Comparison with London would not have surprised the men of Liverpool. To at least one foreigner the place seemed as new and as drab as any other drab new town: 'rien n'est plus triste à voir que Liverpool.'[1] But its old, inner, conservative society was definitely and consciously aristocratic. There were those dress coats and those cravats on 'change. There were the Wellington assembly rooms, dating from 1814, to which only families of 'position and standing' were admitted. Six or seven assembly balls were given in them each year. The strictest propriety, we are told, was enforced and 'vigilant stewards' checked any trace of roughness in the dancing. There was a reserve, dignity, and careful courtesy of manner among these leading families—Gladstones and

[1] Faucher, L., *Études sur l'Angleterre*, 1845.

others older. Some had already bought places in the country; some kept London houses, were merging in London society, and adopting its ways. It is doubtful whether in any town outside London Harriet Beecher Stowe would have found herself invited, as she was on landing at Liverpool in 1853, to a breakfast party 'on a large scale' at which 'ladies kept their bonnets on and were not dressed in full toilet'. The riding, the yachting, the 'marine villas', the charity balls, the breakfast parties, the places being bought in the country, all suggest an approximation to metropolitan habits which was much rarer in the manufacturing towns.

Manchester had no assembly rooms with their faint flavour of an old county capital and Beau Brummel. 'Amongst the higher classes,' a visitor of 1839 reported, 'though there were few amusements, dinner parties appeared to be particularly in vogue.' He complained that the dishes were always the same; boiled fowl with white sauce, cod, and roast beef. There was still champagne, marvellous dessert, and abundance of port and mahogany. On these occasions people whose normal dinner hour was 1.0 would sit down at 5.0 or 6.0. 'Omnibuses are organized to take dinner guests from house to house or villa to villa.' That was when Manchester had no cabs and few private carriages. But even when the cabs had come and the carriages risen to a thousand, an occasional dinner party, very splendid, very formal, held at an hour at which you did not usually dine, remained the set piece of entertainment for all who could afford it. On those rare nights the drugget was pulled up in the drawing-room and the covers taken off the chairs: 'the appartment blazed forth in yellow silk damask and a brilliantly flowered carpet. Every corner seemed filled up with ornament . . . and presented a strange contrast to the ugliness of the look-out—' which in this case is Mr. Thornton's mill-yard as drawn by Mrs. Gaskell in the fifties. The Thorntons visited 'wi' a' th' first folk; the Mayor hisself dines there, and the members of Parliament an' all'.

Below that level you soon came to the informality of six o'clock tea and a quiet evening of talk, a little music, and—if you did not disapprove—a little card-playing with a handful of friends before supper. Very many people gave at least one evening a week to religious meetings; many perhaps an evening a month to some musical, literary, discussion, or 'mutual improvement' society. Now and again, massed together and enthusiastic, politically minded townsmen could hear Cobden overwhelming the Corn Laws with argument and invective, or John Bright speaking like a prophet against the Crimean War.

After all—seriousness, few amusements, religion, and work were the hall-marks of the middle class in the new towns, where all that was not labour was middle class. The Frenchman who found Liverpool so *triste* warned his readers not to expect museums, theatres, culture there: 'la pensée religieuse est jusqu'ici la seule inspiration qui ennoblisse ces rudes natures': you found churches and chapels at every step. Manchester was 'in some ways the most monstrous aggregation that the progress of society had yet improvised'. There were no amusements. All was hurry and work. What drama there was, was vulgar; the religion dissenting and radical—vulgar too, one is left to infer. But he would rather have lived in Manchester than in Sheffield or Leeds—where the sun only got through on Sundays. He did not see everything, or always see quite true, but he saw what was most visible.

Of Sunday, except for its daylight in Leeds, he could hardly trust himself to write. But it is to be remembered that for the serious Englishman—using the word in its special early nineteenth-century sense—for the serious, whether young or old, the early Victorian Sunday was not gloomy. It was the day of rest; that is already much. It was also, in the words of Christopher Wordsworth's new hymn, the day of gladness; which is more. That children generally found Sundays 'sadly dull days' is true; but those who put away the toys with the newspapers did want to turn their own minds from the last political squabble and the price of cotton twist. That grown people whom the 'inspiration' of religion did not 'ennoble' found the long slow Sunday hours good mainly for sleeping or drinking is also true. And the serious were always a minority, doubtless to be blamed when they put away the toys or put down the bands of music in Manchester parks, but otherwise to be understood.

Their life of work had begun early, which made their appreciation of rest and inspiration the keener. Labouring children, as every one knows, often started at seven years of age or younger; the most fortunate of them at twelve. Between these last and the average middle-class child there was no great gap. 'The prevalent opinion was that boys must be caught young. . . . Most of the manufacturers placed their sons in situations at fourteen or fifteen.' Before that they may have gone to the local grammar school or—much more probably—to one of the many private 'colleges', 'academies', and 'high schools'. The fashion of sending boys to the great public schools had not so much as begun among the mass of business families, though a Peel had long since gone to Harrow and a Gladstone to Eton. As to the University —'if he went to the Scotch Universities', where he could enter very young, 'he came home unsettled for commercial pursuits: how much more if he went to Oxford or Cambridge, where he could not enter until he was eighteen'. That was the dominant opinion, reported correctly by Mrs. Gaskell.

If it was the mill or the works, the boy would be there at 6, like the rest; if the bank, office, warehouse, or shop, as soon as it opened or a little sooner. He stayed until business was done—which at rush times in a shipping office 'meant anything up to 12 o'clock at night and sometimes later'. And, boy or man, he might do his long day's work in conditions almost as insanitary as those in which the very poor lived. His warehouse or office might be in a court 'surrounded by a number of tumbledown, old-fashioned-looking places of business', say, between Deansgate and the Irwell, with a look-out on 'the black, dirty river, crawling sluggishly along'. (Friedrich Engels' classical account of its foulness applies to a point upstream of this.) You would find 'odd corner offices made out of landings and pantries, and warehouses manufactured out of ancient bedrooms, with rats and mice in abundance. Such', the memoir-writer concludes, 'were the ordinary places of business of many of our even wealthy Manchester merchants.'[1] Remain the places of the poor and struggling and unsuccessful, not described. And there is no reason to suppose that Manchester business men were worse housed than others. Their river was certainly not fouler than the Aire at Leeds, if perhaps rather greasier than the Don at Sheffield. That they were trying to get farther out of town for sleep and Sundays was a misfortune, in so far as it led to a more complete social separation of the classes, but nothing in history is more easily explained.

[1] Hayes, L. M., *Reminiscences of Manchester from the year 1840*; the memoirs quoted several times above.

V

COUNTRY LIFE AND SPORT

I. COUNTRY LIFE.

§ 1. THE COUNTRY.

§ 2. THE COUNTRY HOUSE.

§ 3. THE GARDEN.

§ 4. COUNTRY SOCIETY.

II. SPORT.

V

COUNTRY LIFE AND SPORT

By BERNARD DARWIN

§ 1. THE COUNTRY

SOME little while before 1830 the life of the English country gentleman had been described by a literary person called Goethe, of whom he had probably never heard. 'That insular life', remarked this intrusive foreigner, 'which is based on boundless wealth and civil freedom, in universal monotony and manifold diversity, formal and capricious, active and torpid, energetic and dull, comfortable and tedious, the envy and derision of the world.'

Had he known of this description the country gentleman would certainly have demurred to it, and particularly to the 'boundless wealth'. He would have complained of the bad times not merely on general principles but because there were, just distant enough to lend the greatest possible enchantment to the retrospect, those piping times of war which had been sent by Providence as a reward to virtuous landowners. Let us see by way of contrast to Goethe what a fine type of the old English country gentleman thought of it all on New Year's Day, 1830. This was General William Dyott, who kept a diary between 1781 and 1845. He was a gentleman of good old family in that county where good old families remain deep rooted in their own land for ever and ever, Staffordshire. He had been a soldier not without distinction; he had seen a good deal of foreign parts and had mixed in royal circles; now he had come back to live at his own beloved home of Freeford, near Lichfield. He was not a rich man but he was sufficiently comfortable, and lived and dined, shot, and sat on the bench on an equality with the magnates of his county. In 1830 he had reached the age of sixty-eight, not one at which anybody and least of all a General is likely to be elastic in his views or to praise the present at the expense of the past. Indeed, whenever he went to London he was struck afresh by the rise of the moneyed as opposed to the landed interest, and used to wonder and wonder who lived in all the big rich houses that he saw. 'Commerce', he wrote when he was safe back among his own fields at Freeford, 'has produced a class of the community almost unknown fifty years back.'

Here then is the entry with which the General begins his diary on January 1, 1830:

> 'Again a new year opens to the world; I believe a year never opened with less cheering prospects to a country than the present for old England; distress attending all classes of the community. Agriculturists particularly from the low prices. Wheat 8*s.*, barley 4*s.* 8*d.*, oats 3*s.* 3*d.*, beef 4½*d.* to 5*d.*, mutton the same. Meetings held in various parts of the Kingdom to represent the distress of the country. Unless the minister can remove the mill-stone (the national debt) from the neck of the constitution, no abundant relief can be afforded, I fear.'

This question of low prices had been troubling him and his fellows for several years before that New Year's Day. With the gentlemen he felt a natural sympathy in the matter. As to the farmers, they had been getting above themselves and must find their own level. Eight years before, he had written—and his words, he felt sure, were just as true now—that these farmers 'had been acquiring vast profits, the natural consequence of which (encouraged as they had been by the familiarity of their superiors) gave them habits and feelings beyond the rank of life to which they belong, and instead of, as formerly, being the respectable yeomen, they usurped the class of character, now almost extinct, of country esquires'. For them there need be no unnecessary sorrow. There was nothing for it but for them to take their grand coats off and be industrious and frugal as their forefathers had been. The example for them, he would have thought had he known of him, was Miss Matty's old lover in *Cranford*, who refused to allow himself to be called anything but 'Mr. Thomas Holbrook, Yeoman'.

Whoever was at fault, things were very bad. Landlords were borne down by mortgages and rent charges, tenants by borrowed capital. Rents and rates went unpaid. The belief that there was 'Nothing like muck' did not make the crops grow. The land was undrained and there was no money to drain it. The clay farms suffered worst of all. There were deep pools in the furrows, which in their turn were so deep that if a man stood in a Gloucestershire furrow watching another man cross a plough towards him, he lost sight of

THE RURAL SCENE—*BIRKET FOSTER*

him each time he descended into the fresh valley and saw him only on the hill-tops. With 1836 this lamentable state of things began to mend a little. James Smith of Deanston, patronized and encouraged by Sir Robert Peel, made experiments on his farm and taught farmers his new and enlightened ways. He invented the subsoil plough, and 'to deanstonize' became a verb in common use to signify deep ploughing and thorough draining. In 1838 the Royal Agricultural Society was founded and that was a sign that science had begun to come to the farmer's aid and that farming was ceasing to 'depend for its advances on the chance-directed discoveries of unlettered rustics'. The better times, however, were only beginning.

It was not only agriculture that was depressed: so were trade and manufactures. Not only agricultural labourers but gardeners and bricklayers' labourers were 'in the most wretched state of misery' and, in 1830, had 'cruel hard weather' to make things worse. 'Comfortable' was another of that man Goethe's epithets to which any country gentleman would have objected strongly. Times were in fact confoundedly uncomfortable. There was unrest in the air: yeomanry and dragoons were standing ready: in Kent and Sussex, Hampshire and Wiltshire, the labourers had been burning the farmers' ricks and threshing-machines: nobody could tell what might be going to happen. 'Well, you know,' said Mr. Brooke of Tipton to the Middlemarch grocer, 'this Reform will touch everybody by-and-by—a thoroughly popular measure—a sort of A, B, C, you know, that must come before the rest can follow.' What was going to follow? It was all very well for Mr. Brooke, who, though he did not approve of fancy-farming, 'electrifying your land and that kind of thing', was by way of being a liberal-minded man. Other country gentlemen were not so liberal-minded and the last thing they wanted was a popular measure. The people had always been ruled: now, it appeared, they were to rule and 'a few Birmingham buckle makers' were to 'promulgate laws for their own happy country'. Even Mr. Brooke himself must have had his doubts when he found himself taunted by Dagley, one of his own tenants, and told that when 'this Rinform' came in the landlords 'as never done the right thing by their tenants 'uld be treated i' that way as they'll hev to scuttle off'. That was an exaggerated view, for poor Dagley was not only sunk, as were many of his kind, in abysmal ignorance but had been dining just too well at the ordinary at the 'Blue Bull'. Still Mr. Brooke's fellows, had they been there, would have said 'I told you so'. It only showed that to touch Old Sarum was to open unknown floodgates and ruin the country.

There was another uncomfortable and puzzling thing, the coming of the railways. Nobody could tell what would be the end of that. It might be a wonderful thing but it would render 'roads, horses, and canals useless' and would ruin the holders of canal stock. The big paddock would probably be cut in two and spoilt, the mares in foal would be frightened out of their wits, and a herd of ruffianly navvies would be let loose on the countryside. The views of many a country gentleman about the iron roads were very much those which Jasper Petulengro expounded to the Romany Rye. 'I thought to myself what a queer place such a road would be to pitch one's tent upon, and how impossible it would be for one's cattle to find a bite of grass upon it; and I thought likewise of the danger to which one's family would be exposed of being run over and severely scorched by these same flying fiery vehicles.' It seemed that life would be utterly unsafe. Why, even at Eton, which was quite near London, where people knew what was what, the school authorities objected to the railway because the boys would certainly wander on to the line and be killed. Dr. Hawtrey knew of boys who threw shillings on to the rails in order to watch the train go over them. To be sure there would be compensations. Good prices could be got for the ruined land and the uttermost farthing should be extracted, but there was something unsettling and sinister about the whole affair. It had some vague connexion with those Liberal ideas which made the lower orders discontented with their masters. That at any rate was the view of the genuine unchanging Tories. 'He is a decided enemy to the railroads,' wrote our General of a praiseworthy neighbour, 'and joins us as a good conservative to frustrate the knavish tricks of the growing democraticks.'

To such good Conservatives it seemed the more perverse and unnecessary of people to want railroads just when roads and coaches had attained such a pitch of perfection. It had not been so always. There had once been much grumbling at the badness of the roads: there had been walking

THE RURAL SCENE—*BIRKET FOSTER*

up the hills. When Nimrod was a Rugby boy the coach between Shrewsbury and Chester, the 'Highflyer', used to take from eight in the morning till eight at night to cover the forty miles. If a passenger wanted to pay a call or do a little business on the way there were no crude hustling objections taken; the coach waited. Two hours were allowed for dinner and the coachman was always ready to be indulgent to any gentleman who desired another bottle. Now all was changed. London to Shrewsbury took 16¼ hours instead of 27. The 'Comet' on the way to Exeter covered its first stage from Piccadilly to Hounslow in 55 minutes and only one minute was allowed for changing horses. It was trotting all the way to Devonshire except when it was galloping. Walking had been done away by McAdam, the 'Colossus of Roads'. The 'Comet' was timed to do its ten miles an hour to Exeter and it ran to time, but the 'Quicksilver', which started later in the day, kept up its eleven miles an hour, and so—very nearly—did the mail from London to Edinburgh, for including stoppages it covered 400 miles in just over 40 hours. As for what private gentlemen could do with a chariot and four, Lord Londonderry had made a speech in the House of Lords one night and been in his own house in Durham 250 miles away the next. That to be sure was something altogether out of the ordinary—a rich man, additional relays of horses, and no expense spared—but even the slow coaches were timed to do eight miles an hour. What in the world did people want faster than that? Why, a man's wig had been blown off when he put his head out of the window. And now those perfect roads would go inevitably to rack and ruin.

There was another trouble which greatly worried the country gentleman of 1830, had worried his predecessors and has never wholly ceased to worry his successors. This was the trouble of poachers. The poachers killed his game and assaulted and shot at his keepers. There were often murderous affrays and in some parts of the country the law-breakers were so bold, so dangerous, and went about their work in such large bands, that 'unless a country gentleman could support battalions of keepers he must rest content with having his game carried off'. The penalties were exceedingly severe, but the temptation and the profit were great enough to make the poacher's risk worth the running. Sometimes the poachers actually beat the gentlemen, who in despair gave up preserving. This was not only an outrage against the rights of the property owner, but it was an intolerable nuisance and expense. Moreover, in the view of the more enlightened, it was a thoroughly bad thing for the countryside. It made bad blood between rich and poor and produced a number of idle and vicious characters. Once a man had experienced the stolen excitements and rewards of poaching he became a bad lot and a bad citizen not easily to be reclaimed.

This state of things had been for some time growing steadily worse. It was due directly to the Game Laws, which seem to us nowadays to have been of a fantastic absurdity, and indirectly to the gradual increase in wealth of classes other than the landed gentry and the consequent increase in the general luxury of living. Once upon a time the country gentleman had had his own game on his own table and had given of his superfluity to his friends. The rest of the world, the prosperous merchant or manufacturer, had not wanted game or had regarded it perhaps as something above his station. With the nineteenth century, however, all this had changed. The rich man who was not a landowner now insisted on having game as a second course; he would have it not only at his private table but at one of the big taverns where he went to some public dinner. It was all due, in General Dyott's words, to 'the prevalence of the human mind to cope with and imitate those above us in rank and station'. There were 'persons in life, heretofore unused to indulge in providing game for their guests', and now these persons thought themselves gentlemen and game became as regular a need 'for the pampered appetite of the moneyed merchant as for the ducal board'. If the poulterers would not supply this need they lost custom; and so the poulterers had to go to the poachers.

The law was briefly this. In order to be qualified to carry a gun or keep dogs for the killing of game a man must possess lands of inheritance of £100 a year or leases to the value of £150 a year. Lords of the manor could by writing appoint game-keepers who might kill game. There were penalties against people, whether qualified or unqualified, who should buy or sell game. Therefore to sell game was illegal, whether for a landowner or anybody else. The results were obvious and inevitable. The tenant who had not the required qualifica-

THE CLUB WALKING; THE WAITS—*BIRKET FOSTER*

tions naturally encouraged poaching since it saved his crops. The landowner himself was tempted to destroy superfluous game in the egg in order to save himself from the plague of poachers. As to those who supplied the large illicit demand for game, a whole string of persons was corrupted. There were, to begin with, the porters at the coach offices. They were in league with the poachers and also with the guards of the night coaches, who filled the boot with contraband. Sometimes after a succession of moonlight nights there would be a glut of poached game. Then the porters exhibited a touch of humour. They took the labels off the birds which the country gentleman, in all the glory of strict legality, was sending to his friends by the mail, and attached the label to their own poached game that was no longer quite what it should have been. So the Squire's friends to his great indignation received uneatable birds and the wicked poulterer provided good ones for his customers. In short there was, though on a much smaller scale and with far fewer ramifications, a corrupt industry comparable to that of 'bootlegging' in America.

The Committee of the House in 1818 came to the conclusion that the law was thoroughly bad, and they went so far as to make a recommendation that 'all game should be the property of the person upon whose land such game should be found'. Meanwhile some members, whom we should now call 'die-hards', conceived a plan of ingenious impudence. Actually while the Committee were sitting they tried to smuggle through the House a Bill enabling magistrates at quarter sessions to convict summarily persons found by night with intent to take game and transport them for seven years. They nearly succeeded, for the title 'Rogue and Vagabond Bill' had the sound of some trivial regulation about tramps and vagrants. Luckily somebody took the trouble to read the Bill and protest. Even so it was passed subject to an alteration that gave the poacher the comparative safeguard of a jury. It was hardly to be wondered at that there were threatening letters abroad. 'Now we do swear to each other', ran one of them, 'that the first of our company that this law is inflicted on, there shall not be one gentleman's seat in our country escape the rage of fire.' In fact no country house lit up the sky with its flames, but neither was this monstrous penalty exacted, and the new Act became in effect a dead letter. Still nothing was done to remedy the law which was at the root of the trouble.

Not till thirteen years after the sitting of the House of Commons Committee was there passed the Game Act of 1831, which, amongst other things, instituted game certificates (now licences) and gave the tenant the right to kill game unless it was reserved to the landlord or his assignee. Most important of all, it allowed persons holding game certificates to sell game to persons licensed to deal. The law thus became infinitely more reasonable than it had ever had been before, but it did not stop poaching, which indeed at one time seemed to flourish more than ever. Poor old General Dyott, who was over eighty and had long suspected that the world was going to the dogs, recorded in 1843 that 'the existing game laws have done more to encourage vice amongst the lower orders than can be imagined'. Poaching did not seem to diminish and the poacher had a certain amount of sympathy, no longer because he supplied a felt want but because he was by some people invested with the glamour of a gallant outlaw as a modern Locksley. Other and much more sensible people felt for the wretched conditions of the agricultural labourers from whose ranks poachers were recruited. Kingsley was by instinct and bringing up a country gentleman, but in *Yeast* in 1851 he attacked game laws with a vigour to make dead and gone country gentlemen turn in their graves. *Tom Brown at Oxford* appeared ten years later, and here also is to be found something of the same feeling for the underdog who turns poacher half in revolt against the injustices of society. It will be remembered that Harry Winburn, who had been Tom's friend among the country boys at home and the model boy of the village, is ill used over his cottage by an overbearing landlord and is caught poaching by Tom. The reader is clearly meant to sympathize with Harry, who, by the way, afterwards reinstates himself by heroic behaviour in war. Yet Hughes was by breeding a country gentleman through and through who must in boyhood have been brought up to believe that all poachers should be hanged, drawn, and quartered.

§ 2. THE COUNTRY HOUSE

It was not only the small country gentleman, more or less immobile under the shadow of his own hills, who was

A COUNTRY HOUSE GROUP, 1855, READING THE FALL OF SEBASTOPOL

rendered uneasy by these new and tiresome things. There was also the great country gentleman who was living in a condition of feudal splendour with an immense 'stake in the country'. Of him and his glories just before the Reform Bill a countryman of Goethe's gives a picture well worth studying. This was Prince Pückler-Muskau who toured England and Ireland at the end of the 1820's and wrote four volumes of his observations. He is said to have been the original of Count Smorltork at Mrs. Leo Hunter's party, who in a visit of three weeks had collected a large book full of notes, 'music, pictures, science, potry, poltic: all tings'. An intelligent foreigner is always and no doubt rightly a ridiculous object to the British eye, and Pückler-Muskau, is now and again absurd enough, but he *was* intelligent and he wrote in many ways a genuinely amusing and interesting book.

His particular fancy was for palatial houses, their parks, and amenities. Being a gentleman of noble family with good introductions he had plenty of opportunities of indulging this taste, and even when he did not know the owners he clearly had a way with him in regard to housekeepers and bailiffs. In any case it was usually the housekeeper with whom he had to deal, for there seemed to be a fate against him; whenever he went to a house the earl always had the gout and, possibly forewarned of his visitor's intelligence by a previous victim, regretted that he could not personally show him round. He made a grand tour of houses during which he was at once wholly delighted with their beauties and half-indignant at their insolent luxury, such as even a German sovereign could not possibly afford. He started with Cassiobury, which he was told—and it was probably an under-estimate—cost £10,000 a year to keep up. Then he went on to another great Hertfordshire house, Ashridge, which was like Cassiobury in its splendours, only more so, but he very properly disliked the ugly gothic. Next he went to Woburn and this seemed the culmination of all earthly gorgeousness with its aviary and riding-school and ball-room and galleries full of statues and pictures. Nothing could be more opulent and the park was 'four German miles in circuit', but he cared no more for Woburn when he saw Warwick, which was an enchanted palace. 'Figure this to yourself,' he wrote to his unnamed female correspondent. 'Behold the whole of this magical scene at one glance;

connect with it all its associations; think that here nine centuries of haughty power, of triumphant victory and destructive overthrow,' and so on and so on. 'Is there', he ended, 'a human being so unpoetical as not to feel that the glories of such memories, even to this very day, throw a lustre around the feeblest representative of such a race?' Every drop of his own aristocratic blood tingled in sympathy, and he proceeded to make a ground plan of the Castle, specified the thicknesses of the walls and the liveries of the servants, and described a number of the Holbeins and Van Dycks at considerable length.

Warwick had spoilt him for Eaton, of which he thought little, but it had not impaired his appetite for houses. He saw four of them in one day, three of minor importance, and Blenheim to end with. Here there were forty men hard at work mowing. At Syon House there had been men mowing all day, but this was even more overpowering, and Capability Brown was the 'Shakespeare of Gardening'. He passed on to Oxford, but there was nothing quite ducal enough there, and what he seems to have liked best was a bas-relief of a knight in splendid gold-green armour made of beetles' wings. 'Our modern knights', he was tempted to remark, 'might be very handsomely represented in steel-blue armour made from the wings of the dung-beetle.' After a night's repose he travelled to Stowe, 'another specimen of English grandeur and magnificence'. He rested a short while in London and then went on to stay with Lord Darnley at Cobham. Lord Darnley had the gout but roused himself after dinner to receive the visitor, while lying on a sofa, covered with a Scotch plaid. Out of gratitude for this delicate hospitality both he and his house were only alluded to under initials in the great book.

That was the end of this particular tour, but by no means the end of the Prince's sightseeing. He would have liked to go on seeing parks for ever, but he realized that the task was a hopeless one. He calculated that the lady to whom he wrote would only be able to see a quarter of a park a day since she was averse to walking, so that 'it would take you at least four hundred and twenty years to see all the parks in England, of which there are doubtless at least a hundred thousand, for they swarm, whichever way you turn your steps'. Doubtless there were not so many and the

A COUNTRY HOUSE GROUP, *c.* 1860

magnificence went sometimes a little to his head, but, allowing for exaggeration, it was a good time for the grand seigneur, who lived in a style of almost regal splendour, so well satisfied with himself and England that 'even the least of lords in the bottom of his heart thinks himself a greater man than the King of France'. It could not go on, the Prince thought; the owner of Blenheim with seventy thousand a year was so much in debt that the property had to be administered by his creditors. It would be the same with them all sooner or later, and the Prince gave them only a few more years, but the glory survived longer than he expected.

Whether the country gentleman lived in a palace or whether he lived merely in the best house in the village which carried with it the title of Squire, life was arranged on much the same plan though on very varying scales. Breakfast, unless there was something particular afoot, was at an easy-going hour, very likely approaching ten o'clock with the ladies of the household to do the honours for any guests. It was a formidable meal, with eggs as a rule for the hot course, but rounds of cold meat as the real backbone and foundation. It was eaten leisurely with plenty of cups of tea and prolonged by a reading of the newspapers. A solid, uncompromising, inelegant meal it was, with this justification that its effects had to last some time. After it the men went out to their sport or to their business. There was the library for writing letters and the justice room for any magistrates' business. If they had luncheon it was usually in the brief and manly form of sandwiches. The luncheon that was served in the house was for the ladies who, it was sometimes hinted, liked to affect only a slender appetite at dinner and had to lay their plans accordingly. The men were no more seen till some half an hour before dinner, when the company assembled in their evening dress. After dinner the men drank as much wine as they wanted and then went in search of tea, coffee, and ladies. Thus reassembled the company spent several hours together. Our German Prince, with a passion for detail for which we cannot be too grateful, observed carefully what every one was doing one evening after dinner at Cobham.

'Our suffering host lay on the sofa, dozing a little; five ladies and gentlemen were very attentively reading in various sorts of books (of this number I was one, having some views of parks before me); another had been playing for a quarter of an hour with a long-suffering dog; two old members of Parliament were disputing violently about the "Corn Bill"; and the rest of the company were in a dimly-lighted room adjoining, where a pretty girl was playing on the piano-forte, and another, with a most perforating voice, singing ballads.'

At last the *Keepsake*, the *Book of Beauty*, and *Forget-me-not* had been exhausted; the ladies went to bed, and a little before midnight came a further alleviation; a light supper of cold meat and fruit appeared. Everybody helped himself to what he wanted and then to one of a row of small candlesticks, and so to bed amid chintz curtains and under an enormous canopy.

Another entertaining account of the country-house life of splendid idleness was written by a Mr. Willis, an American journalist who went on a visit to the Duke of Richmond at Gordon Castle. It is to be found in Howitt's *Rural Life of England*. He was in transports over the kindness and civility of his host and hostess and everybody else, though he sometimes felt a little guilty because he was happier in this private paradise than if he had been amid the open and more democratic beauties of his native land. Happy he certainly was, since with 'the whole visible horizon fenced in for the enjoyment of a household of which I was a temporary portion, and no enemy except time and the gout, I felt as if I had been spirited into some castle of felicity and had not come by the royal mail coach at all'.

There were always at least thirty people at the Castle during his stay and a constant and unobtrusive melting away of guests to be almost mysteriously replaced by new ones. It was at dinner that he first met the house party and dinner was at seven o'clock. There was a band which played until the ladies left the dining-room. Then the 'gentlemen closed up, conversation assumed a merrier cast, coffee and liqueurs were brought in when the wines began to be circulated more slowly'. It was not till eleven that a move was made to the drawing-room. 'Cards, tea, music, filled up the time till twelve, and then the ladies took their departure, and the gentlemen sat down to supper.'

Mr. Willis did not go to bed till two and was late next morning, finding a large party already assembled. He was

A COUNTRY HOUSE GROUP, *c.* 1860

struck with the contrast to the night before—no servants to wait, no smartness, no jewels, the men in fustian coats and hob-nailed shoes and an almost unbroken silence: 'the ten or twelve noblemen present were engrossed with their letters or their newspapers over tea and toast.—Nothing could be more easy, unceremonious and affable than the whole tone of the meal.'

Between breakfast and lunch the ladies were more or less invisible, going off for walks in the park by themselves: the men went to shooting or to billiards, and Mr. Willis himself was taken on a solemn visit to the kennels. At two came luncheon—'a dish or two of hot game and a profusion of cold meats were set on the small tables in the dining-room, and everybody came in for a kind of lounging half-meal, which occupied perhaps an hour.' Then to the drawing-room under the windows of which there had been magically assembled a vast array of carriages 'with grooms, outriders, footmen, and saddle-horses'. Parties were made up and off they went, and wherever they went there were gates to fly open and a general touching of hats 'with the delightful consciousness that, speed where you would, the horizon scarce limited the possession of your host'. It all sounds and no doubt was delightful. Well might Howitt rapturously exclaim: 'Let every man who has a sufficiency for the enjoyment of life, thank heaven most fervently that he lives in this country and age.'

§ 3. THE GARDEN

In his account of this gorgeous paradise Mr. Willis said nothing of the garden and very likely he did not see one, for the 'flower garden' is to this day in Scottish country houses apt to be tucked far away out of sight of the house.

In any case the country gentleman was not as a rule what we should call to-day 'a great gardener'. His predecessors had probably been more interested in this subject than he was, for Cobbett, who had started life as a garden boy in Surrey, said in 1835 that 'the taste for making pretty gardens had been declining in England for a great many years'. If he was a big country gentleman those predecessors had probably been swayed by a series of fashions and so passed on his estate to him, bearing traces of the various tastes of successive generations.

His ancestor, for instance, of the early eighteenth century had liked everything extremely formal and rectangular, but he had also liked a view. In front of his house had been formal parterres and clipped alleys. Farther on he had caused to be made through the park and the woods radiating glades, vistas, and avenues. If he was a Duke it might even be that his neighbours had obsequiously cut and trimmed their property, as the late Mr. Avray Tipping said in *English Gardens*, 'to humour his vistas'. The great Mr. Pope and Mr. Addison had laughed at this geometrical beauty and unsettled the country gentleman in his mind. Then there had come the ingenious Mr. William Kent, who made everything 'elegant and antique' and, as Horace Walpole said, 'perfectly classic'. Our country gentleman of 1835 may have possessed certain relics of Kent and his school, perhaps a little neglected and the worse for wear, a cascade silted up with dead leaves, or a figure of Pan grown green and mossy. It is more likely, however, that the estate bore marks of Capability Brown or one of his imitators.

Brown had professed to copy Nature, but he had done it in an extremely regular and methodical way and had grown as mannered as an Academy painter who has yearly to produce sheep or soldiers or birch trees and a pool. 'With Brown', says Mr. Tipping, 'avenues merely gave way to clumps and belts, canals to serpentines, straight paths to winding walks, terrace parterre and labyrinth to tree-dotted lawns that carried their undulations up to the drawing-room windows.' Much of what Brown had done survived, perhaps with some additions made by those who thought that he was a trifle dull and did not sufficiently appeal to the emotions. So there may have been a romantic rock or a ruined and ivy-clad castle; or even a sham church spire to produce sentiments of rustic tranquillity. Repton had followed Brown, and many of the works remained, but the early Victorian owner, if he was interested in the matter, had begun a little to revolt against the 'landscapists'. He thought perhaps that the park and the trees had encroached too far and that, at least close to the house, something in the older and more formal style was becoming. A new sort of parterre was invented 'with annuals and greenhouse plants'. In the late fifties and sixties there arose Eden Nesfield, who not only built houses and designed furniture but also designed gardens.

SHRUBLAND PARK
Garden by BARRY

He was a gentleman by birth, for his father had been at Winchester and he at Eton, and so he could presumably dictate to his clients as man to man. He made them have large formal gardens with coloured sand, and elaborately cut box and parterres, full of symmetrical and—one may venture to add—hideous curleywigs.

What was in the greenhouse was, however, often regarded as more important than what was outside it. There was a decided taste for anything that was rare, tender, and exotic. There was a certain Mr. T. James who lived somewhat before his time and lamented bitterly that the true gardener's art was forgotten in the cultivation of the mango and the mangosteen, of anything in short that was strange. 'To be the possessor', he wrote, 'of a unique pansy, the introducer of a new specimen of the Orchidaceae, or the cultivator of 500 choice varieties of the dahlia, is now the only claim to gardening celebrity.'

Now and again there was a country gentleman who not only disliked Capability Brown but formal parterres as well and longed for what Mr. James had called 'the real beauty and poetry of a garden'. There was, for instance, Mr. Edward Hussey of Scotney Castle in Kent. He had come into his kingdom as a boy of ten in 1817, and when he was grown up he became a disciple of Sir Uvedale Price, who had hated the landscape gardeners and written against them. So he made those then very rare things—a wild garden and a rock garden. He had not many followers. People were seldom genuinely fond of plants and flowers, and the shapes of the flower beds were more important than what was in them. Any real revolution in favour of wild and natural gardens, as we know them to-day, did not break out till some time after 1865.

These remarks apply mainly to the big country gentleman who could have a big garden and spend money on it. The smaller man was more fortunate in that his garden had remained comparatively untouched. Even if he had the money his ancestor had not as a rule had the space to try 'landscaping' antics. Consequently the small Victorian garden was still much as it had been for years: the pleasant old sheltering walls remained and the cut hedges, and the owner walked to a point by the direct way and did not have to meander down a serpentine path. Flowers had played the most secondary part in big gardens, but the care and the love of them survived, to some extent at least, in small ones. One may doubt whether garden owners were often so passionately attached to them as they are to-day, whether they thought of their flowers not merely as individuals but as dear friends. Were there many people who, like the ladies of Llangollen (they were to be sure a little early for our period), not only supervised but took part in the work in their gardens? It is difficult to say, but the novels of the time have not much to say about gardens. Though the date is too early it is pleasing to recall that Mr. Collins worked in his rectory garden, that it was one of the 'most respectable pleasures' and his wife wisely encouraged him in it. But did anybody garden in George Eliot? Dorothea was too busy over good works and good cottages and would perhaps have thought caring for flowers almost as bad as caring for jewels. One cannot remember any gardeners in Dickens, but Laura Bell was wearing a pinafore and gauntlets as she worked among the rose bushes when Arthur Pendennis proposed to her. Sergeant Cuff, the detective in *The Moonstone,* used to argue with Lady Verinder's gardener about roses, and no doubt there are other instances, but generally speaking gardening plays a greater part in modern novels or for that matter in to-day's *Punch* than it did in the early Victorian era. It was an era not of flowers but of the rolling of gravel walks.

§ 4. COUNTRY SOCIETY

The ecstatic Howitt was, as we have seen, more optimistic about the English country gentleman than Pückler-Muskau, and his judgement proved the sounder, for the good days lasted much longer than the German prophet had foretold and became even more golden and unruffled so that they seemed likely to see the very stars out. The agitations of reform bills and corn laws passed, and at the end of our period the country gentleman reached perhaps his zenith. He was in himself a better man, more cultivated, more interested in public affairs, more anxious to do his duty. Public schools and railroads had helped to take him away from his own valley and to widen his mind. There were more men of the type of Philip Pusey, who, while a member of Parliament, a fellow of the Royal Society, a friend of the leading thinkers and public men of the day, yet found time to be an agriculturist of an extremely practical kind and an admirable landlord who built better cottages for his tenants.

With the improvement in the squire there kept pace an improvement in the parson. The country parson early in the century had often been a gentleman of very good family, since that is what family livings were made for, but on the whole he had hardly risen to the occasion. Perhaps the hunting parson looms disproportionately large in the memoirs of his time. Sometimes no doubt he was an excellent man, but those of whom we hear were not wholly creditable. There was the one, for instance, in Osbaldeston's autobiography, who, when dining in a lady's house, passed the Squire a note under the table, telling him that their hostess was his mistress and giving him some extremely odd evidence to that effect. He was perhaps an exceptional parson, but there were many who, when they had a fall into a brook, need not be rescued because they would not be wanted till Sunday. Such, we may imagine, were two who hunted with the Duke of Beaufort in Nimrod's day—the Rev. John Wallers, who was 'the hardest old man in England', and the Rev. 'Zack' Taylor, 'a very fine horseman but perhaps somewhat too convivial in his tastes'. There were plenty of spiritual descendants of Bute Crawley. There seems something priggish in condemning them, but they cannot have been very good clergymen and on the whole their successors were better. As time went on probably fewer younger sons went as a matter of course into the Church, and as clergymen became less genteel they grew apparently better at their work. Moreover, public opinion turned gradually against their laxities, sometimes to a ridiculous extent. In the early days of archery we hear of a parson who excelled at it and yet had to give it up to placate his parishioners. By way of compensation he indulged in leaping, but secretly as if it were a sin. He may have taken his parishioners too seriously, for the great Thring of Uppingham played football with his sixth form and held that his dignity would suffer no more than his shins.

Thus between 1850, let us say, and 1865 we have a better gentry and clergy and at any rate less audible growlings of chartists and rebellious persons. Never had the great or the little country kingdoms seemed so stable and so prosperous.

Life was a long tranquil sunshiny afternoon, not wholly idle, but with pleasant duties to be performed towards well-affected vassals. Of the great kings it would be hard to find a better sample than the eighth Duke of Beaufort, whose life has been written. The picture of Badminton in his early days is at once gorgeous and idyllic. He was pre-eminently a country gentleman and lived on his own land among his own neighbours. He was master of his famous pack; he farmed on a large scale practically and with real knowledge; he had a flock of Southdown sheep and showed them and took prizes; he did good work in stock-raising and horse-breeding all round Badminton. Over his hunt he ruled undisputed but as generously as he did splendidly, like a kindly god stepping down from Olympus. It was said that the hunt was 'a sort of open-air club' where 'every one could do what he pleased save to ride over the hounds'. Everything was at the Duke's expense and he alone could confer the honour of the blue and buff uniform. His coach drove to the meet loaded with his friends and guests. His children all hunted, though not, as they explained to a visitor, more than three times a week till they were five years old. Everywhere hospitality and friendliness reigned: tenants were content and respectful, servants adoring. Royalty was royally entertained. Everything was as it should be, and everything was going on in the same way for ever and ever.

The Duke lived more than long enough to know the hard times of agriculture, but the early days of his reign were spent in perhaps the best times of all. He came to his throne in 1853 and thus escaped a spell of uncomfortable years. After the Corn Laws came a period of depression for agriculturists and this was made worse by the commercial depression which in 1847 followed the pricking of the railway speculation bubble. In 1849 and 1850 the price of wheat sagged down and down, and farmers who only paid their men seven shillings a week were threatening to reduce even these wages. Landlords refused in general to reduce rents and farms were thrown back on their hands. Of 5,000 acres belonging to the Duke of Marlborough most were left derelict, for the Duke would grant no abatement and the farmers fled. All forms of ruin and disaster were prophesied, and yet in a few years everything was bounding upward again. Trade revived, the price of corn went up, and with the Crimean War, which began in 1854, farmers began to make fortunes. There was now and then a falling off, but, says Traill's *Social England*, 'Taking all things into consideration, the period of ten years ending with 1862 was probably the most prosperous decade ever enjoyed by British agriculturists'.

Nine years out of those ten were the first nine years of the Duke of Beaufort's reign. No wonder that Badminton was happy and glorious, and country gentlemen everywhere were basking, according to their degrees, in the same sunshine. Moreover, they were, most of them, doing their best to deserve success. The alarming though temporary drop in prices before 1850 had roused agriculturists from lethargy and urged them to drain and otherwise improve their land. There was a steady and striking advance in agricultural machinery; good work was done in breeding; farmers' clubs grew and flourished, discussed interesting questions and extracted a grudging imitation if not approval from those who hated new-fangled ways. Only at the very end of our period between 1862 and 1865 was there a real set-back with the coming of the cattle plague and a serious drop in prices. It took more than three years, however, for any writing on the wall to stand out in unmistakable letters, and, as one small example of complacency, the Duke of Beaufort, who had to all intents and purposes given up racing for some years, took to it again in 1870 and was extremely successful. So in 1865 the world seemed still to be going very well for the country gentleman. No creepy, sunset breeze had yet begun to chill the long golden afternoon.

SPORT

In the world of Sport the Georgian era had been rich in resplendent figures. When George IV died the great men were growing old and there seemed for the moment few to succeed them. In 1830 there must have been many illustrious contemporaries each of whom thought of all the others that they were not quite the men they had been.

It was now twenty-one years since Captain Barclay Allardyce had walked his thousand miles in a thousand hours on Newmarket Heath. He could still, and for years afterwards, lift a full-grown man on to a dinner-table with one hand, but his zenith was passed; he was over fifty years old. And what had befallen the master had almost befallen the man. Tom Cribb, whom Barclay had trained to beat the black menace Molyneaux, was forty-nine and had long since left the ring. He had been allowed to call himself Champion as long as he lived and now held his court in his own bar parlour at the 'Union Arms' in Panton Street. Tom Spring, his successor, had retired too, to the 'Castle' in Holborn. John Gully, two years younger than Cribb, had cut away the inn-keeping rung of the ladder and, like John Jackson, had 'practically realized the position of a gentleman'. Two years later he was to win £85,000 on the Derby and the St. Leger, and become member for Pontefract. He had almost forgotten how he had beaten Gregson, the fight seemed so far away, and perhaps he thought pityingly sometimes of two other young men who had come out of Bristol, Jem Belcher and the Game Chicken, dead long ago. They had drunk and had not looked after their money as he had—but there were no such men in the ring nowadays.

The heroes of the hunting field had a longer run for their money, and George Osbaldeston, one of the two greatest of them all, was still Master of the Pytchley and had yet before him his ride of 200 miles on Newmarket Heath, and his victory over Dick Christian in the match between Clasher and Clinker. He was, however, nearly forty-five and his cricket and his rowing were done. Assheton Smith, of whose even mightier fame Osbaldeston had always been a little jealous, was older; he was fifty-four but still hunted his own hounds four days a week in Hampshire. Jack Mytton ought to have been almost at his best, for he was only thirty-four, but he had tried himself too high, the splendours of Halston were past, and he was on the eve of flitting from his creditors to Calais. Of all the great ones only Captain Horatio Ross, pigeon shot and walker and steeplechase rider (although Osbaldeston said he rode like a tailor), was really young. He was twenty-nine, with thirty years ahead of him, before he made the best score for Scotland in the first Elcho Shield at Wimbledon.

Then take cricket, in a comparatively small way as yet. Mr. Gully had by the way at one time taken an interest in it, when the bookmakers stood outside the pavilion at Lord's, but somehow he had never managed to get the hang of the game or had thought horses safer to bet about than men. Cricket was not quite what it had been. The immortal

Beldham was sixty-six now and that was too old even for him. The perhaps even greater Lambert had been warned off Lord's thirteen years since for selling a match at Nottingham and, though he could still make plenty of runs round Reigate, he was over fifty. David Harris was long dead, and Lord Frederick Beauclerk, who said that David's bowling was the grandest thing he had ever seen, had put his bat away after thirty-five seasons. He was now a respectable clergyman at St. Albans and only watched at Lord's, where he was exceedingly autocratic. William Lillywhite was making cricket history by his still illegal round arm bowling, but his fame had not yet reached its zenith. Certainly there were fine cricketers, but the stage was an intermediate one; the glory of Hambledon had departed and the sun of Kent had not quite risen; it was two years before Alfred Mynn was to appear at Lord's. The North was as yet inconsiderable.

At just about this time of change and vacant thrones there was setting out for his first school one who was destined to preach a new and different gospel of open-air glory. In 1831 Tom Hughes went with his brother to a small boys' school at Twyford to be prepared for Rugby. Probably Tom Hughes read his Bell's *Life* and admired those of whom it told him, but, if we imagine him in 1831 a grown man, he would have looked on those heroes with different eyes. He would not have thought them good examples for English boys ('God bless their bright faces and kind hearts' he might have added) and would have called many of the things they did 'low and blackguard'. And the aggravating part of it is that in many respects that great and aggravating man would have been right. When the First Gentleman in Europe died, the standard of sporting morality among English gentlemen was, as we should now regard it, a low one, and we who love our ancient heroes can only say that these things all depend on the point of view.

'Large sums could have been won by backing Rattler to trot one mile under three minutes, as he could do it in two-and-a-half minutes; but Jackson let the cat out of the bag and could not make matches for the horse.' That sentence in George Osbaldeston's autobiography about the trotter Tom Thumb is indicative of the spirit of the age. The chief thing was to make a match and to make money. Osbaldeston was, according to the famous Mr. Budd, 'a noble fellow, always straight'; he was one of the bravest as he was one of the most soft-hearted of men, and I do not believe he ever did a thing which he thought unworthy of a gentleman, but according to our views he did some very odd things. He deliberately pulled a horse in one race in order that he might win another, and he did not in the least mind letting that cat out of the bag. He said he had done it to show the handicappers and their friends that he had seen through them, and that what was sauce for the goose was sauce for the gander. His only concern was that his closest friend, whom he had trusted to put the money on, had got the best odds for himself and not for George Osbaldeston.

In that case the Squire pushed matters perhaps to extremes, but if a few straight-laced and arrogant persons thought a little the worse of him, he did not think the worse of himself. Life for the sporting man consisted in backing himself or his side. Honour and glory were all very well, and doubtless all Hampshire hearts were with little Hambledon when they met All England, but Mr. Dehaney and Squire Paulet, who had founded the club, had got their money on it, and sometimes they hedged and laid their money on the other side. It was an age of match making and of play or pay. It was the other man's business to understand the terms of the match; if he did not grasp all their possibilities, so much the worse for him. If he betted that he could drive a coach and its passengers, then the passengers could be the twenty largest available Life Guardsmen. If he was ill in bed when the day came there was nothing to do but pay. No quarter was given or expected. It was a simple code clearly understood by all parties. It is arguable that it was the best possible code, because it left no room for doubt or dispute. Yet in some unaccountable way disputes did arise. They were always arising, and some of the most famous matches between gentlemen of the most unquestioned honour were left drawn because nobody could agree as to who had won them.

There were no finicking notions about amateurism to complicate the issue. Captain Barclay ran a long distance race against the best professional of the day, Abraham Wood, and ran him 'off his legs'. Osbaldeston played single wicket against professionals and rowed races with and against Thames watermen. A clergyman and the son of a Duke confessed that he reckoned on making £600 a year out of his cricket. It sounds beautifully simple, a perfect age of innocence, and yet somehow or other things that ought not to have happened did happen; there were always people who did not know exactly where the line should be drawn.

Pückler-Muskau probably overstated the case when he said that 'cheating in every kind of sport was as common in England as false play was in the time of the Count de Grammont'; but anybody who reads the history of sport in early Victorian England must, however regretfully, grasp the fact that the sporting morals of our ancestors were not quite those that we like to believe our own to-day.

Future historians of the nineteenth century will no doubt lay great stress on the popularity attained by games and athletic sports, of the public interest taken in them, the big crowds assembled to watch them, and the ever-increasing space given to them in the newspapers. For the most part, however, they will devote their attention to the last quarter of the century and our period will play a comparatively small part. At the beginning of that period and, generally speaking, even at the end of it games and athletics were, to a large extent, what some people think they ought essentially to be. That is they were comparatively unorganized, local and rough and ready in character, with but little money spent on them. Naturally as means of travel improved, so both players and onlookers could go farther afield, and rivalry became possible between other than near neighbours. Yet even in 1865 the great tide of popularity had not begun to surge, and of the pursuits which to-day bring the biggest crowds and fill the most columns, some were still inchoate, and though old in years yet practically in their infancy, while others did not exist.

We may take as a starting-point the five pastimes which are still regarded as giving the most cherished blues at the University. They are almost beyond cavil, cricket, the two footballs, rowing, and athletics. In case this appears disrespectful to a number of others, let us first say a brief and propitiatory word about those others and clear them out of the way. It must be remembered that in 1865 golf was, save for Blackheath, a purely Scottish game, and lawn tennis had not yet sprung into the ingenious mind of Major

Wingfield. Tennis, a noble game of illustrious ancestry, was confined to a small circle by the fewness of its courts, and the same may be said of rackets. Tennis had produced in France the ever famous Barre, who remained a great player for an incredible number of years, and he was something more than a local celebrity. Fives had had its Cavanagh, deemed worthy to be made immortal by Hazlitt, and rackets had had its moments through the circumstance of being played in the yards of debtors' prisons. In 1832 Pierce Egan could enumerate several players of fame, the two Pittmans, Tom and John, who were at least unofficial professional champions, a certain Major Campbell who had attained to almost professional skill through fourteen years of imprisonment, and a one-eyed man, name unknown, who would 'contend against any man in England playing under his leg'. In the Fleet a debtor, by name Hoskins, who like Mr. Pickwick would not pay a debt on principle, was called the Racket Master, and, in what Egan called the 'swellish times', young sprigs would entertain their friends who came to see them in prison with an exhibition of rackets.

All this did not amount to much. Yet, as regards popular fame, these games were far ahead of football, for the history of football is at once very venerable and very modern. Football as essentially a game of the people went back into the mists of time for at least five centuries, but it was not so much a regular game as one to be played during some particular holiday or jollification, like the backsword play and wrestling at the 'veast' in *Tom Brown*. Such was the match at Corfe Castle played on Shrove Tuesday and Ash Wednesday, from Corfe to Owre Quarry, in which every one joined in the fray and at the same time maintained an ancient right of way for the Marblers of Purbeck. There were several such contests, generally taking place on festival days of the Church, but by the nineteenth century they had become interesting survivals rather than sporting events, and cheerful free fights rather than matches under any ascertainable code.

Football had been, though by no means universally, adopted by schools, presumably both because the boys had seen it in their country homes and because it is so obvious and natural a game as to spring unbidden into being. Every school had its own variety of the game, not from any excessive thought devoted to the matter but because it was a game for the playground, and playgrounds varied in size and shape. The ball, as we know from *Tom Brown*, used to hang round the Three Trees, as it still hangs round the Wall at Eton. In the old rustic fighting games collaring and carrying the ball had been allowed, and if it ceased to be allowed in most of the school games it was only because it was dangerous to limbs and clothes. Therefore incidentally when William Webb Ellis, 'legibus splendide spretis', first ran with the ball at Rugby he was not so much an innovator as an unconscious reviver.

In the forties and fifties there came an increase in school games because there was a great increase in public schools. Marlborough, Cheltenham, Radley, Lancing, and Rossall were founded in the forties, Wellington and Bradfield in the fifties, Malvern and Clifton in the sixties. Some of them had strong leanings towards a particular model, notably Marlborough, which began with a great feeling for Arnold and Rugby traditions. This would no doubt make for some similarity in football rules but the game was still in each case a domestic one. Old boys from a particular school naturally enjoyed an occasional bout of their particular game when they went on to the University, just as Old Etonians to-day still play their Field Game at Cambridge; but the first formal club of grown-up men to play football did not exist till 1858, when some old Rugbeians and old boys from Blackheath School founded the Blackheath Club. Sheffield had a club playing in 1860 its own peculiar rules, which lasted for nearly twenty years afterwards. In 1863 the carriers and the dribblers, the Rugbeians and the Football Association, definitely split, but it may be said that it was not till 1870 that football became definitely more than a school game, and it was not till some time after that year that it became a game of the people. The upper and middle classes in the shape of the schools borrowed the game from the people, and in the end the people took their own game back again, but the far-reaching victory of the working men of Blackburn Olympic over the Old Etonians in the Association Cup is much too late for us here. In short, football as a national game does not belong to early Victorian England.

The story of foot-racing and athletic sports runs on lines not dissimilar. Foot-racing is of course as old as the world, but it is comparatively modern as an amusement in which large numbers of people take part. All through the nineteenth century there were periodical outbreaks of matches between professional runners, and sometimes the amateurs took fire from their example. They made matches against each other for money, and if they were good enough, against the professionals also. 'An amateur meant a gentleman', says Sir John Astley, 'whether he ran for money or honour or both,' and he himself was running matches in the fifties against any one he could find to meet him. He went to Spain and challenged any man in Madrid at 100 yards. He stayed with a friend in Norfolk and sent a message into Norwich, that he would run any one in the town for £5. He took about as a retainer a pedestrian known as the Flying Tailor, and the two would practise together, taking care to beat each other alternately 'lest people should know too much'.

This, however, was 'pedestrianism', which had its own heading in Bell's *Life* in 1838: it was not amateur 'athletics', which did not exist till 1850 and did not flourish till some time later. The Crick Run at Rugby was founded in 1837 and, as we know from *Tom Brown,* there had been Big Side Hare and Hounds before that; but except for one solitary and abortive meeting at Sandhurst in 1812, the credit for the first Sports belongs to some undergraduates of Exeter College, Oxford, who held the Exeter Autumn Meeting in 1850. This was about the time when pedestrianism was at its height. George Frost, the Suffolk Stag, one of Sir John Astley's stable, was winning races before great crowds, when it paid him to do so. He may have been the inspiration of the Exeter meeting, but the form of the programme, in which nearly all the races were called sweepstakes, was rather on horsy lines. It may be studied in the late Sir Montague Shearman's most entertaining historical chapter in the Badminton book. Woolwich began at the same time, Harrow three years later, and then followed several colleges at Oxford and Cambridge. About 1860 there came the Volunteer Movement. There had been the Indian Mutiny, the country had been denuded of troops, France was hostile, and there was a patriotic panic. Within a few months 120,000 men were raised and Lord Elcho revived in the National Rifle Association the ancient pastime of practising at the butts.

A SPORTING HANDKERCHIEF

Large bodies of young men thus associated may well have looked about for new ways to amuse and exercise themselves. The feats of the famous Deerfoot were just causing another running 'boom' and sports naturally suggested themselves. The Honourable Artillery Company had already held a meeting in 1858, and in 1862 we hear of the first Open Meeting, though it seems that a certain suspicion still hung over the track, for the amateurs frequently ran under assumed names. In 1863 the Mincing Lane Athletic Club was formed, the first of its kind; in 1864 came the first Inter-University Sports and the Civil Service Sports. The fire quickly spread to the provinces and two years after 1865 there were over a hundred meetings held in the year. More or less as in the case of football the end of early Victorian England synchronized with the beginning of Athletic Sports.

The situation of cricket in 1830 was a very different one from that of any other of the games which are to-day so popular. It had already got a firm hold on certain parts of England, not merely as a spectacle in which celebrated players took part but as one of the active amusements of the people. John Nyren had written the best book that ever was or ever will be written about cricketers. Seven years later the Rev. James Pycroft was to go down into Hampshire with Nyren's book and Mr. Mitford's manuscript in his pocket and 'his inkhorn at his button' in order to talk to old Beldham of past Hambledon glories and thus begin the labours which culminated in 'The Cricket Field'.

Moreover, just about 1830 the game was passing through a political crisis. In 1822 Mr. John Willes, who had revived the almost forgotten 'throwing bowling' of Tom Walker, had mounted his horse in a huff and ridden out of Lord's ground and out of cricket history, but a much greater than he had taken up the struggle on behalf of round arm. William Lillywhite, the 'Nonpareil', with the 'foxheaded' Broadbridge at the other end, was tacitly breaking the law by raising his hand to the height of his shoulder, whereas the rules allowed only the height of the elbow. Sussex could beat England with these two great and lawless pioneers to help it: the umpires said nothing, with the general sympathy of the public, and it was clear that another concession by the Marylebone pundits must come. And here it may be mentioned, out of chronological order, that the end of our period was destined to see the final liberation of the bowler. In 1862 another dauntless Lillywhite deliberately tried to force a decision by 'no balling' Edgar Willsher at the Oval, and two years later the triumph of overhand was open and complete.

To return to the general popularity of the game: what Mr. Pycroft wrote of it, as it was in 1800, was probably still true, without emendation, in 1830. 'Cricket had become the common pastime of the common people in Hampshire, Surrey, Sussex, and Kent, and had been introduced into the adjoining counties, and though we cannot trace its continuity beyond Rutlandshire and Burley Park, certainly it had been long familiar to the men of Leicester and Nottingham as well as Sheffield.' In the southern counties named it was everybody's game, probably more so than it is now. Quite apart from the grand matches there were constant tussles between parishes and great local rivalry. In the north it had not yet reached the same position. Nottingham had always had some good cricketers, and there were occasional big matches for big money in which famous southerners exhibited themselves, but these were played in towns and cricket was not yet a village game as in the south.

Miss Mitford began to write her experiences of *Our Village* in 1819. She lived between Reading and Basingstoke and, though it treats of a time just a little too early, her book probably gives a sufficiently exact as it certainly does a most engaging picture of a village cricket match.

'I doubt', she wrote, 'if there be any scene in the world more animating or delightful than a cricket match. I don't mean a set match at Lord's for money, hard money, between a certain number of gentlemen and players, as they are called—people who make a trade of that noble sport and degrade it into an affair of bettings and hedgings and cheatings; nor do I mean a pretty fête in a gentleman's park, where one club of cricketing dandies encounters another such club and where they show off in graceful costume to a gay marquee of admiring belles.—No! the cricket I mean is a real, solid, old-fashioned match between neighbouring parishes, where each attacks the other for honour and a supper, for glory and half a crown. If there be any gentlemen among them it is well; if not it is so much the better. Here and there, indeed, one meets with an old Etonian who retains his English love for that game which formed so considerable a part of his education; some even preserve their boyish proficiency; but in general it wears away like the Greek, quite as certainly and almost as fast. A few years of Oxford and Cambridge or the Continent are sufficient to annihilate both the power and the inclination. No! a village match is the thing where our highest officer or conductor—to borrow a musical item—is but a little farmer's second son; where a day labourer is our bowler and a blacksmith our long stop—where laughing and shouting and the very ecstacy of good humour prevail.'

That passage is worth quoting not merely for its own sake but because it gives in more than one respect a good general view of cricket at the beginning of our time. For one thing it had been played too much for 'hard money', and there had been a series of unpleasant revelations. Matches had been bought and sold outrageously. By 1830 things had decidedly improved, but this had been due not to virtue but to the fact that 'the rogues had spoilt their own market'.

Again, Miss Mitford's rather bitter remarks about gentlemen cricketers had some foundation. Eton and Harrow had played their match, not quite uninterruptedly, since Byron's time, and the Universities had begun, broken off, and then begun again at Mr. Pycroft's instigation. There were and had been one or two really fine gentlemen players such as Lord Frederick Beauclerk, Mr. Budd, and Mr. Ward, but as a rule the gentlemen were not skilful enough for the best company, and the backbone of good cricket as of village cricket was the countryman, the genuine rustic player of whom Beldham said, 'It was easy to tell the Kent boys as they came staring into the Green Man'.

It must not be thought that the gentlemen did not play, for they did at any rate at school. There was the Wellesburn match and the Marylebone match at Rugby in Tom Brown's day. In the forties at Eton there were three school matches against Westminster, Winchester, and Harrow; what is more, there was a fourth-form club of lower boys, and one of the Eleven used regularly to go and watch the game in search of talent; but the game seems to have been uncommonly casual. Everybody knows the passage in *Tom Brown* describing how Tom, the Captain of the Eleven, does not know the batting order in which he has written down his own team, how he changes it to let the swiper, Jack Raggles, go in, and how Jack waves his bat to the assembled company. In Mr. A. D. Coleridge's *Eton in the Forties* is told the story of a real scene rather similar. Eton and Winchester were playing at Lord's and at a crucial moment the last Winchester man came in. Macniven, known as Snivey, afterwards a famous Cambridge batsman and a great character, was fielding at long slip, and as the nervous batsman approached he roared at the top of his voice, 'Hullo, 'ere comes Jones Bateman, to get thirty runs; I know's I shall catch him out, as 'ow his brother boards at Mrs. Ward's.' The process of reasoning was peculiar, although it proved perfectly sound, but not so peculiar as the standard of behaviour, judged by the scrupulous silence and solemnity of a modern match.

Cricket had not yet become solemn. Mr. Coleridge states, half defiant and half ashamed, that in his day at Eton waves of enthusiasm for more childish pursuits such as tops, leaping poles, and cross-bars would for a time put the noses of serious games out of joint. Sir John Astley at about the same time would at once be playing cricket in Sixpenny and spending much time on the river, as well as chasing the deer and dodging the keepers in Windsor Park.

Charles Box, in describing the glories of Kent in its greatest days—in the thirties and forties—emphasizes the fact that the gentlemen were hardly good enough.

> 'It has been repeatedly said that a young amateur from a public school or university would grow inches if he had the honour to be asked to play in a county match; but not the wealth of the Indies, or the interest of both Houses of Parliament put together, would have gained him admission into the county ranks, unless he could pass muster with the experienced hands who had charge of the management. It was no joke to miss a ball, much less a catch, with the Kentish yeomen watching and backing their county. The wealthy and well-to-do found the money and guaranteed each match and the honour of the county was usually entrusted to Alfred Mynn, Felix, Pilch, Wenman, or men of such a stamp.'

Felix was a schoolmaster and a man of education; but Pilch was a village tailor, Wenman a village carpenter, and Mynn a yeoman farmer.

The Players in the nature of things will always, year in and year out, be better than the Gentlemen, but the farther we go back the greater seems the disparity. Tom Hughes regretted that the Rugby boys after his time had had a professional coach. When this became the usual course at public schools schoolboys would obviously improve and no doubt they did.

The foundation of the I Zingari in 1845 was a sign of

amateur enthusiasm, but a more far-reaching event a year later was the birth of the first All England Eleven under William Clarke. Here was a cricket evangelist who spread the gospel on business lines. His team was made up of the best professionals of the day with an occasional amateur (the great Mynn played in the opening match at Sheffield), and in the course of its first three years it visited about forty different districts, playing as a rule matches against local twenty-twos. After a few years there was a quarrel and some of the players broke away and formed on the same lines the United All-England Eleven. There was room for both if not for some further imitators who soon collapsed, and these two teams, regularly touring the country in their check shirts and billycock hats, fired enthusiasm and raised the standard of play. To play against one of the Elevens was the height of ambition, to withstand an over or two or to take a wicket was to make a local cricketer 'only a little lower than the angels'. It is all summed up in John Leech's picture of the pride of the village coming home with a black eye and an arm in a sling to utter the famous words beginning, 'I had a hover of Jackson'. The two rival sides so far composed their differences after a time as to meet in an annual match which was *the* match of the year: they were still flourishing in 1865, so much so that in that year a third, and this time a serious, rival sprang up in the United South of England Eleven.

These were the players who were talked about in the fifties and early sixties, but meanwhile, in a Gloucestershire orchard, there was being played a quiet serious family game destined to be of far greater import. Here there practised daily a local doctor and his sons and his brother-in-law, with a mother and sisters to look on and lend a hand in the fielding. The sound of their strokes among the Downend apple trees, the barks of delight of that immortal trinity, Don, Ponto, and Noble as they rushed to retrieve the ball, still echo through the world of cricket. One of those sons had been taken as a treat to see the All England Eleven play when he was six years old in 1854. In 1863, at fifteen, he was playing against them and made two and thirty runs against Jackson, Tarrant, and Tinley. In the next year he first played in London, at the Oval, and John Lillywhite's *Companion* committed itself to the guarded statement, 'Mr. W. G. Grace promises to be a good bat'.

Thus the end of our period marks in cricket the beginnings of another. John Small, the Elder of Hambledon, was said to be the man who 'found out cricket', but it was W. G. more than any other man who made the English world find it out and turned it from the game of two or three southern counties and Nottinghamshire into that of the west and the north, the game not only of all England but of Australia as well.

> It is Glo'ster coming North, the irresistible,
> The Shire of the Graces, long ago!
> It is Gloucestershire up North, the irresistible
> And new-arisen Lancashire the foe.

That was written of 1878, but the arising of Lancashire in its might had been predestined fifteen years before when a lanky boy, with the first down of a black beard on his chin, first knocked off Tarrant and then hit a lob of Tinley's into the scoring tent.

To-day we regard cricket and rowing as incompatible if not antagonistic pursuits. Between the dry bob and the wet bob there is a gulf fixed; the dry bob looks across it rather arrogantly at his wet brother, deeming him one who would have hit a ball if he could and took to clumsy feats of strength because Heaven had not granted him an eye. Not long ago a preacher at his old school trying to explain that he understood the ambitions of boys, said that he himself had been 'in the eleven and the eight and that kind of thing'. A gasp was heard throughout the chapel and the poor man was regarded as the most colossal and unblushing of liars. Once upon a time his statement would have aroused no surprise; cricketers thought no shame to try to excel with the oar and a double blue was not an uncommon phenomenon. Frank Fairlegh, it may be remembered, could 'cross a country, pull an oar, or handle a bat with the best of them', and Tom Brown, though he had been Captain of the Rugby Eleven, wanted no persuading when he went to Oxford to take to 'pulling', and rowed in his college boat in his first year though quite new to the art.

There is a good deal about rowing in *Tom Brown at Oxford*. It seems in some ways very casual and in others very earnest; it is certainly very long drawn out before the virtuous Sizer Hardy is substituted for the dissipated Drysdale, and the boat is left safely at the head of the river. A far better book

—and indeed that is not saying a great deal—is the same author's *Memoir of a Brother*. George Hughes, apart from being a fine athlete, was clearly a remarkable man; he accomplished little in life but had a great power of inspiring both affection and admiration. The book is worth reading for its picture of an early Victorian country gentleman, of decent family and modest but sufficient means, brought up at a public school and university. Here, however, we are concerned with its picture of early rowing.

George Hughes went up to Oxford in 1840 and his younger brother Tom was shocked to hear that he had given up cricket for boating. 'I expressed my sorrow at this and spoke disparagingly of boating, of which I knew nothing whatever. He declared that he was as fond of cricket as ever, but that in the whole range of sport, even including hunting, there was no excitement like a good neck-and-neck boat race, and that I should come to think so too.' It was an exciting time at which to take to boating because after some years of Cambridge supremacy a saviour of Oxford had appeared. This was Fletcher Menzies of University, who trained his crew on a then new principle, 'the substitution of the long stroke with sharp catch at the beginning for the short, digging, waterman's stroke'. George Hughes was in this crew which duly beat Cambridge over the six miles' course between Westminster and Putney Bridges and proved Menzies to be right. A curious little piece of inside history is that Hughes was becoming faint with the heat of the sun—the race was in summer—when the cox reminded him that he had a piece of lemon and Menzies took off his own hat and gave it to him. That was in 1842 and in 1843 came a greater exploit. Menzies's crew was to row Cambridge at Henley. At the last moment he was taken ill, and on a legal point the stewards decided that his place could not be filled because only those might row whose names had been sent in. It was decided to row with seven oars. George Hughes was moved to stroke and Cambridge was beaten, whereupon all Henley became justly delirious and 'headed by a small, decorous, shy man in spectacles' threw a heavy toll gate over the bridge and into the river.

The heroic story of the seven oars had a notable effect on Oxford rowing. Tom Hughes says, 'It made rowing really popular, which it had not been till then,' and he himself was entirely converted and helped his brother to win the fours for Oriel, after nearly destroying it by catching a crab. Oxford never went back on the reforms of Menzies and the coaching of watermen disappeared for ever. Cambridge were not wholly convinced, and in 1852 they engaged a waterman to the fury of their famous coach, Mr. Egan, who thereupon went over to the enemy and coached Oxford, thus teaching a lesson never since forgotten. It is to be remembered that in early days the parts of cox and coach were generally doubled and Mr. Egan did so for Cambridge in the race of 1836. That was the second University race in history, the first having been rowed in 1829. From 1856 the race became an annual one.

Apart from the University race we have seen that Henley was flourishing early in our period. So was Leander, which had celebrated crews in 1837 and 1838. There were also of course rowing schools, and Eton and Westminster first met in a race in 1829. Then there were the professional watermen who would row races if anybody would put up the money, and it is worth noticing a sudden incursion into this new field by Squire Osbaldeston. He may have rowed a little as an Eton boy but never since, and in 1829 he was in his forty-second year. Yet he first collected an amateur crew to beat a crew of Guardsmen for a bet, and then for the next year or two he plunged into professional rowing, took part in 'Randan' races with watermen and became a 'Leading Patron of the Aquatiques'. There was a certain pleasant casualness even in the races for money; when Lord Ranelagh, rowing in a pair-oared race with a waterman, exclaimed, 'May I be damned if I can row any more,' Osbaldeston came alongside, took his oar, and finished the race.

The backbone of rowing throughout our period was, however, as it is now, amateur rowing, and since it had at Oxford and Cambridge far fewer rivals than it has now, it had attained if not its zenith yet a great popularity in the sixties. With football and athletic sports still in their infancy, rowing was the one thing for a man who wanted exercise. It was an obvious and a universal pastime in a way which it never can be again.

While certain games and sports were growing steadily in fame and popularity one that had been the greatest of them all, and generally supposed to have made one Englishman worth two Frenchmen, was in a decline. The ring was beginning to be regarded as decadent and corrupt. In 1822 Tom Cribb had retired and handed over the championship. He had, to be sure, a worthy successor in Tom Spring, but Spring's two fights with Langan were the last of their kind and they were over before 1830. It was symptomatic that John Jackson, Byron's 'Emperor of Pugilism', had given up his Bond Street rooms in the year of his patron's death, 1824. Jem Ward was the champion in 1830, and he had been once expelled the ring for fighting a cross and afterwards forgiven. There were too many crosses and then, by an unlucky chance, there came two deaths. In 1830 McKay died after his fight with Simon Byrne. Three years later Byrne himself died after a long and desperate fight with Deaf Burke. There was another fatal fight in 1838, and though juries were as lenient as they could be, the ring, already fast growing discredited, could not survive such shocks.

The story of the succeeding champions such as Deaf Burke and Bendigo is but an ignoble one. The honesty of the fighters became more and more suspect: there were more and more fights won on fouls and the whole business became a tainted and hole-and-corner one, with secret battle-fields and mysterious trains that started for nowhere in the middle of the night. 'Owing to the puritanical persecution to which the ring had been for some time subjected,' wrote a sporting writer of the time, 'a line of country had to be selected which had for a long time been untried.' Gentlemen still went to see fights but they had to struggle for railway tickets with a mob of ruffians. Gone was the time when Bob Gregson in an Earl's barouche was openly escorted to the battle-field by a body 'of noblemen and gentlemen'. In the last fight between Caunt and Bendigo the Nottingham 'lambs' gathered in one corner with their bludgeons and aimed blows at Caunt when he came within reach. The fight was a farcical and disreputable business carried on amid an uproar.

And then in the squalid darkness there came one bright and final splendour, the fight between Tom Sayers and the Benicia boy in 1860. It was surrounded by the same atmosphere of secrecy, but for once the secret was no secret at all: every one winked at every one else: respectable citizens left their houses at one o'clock in the morning to find their way to London Bridge; every policeman on his beat knew where they were going and wished that he was going too. All England that could not go, its dying interest suddenly called back to life, waited eagerly for the news. The fight was a fair stand-up fight in which both men, Sayers the English David and Heenan the American Goliath, showed that courage which no man can despise. We have all been brought up to believe that Sayers with one arm broken would have won had the fight gone on. As sang the *Punch* poet, supposed to be Thackeray:

> Fain would I shroud the tale in night—
> The meddling Blues that thrust in sight—
> The ring-keepers o'erthrown;
> The broken ring—the cumbered fight—
> Heenanus' sudden, blinded flight—
> Sayerius pausing, as he might,
> Just when ten minutes used aright
> Had made the fight his own!

There is another view, and it may be that the police only interfered when the Englishman was in jeopardy. Be that as it may, no one has ever impugned the honesty or the bravery of the two fighters themselves. 'The meteor drops and in a flash expires.' The old prize ring ended with Tom Sayers and ended in a blaze of glory.

This shadow by which the ring was gradually eclipsed had much earlier fallen upon more questionable pursuits. There were many cruel things still more or less openly done in George IV's reign, but the general sentiment of decent people had already turned against them. In 1824 General Dyott wrote in his diary that 'refinement in manners and habits of various classes had reached the little as well as the great' and that, under its influence, bull-baiting was sinking to rise no more. Indeed he seemed to think that it only went on at all because it was too 'contumaciously' opposed by indiscreet crusaders. It is likely enough that he was right, for much as we may dislike an ancient custom, we often dislike far more those who decry it and, in so doing, tread incidentally on some corns of our own. In 1825 there was much advertised a coming fight between a lion and a team of dogs. It was very properly denounced as a disgrace to a Christian country, but unluckily those who denounced it were equally strong against the prize fight between Gentleman Cooper and Whiteheaded Bob. So Jasper Petulengro admitted handsomely enough that he had no quarrels with Evangelicals, but he did not approve the putting down 'of all life and manly sport in this here country'. The fight with the lion was duly carried out and so was a fight between a dog and a monkey. The wretched monkey had no fight in him and so Tom Cribb secretly wounded the dog to make the blood flow and winked at Grantley Berkeley as he did it. Something had to be done to give value for money, but the people who wanted this kind of money's worth were growing fewer and more shady every year.

Cock-fighting survived longer, and indeed for those who know where to look for it and are 'given the office', it is said to survive to this day; but even in 1830 it had sunk comparatively low. Pierce Egan had still plenty to say about it in his book of games in 1832 and gave an account of a match as full of fire as any of the ring. 'They were beak point to beak point', he wrote, 'until they dashed up in one tremendous flirt, mingling their powerful rustling wings and nervous heels in one furious compressed mass. The leap, the fire, the passion of strength, the *certaminis gaudia* were fierce and loud.' Nevertheless, as far as 'gentlemen sportsmen' were concerned he was bolstering up a dying game. There were several pits still in London, notably in the Horseferry Road in Westminster, but for the most part it was a game for the miners of the midlands and north. Among them were fought many mains. 'Newcastle may challenge all the world to cocking,' said Egan, and he quoted what he termed a 'flash but rather coarse chant' about the fights and the drinking of the colliers and the nailers at 'Wedgbury Cocking'. A thousand cocks, it was calculated, would die in a season and there was a whole race of professional 'Feeders' and 'Setters-to'. Still such shoddy glory as there had ever been was fast departing. In a few years more it had departed altogether, and if our country gentleman went to a cock-fight he went under the rose and felt, it is to be hoped, rather ashamed of himself. Public opinion had definitely condemned cock-fighting by the time Queen Victoria came to the throne.

For a gentleman the competitive instinct and the love of fame could not find an outlet in the ring to which he could only play the part of a Maecenas. For him to be a sportsman and especially a horseman and a master of hounds was the way to earn the stately praise of Nimrod and to be a great man. And in 1830 there were two very great men whose names still sound stirring, Thomas Assheton Smith and George Osbaldeston. Even to-day there must be a hundred people who have heard of Tom Smith or the Squire for one who can enumerate the modern and local heroes of Leicestershire.

Both were remarkable men typical of their time. They spent their souls on sport and especially on foxhunting with a red-hot passionate enthusiasm, unafraid of ridicule. In a number of ways their lives ran on similar lines and in some respects they must have been very like one another, in others utterly different. On neither account were they likely to be real friends, and perhaps each in the bottom of his heart felt towards the other an equal measure of jealousy and half-grudging respect. Both were of good country gentleman stock, went to Eton and to Oxford, and had at the very beginning of their careers all the money they wanted. Both had great physical strength and endurance, lived temperate and healthy lives, and retained their powers to an advanced age. Each was an accomplished and fearless rider, each hunted his own hounds for years, and they followed one another in the Mastership of the Quorn. Each was for some time, Smith by far the longer, a member of Parliament who voted rather than spoke. Each was a proper man with his hands and would fight any man, 'lout or gentleman', as Tom Hughes would have said. Smith's fight with the gigantic coal-heaver in the main street of Leicester is historic, and the Squire 'with his hackles up' was as formidable as he was light and small. In this respect they seem to have passed almost into the realms of mythology, for there is the same story of each that he struck a man with his whip and on being told that he dared not do that off his horse, instantly leaped down to give battle.

Hunting had with each of them first place, but they were both all-round men and in particular each was a fine cricketer. Osbaldeston is the better known now and for a short while devastated the country in single wicket matches by his tremendous fast bowling, but Smith had a long career as a batsman in the best company. He played for the Gentlemen and could make his forties and fifties with Lambert and Lord Frederick. Both were good shots but Osbaldeston the better:

he was not only one of the best-known game shots of his day but could hold his own at pigeon shooting at the Red House even with Captain Horatio Ross. In the sports which both professed and in which both excelled probably the right verdict was that of Tom Smith himself, that he would like to ride, shoot, box, and play cricket against Osbaldeston, but that he would box first in order to disqualify him for the other three contests.

Osbaldeston's was, at any rate as regards results, the more many-sided talent for sport. He has to his credit a wonderful variety of feats—trotting and coaching, rowing boat-races when over forty, playing tennis against the great Barre with his bare hands. Moreover, the perpetual itch for fame drove him on to feats of horsemanship which Smith would not touch—his riding of 200 miles within ten hours at Newmarket and his winning of single matches across country. Once 'nettled' as he said by the continual praises of Assheton Smith he issued the challenge to ride him a match and Smith refused. Osbaldeston's comment was that he knew he would refuse because he had not the pluck. Smith declared that no man should make a roughrider of him unless he pleased; he had no love for steeplechases because he hated to exhaust a horse.

In that incident we can see one of the outstanding differences between the pair. Smith did not care to do a thing merely to beat the other man and he was never a gambler. The Squire admitted that 'chaffing challenges and the love of fame' were always too much for him; he would back himself to do anything for anything against anybody, though it was rather the greed of victory than of money that drove him on. Each was in his way a very fine gentleman but Smith had the greater balance and dignity. He would not have cared to have it said of him 'Squire of where?—Why, he's the Squire of England', and Osbaldeston's bristling vanity could never have withstood that compliment. Smith could make time to manage his own affairs shrewdly as well as generously and died a very rich man, while Osbaldeston's was 'a life of plunder' and he was only saved from penury by a prudent wife who made him buy an annuity and doled him out a sovereign a day to lose at his club. Smith, we are told, was well read and loved his Horace, and the Squire never read a book in his life. Smith too had a natural genius for boat-building and had at least something to do with the discovery of the 'wave line' principle. Yet Osbaldeston too had something of a natural genius and that for writing. When as an old man he wrote his autobiography to please his wife—and a very odd book it was for that purpose—he showed himself master of a style terse, simple, and vigorous, such as any one might envy. Few men have done better what George Borrow so much admired, namely told a plain story.

It is tempting but perhaps futile to make a comparison between the two in the hunting-field. For either we can find a splendid and sonorous epitaph. For Smith the Druid shall speak: 'He was the mightiest hunter that ever rode across Belvoir's sweet vale or wore a horn at his saddle bow.' For Osbaldeston the Gentlemen of the Pytchley: 'To the best sportsman of an age or country' they wrote on the silver cup they gave him. If there is to be a casting vote I think it must be given by Dick Christian, free from all rhetoric, for Assheton Smith, 'he was certainly the best man that ever came into Leicestershire'. He had paid him, too, the greatest honour in deeds not words that ever was paid to a foxhunter. In 1840 he was sixty-six. For more than twenty years he had not been seen in the Burton country where he had once been Master. Then he was asked to bring his hounds there from Tedworth, and from all the shires, from Quorn and Pytchley and Cottesmore, from fifty miles round, there came 2,000 horsemen and a great crowd on foot, the elders to greet a friend, the younger generation to gaze on one who was still so mighty a name. This was the famous Rolleston Day to be remembered ever afterwards. A fox was found but no huntsman in the world could hunt in such a multitude. Assheton Smith was almost overwhelmed by the tribute and remained for once 'quiet throughout the day'. As one of the old farmers said, 'Ah, there is old Hi, hi! but alas! the hemphasis is wanting.' Still, one thing had been emphasized, that, as Nimrod remarked, 'There never will be such another Mr. Smith as long as the world stands.'

In 1834 Osbaldeston hunted with his own hounds for the last time. Tom Smith was still hunting in his eightieth year in 1856. Both as fine horsemen and famous masters of hounds had inevitably left their mark on hunting but they had not made modern hunting. The change had come earlier than their day with the beginning of the century. It is from then that the historians date hunting as it is known to-day with its elaborateness and expensiveness, its pace and its hard riding. Mr. Meynell could not bear it; the reckless dashing riding of the new-comers made him say that he 'had not had a day's happiness', but hard riding had come to stay in despite of him. Nimrod in his famous *Quarterly* article says that it was Mr. Childe of Kinlet Hall in Shropshire who first set the example of 'hard riding, or, we should rather say, quick riding to hounds', and it was soon followed 'by the leading characters of the Quorn hunt'.

There were fewer people hunting in the Squire's day than there were later; there may or may not have been more fences, but the modern epoch had begun before him and there was no really material change between 1830 and 1865. Famous names came after his in the Mastership of the Quorn—Sir Bellingham Graham, Goodricke, Holyoake, Sir Richard Sutton, Mr. Greene of Rolleston who skimmed over the Whissendine 'like a swallow on a summer evening', but they were masters in an already established tradition.

It may be said that hunting has changed wonderfully little since the early half of last century and that in many respects it had then reached its zenith. Sir Herbert Maxwell wrote in 1898: 'Mr. Maher, the Squire, and Sir Francis Burdett, if they could put in an appearance on a Quorn Monday in the present season, might exchange some remarks about the enormous number present; but horses and hounds would neither exceed nor fall short of their ideal; and they would have nothing to learn about getting a start and keeping it. The "Quarterly Run" might be re-enacted for their benefit, without the alteration of a single detail.'

He then went on to point out how utterly, as compared with hunting, shooting had changed, and tried to imagine the feelings of Colonel Hawker on accepting an invitation to shoot at Blubberhouse on the 12th of August. Not only the weapons but the conditions have changed out of all knowledge. The great Joe Manton perfected the flint-lock about the time of Waterloo, and though the copper cap came into more or less general request about 1830, the flint-lock only gave way to the detonator after a long and bitter struggle. There is a pleasant story in a letter of Mr. Spencer

Stanhope of the early days of grouse driving, which was still in its infancy about 1840. An old cock had come down the length of the line and was at last shot by an old gentleman, Sir William Cooke, with a flint-lock. He took off his white hat in a gesture of triumph and exclaimed, 'There's your copper caps, gentlemen.'

There was another struggle when in 1853 the first breech-loader was introduced from France into England. Five years later there was a public trial of the two and the muzzle-loader was held to have proved itself slightly superior to the intrusive new-comer. In the next few years, however, the breech-loader generally asserted itself, though the *Badminton* records that in 1870 there were still a few well-known shots in Norfolk and Suffolk who stuck to their muzzle-loaders.

As regards conditions, in Osbaldeston's best days there was no driving. In 1831 General Dyott went shooting with his friend Lord Combermere, 'which sport he has in superb perfection. We had nine spaniels to beat the coverts in the highest possible state of discipline and perfection.' Even pheasants were walked up and the stubble was inches thick and gave good cover. When machine cutting came in it was a very different story and 'there is scarcely a stubble field in England at this day that would shelter a mouse'. When the stubble was thick, partridges, it was said, did not see the guns until they were actually shot at. There was, then, some compensation for the inferior weapons, and there is nothing so incredible, as might at first sight appear, in some of Osbaldeston's feats with his 'flint and steel of eighteen bore made by the celebrated Joe Manton'. He killed 100 pheasants with 100 shots and in Scotland bagged 97 grouse with 97 shots, and there were others as good as he or nearly so, Captain Horatio Ross, Mr. Coke, and Lord Kennedy. Perhaps the whole difficult question of comparison may be summed up in the words of the late Sir Theodore Cook—and no man admired the Squire more than he did: 'Our best shots make their records with first-rate guns under conditions often extremely difficult; the best shots of a century gone made their records under easy conditions with very poor guns.'

Unlike its more disreputable relations the turf did not die in early Victorian England, but it passed through a time not of mortal yet of very serious sickness. Perhaps this is not to be wondered at when we remember what singular things could be done by gentlemen of unblemished character. No better illustration is needed than Squire Osbaldeston's own account of the proceedings at Heaton Park in 1835 which led to his duel with Lord George Bentinck. Here it is in brief. It seems that nobody got fair play at Heaton Park except Lord Wilton's own house party and the horses trained by Scott, who was allowed to train in the Park. The handicapper stayed every year in the house and the handicapping was, according to the Squire, an open scandal; so, when it was necessary, was the judging. Osbaldeston did not stay in the house and there was perhaps a touch of jealousy in his comments on the 'aristocrats' who did. An indignation meeting was held of the other owners who did not stay there but they could come to no decision; so the Squire thought of a simple plan of his own, namely, 'to purchase horses with whose qualities they (at the Park) were unacquainted'. He bought in Ireland a horse called Rush, with which to win the Cup.

He rode Rush in a trial, and when he saw people watching he pulled up and let the other horse win. He rode him in a handicap on the first day at Heaton and as he naïvely remarked, 'Rush was such a beautiful horse to ride that they could not detect any roping.' Meanwhile he got on all the money he could for the Cup and amongst other bets he took £200 to £100 from Lord George Bentinck. The great day came and the Squire, having waited on Rush till a hundred yards from the post, won in a canter. The smart ladies in the stand hissed him; Lord Wilton and Lord George Bentinck would not speak to him, but Scott showed perhaps a juster appreciation of the state of things when he cheerfully observed, 'Squire, you have done us this time.' 'Yes,' said the Squire, equally cheerful, 'I am just twelve miles farther north than you are.—This time we have helped ourselves.'

If these things could be done in the green tree what could be done in the dry? No wonder that Nimrod in the third of his *Quarterly* articles spoke strongly though guardedly. He solemnly warned the young gentleman 'who may have imbibed the ambition of shining on the English turf'. Let him remember this, 'that he presents a *broad mark*—that there are hundreds on the watch for him—and that he stakes what is certain against not only all other chances, but the rife chance of fraud'. There was heavy betting both by jockeys and trainers, there were false favourites made by false trials, there was a general bamboozling of the betting public. When St. Giles won the Derby in 1832 the *New Sporting Magazine* openly proclaimed that every horse but one had been 'made safe' and nobody thought it worth while to contradict. Nimrod was careful not to mention names but he had something to say about the owners of St. Giles, who had done that which was regarded as a legitimate thing. These were the famous John Gully of prize-fighting renown and his racing partner—or as it was then rather ominously called confederate—Robert Ridsdale. As confederates they were allowed to 'compromise' and they 'compromised to give the race to St. Giles, although doubtless Margrave could have won it'. This was certainly profitable, for Gully is said to have won £50,000 on St. Giles, and when Margrave won the St. Leger he won another £35,000.

What is now called 'doping' seems to have been rampant. It was a good many years since Danny Dawson had been hanged on Castle Hill at Cambridge for poisoning the watering troughs at Newmarket, but everybody believed that the real villain of the piece was Bland, who had kept Dawson quiet by telling him that he would be reprieved, and Bland was still flourishing like a green bay tree. One of the most blatant of all frauds was apparently the St. Leger of 1834, when according to Nimrod the best horse since Eclipse was made so safe that he was beaten before he had gone a quarter of the distance. At the same meeting the son of a peer, a well-known racing man, was held to have been guilty of forgery in privily adding a name to a list of horses named in a bet against the field.

A Hercules was badly needed to clean this stable, and presently he appeared in the person of Lord George Bentinck. He said of himself that he did not know much but 'I can judge of men and horses'. He had at one time as many as sixty horses in training; he betted heavily and successfully and once declared that he kept so large a stud of horses in order to try to break the betting ring. In those almost universally lax days he had a high standard of honour and was unrelenting towards defaulters or those that he deemed dishonest. He was peremptory, determined, and able, and he necessarily made enemies, but he did much to improve the turf, and was called the 'purger of abuses'. His most celebrated effort was in the case of Running Rein, who was supposed to have won the Derby in 1844. This was a complex fraud, for the conspirators had two strings to their bow, the four-year-old Maccabaeus who was substituted for the real Running Rein, and the five-year-old Leander. They were to have come in first and second had not an accident befallen Leander. Even so the poor villains had what may be called a piece of bad luck. Maccabaeus had been kept at one time on a farm in Northamptonshire. The farmer, a Mr. Worley, came to see the Derby and when shown Running Rein proclaimed stoutly that it was 'his horse' and added, 'Do you think I don't know him when I had him so long? I can swear to him.'

With that the trouble began. Lord George was on the scent and nothing would turn him from his purpose. There was finally an action tried in Westminster Hall and the Running Rein party did very well till the honest Worley went into the box. Not even the famous Mr. Cockburn could shake him. The real Running Rein was hastily ridden away to some secret place and could not be produced, and Lord George enjoyed a great triumph. Not so in his second effort, when he was too precipitate. In 1839 the Derby was won at 40 to 1 by Bloomsbury belonging to William Ridsdale, the brother of Robert, with whom John Gully had long since quarrelled and come to blows. There were whispers and hints and rumours and Lord George was again on the war-path, saying that Bloomsbury was either over age or was not Bloomsbury at all. He could prove neither statement and his action to recover the stakes from Ridsdale failed rather dismally. 'His Lordship', commented Osbaldeston dryly, 'did not get much praise for this proceeding,' but the Squire, though he had been called a robber and had fought that duel with Lord George, had a half-grudging respect for him and owned that he might be 'domineering' but he had done good to the turf. That the turf was abundantly in need of it no one can doubt.

There remains a word to be said of fishing, and the early Victorian fisherman found it easier to practise his art in quiet and unpolluted waters than did his successors of a later time. The waste products of mighty industries in the north had not yet wrought him great hurt. In the south, even as to-day, 'the naiads of the Test still laved their limbs in lucid streams'. No technical disquisition is here possible (the writer is utterly incapable of it), but it may be pointed out that the fishermen of our period did not know the dry fly. From the charming *Chronicles of the Houghton Fishing Club* (at Stockbridge) may be quoted Sir Herbert Maxwell's description of the old ways:

'The old manner was two-fold—either to fish down-stream with two flies of a bulk and build that would send every sane twentieth-century trout within sight to the nearest shelter, or to impale a natural fly—grannom, mayfly, or caperer—on the hook and to present it by "blowing"—that is, to let it float before the wind at the end of a line of floss silk and alight in as natural a way as possible on the water. To do so, of course, required a favouring wind, neither too much nor too little.'

Obviously the dry fly revolutionized the fishing on the Test; yet there is no mention of its coming in the club book. It can only be inferred from an entry in that year that it had not appeared in 1862: 'Wind SW and very strong. So tremendous were the gusts that it was impossible to hold up the blow line rod.'

It would be hard to find a pleasanter, more leisurely picture of the English country gentleman than these annals afford in the club's earlier years, not long after its foundation in 1822. The members were dependent on the weather and they had no trains to whisk them away if that weather was unkind. So they came and settled down for the two regular festivals—the rise of the grannom and of the mayfly. If they had too much leisure they employed it in composing songs, charades, and other *jeux d'esprit* about their art and about each other.

Oh I love to stray by the purling brook
  On a dark and windy day,
With my rod and my line and well-stored book
  In the genial month of May.

So one of them burst out, presumably on a day of bright sunshine in 1840. In the next year sunshine produced a bitterer tone.

'*18th August.* Mr. Penn and Mr. Norman arrived from London by the one o'clock train, having determined, in consequence of the precarious state of the harvest, to secure for anxious agriculturists a few days of that bright and clear weather which never fails to attend upon the labours of the Club. Taking to-day as a specimen of what is to follow, it seems almost certain that their patriotic purpose will be fully obtained. There was hardly a cloud or a breath of wind.'

It was doubtless that railway to Stockbridge which, by reducing the hours of enforced idleness, indirectly reduced the entries in the book. They became much shorter and more strictly to the point. Possibly also the literary fishermen were succeeded by a more businesslike race. One survived all changes, the Rev. F. Beadon, one of the original members of 1822. Forty-six years after the club's founding, in 1868 at the age of ninety-one—and that was ten years before his death—he wrote, 'Yesterday I caught a brace of trout—one 2 lb. 8 oz., and thank God, as my health is good, I shall try to catch more; but, of course, I cannot see, as well as formerly, the fly on the water.'

The sports and games of early Victorian ladies can be dismissed with a more unchivalrous brevity than would be possible in the case of their successors. If the life of the country gentleman was as Goethe thought, 'active and torpid', that of the country lady was apt to be almost wholly torpid. It was not that she could not find plenty of domestic things to do. Tom Brown's mother in the Vale of White Horse not only looked after her house and her children and her servants but 'dealt out stockings, and calico shirts, and smock-frocks, and comforting drinks to the old folks with the "rheumatiz", and good counsel to all; and kept the coal and clothes clubs going for Yuletide'. We hear little, however, of any active open-air employment, and Miss Bingley's views about the absurdity of Elizabeth Bennett walking a few miles on a muddy day survived her for a good many years. Ladies had always ridden and had to some extent hunted. There had been at any rate one dashing horsewoman who would not have cared for a hundred Miss Bingleys. This was the great Mrs. Thornton, who had made her match on the Knavesmire against Mr. Flint, as long ago as 1804. She was presumably deemed unwomanly to ride the race and poor Mr. Flint was deemed ungallant to win it: so nobody was much the better. *Vixere fortes*, even before Mrs. Thornton: a Lady Salisbury of the eighteenth century had kept a pack of dwarf foxhounds at Hatfield with sky-blue uniforms for the hunt, and in the same century we read of a famous Miss Draper, the daughter of a Yorkshire squire.

Her Christian name was Diana, a more refined tribute to the chase than the name of Jack Mytton's god-daughter, Mad Foxhunting Moll.

Generally speaking, however, the hunting of ladies was of a comparatively subdued type. We hear of Tom Smith going to the tea and card parties of the Melton ladies, but we do not hear of them out with the Quorn. Not one of them is named in the 'Quarterly Run.' The real hunting woman of to-day, living for hunting and for nothing else, did not seem to exist. There were good horsewomen, and in 1856 the Duke of Beaufort recorded in his diary, 'Lady Adelaide (Curzon) rode Evangeline and Viscount and as usual went splendidly on both.' When Mr. Punch arises as a star to lighten our darkness as to social customs we find some hunting ladies in John Leech, but more of them riding in the Row with bewitching feathers in their hats. In 1857 there are ladies depicted as present at a hunting breakfast, and in 1860 there is a heavenly picture in which 'Miss Diana slips off at a fence and leaves the better half of her habit on the pummels of her saddle'. Four years later there are two Dianas discussing the proper headgear and one remarks, 'If you want to look like going across country the chimney pot all to nothing.' Leech laughed at the hunting ladies a little but he made them look charming, and to be a good horsewoman was an attractive accomplishment. It was on the list which Sir John Astley gave of the charms of his betrothed in 1850:

'She was comely to look upon, ten years younger than I was, a beautiful mover and a perfect horse-woman, fond of music, good-tempered, and cheery. "What more can a man want?" I hear you say. "Well! right you are," but still there are other points, minor details I admit, yet not to be despised. She was the only child of a well-to-do and well-born squire, who was not only a perfect gentleman, but rode straight to hounds, and was as highly respected at Quarter Sessions as he was in the House of Commons.'

There is very little talk of the ladies going out with the guns and this habit probably only became at all common when ladies began to wear more sensible clothes and boots, and shooting lunches became more elaborate. If, however, they did not watch men shoot they themselves shot with bows and arrows. Archery had begun to enjoy a revival at the end of the eighteenth century. In 1785 the Woodmen of Arden had awakened again after a long sleep. In 1781 the Royal Toxophilite Society had been founded, and fifty years later it built its Archers' Hall in Regent's Park. Those who know their Miss Edgworth will remember the horsy lady, Lady Diana Sweepstakes, and her archery meeting and the tragedy of the green and white uniform in 'Waste not, Want not'. Rather later than Miss Edgworth's stories comes General Dyott with a mention of a smart archery party at Lord Bagot's with tents pitched and a band to play and all the pretty ladies of the county. Later on in the thirties there is the same thing at other big Staffordshire houses, and archery had clearly become a way for people both to entertain themselves and to entertain other people.

Here is a pleasant extract from a letter from Mrs. Josiah Wedgwood the younger, whose daughter Emma afterwards married Charles Darwin: 'Jessie really is uncommonly pretty. She went with us to the Archery and was much admired; and what is more, she got the first prize, a beautiful pair of earrings. . . . As for Fanny and Emma, they are quite dragonesses, but nothing pleased me so much in their success as the sincerity with which they tried to waive their glories in favour of the other competitors.'

Nobody could possibly say, as was said years afterwards of lady golfers, 'We take leave to observe that the posture and gestures requisite for a full swing are not particularly graceful when the player is clad in female dress.' Archery was statuesque and elegant, and Mr. Punch made his shooting ladies look as pretty as his hunting ones. It spread wherever the banner of England flew, as witness Mr. Kipling's story of 'Cupid's Arrows' and the Diana of Tara Devi in the ancient India of pre-croquet days.

That croquet should have put the nose of archery out of joint is not to be wondered at, for a ball has a unique attraction, and ladies who had perhaps been unconsciously hungering for a ball game since the days of Nausicaa now found that they could play. The credit of its introduction belongs historically to an Irish lady, Miss Macnaughten, who is said to have discovered it or something like it in the south of France soon after 1850. Under her auspices it was first played in England on Lord Lonsdale's lawn in 1852. Whether her implements were imported from France or were home-made is not recorded, but in 1856 Mr. John Jaques, a purveyor of all sorts of games, saw the game played and realized its merits. The croquet set—complete in a box—soon made the game popular. In one of the original green numbers of *Our Mutual Friend*, published in 1864, may be found an advertisement of Mr. Jaques with the statement that he had won two prize medals. It is adorned by a picture of a pretty young lady in a crinoline holding her mallet with the left hand below the right, with one elastic-sided foot placed victoriously on her own ball while she is preparing to croquet her enemy far away. That was one year after *Punch* had taken judicial notice of the game by a delightful early Du Maurier drawing of enthusiastic ladies playing in a snowstorm. In 1864 there was a poem on the subject and the game was fully launched, nor had it any serious rival till lawn tennis appeared in the seventies. As a social amusement it was probably best in its infancy with its enormously wide hoops and its jingling bell in the middle. It was admirable for keeping people amused as an adjunct to a summer tea-party: everybody could take a hand; the mallets were small and light enough for the most delicate females: nobody played very well or very seriously, and the game was an agreeable vehicle for mild flirtation. If the ball crashed away deep into the laurel bushes it could presumably be sought for by a pair of partners as leisurely as was Sam Weller's hat by its owner and the pretty housemaid when 'there was something behind the door, which perwented our getting it open for ever so long'. Soon, however, the inevitable happened: players became too good and either went round and round monotonously or became cross if they did not. The end of early Victorian England saw the end of the first fine careless rapture of croquet, for two years later there was a public match at Evesham: in 1868 the All England Club was formed and the game was up.

VI

THE NAVY

§ 1. SHIPS AND ARMAMENTS.

§ 2. OFFICERS AND MEN.

§ 3. DISTRIBUTION AND ACTIVITIES.

VI

THE NAVY

By ADMIRAL G. A. BALLARD

Of an organization on so technical a foundation as an armed sea service it is impossible to write anything in the nature of even a moderately complete account without including much that is apt to be laborious and uninteresting to the general reader. But as that applies to the material in the composition of a war fleet much more than to the human element, and as the two are largely capable of independent treatment, they are presented in separate sections in this chapter. The first of these deals with ships and armaments; the second with officers and men. A third is added as an account of the naval distribution and activities of the early Victorian sea forces, with a brief description of the principal historical events which had a naval aspect.

In so far as is possible, however, the section dealing with material has been worded with an economy of technical language in an endeavour to make the contents clear to those who have little knowledge of the service for which their ancestors had to pay. And even if not studied with close attention it ought at least to be glanced over, if anything approaching to a correct idea is to be formed of the closing phase of an order of things belonging as utterly to vanished ideals as Phoenician galleys or Plantagenet archers. The main point to be recognized in correctly appreciating the extent of the profound transformation in the conception of water-borne force that occurred in the Victorian age, is that at its beginning the gun was mainly designed to suit the ship, but at its end the ship was entirely designed to suit the gun. In the human element by far the most important change was the establishment of 'continuous service' for the lower ratings, whereby the Navy became a standing force in men as well as officers for the first time.

Descriptions of ships have been entirely confined to the armed classes, as space does not permit the inclusion of the numerous unarmed pennants employed on various important auxiliary services such as transports, storeships, surveying vessels, government mail packets, &c. All statements and details are taken direct from official documents in charge of Mr. Bonner Smith, the Admiralty librarian, whose assistance has been invaluable in producing authentic sources of information. The only private authors consulted have been Sir Vesey Hamilton on Naval Administration, and Sir Howard Douglas on Naval Gunnery.

§ I. SHIPS AND ARMAMENTS

For almost exactly a century after Bonaparte looked his last on France from the poop of a British seventy-four, the people of Great Britain remained absolutely free from hostile molestation to their domestic hearths or imported daily bread. That long immunity more than covered the entire record reign of Victoria, and arose from a sound national instinct—definitely voiced in an Act of Parliament—whereby this nation realized the advantages of its natural environment. As it was a geographical certainty that the homeland was completely encircled by deep water, it followed that no enemy could offer violence to their lives or property without first putting to sea. Any aggressive intentions on his part therefore might be frustrated before he ever arrived, if a full use was made of the force inherent in the highly specialized type of naval architecture known in early Victorian days as the 'ship-of-the-line'. Herein lay consequently the prime reason for the maintenance of a British navy in the peaceful years of the nineteenth century, just as much as in the war-disturbed passage of its immediate predecessors.

In composition the sea service upon which the national security mainly reposed was somewhat complex, though not because its responsibilities were in the least obscure. Stated in the plainest terms, the main function of a fleet is to stop all the sea movements of a hostile Power great or small; whether the enemy ships are undertaking the conveyance of armies bent on invasion, or the multifarious commodities of ordinary trade and exchange. To be suitable for carrying either, the vessels employed must belong to the ordinary mercantile description, wherein structural appropriation of space for passengers or cargo leaves little room for defensive equipment; and if the specially-built fighting ship had only such adversaries as these to deal with, her design might be comparatively simple; demanding merely the speed to overtake a defenceless object of pursuit with the very modest armament needed to enforce its surrender or destruction.

But as these carriers may move under the protection of specially-built fighting ships themselves—either in the shape of close escort or distant cover—the whole problem of intercepting their activities has for centuries been raised to the higher plane of fighter against fighter; which in the past caused incessant rivalry through the efforts of different countries to build more and more formidable types. This competition only ended in a virtual condition of stalemate when all reached about the same point, beyond which it was impossible to go with the available materials of the age. With timber only for hulls, and cast metal for guns, it produced the ship-of-the-line in the particular form which she happened to take at any given date between the Stuart period and the mid-Victorian, and with iron and steel the armoured battleship of the Great War; types, which though utterly dissimilar, were launched for exactly the same duties, and may for the sake of brevity and convenience both be referred to hereafter under the general heading of 'capital ships', as the maximum embodiments of sea force of their respective ages. These were not the only classes of vessel required for maritime war. Certain considerations to be presently set forth demanded a whole series of accessory units and complicated the organization of a fully constituted war navy still further. But as the prime factor the capital ship stands entitled to first attention in any description of an armed assemblage centred on her presence.

Nominally the period to be surveyed here is the Early Victorian. As, however, the opening stage of Victoria's reign did not chance to coincide with any important naval events or progress, whether arising from operations of war or preparations in peace, it is perhaps more interesting to start a little further back. And in that case the nearest antecedent year of rather special naval association is 1827, for that witnessed in Navarino Bay the last occasion on which British wooden capital ships engaged their own kind. It was not their last fight of any sort, but those which came after—few in number—were all conflicts with land defences.

At the time of the battle of Navarino the British Navy was in the drastically reduced condition as regards men that always followed the conclusion of an exhausting war in the days before the establishment of 'continuous service' for the lower deck element. About 60 per cent. of the ships were laid up in ordinary, bereft of crews, dismantled aloft and disarmed below; while thousands of their guns congested the ordnance wharves in endless rows. But vessels and weapons lasted so long in those days, and changed so little, that both remained available for effective service if refitted and manned; and in quantity the British stock in both exceeded that under any other flag. Incidentally all foreign fleets were in a similarly demobilized condition.

In that year the British capital ships numbered 95 all told, of which all but 17 were laid up. All these were timber-built sailing-vessels with cast-iron smooth-bore armaments of 74 to 120 guns; and all could be grouped as two-deckers or three-deckers, according as to whether their main armament was carried at two levels or three. Actually the so-called two-decker had four decks and the three-decker five; but of these the highest was only lightly armed and the lowest carried no guns at all. Excepting such as were prizes of war, or the few built of teak in India, the whole were British-grown oak in structure, of which, providentially for the realm, the southern counties afforded at that period a sufficient natural supply. On an average about 900 acres of forest, containing 3,500 full-grown trees, came under the axe to build a three-decker. After felling, the logs were hardened by twenty to thirty years' seasoning in the timber ponds before being sawn up. For sails, masting, and rigging, 50,000 square feet of canvas, 80 tons weight of spars, 900 blocks, and 34 miles of rope were required, the largest rope being 6 inches thick. All capital ships of the early Victorian sailing era were 3-masted, with 11 square sails, 3 jibs, 4 stay-sails between masts, 10 stunsails, and a spanker. These 29 sails were cut to the same plan always, varying only a little in scale between a two-decker and a three. The rigging plan was identical for both, but varied in scale also. Two suits of canvas were carried. Judged by frigate or clipper standards the capital ships were not fast, rarely exceeding ten knots even under a sail pressure of many tons; but good speed lines are not compatible with the robust buoyancy required for carrying a great burden of armament. On the other hand they were excellent sea-boats, fit to face any weather, safe under a press of sail, and easy to steer for their size.

The early Victorian Navy was graded—exclusive of its smallest classes—in a descending sequence of six 'Rates' according to size, of which the First Rate comprised its 16 three-deckers. Of those the largest examples were 205 feet long on the lower gun-deck, with a displacement of 4,500 tons. Such figures sound very modest now, but the towering height of their hulls presented an extremely majestic appearance, notably enhanced by a triple row of guns conspicuously displayed along the three white bands of their chequered sides. In the days of solid roundshot the guns were designated by the weight of the projectile instead of the diameter of bore as now; the change being due to the later adoption of hollow shot in which weight gave no indication of calibre. Thus the larger three-deckers of the period carried 114 guns known as 32-pounders, two as 68-pounders, and four as 18-pounders. Though all firing the same-sized ball the 32-pounders themselves were in four different weights of gun from 63 to 25

H. M. S. HOWE

cwt., with powder charges and ranging power in proportion. These 120 weapons in all were cast-iron muzzle-loaders on wooden mountings, trained by handspikes, elevated by quoins, and checked in recoil by stout rope breechings. The shot were loose enough in fit to roll down the bore by their own weight, and were kept down by wads of oakum rammed home with them, double shotting being permitted in close action. Powder charges were made up in flannel bags in the magazine from the powder barrels, and were fired by a flint-lock or percussion lock on the gun, which the gun-layer pulled by a long lanyard. In the early thirties the British Navy had 8 three-deckers out of its total of 16 armed in this way, throwing a broadside of 1,928 lb., and carrying 900 officers and men each, typical examples being the *Britannia, Howe,* and *Prince Regent.* The other eight were slightly smaller vessels carrying 104 to 112 guns.

The three-decker represented the maximum concentration of power attainable in one unit of flotation of timber structure, but the nature of maritime war often demands a dispersion of force requiring considerable numbers of ships. The three-decker could only be in one place at a time either tactically or strategically, and was much too expensive for any country to build except in strictly limited quantity. All maritime States therefore aimed at obtaining a numerical sufficiency of vessels for their needs by falling back on types of lesser individual size and power; and thus it came about that the main body of all the battle-fleets in the early nineteenth century consisted of the two-decker grade of capital ship instead of the First Rate; of which the former only cost £70,000 to build against an outlay of £120,000 for the latter. In the Georgian era it was the historically celebrated two-decked 'seventy-fours' that in reality won every great battle (even when the more powerful three-decker was present), corresponding on the water to the infantry of the line on the land, as the central force to which all other combatants were supplementary, and genuine heavy weights even if not actually in the very limited champion group. In Navarino year the bulk of the British battle-fleet consisted of 80 two-deckers; fourteen of which were vessels mounting 80 to 92 guns, classed as Second Rates, and 66 vessels mounting 74 guns classed as Thirds. As a general type the two-deckers varied in size from 2,900 to 3,800 tons, and in complement from 600 to 750 officers and men. The broadside of a seventy-four weighed 1,028 lb.; from which it will be realized that her blow had little more than half the force of the largest First Rates. Having finer lines as a rule than the bigger type the two-deckers were usually faster, but exceptions on both sides existed. Typical ships of the two-decker design were the *Rodney*, *Powerful*, and *Cumberland*.

In war the capital ships furnished the chief security of the British realm; but in peace they were mostly dismantled and laid by in the upper reaches of the Admiralty harbours. Having the special office of standing guard for the homeland by keeping a close watch on the main strength of an enemy, they represented the principal of massed force at the focal points of strategic disposition; not merely in their individual construction but in their assemblage; whether brought out in wholesale combinations in the hour of danger, or set aside by the score when the cloud had passed. A few were employed on detached duties both in war and peace, but the great majority never knew any service away from the immediate company of their own exalted rank.

Below the two-decker the term capital ship or ship-of-the-line ceased to apply and the description of vessel known as a frigate followed. In her functions she was the predecessor of the modern cruiser. All frigates at that period carried their main armament in a single tier, but apart from that feature varied so much in size that they comprised the Fourth, Fifth, and Sixth Rates. As instruments of war they only differed from the capital ships in scale and simplicity of design, being wind-propelled timber fabrics carrying cast-iron guns. But from having a larger sail area in proportion to tonnage they were the fastest craft afloat, able to escape from a ship of the line or capture a sloop or merchantman. In Navarino year the British frigates numbered 124 in the aggregate of their three Rates, varying from 700 to 1,700 tons, from 28 to 50 guns in armament, and from 180 to 460 in complements of officers and men. In weight of broadside they ranged from 380 to 550 lb.; that is to say roughly averaging half that of a two-decker, just as the latter had roughly half the broadside of the larger First Rates. Typical examples of frigates were the 50-gun *Winchester*, the 36-gun *Flora*, and the 28-gun *Sapphire*.

Next after the frigates came the sloops, which carried no

H.M.S. SOUTHAMPTON

H.M.S. OSPREY

guns below and were not a Rated class. Within their own limits of size and armament these minor craft varied even more than the former, but officially they were only divided into two general groups as 'ship-rigged' or 'brig-rigged'. Some were merely converted coasters. At the beginning of our period the British sloops totalled about 110 effective vessels, varying from 280 to 550 tons, with armaments of 10 to 20 light carronades firing an average of broadside equal to approximately half that of a medium-sized frigate, and carrying 70 to 150 ranks and ratings. Sloop types were represented by such vessels as the 20-gun *Columbine* and the 16-gun brig *Bittern*. Last and smallest of all British armed hulls stood seventeen cutters and schooners with 6 to 12 of the lightest carronades manufactured.

It has been remarked that capital ships nearly always operated in combination; but that was otherwise where frigates and sloops were concerned. On these lesser craft devolved the responsibility of protecting the widely scattered British property on distant oceans from foreign raiders of their own class—plentiful and ubiquitous in war—and though more than twice as numerous as the capital ships they nearly always acted alone, because required to meet an extensively diffused form of menace impossible to frustrate effectively in any other way. Being moreover far less expensive in commissioned upkeep than capital ships, and quite equal to the secondary duties of a navy, such as the prevention of piracy and disorder on the seas, the frigates and sloops were much more employed during time of peace than their bigger consorts. Under normal peace conditions about forty-five frigates and seventy sloops were in commission at any given date during the twenties and thirties of the nineteenth century.

Apart from all other categories in Navarino year stood a pair of little craft of prophetic significance quite unrealized at the time, which were officially designated 'steam engine vessels' and regarded by the rest of the Navy with extreme curiosity mingled in some quarters with distrust and in others with approval. One of these, named the *Comet*, was specially built as a steamer and carried four 9-pounders, while the other was the converted brig *Echo*, carrying only a pair. Each of them was provided with a boiler raising steam to a pressure of about 3½ lb., a long bell-mouthed chimney, and a single-cylinder reciprocating engine pointing upwards and slowly turning a pair of unboxed paddle-wheels; the whole contrivance being hand-made in hammered iron by blacksmiths and giving a speed of four to five knots.

As a summarized statement of force embodying all the above-mentioned Rates and classes, but excluding all unarmed vessels such as storeships, surveying ships, packet ships, &c., the British Navy at the end of 1827 might be counted as 349 hulls in effective condition for service, with 15,710 guns. To these a large but indefinite number of wholly or partly worn-out ships might be added as national property of no war value. In round figures the serviceable total had cost about £14,500,000 to build, spread over about forty years. In cost of maintenance the fleet of 1827 was paid for (inclusive of new construction) by estimates standing at £6,126,000, which were freely criticized as erring on the extravagant side.

As the memory of the past wars faded and a new generation arose, so the Naval Estimates were insistently reduced. Public interest in national defence declined in the long peace, old ships were broken up wholesale without replacement, work in the dockyards was slowed down to the point at which a new ship took a full dozen years to build, and the Navy dwindled to half its old strength within fifteen. But though reduced to great straits for money the Admiralty was forced to watch the situation abroad which had certain causes for anxiety. The French were paying special attention during the thirties and forties to two new and portentous lines of naval development. Of these one was the extended application of steam—to private tonnage as well as national —while the other was the adoption of explosive projectiles. Either of these in itself had alarming possibilities. Such money as was allowed by the politicians for naval defence therefore was devoted to following the French lead. So long as other countries had remained content with canvas, a sailing navy answered British requirements; but that was a rapidly changing state of affairs, and the production of a steam branch had become imperative. By 1840—the year of the battle of Acre––though still small, it included two vessels of frigate measurements, the *Cyclops* and *Gorgon*, besides twenty-one sloops and fifteen so-called 'gun-vessels' of ketch size only. But as the earliest form of steam propulsion was

H.M.S. GORGON

H.M.S. ROYAL OAK

practically confined to paddles, all of these except one suffered from the serious drawbacks of that type of drive for a fighting hull, of which the most serious was the drastic reduction in armament due to very heavy engines and absorption of broadside space by the wheels. Thus although frigates in tonnage, the *Cyclops* and *Gorgon* only fired the weight of broadside of a small sailing sloop, while the broadside of a steam sloop could easily be carried by one man.

In a country relying so much on naval protection as Britain such defects could not be ignored and the Admiralty was compelled to proceed with caution. Two arguments, however, outweighed all objections. Firstly came the decisive fact that no sailing fleet could stop a steamer's movements in open sea. And secondly, whatever the disadvantages of steam in certain directions might be, they were shared by the steamers under foreign flags. To minimize the loss of broadside fire the principle of heavy upper-deck pivot guns was introduced in all paddlers, thus initiating the policy of centre line armaments capable of full use on either side. Patterns of machinery varied very much (though the side lever description predominated) and speeds ranged from six to nine knots. Consumption of coal was very extravagant for power obtained and necessitated large bunkers. The one screw steamer in the British service in 1840 was the *Phoenix*, which enjoyed the distinction of standing first in Admiralty documents with the notation 'screw' to her name. But the adoption of that epoch-making invention was tardy at first through insufficient realization that it demanded special lines of after-body to give satisfactory results.

French example also forced the pace in ordnance. A scheme to simplify British naval armament by reducing its variety to four standard calibres was begun in 1831, but moved so slowly that it was barely complete when scientific attention to gunnery on the Continent abruptly started to advance in strides. Within a single generation the rapidity of its progress had revolutionized from top to bottom not only the designs of the weapons but the designs of the ships that carried them. In this momentous transformation the first move was not so much a change in the gun itself as a change in its contents. The French led off in 1837 by a decision—long pondered and delayed—to adopt the kind of projectile for their fleet known in England as a shell, already in use for years in the Army. It depended for effect on devastatingly violent explosions inside an enemy's ship instead of the mere perforation of a solid shot, but had always been regarded as dangerously unreliable for sea service through the bad impression caused by some terrible accidents due to inexperienced handling during much earlier trials in both the French and the British fleets. Each continued to realize, however, that these volcanic appliances might be used to shatter an enemy's ship like a destroying angel provided that the user himself was not shattered first; and at length, after some twenty years of hesitation, the French armed their ships with a proportion of Paixhan's *obusiers* or shell guns, so named after their designer. By that step the minds of the British authorities were made up for them, and a percentage of shells was added to the ammunition allowance of all British ships. A certain previous measure facilitated this move, since solid roundshot had already been partly superseded by hollow, which could be made in larger diameter without adding to weight and thus strike a larger hole for the same poundage. The guns specially cast for their use were known as the 8-inch and 10-inch and now became shell firers.

But the French had secured a long start while the British were arguing about corn laws; and knowing their superiority in steamers and shells assumed a suddenly truculent attitude for the first time since Waterloo, when a diplomatic wrangle broke out in the middle forties over affairs in the distant Pacific. After twenty years indifference, therefore, the British public were startlingly awakened to a realization of danger and the usual hurried measures followed. Panic shipbuilding commenced, exhausting the stock of seasoned timber already depleted through national parsimony. But as the Treasury doors were now wide open the Admiralty were permitted to try iron—never hitherto used in the Navy—and contracts were placed for six iron-hulled frigates in private dockyards, where iron tonnage had been launched for the merchant service during several years, though it was very brittle stuff in those days of primitive smelting.

Before these frigates were completed, however, experiments demonstrated that they would be useless for war. It was found on trial that the impact of cast-iron shot on thin wrought-iron plates caused a smash-up of both, sending showers of scrap flying in all directions behind the target. Malleable iron of the only known purity at that period was condemned at once as material for naval war designs therefore, and foreign countries took note of the tests—of which no secret was made—and accepted their teaching. Timber retained its ancient monopoly for the time and the scare passed with diplomatic honours for France.

But if the haste of the occasion imposed a check on iron shipbuilding for the fleet in this way, it stimulated genuine progress in the further adoption of steam. Foremost among the projects openly discussed in Paris was a plan for a descent on the English coast by an army taking advantage of the French numerical superiority in steamers; which raised in the British Isles once more the terrifying spectre of invasion, dormant since Trafalgar forty years before. Eminent statesmen and others, with no sea knowledge, made the announcement that 'steam had bridged the Channel'; which to the ignorant seemed to have a knowledgeable ring about it, and like all terse declarations of a sensational tone found much ready credence; the more especially as the resonant voice of St. Vincent was no longer present in the House of Lords to reassure what he called the old women of both sexes.

But professional seamen of the day realized very quickly that if steam had bridged the Channel it could at least with equal certainty be made to bridge the ancient difficulty of keeping a sufficiently close watch on the enemy's movements to ensure their interception—a difficulty that had led Nelson on a vain search of 10,000 miles. If the British tax-payer would provide enough steamers, the old danger that a shift of wind might decide the fate of England would vanish. And the tax-payer did; for although the alarmist note of certain extremely prominent public characters was chiefly uttered to justify a great scheme of coastal defence, its main result in the end was to strengthen the hands of the Admiralty in a wide extension of steam to the fleet. Screw engines were installed in several two-deckers, which was a great step forward. Their machinery was only powerful enough for the slow speeds of local operations; but its successful application refuted the long-maintained belief that steam could never be adopted for use in anything larger than a frigate, and thenceforward its full and universal acceptance for even the largest classes was only a question of time. The French took note of this and the talk of invasion ceased.

A few years later the whole British Navy, except its most obsolete vessels, was in commission for the first time on a full war footing since the peace settlement after Waterloo in order to prosecute hostilities with Russia. Since 1840 the superiority of steam over sails for tactical movement had become so generally recognized that no sailing ships pure and simple had been launched for any important navy for some time; and even those originally begun as such had been converted into steamers before taking the water. Not that sails had disappeared. Every steamer in the British fleet was masted, and the majority were just as fast and easily handled under canvas as their steamless predecessors. Oceanic passages were always made with screw hoisted and funnel down; but the day had gone when any British ship would ever fight without using steam. Paddles, however, had become obsolete for fighting tonnage within twenty years of their first appearance and were to die out.

In main features of construction the British fleet of 1855 still adhered to the fashion of centuries as to main types, only differing in the average hull-dimensions of each particular Rate, which had gradually increased during the previous twenty years till all had become half as large again in tonnage. Wood still held its monopoly, though the home-grown supply was no longer adequate, and great quantities were purchased abroad by Admiralty agents. The ordnance of the service had become very simple, four patterns providing virtually the whole supply. These were the 8-inch and 10-inch guns for shell and the 32-pounder and 68-pounder for shot, both shot and shell firers being about equally in use, though the lighter pair were about fifty times more numerous than the heavier, taking the Navy as a whole. The 10-inch and the 68-pounder were always upper-deck pivot guns, while the 8-inch and 32-pounder were usually carried on the broadside except in very small vessels. But though the varieties themselves were few the variety in their allocation to different ships was almost endless. About twenty different combinations existed in capital ships and frigates quite apart from lesser craft; and in several instances among paddlers the armament was peculiar to the individual ship. No standard for paddle frigates in fact existed, and that class were rated solely by tonnage.

By 1855 the sailing branch of the service, though still in use, was too obsolescent to merit further attention here. But the steam branch possesses an historical interest as being composed of the last eventually surviving wooden vessels under British colours ever to exchange shots with a European opponent. It numbered 3 three-deckers, 24 two-deckers, 24 frigates, 77 sloops, and 34 gunboats.

The twenty-seven capital ships were all screw, as paddles were never installed in any vessels of that category. Of the three-deckers the largest was the *Duke of Wellington* of 6,070 tons, carrying 131 guns with a broadside of 2,732 lb. and 1,150 officers and men. Her full steaming speed was 11½ knots. Fifteen comparatively new two-deckers were graded as Second Rates of 4,500 tons and 91 guns. These had a broadside of 1,820 lb. and a crew of 880. Nine old seventy-fours converted to steam comprised the Third Rates, with revised armaments of 60 guns, a broadside of 1,500 lb. (much heavier than before), and a crew of 615. Though old they were much sounder than some of the newer and larger vessels hurriedly built of unseasoned timber; but being the earliest capital ships to receive engines they could only steam six knots and were officially known as blockships. The frigates as a whole were a very heterogeneous lot of 1,200 to 1,850 tons, eight being screw steamers and sixteen paddle, with broadsides of 300 to 984 lb. and complements of 200 to 450. The sloops ranged from 480 to 1,130 tons, twenty-one being screw and fifty-six paddle, with broadsides of 64 to 620 lb. and complements of 90 to 170. Lastly, the gunboats were little craft of 220 to 480 tons, fore-and-aft rigged, all screw driven, with 2 to 4 pivot guns and 30 to 60 officers and men. As many as 150 more of them were built eventually for this particular war.

It was the first clash of arms to illustrate the murderous efficiency of shells in shattering wooden ships, though seventeen years had elapsed since they were added to naval ammunition. While the storm was brewing, but before the British or their French allies had passed the Bosphorus, the Russian Black Sea fleet, armed with Paixhan's *obusiers*, fell on the Turkish armed with solid shot only, while anchored in an open bay, and annihilated them so completely with no appreciable loss to themselves that this perfectly legitimate act of war was roundly denounced in England as the 'massacre' of Sinope. A few months later twenty-one British and French capital ships tried conclusions with the sea-forts of the Crimean peninsula only to find that in face of the Russian shells they could effect nothing without courting disaster. Thus the lesson of Sinope was carried a step farther, for this second demonstration was not a test of shell against shot, but of shell behind wood against shell behind stone. And the cause of failure pointed to the remedy in a more instructive fashion than would have been the case in an engagement between shell-firing fleets on both sides; for it was observed that when they struck stone they exploded almost harmlessly outside, whereas on striking a wooden ship they penetrated and burst internally as intended. That attracted the notice of a certain artillery officer with a natural gift for problems in gunnery, and as he happened to be the Emperor of the French his methods for solving them received immediate trial. As the author of a scientific treatise on ordnance he knew that thick cast-iron plates had been tested as a protection for fortresses years before and failed. But whereas cast metal is brittle, rolled metal is tough, and such great progress had been made in rolling iron since those experiments that it was virtually a different substance. Rolled plates 4½ inches thick were ordered accordingly from the makers, in sufficient quantity to cover some specially built vessels designed in the form of gigantic decked steam barges of shallow draught, intended for further attempts against land defences. These were designated 'floating batteries', but a better name would have been 'coast attack ships' since every fighting ship at that period was nothing else but a floating battery for the simple reason that she was launched for the sole purpose of carrying guns on the water. But that was a minor point. What really mattered was their complete success on the only occasion they had of proving their value. Britain copied them too late for use in that war, though if they had been available at its commencement there is little doubt that the whole history of the siege of Sevastopol might have been different.

As soon as it appeared reasonably evident that efficient shell-proof plating could be produced in rolled iron an extension of that form of covering to the line of battle was sooner or later inevitable, and once again the French pressed their own lead by being the first to armour a capital ship, though still adhering to a wooden hull as the structure to be protected. Then Britain drew in front for the first time, by one of the most far-reaching decisions in the history of naval architecture; which consisted in an abrupt and uncompromising abandonment of the so far universally accepted belief that even if thick iron was required as a protection, the thin iron which afforded the only possible alternative to timber as a hull substance was unsuitable material for war tonnage. Realizing from the advice of their Surveyor's experts that the improved quality of malleable iron had removed its former drawbacks, the British Admiralty accepted the suggestion they advanced that thin iron behind thick was better than oak behind thick, as being not only less inflammable but as permitting vast advances in hull design. Two forcible considerations supported the argument. Suitable oak was no longer plentiful in England, whereas iron was abundant. And the extremest limits of seaworthy size producible with even the finest timber had been reached in ships already afloat; perhaps passed, as the longest of these were suffering from longitudinal distortion.

No half measures marked this step either in the proposals of the Constructor's staff or the approval of the Board. Composite building of the type then coming into fashion elsewhere was set aside as unsuitable for capital ships; and once freed from the limitations imposed on their work by the nature of wood as a substance, the Admiralty designers, with the most valuable help of private builders expert in iron merchant-ship construction, immediately added 140 feet to the previously normal length of a capital ship in one jump, in a plan for a wrought-iron hull in keel, ribs, beams, stanchions, posts, and shell, with an armour covering over the main portion of the single gun-deck. This was the *Warrior*, in some respects the most interesting vessel in the history of British naval architecture as applied to belligerent purposes. She was built at Blackwall and launched in December 1860, being half as large again as the largest three-decker in the world.

Having taken this momentous step, the Admiralty gave it full scope by ordering five more iron-hulled capital ships to be laid down within eighteen months, and cancelled the commencement of any more in wood. Like the *Warrior*, these five had to be built by contract in the absence of the necessary plant in the Crown dockyards. Though differing in measurements among themselves the whole six had their main features in common, widely contrasting with all previous ideals. As the added weight of the armour was all carried above the water-line, stability could only be preserved by lowering the centre of gravity of the ordnance in mass; and that was only feasible by mounting it all on one deck instead of piling it up on two or three. Such a change unavoidably diminished the number of guns for which space was available; but loss in offensive power was averted partly by increased longitudinal space and partly by including only the very heaviest calibres in the armament not only as pivot guns but on the broadside. This instituted the policy of a small number of large guns instead of a large number of small, and as guns at this period grew even faster than ships in size they soon dominated the design of the latter in place of being subordinate to it. So far was that carried that within sixteen years of the launch of three-deckers carrying 130 guns the superlative example of a capital ship under construction was to carry only four, to suit which she had to be specially built. With these first six armoured vessels the process of increasing size and reducing numbers operated on their individual cases, since all ended their service carrying far fewer but much heavier weapons than when they began. For protection all were plated over the main battery by 4½-inch armour. Four more were begun soon after the original six.

The abruptness of the transfer from wood to iron raised a question as to what was to be done with eight partly built wooden capital ships on the stocks in the Royal dockyards. Little time was lost in settling it. To finish these vessels in their original design whether as two-deckers or three-deckers was out of the question now if armour protection was to be essential to battle-fleet rank. But as much money had been spent on them already the Admiralty decided to complete them as wooden hulls of modified form with only one gun-deck, but with armour protection of the same thickness as in the iron ships covering them entirely from bow to stern instead of merely over the battery. One of them, however—and that the largest—was even more thoroughly transformed into a coast defence turret vessel, thereby initiating a radically novel method of carrying guns at sea. Moreover, as a surplus stock of oak remained in hand it was reduced by specially building a last pair of wooden hulled but heavily armoured ships, in which the Admiralty were largely influenced by the armoured shipbuilding activity of the moment in France. Iron hulls would have been preferred as in keeping with the new ideals, but no further contracts could be accepted just then by private yards capable of launching them.

Huge developments in ordnance at this period accompanied—and in proportion even far surpassed—the remarkable advances in naval architecture. Both had their origin in an identical cause; for it was progress in the production of pure quality iron that enabled guns to be forged instead of cast. Old restrictions as to size were thereby removed, with the result that they increased about twenty times in weight in the same interval as capital ships had doubled. Moreover, the greater strength of forged iron allowed much heavier loading in proportion to weight of gun and increased ranging power threefold. And lastly, rifling the bore—thus far confined to manual firearms—was extended to artillery, with a correspondingly enhanced accuracy in shooting. For a short time breech-loaders were adopted in the British service from 1860, of the original Armstrong pattern; but proving unsatisfactory in breech mechanism were replaced by rifled muzzle-loaders, which for twenty years thereafter provided every size in British naval ordnance from the largest down, and were in full use to the exclusion of all else except a remnant of small Armstrongs in 1865, when the period covered by this description ends.

The building of the *Warrior* and her contemporaries, with the tremendously increased destructive power of armaments, set a new standard of war values by which the capital ship of a brief three years before simply ceased to count. No exaggeration is involved in saying that the whole combined battle-fleets of the Russian war era would have had as little terror for the *Warrior* as a flock of sheep for a wolf. They had no means of harming her, whereas she for her part could have executed them wholesale granted enough ammunition. And the same might be said of at least all the larger armoured ships built thereafter. Hence British sea-power in

1865 was founded on an armoured main force, and no correct presentation of the principal elements in its composition was obtainable under the old scaling by Rates, which had become very misleading as an index of power. With the whole service undergoing such a transformation as occurred in the sixties, however, no precisely descriptive system of classification could be substituted, as the Admiralty themselves found. It is only possible to say that a definite standard for a true capital ship of the new style is legitimately applicable by drawing a line at a figure of tonnage not below that of the largest three-deckers of the old order, and adding the qualification of ocean-keeping ability. Eighteen vessels out of a very diverse assortment of 32 armoured hulls in all answered to that test. The remainder consisted of 6 coast defence craft, 4 floating batteries, 2 corvettes, and 2 sloops.

Those eighteen armoured ships were the true successors of the two- and three-decked ships of the line reaching back to the seventeenth century. Ten were iron built, namely the *Warrior, Black Prince, Achilles, Hector, Defence, Valiant, Resistance, Minotaur, Agincourt,* and *Bellerophon.* Eight were wood, namely the *Prince Consort, Caledonia, Ocean, Royal Oak, Royal Alfred, Lord Clyde, Lord Warden,* and *Zealous.* But all of them, whether iron or wood in main structure, were single gun-decked broadside-armed designs, varying from 250 to 400 feet in length, 54 to 59½ feet in beam, and 6,000 to 10,600 tons in displacement. Twelve were covered either wholly or partly by 4½-inch armour, five by 5½-inch, and two by 6-inch. The *Bellerophon* was specially built to suit the new 9-inch rifled muzzle-loaders of 12½ tons, which fired a shell of 250 lb., nearly four times the weight of the heaviest of only five years before. The rest were armed with from sixteen to thirty-two rifled muzzle-loaders of 7-inch and 8-inch in combination—throwing shells of 120 lb. and 180 lb.—and manned by complements of 450 to 700 ranks and ratings. All these guns were slide mounted and arc elevated; and iron mountings were used for the 8- and 9-inch, being the first in the British service. For machinery the whole of these ships were horizontal engined with rectangular boilers, speeds ranging from 11½ to 14½ knots on trial, and all were square rigged. Two had five masts. As a group they constituted the battle-fleet of the White Ensign in 1865, and had cost in all about £6,500,000.

H. M. S. WARRIOR

Of the fourteen less important armoured units little need be said. The ten in the coast defence and floating battery divisions (known in the Navy as 'flat irons') belonged to categories which have never been otherwise than temporarily represented in the British service, and passed nearly all their existence lying up dismantled. But four of them had a feature of considerable interest nevertheless as the initial carriers of a centre line armament mounted in turrets above the hull instead of internally on the broadside; a change of supreme importance that was extended to the most powerful new types of capital ships in the near future. The four armoured corvettes and sloops had little value, for although they were quite safe from any unarmoured enemies, their own striking power was insufficient to find a proper place in the battle-fleet and their speed too low for useful cruiser duties.

Viewed in its entirety the armoured section of the British Navy at this stage of history illustrated very comprehensively the early Victorian process of transformation in four cardinal attributes pertaining to the water-borne power of previous centuries. Firstly the transition from sails to steam engines was conspicuously at its half-way point, for all capital ships had adopted the new motive agency without as yet relinquishing the old. And the same may be said of the change from wooden to iron hulls, for of the total number in the line of battle about half were of each substance. Thirdly, as regards offensive power, though the substitution of forged ordnance for cast was complete, the transfer of main armaments from the internal broadside to the external centre line was just beginning in the design of the coast defence vessels.

Of the unarmoured portion of the Navy nothing above frigate class had any war value now, for ships of the line of the old description were no longer line fighters, nor suitable for other work. The *Victoria*, the last and finest of British three-deckers, only served one commission. Below the capital ship standard, however, all unarmoured types still remained suitable for the duties of a world-wide cruiser force under the prevailing conditions; though the long-famous frigate was gradually giving way to a mixed collection of masted vessels which were classed indiscriminately by the Admiralty as 'corvettes', a term of French origin denoting a large sloop.

Properly, therefore, it only applied to vessels carrying their whole armament on deck, and in that sense it came into the British Navy with some prizes, though for half a century it was very sparingly used. But Admiralty nomenclature has always been consistent only in its inconsequence. By the fifties the title 'corvette' was being bestowed on a numerous new class of twice the tonnage of a sloop, and by the sixties on ships exceeding the size of a Georgian frigate. Before the seventies the original meaning of the word as indicating a craft with no guns carried below had ceased to apply; and every new unarmoured hull intermediate between 1,000 tons and 5,000 tons was officially dubbed a corvette, the term 'frigate' being abandoned altogether before the eighties, by which period vessels of the tonnage of the *Victory* were on the corvette list.

In 1865—the closing year of this survey—thirty-eight frigates were still on the effective list, to twenty-six ships then classed as corvettes. Both categories were entirely composed of timber-built broadside-armed fully-rigged ships, all of which were faster ships under sail in a good breeze than their best speeds under steam, and several of which were the fastest sailers ever built for the British Navy, with speeds of fourteen to seventeen knots in a gale. The frigates varied from 3,000 to 4,500 tons, and the corvettes from 1,000 to 1,700. Both carried mixed armaments of rifled guns and smooth-bores. The sloop class were in process of extensive replacement by the type officially listed as 'gun-vessels', which were on the average just as large as the sloops of twenty years before. But thirty heavy sloops still remained of 480 to 970 tons, all three-masted, as brigs were no longer built. Of gun-vessels and still smaller 'gunboats' about 135 were afloat in condition for service, ranging from 210 to 690 tons, all armed with pivot guns and rigged as barques or three-masted brigantines. At that period even the smallest of these carried guns of the same calibre as the largest frigates, but only two instead of forty.

No descriptive treatment of the British fleet at any stage of history can be considered as in any degree comprehensive without at least some brief reference to the industry under which its material elements were produced and maintained in fit condition for use. In early Victorian days the nation was far less disposed than in later times to resort to private assistance towards providing and repairing the instruments of a sea defence. No three-decker was ever launched from any but a Royal dockyard, and extremely few two-deckers. The main line of battle therefore was placed afloat by nationally organized labour, supplemented by the co-operation of private shipbuilders in aiding with the production of accessory units. All repair and maintenance was carried out in the establishments of the Crown. To meet the demands of the fleet under this system of administration six State dockyards existed in the early Victorian period at Portsmouth, Chatham, Devonport, Woolwich, Sheerness, and Pembroke. In these the number of workmen necessarily varied to some extent with the amount of building and repairing in hand; but an established nucleus of not less than 6,000 remained even when expenditure was at its lowest, because when a large part of the fleet was laid up dockyard labour was necessary for the preservation and care of the vessels so transferred to dockyard charge, every one of which, among other things, required periodical pumping out. In the panic periods as many as 12,000 to 15,000 hands were employed, and since neither seamen nor ordinary labourers would handle coal in those days, convicts were used in the dockyards to coal the fleet.

Collectively the Crown yards possessed forty-four building slips, of which thirty were large enough to receive the keel of a capital ship. But though the State itself produced nearly all its vessels in that era, the very opposite was the case with their weapons, for which it relied almost entirely on private industry. By an antiquated arrangement, largely connected with political patronage, the Admiralty had to arm the Navy through the authority of the Master-General of the Ordnance, a functionary over whose department they had no control, and from whom every gun on board a ship was legally on loan. The Ordnance branch for their part procured the guns and shot by contract from private foundries, under which arrangement the cost of the heaviest cast-iron smoothbore complete with mounting and appurtenances was about £45. The price of a roundshot of the same calibre was about 6*s*.

When, however, towards the end of the fifties the Admiralty and the Ordnance authorities alike availed themselves of the great improvements in the quality of wrought iron a curious reversal of former practice occurred; for whereas the sea service began to rely much more on private co-operation the land service began to rely much less. Neither had the plant to undertake iron forging on the scale they now needed; but that presented little difficulty where ships were concerned, as a score of private yards were engaged by that time in iron mercantile ship-building, any of which were prepared to accept Admiralty contracts. But as nobody had hitherto wanted such a thing as a wrought-iron gun no firm had the machinery for making them, and in that respect the private iron-founders were no better off than the State. Two engineering firms only were able or willing to help, which was nothing like enough. The new demand therefore was met by a very large extension of the Royal Arsenal; and thus by the year 1865 eight of the ten iron-hulled capital ships afloat had been built by private labour, while eight out of every ten guns they carried had been forged by the State. A very few years before those proportions would have been more than inverted for both.

The first iron-hulled vessel ever to be built by any government in the world in a yard of its own was the *Achilles*, whose keel was laid at Chatham in 1861. Several years elapsed before iron hulls were put in hand at any other British Royal dockyard, and none were ever launched from Woolwich, which was closed down altogether in 1869 after existing since the reign of Henry VIII. As regards machinery all engines and boilers for the Navy were made by private manufacturers for nearly fifty years after the *Comet* received the first set. A few large firms who specialized in the particular types of engines most suitable for war designs practically monopolized Admiralty orders; and even repairs were largely undertaken by contract.

Space does not permit here of further details regarding the ships and armaments of the middle nineteenth century. But from the above general account some idea may perhaps be gathered of the profundity of the change that overtook their forms and dimensions during the first half of the reign of Victoria—a change so revolutionary and all-embracing within a single decade that nothing like it or even approaching to it had occurred in the annals of fighting-ship construction during the three previous centuries of the history of British maritime defence.

§ 2. OFFICERS AND MEN

The administration of a fighting fleet is a task of gigantic complexity, which in the case of the British service has been on a larger scale than any other since the conclusion of the Anglo-Dutch wars of the seventeenth century. Not only must it control the manufacture of a much vaster mass of scientifically designed and laboriously produced structure than that created by other agencies either afloat or ashore, whether national or private, but it must apply the units of the finished whole to their many separate purposes, and to that end assemble, organize, train, pay, and feed many thousand skilled servants. It combines the functions of shipbuilder, shipowner, and professional instructor—which in private maritime industry are usually distinct—and adds to them those of the strategist, tactician, cartographer, and maritime law enforcer. And finally it must render a meticulously detailed account of the immense sums of public money expended on all these forms of activity.

In England naval administration began with the appointment of Keepers of the King's ships in the thirteenth century, from which the office of Lord High Admiral eventually arose. This great responsibility fell to a long line of exalted servants of the Crown and ultimately passed to Prince George of Denmark as husband of Queen Anne. But he did not prove a great success, and at a later stage the duties were handed over to a council of naval officers presided over by a cabinet minister, styled 'Commissioners for executing the Office of Lord High Admiral' but holding civilian status; and except for a brief interval of eighteen months in the reign of George IV the office has been in that form of Commission ever since. But whereas the First Lord Commissioner was usually a professional seaman of long experience up to the end of the Napoleonic wars, he was always a civil politician thereafter, whose only qualification for heading a service which knows no party adherence lay in the fact that he was an ardent and capable party servant.

It so happens that the brief temporary revival of a Lord High Admiral's authority in a single individual coincided with the commencement of the period under review here, for it was in 1827 that the Duke of Clarence (afterwards William IV) was so appointed by his brother, then on the throne, with the members of the dissolved Board of Commissioners reduced to the position of his counsellors. Next year, however, when Wellington became premier, he demanded the Duke's resignation; who, although very conscientious in attending to his functions, saw them mainly in the light of a truly regal ideal of hospitality at his own expense, whereon, according to Sir John Barrow, he lavished £20,000 in eighteen months. On his resignation Commissioners were again installed, first with Lord Melville at their head—who had served for fifteen years in a similar position under former governments—and then Sir James Graham. The latter reconstructed the whole system of naval administration in 1832 on a model remaining in force with very little alteration to the end of the century. By his reforms thirteen outside and practically independent departments which had come into existence from time to time for conducting various branches of naval supply (with much overlapping and delay) were all absorbed under immediate control of the Board under a well-devised plan of co-ordination.

The wide powers vested in the Commissioners as representing the Lord High Admiral in matters of authority over officers and men were based on the Articles of War as laid down by Parliament; but the Commissioners themselves were held to be civil servants while in office, and as such not subject to naval jurisdiction even though holding the King's Commission as naval officers. In 1827 the Articles of War were still those framed in 1749, which prescribed twenty-two offences for which any court martial could pass sentence of death, including ten where such a sentence was compulsory. Flogging and long terms of imprisonment could be ordered by any captain on his own warrant. In 1860, however, Parliament amended the Articles of War for the first time in 111 years, reducing the offences in which a death sentence was permissible to seventeen, and those in which it was compulsory to treason and murder only. Flogging was to be a court-martial punishment, and a captain's power of imprisonment was to be limited to three months. Minor summary punishments were regulated by code for the first time. Apart from their penal clauses the Articles of War laid down certain definite instructions for the regulation of the service, whereby among other things the Admiralty were empowered to make such rules by Orders in Council as they might consider necessary, which obviously gave them very autocratic authority indeed over all questions of the employment and promotion of officers. Against their decision in such matters there was no appeal as long as an officer was in receipt of the pay of his rank.

Of the Navy as a whole it may be said that during the forty years' interval between the end of the Napoleonic wars and the mid-century conflict with Russia its position was rather that of a large standing reserve than an active force, since more than five-sixths of the officers were idle on shore, and the men were not entered for permanent service but simply hired and discharged as needed, in the same way as in the mercantile marine; except those who engaged to train for the higher gunnery ratings, and even they were only on a seven years' contract. The officers were organized in four branches; but only one branch held the King's Commission as members of the profession of arms, the other three serving for purely non-combatant administrative duties under rank granted by a warrant from the Admiralty. Commissioned officers were styled the 'military' branch, and comprised the Admirals, Captains, Commanders, and Lieutenants. On them rested all responsibility for conducting operations of war, and all executive authority. Under training to rise to commissioned rank were the Mates, Midshipmen, and so-called Volunteers. Between the mates and midshipmen the only difference was that the former had passed the qualifying examination for a lieutenant's commission and were waiting the good pleasure of the Admiralty to receive it—which might never come—and the latter had not passed, and perhaps not even tried although in possession of the six years sea time entitling them to do so. The volunteers corresponded very much to the modern naval cadet in some respects, being boys under fourteen, but serving without pay. Some were entered direct from the shore by nomination of the captain of the ship, while others were sent afloat by the Admiralty from the old Royal Naval College in Portsmouth dockyard, an establishment on the lines of an ordinary preparatory school for 100 boys under twelve, maintained officially through a scale of fees payable by their parents, to which the sons of gentlemen were nominated by the First Lord. That was the first rung of the long ladder before them.

Mates, midshipmen, and volunteers were only rated as

petty officers, and were therefore discharged to the shore whenever their ship paid off, just as the men. Once on shore the Admiralty had no power to appoint them to another ship unless they applied for it, and those who found the prospects of a shore career more promising left the sea altogether. Others, who either could not or would not pass for a commission, or who were not considered suitable for one by the Admiralty even though passed, simply continued to serve in ship after ship in the same rating till men of middle age. Bald or grey-headed midshipmen were sometimes seen accordingly.

The military branch in a three-decker when Victoria became Queen was made up of the captain, eight lieutenants, twenty-four mates and midshipmen, and five volunteers. At the opposite extreme of tonnage a brig or cutter carried one lieutenant and one mate or midshipman. From the forties on, a commander as well as a captain was carried by all ships of the line in place of one lieutenant, but otherwise these officers' complements remained practically unaltered till the ships of those types died out.

A marked distinction was officially drawn between the commissioned branch and the other three, consisting of the Masters, Pursers, and Surgeons. The first-named of those were professional master mariners transferred from private employment to naval service by grant of warrant rank, and to them—under the captain—was entrusted the navigation and pilotage of each ship; obviously a supremely responsible charge. Expert seamanship was their special qualification as distinct from any knowledge of gunnery; and it was not asked of them to be able to recognize a gun when they saw it, except as an article that might affect the accuracy of the compasses. But every ship in the Navy from the largest to the smallest carried a representative of the masters' branch, and as their station in action was beside the captain they had their full share of exposure to danger and ought in justice to have been granted commissions. Second masters and masters' assistants formed the lower ranks in this line, the latter being rated petty officers like the midshipmen.

Pursers were the accountant and victualling officers responsible for provisioning and clothing the men. They held rank under warrant from the Accountant-General at the Admiralty and were usually drawn from the civil class of minor clerks and retail tradesmen. Though in receipt of a lower scale of pay than a lieutenant—and at a figure that was exactly the same in every ship large or small—their official profits on victualling and clothing contracts and issues were so extensive that their actual income usually exceeded that of any officer in the ship including the captain. In naval literature the purser is caricatured as an unattractive figure; and perhaps not quite without reason, for though it would be a wicked libel to suggest that the majority were other than straight by the standards of the time, it would be equally absurd to maintain that none ever fell before the temptation of making an unscrupulous use of the regulations governing contracts, which were so peculiar as to offer direct incentives to sharp practice. Every vessel carried a purser.

Of the medical branch it need only be said here that they were qualified surgeons or physicians appointed by warrant from the Medical Director-General. A First Rate ship carried three, and the lower Rates two or one in proportion to complement. In the unsanitary conditions of early Victorian sea life the medical officers were a hard-worked body during peace as well as war, especially on unhealthy tropical stations, and large numbers fell victims to duty in combating epidemics of yellow fever and infectious disease.

In 1826 the engineers appeared, but not on a permanent list, being then only factory foremen lent by the contractors for making the engines, and given temporary warrant rank. As machinery became more and more important, however, they were established as a permanently registered branch of warrant officers entirely in the public service like the others, and ranking next to the carpenters. Later still they were raised to the same status as the master and purser branches and organized in four classes.

Officers' quarters varied extremely with their rank. For admirals and their personal staffs special accommodation was erected on the main deck; and in a ship of the line even the captain's suite of cabins was almost as spacious as the quarters of all the other officers combined, with a dining cabin where he could easily seat a score of guests. He lived alone as now. Lieutenants, masters, pursers, surgeons, chaplains, and chief engineers messed together in the Ward Room, and in most cases occupied separate cabins which they had to furnish themselves. Mates, midshipmen, volunteers, and juniors of the civil branches lived in a space partitioned off in the cockpit (lit by candles alone), slept in hammocks, washed in buckets, and kept their scant kit in diminutive chests. Officers were entitled to exactly the same rations as the men, but in the Ward Room those were supplemented by a private system of a common table. As a rule the mates and midshipmen had to be content with rations alone.

But all ranks suffered in that age from a common lack of professional employment, and the higher the rank the worse the evil. Naval officers were servants of the State in title rather than in fact, for though holding commissions or warrants on permanent lists debarring them from accepting work in other directions, the demand for their presence afloat under the pennant was so excessively limited for forty years after the Napoleonic wars that their occupation was almost gone, and with it their proper pay. In the thirties the Navy List contained on an average the names of 200 flag-officers, 1,500 captains and commanders, and nearly 3,000 lieutenants, of whom fourteen admirals out of fifteen, nine captains and commanders in ten, and five lieutenants out of six were rusting ashore on a starvation scale of emolument for the juniors. The ordinary run could only hope for about five years' full pay to twenty of enforced idleness; and a legend exists that one officer caused a sensation by sweeping the Whitehall pavement outside the Admiralty in full dress to call public attention to the plight of his profession. Moreover, as there was no compulsory retirement for age the lists got hopelessly blocked. Flag-officers and captains of ninety and lieutenants of eighty were all to be found on the Active List liable for sea duty. Promotion to rear-admiral only came after about thirty-five years on the list of captains.

A further great handicap to advancement arose from the regulations whereby (very properly) a certain number of years had to be spent at sea in each rank before an officer could be promoted to the next. That ended in leaving the prospects of all a good deal in the hands of such admirals as were fortunate enough to be sent to sea themselves, because when one of these hoisted his flag he could in practice select most of his flagship officers, and so help their futures by giving them the necessary qualifying time; in addition to which his flag-lieutenant was promoted straight away when the flag came down. Naturally enough, they chose their own sons and nephews first, and then those of other admirals who could return the same favour; with the result that in early Victorian days naval careers were almost a monopoly of certain families, and in a gradually lessening degree this continued for quite fifty years more. Probably the interests of the country did not suffer much as the lineage was good stock; but in some notorious cases it failed to breed true, and right to the end of the century officers were to be found who had obviously reached the higher ranks through their name and not their merits. Old satiric naval prints show these favourites of fortune walking straight through the half-pay officers' waiting-room at the Admiralty, in which brother officers grew grey-headed during futile years of patient attendance.

From time to time as the early Victorian age ran its course the Admiralty resorted to various expedients and remedies for relieving the utter stagnation in the general prospects of the younger officers by sweeping schemes of compulsory retirement. An improvement arose through the commissioning of all effective ships for the Russian war in 1854 but it was only temporary, and with the return of peace matters were as bad as ever. Eventually after a Parliamentary inquiry and report the government of the day cut down the permanent list to a fixed number of 100 flag-officers, 300 captains, 400 commanders, and 1,000 lieutenants, the civil branches being reduced in proportion. A wholesale clearance was made of all the rest, but the prospects of those who escaped the axe were so much improved that even in a year of peace such as 1860, about half the captains and commanders and three-quarters of the lieutenants were at sea on full pay. Mates had become commissioned officers with the title of sub-lieutenant and volunteers were now known as naval cadets. A training ship had been established for all officers entering the 'military' branch, and all ranks were established on permanent lists. Compulsory retirement had been introduced at a fixed age for each rank.

Corresponding changes were made in the civil branches, which were all raised by a succession of stages extending over some twenty odd years to commissioned rank before the middle of the reign of Victoria, and in certain cases granted new titles though never invested with disciplinary authority. Thus the masters' branch became staff commanders, navigating lieutenants, navigating sub-lieutenants, and navigating midshipmen. The pursers became paymasters, assistant paymasters, and clerks, and were placed on a much higher rate of pay but deprived of the former percentages on issues and contracts. The engineers, however, still formed a separate mess socially and were by regulation debarred from inclusion in any civic or social courtesies or hospitalities extended by the shore to the officers of the fleet. At this period they were mainly of dockyard artisan or lower deck parentage; and although professionally highly competent and reliable servants of the State it must be admitted that they appeared more frequently in the court-martial returns on charges of insobriety than the other officers, though in early Victorian days that tendency was much more common in all branches than it was after.

At the beginning of the nineteenth century the uniform of naval officers was about as unsuitable for sea life as could have been devised, with its white knee-breeches, waistcoat, stockings, and cravat, buckled shoes, cocked hat, and open coat blown about by the least wind. Epaulettes and gold lace rapidly tarnish in damp sea air. But by 1830 the knee-breeches had been abolished in favour of trousers—white or blue according to season—and a buttoned ship-jacket without epaulettes was worn for ordinary duties with a stiff black wide-rimmed and glazed hat having a side cockade and gold loop. Black cravats replaced white. The full-dress coat was cut to button up and scarlet facings replaced white; the sword-belt being changed from black watered silk to black leather. Up till 1832 the civil branches wore warrant officers' uniforms with distinctive collar badges, but no epaulettes. From that year, however, their dress was similar to the military branch but with a single- instead of a double-breasted coat.

In 1847 the undress uniform was completely changed into a cut more in accordance with the general fashion of the day in men's attire. A double-breasted frock-coat replaced the cut-away ship-jacket and a straight-peaked, narrow-crowned, gold-banded cloth cap the hard hat. Gold lace rank stripes were put on the sleeves, and white facings restored to the full dress in place of red. A crown was worn as cap badge but no anchor. In 1856 the gold cap band was abolished and a black one substituted, an anchor and laurel wreath being added to the badge. The 'curl' was introduced in the rank stripe of the military branch. In 1869 the Navy was allowed to grow a beard, and did so in voluminous form. But never during the early Victorian age was any uniform suitable for hot climates introduced; and in the full glare of the tropics a naval officer was dressed from head to foot exactly as in Portsmouth harbour except for white trousers.

At the beginning of the Victorian period the Navy was only a standing body as regards the officers. The seamen were not entered for a long term of continuous service like soldiers, but engaged as servants of the nation only for the period during which the ship they chose to join from the shore was in commission and for a five years' maximum at that. When a captain was appointed to commission a vessel in reserve, therefore, he had to begin by finding himself a crew, which might take months if seamen happened to be much in demand at the moment. And as the ship was an empty shell without masts, armament, or stores of any kind, his next task was to fit her out by degrees as he obtained competent hands.

Once engaged the men earned their wages under the regulation scale, but as a precaution against mutiny or desertion the money was never handed over till the ship returned home, when they were paid off with the whole sum due for three or four years in a lump (speedily dissipated) and remained their own masters until they chose to join a fresh ship. While serving, however, a man was permitted to allot his wages, in whole or part monthly as they fell due, to his wife or any friend permanently resident in the United Kingdom, such allotments being paid direct to the recipients by the Admiralty. Under that arrangement he could provide for his dependants in his absence, even though the check against his desertion held good. That suited service requirements in more ways than one, as such men had very little cash to receive on paying off, and empty pockets soon drove them to rejoin. When by a succession of commissions served under this system—all recorded on his certificate—a seaman had accumulated twenty years under the pennant, he was entitled to a pension however long his intervals of absence from the Navy might have been; though only a very small proportion ever reached it. Often they joined the merchant service for a time, especially during the dearth of naval employment during the thirties and forties when four-fifths of the fleet were laid up.

The early Victorian Navy was essentially English manned. Out of 100 seamen taken at random on any date about 83 would be English bred, and only 11 Irish, 4 Scotch, and 2 Welsh. And three-fourths of the English element came from the southern counties. Taken in the mass they were a rough, illiterate, muscular lot under twenty-five years old, drawn chiefly from the poorest quarters of the Royal dockyard towns; ill fed, remorselessly worked and drilled, and leading a life of chronic over-crowding and hardship under an exacting discipline. On foreign service they often passed three or four years without ever setting foot ashore, as no leave was granted in alien ports, and they had no money to tempt them to land in colonial. But most of them knew no other existence, for a lower deck career was almost traditional with the lads born in the alleyways of the great naval ports, who were creditably proud of it as a skilled trade, and patriotically amenable to discipline when administered with justice from a full consciousness of belonging to the premier service of its particular kind in the world. In every ship, however, a few ruffianly characters were sure to be included, who feared no punishment but the gratings and were always ready to foment trouble. Flogging was a terrible ordeal, leaving the back scarred for life, but in Victorian days the better class among the men themselves always insisted that in critical situations it might often be the last sanction for discipline and general safety; and at that period of naval history a stage had been reached in which the Admiralty never tolerated its abuse by commanding officers.

With the general public the seamen of the Navy were popular, partly because of their importance to national security, and partly because when seen on shore they were generally in convivial holiday mood with open hands. But it was a superficial sentiment, never extended to any direct interest in their welfare, of which Parliament and the Press were alike oblivious. Scandalous victualling contracts and such-like passed unheeded unless matters were so bad that seamen were unobtainable in sufficient numbers on occasions of national uneasiness or emergency. And it was this uncertainty of getting the fleet expeditiously manned in times of political unrest that eventually altered the old system. In former days the remedy lay with the press-gang; but Victorian ideals were not in accord with such crude prescriptions, and after a succession of national alarms connected with developments of the French fleet the Admiralty announced in 1855 that it had become 'highly important to give the Navy a more permanent organization'. A half-step towards that end was taken accordingly by an order that thenceforward all new entries of men under eighteen years of age were to be regulated by their engaging to serve for ten years in continuity, passing direct to the guardship at the port when paid off from one vessel (instead of being discharged to the shore) so as to be in readiness for drafting to another whenever needed, and retaining any higher rating they might have reached instead of losing it by discharge. An interval of paid leave was to be allowed between ship and ship, and wages were to be paid half-yearly both at home and abroad instead of held up till the end of a commission. On completing a first ten years they were to have the option of engaging for two further periods of five years each and so complete the twenty years entitling them to a pension.

But men over eighteen could still join under the old system though permitted to join under the new; and because it was only a half measure as tried thus, 'the more permanent organization' was only partly attained. To many the complete release from the bondage of discipline enjoyed on each discharge to the shore appealed very strongly. As a further inducement to enter on the new terms, therefore, the whole Coastguard Service was transferred in 1856 to the Admiralty and opened to continuous service men of good character, who were enabled thereby to obtain permanent wages and free quarters for themselves and families while remaining available for the fleet in war or emergency. But even that failed to produce sufficient numbers, and at length in 1862 continuous service was made compulsory for all men joining thereafter, the seamen being entered first as boys in one of five harbour training-ships specially established, and the stokers entered direct in the port guardship. The Navy had now for the first time in its long history as a constitutional force become a standing body of men as well as officers.

Up till the year 1857 no regulation uniform existed except for the officers. The men had to make and pay for their own clothes from materials in the pursers' 'slops'. A general similarity of colour prevailed throughout the fleet since the materials were the same in all ships; but each captain had his own fancies as to cut and trimmings, and this lack of uniformity was one of the men's objections to continuous service, as a direct transfer from ship to ship often entailed a new outfit. To meet this difficulty therefore a uniform for the whole service was established in 1857—still at the men's expense—to which pattern they were compelled thereafter to adhere in making their clothes. It did not differ very much from that which is still worn, but the upper garment was tucked inside the trouser waist like a shirt, and known as a 'frock', and straw hats were used as well as caps. For inspection and ceremonial kit a stiff blue cloth outer jacket was put on over all, officially known as a tunic, though only reaching down to the waist and open fronted. Trousers were blue cloth instead of serge as now.

In complete contrast to all conditions governing the service of the professional sea officers and men stood those which regulated the Royal Marines, who formed part of the general force administered by the Admiralty, although ranked, raised, organized, armed, and attired on the army model and trained purely as soldiers. This was a standing corps from top to bottom, inspired by a very high standard of discipline and loyalty, and performing duty alternatively in the fleet and ashore as part garrison of the three chief naval ports. The officers therefore knew nothing of the evils of long half-pay unemployment, and the men were recruited and trained in their barracks on the same general system as the land forces. But neither officers nor men had any knowledge of technical seamanship, whether in its higher scientific application or in its skilled labour; and the inclusion of such a body in a fleet organization was confined to the British and United States navies as a consequence of their casual method of engaging expert seamen, who in other countries served under conscription. Hence arose the time-wasting anomaly that when a captain and his officers were appointed to a ship in reserve, and had to rig and arm her for service, the only men to be put on board at once were her marines from barracks, who were useless for fitting out however excellent as a foundation for discipline. Long delays often resulted, which were only avoided when the policy of continuous service was made generally applicable.

In the early Victorian days the marines were divided into artillery and light infantry, the former being fully instructed in all forms of naval gun drill but the latter only in the use of musket and bayonet. As a standing corps they underwent much less fluctuation in numbers than the seaman element, and in peace therefore formed a much larger proportion of the Navy as a whole than in war. For example, during the Napoleonic conflict they constituted about one-sixth of the total muster under Admiralty administration, whereas twenty years after, when that total had been forced down to 30,000, they provided almost one-third. In uniform and appointments they corresponded very closely to the regular army, and when not required afloat they were subject to the Army Discipline Act though always at Admiralty disposal.

§ 3. DISTRIBUTION AND ACTIVITIES

As the chief protection of the British Isles against invasion, the central mass of the Navy was never out of European waters in peace or war unless some great strategic movement of an enemy's forces was in progress, such as the French concentration in the west Atlantic planned by Bonaparte before Trafalgar. But the security of the colossal aggregate of British goods and property scattered over many million square miles of water has always demanded the stationing of detached forces, and as the necessity for their protective presence becomes instantly urgent on the outbreak of war with any maritime Power—when no time is available to organize and spread them—their permanent retention within their allotted areas of vigilance is just as unavoidable even in time of peace as, for instance, the permanent presence of British troops in India. More than ever did that apply in early Victorian days, before either radio or cable messages could pass to give intelligence of the discovered whereabouts of hostile raiders, and when independence of coal supplies afforded an enemy unfettered freedom of movement denied to the German cruisers of the Great War.

In those days, therefore, as now, such portions of the Navy as happened to be in active commission were always extended over enormous distances and areas, even when no nation was on terms of hostility towards the British flag.

But while so distributed they were by no means idly waiting on the possible advent of war, for the risks from irregular enemies on the sea are never absent even when quiescent. Right down to our own times history has told the same tale, that in countries with a coast-line whose government is ineffective or semi-civilized, endemic piracy invariably exists unless suppressed by outside force. For example, the fifty million Chinese engaged in sea-fishing or coastal junk traffic are pilferers almost to a man (as every one conversant with that littoral knows), always disposed to turn pirate given arms and immunity against retribution. The same applies to the whole population of the Malay Archipelago where not under European colonial administration, and to at least a portion of the very mixed breeds inhabiting the regions round the Caribbean. The seafaring Arabs again are by tradition slave-dealers and weapon-sellers whenever such commerce is not made too risky. Nor are these various illicit activities confined to coloured operators, for the gun-runner and his like in east or west is often financed by white rascality.

At the Navarino period the main branches of British ocean trade requiring secure conditions for prosperity were the West Indian and North American in the occident and the East Indian and Malayan orientally; the first two open to all shipowners, but the last two a monopoly of the East Indian Company, whose enterprises extended to Canton, the only port in China then open to foreigners. Japan was closed except to the Dutch, Australia still too undeveloped for regular commerce, and the Pacific only sailed by American whalers. Beyond Cape Horn in one direction, therefore, and the Straits of Malacca in the other, the British Navy had nothing to watch over in 1827, although plenty under its charge in the Atlantic and Indian Oceans.

In that Navarino year nine two-deckers, thirty-three frigates, and sixty sloops were distributed between eight foreign stations, each of which was a separate command under a flag-officer or commodore: namely North America, South America, West Indies, East Indies, Mediterranean, West Africa, Cape of Good Hope, and Lisbon. Three of the capital ships were employed in support of British policy in South America connected with the rebellion against Spain; four others were on the Lisbon station, also for political reasons of the moment, and the remaining pair in the Mediterranean, which in the days before it gave through passage to the east, or was flanked by a great French colonial dominion, formed not nearly so important a command as it became later. The slave-trade was flourishing on either side of Africa and boat actions with Malay and Arab pirates were frequent.

In addition to its other duties at that period the Navy was charged with carrying the oversea mails, except to Indian Ocean ports, where that responsibility rested with the vessels of the East India Company. The mail packets were all partly disarmed sloops organized for separate routes, of which the transatlantic services based on Falmouth required the greatest number. These packets were the only ships of the Royal Navy, moreover, that were ever regularly employed in carrying private passengers at a fixed schedule of charges.

By 1840—the year of Acre—the total force on foreign service was sixteen two-deckers, twenty-five frigates, and ninety-four sloops, of which by that time thirteen were paddle-steamers. The Mediterranean had become the very important station it has remained ever since, partly on account of the new French policy of large-scale conquest in North Africa, and partly through an increasing British interest in the development of a route to India by Egypt. The vast Pacific had become a new station following on the expansion of the Cape Horn traffic, and the responsibilities of the Cape of Good Hope squadron had been extended to the east and west coasts of Africa, where the suppression of the slave-trade took its toll in British lives. The East Indies command was also enlarged and now included China and the Malay Archipelago, in both of which areas increased trade stimulated increased coastal piracy on a regularly organized basis, resulting in some severe cold steel work for the boats of the squadron. On the other hand, South America had been reduced to a Commodore's station known as the Brazils, and the North American and West Indian commands had been combined to make one. A general period of quiet lasted through the thirties, but the long succession of minor wars in which the Victorian Navy bore some part were on the eve of beginning.

In the forties and opening fifties, besides the battle-fleet engagement at Acre, and some forcible intervention to protect British interests suffering from perpetual internecine conflicts in South America, the Navy participated in the first China war—which brought Hong-Kong under the flag—and the second Burmese war. Then came hostilities in Europe (with the French and Turks as allies afloat and ashore) against Russia. That mobilized the whole effective fleet lying in ordinary reserve, but made no difference to the disposition of the forces on distant stations, which were always in their war areas. And because British commerce was thus adequately guarded the Russians left it alone, unlike other Powers when at war with Britain before or after. Had that been otherwise it would have suffered something akin to the experiences ten years later of the defenceless mercantile tonnage of the Northern States of America, when ruthlessly destroyed by a single Confederate cruiser built and sailing from a neutral port.

Between the close of the Russian war and the end of the sixties, vessels of the British Navy were engaged in the Persian war and the second Chinese war—in which the gunboat flotilla suffered a sanguinary reverse in trying to force the entrance to the Peiho—besides carrying out reprisals for outrages in Japan. Permanent patrols were also established on both sides of Africa for the suppression of the slave-trade, and although the Malay pirates had been exterminated, the Chinese pirates remained always a source of trouble. In the middle sixties the total force on foreign stations comprised six capital ships, thirty-one frigates and corvettes, and sixty-three sloops and gun-vessels, the whole being steamers by that period,

On the five occasions between 1827 and 1865 in which British squadrons of large vessels were under fire only the first was a purely naval battle, and that was Navarino. The others were engagements with land batteries at Acre, Sevastopol, Kagosima, and Shimonosaki. Each was the outcome of a situation distinct from the others, and only the last two aimed at a similar immediate object. Navarino stopped a land campaign by cutting off the sea supplies of an invading army with no duplicate line of service. Acre halted the coastal marching of an army unable to move by any alternative route. Sevastopol was an abortive attempt to intensify the pressure of an already existing blockade in order to support land operations. And finally Kagosima and Shimonosaki were reprisals for attacks which ceased thereafter.

Navarino was not a premeditated encounter, nor waged in

DECK OF A CORVETTE, ABOUT 1856

defence of any direct British interests. It was a result of diplomatic intervention in the inter-racial quarrels of the subjects of an alien State. The Greek population were in open rebellion against their Turkish masters, and giving them such trouble in the Morean mountains that the Sultan summoned help from the celebrated Mehemet Ali, his Viceroy in Egypt. The latter accordingly dispatched a well-trained body of troops in a large convoy of transports escorted by his efficient fleet, the whole being under his son Ibrahim Pasha. This expedition made for Navarino Bay, the superb Morean harbour used as a base for the Turkish land operations, where the fleet from Constantinople was already lying. But Britain, France, and Russia had agreed to espouse the rebel cause diplomatically, and though vague as to procedure had each sent a squadron to the Morean coast to demonstrate against the Egyptian measures. It was precisely the kind of situation in which naval officers of every country may expect to find themselves the scapegoats of ambiguous orders issued by nervous politicians; and those issued to the British admiral, Sir Edward Codrington, were simply fantastic, as he was directed to prevent Ibrahim's movements though not to use his guns.

Codrington did his best by way of persuasion accordingly, aided by his French and Russian colleagues, but without effect; and hearing presently that Ibrahim's methods were brutal the three admirals sailed into Navarino Bay in company to emphasize their protests, anchoring at two o'clock on the afternoon of October 20 with the British flagship *Asia* leading. Codrington's orders against using his guns were passed to the others and rigorously observed as they entered the harbour, but the Moslems were already at quarters, and becoming alarmed at the proceedings of one or two British boats lowered to take soundings yielded to panic and opened fire. This naturally provoked retaliation in self-defence, whereby a furious general action was started lasting till evening, by which time about half of the 120 Moslem warships and transports had been destroyed. Next morning the admiral sent a prisoner ashore to warn Ibrahim that the remainder would suffer a like fate if they displayed further hostile intentions; and being a shrewdly competent commander the Egyptian accepted defeat and eventually re-embarked for home.

The British squadron comprised 3 two-deckers, with some frigates and sloops, the French and Russian being rather smaller. In France and Russia the news excited unlimited enthusiasm, but British public opinion was divided in sympathy between Turks and Greeks. Whatever views were held in the matter, however, it remained beyond dispute that the outcome was most decisive politically. It laid the foundation of Greek independence and began the gradual recovery of European soil from the Turkish conquest of the Byzantine Empire.

The next British naval engagement was the battle of Acre in 1840, which was a somewhat remarkable swing of the pendulum in the opposite direction, being fought on behalf of the Sultan's authority over Mehemet Ali himself, who was now the arch rebel. Under Ibrahim's brilliant leadership the Viceroy's army had wrested Syria from their Turkish suzerain, marched through Asia Minor, and threatened the Sultan's own capital. Throughout this campaign they were largely dependent on sea transport for munitions, and the Turkish fleet sent to cut these off had deserted to the rebels. For political reasons it did not suit the Great Powers (France excepted) that all the Near East should be ruled from Cairo, and as the conditions were favourable to naval intervention it was agreed that Britain should take hold. The Mediterranean fleet under Sir Robert Stopford received orders to blockade the Egyptian fleet in Alexandria accordingly, and to seize Beirut, which was Ibrahim's Syrian landing port for supplies. Being thus deprived of his sea communications he became entirely dependent on the long coast road by the Isthmus of Suez and Palestine, as the hills farther inland prevented any alternative northward line of advance; and on this road stood the massive fortress of Acre. It was now in Ibrahim's hands as the key to his whole power of movement, and as it mounted 200 guns on its sea faces its reduction promised to be a formidable enterprise.

Stopford undertook it with seven two-deckers and some frigates and sloops, four of which smaller vessels were the first British steamers ever under fire. His flag was in the *Princess Charlotte* and he was supported by three Austrian ships and one Turkish. Two days before he attacked, his frigates took soundings opposite the fortress, but without drawing fire, as the Commandant assumed that the mark buoys they dropped were to indicate berths for the bombarding ships, and when the frigates left he measured the ranges and sighted his guns accordingly. On the morning of November 3 the fleet arrived in position and anchored—being the last British squadron ever to enter action under sail—whereupon the whole fortress instantly flamed into a roaring cannonade. But as the batteries had ranged by the depth buoys, whereas the ships came much nearer, nine-tenths of the shot merely hummed overhead, saving the fleet from sanguinary losses, while the rapidity of their return fire pulverized the defence. After some three hours of close hard hitting a British shell exploded the main magazine, wrecking the interior of the whole fortress and throwing up a dense belch of smoke a thousand feet. All firing then ceased. During the night the survivors of the garrison stole away leaving 1,500 dead, and next day landing parties from the ships occupied the ruins. The fleet casualties only amounted to 58, and Mehemet Ali abandoned all his ambitions. It is impossible to conjecture what political changes might have sprung up otherwise; but the possibility of the rise of a formidable Moslem State governing all the Near East from the ancient capital of the Caliphs was obviously a matter which the rulers of Europe viewed with considerable misgiving, to judge by the unanimity with which they acted.

Meanwhile a shaky Turkish realm had been propped up, and fourteen years later that process was being repeated by Britain, with Russia now as the enemy and France as the ally. This time it was wholesale war by land and sea, since naval action was not sufficient to force a decision alone, though necessary as a first step. A long diplomatic wrangle preceded the resort to force; but of that it is enough to say here that the Tsar and the Sultan came to blows in 1853, that British foreign policy was obsessed with the supposed urgency of keeping Russia out of Constantinople, and that the French Emperor was jealous of Romanoff influence in the Near East. The joint enterprise that ensued was a curious adventure, blundered into without much foresight but productive of fine heroism in the land actions. No suggestion ever arose that on a declaration of war it was conceivable that the great Russian army might invade England instead of the small British army invading Russia; and Britain and France dispatched a fleet and army to the Black Sea, the

British ships being under Admiral Dundas. It was nothing new of course in our own services for the Navy to 'carry the army on its back', as that was invariable whenever British troops went to war. But it was a novel experience for them to cross salt water alongside French comrades in arms; and for the latter it was a novel experience to find themselves seasick as a preliminary to encountering a European enemy, although in its time the French army had fought against almost every country in Europe. The majority of those now embarked had never even seen the sea.

After some undecided landings and re-embarkations the armies were put ashore on the Crimean peninsula, where they passed a year in battering down the great dockyard fortress of Sevastopol, across the entrance to which the Russians had sunk their Black Sea fleet. It was blockaded by the Allied sea forces throughout the operations. At an early stage the French Marshal—being in command of their fleet as well as army—directed his Admiral to support the land bombardment by engaging the 700 guns of the sea defences at long range, and the Admiral asked Dundas to assist. The latter strongly urged that the best plan was to thrust right in to close attack as at Acre, Algiers, and Copenhagen; but the French insisted on distant engagement, to which Dundas submitted rather than destroy loyal co-operation. Eleven French, ten British, and two Turkish capital ships, supported by frigates, attacked accordingly on the afternoon of October 17, 1854, but retired at nightfall, having suffered 600 casualties, received considerable damage, and almost exhausted their ammunition, without silencing a single battery, partly through remaining at indecisive range for fortress demolition, and partly because the Russian shells proved just as destructive to wooden ships at long range as at short. For the remainder of the war, therefore, the allied fleets remained a purely blockading force, though landing their heaviest guns to help in the trenches.

Concurrently with these operations on the shores of the Black Sea, the allies sent a combined fleet of thirty-two capital ships to the Baltic, with sixty-five frigates, sloops, and gun-vessels, besides mortar boats. This was in reality a futile misdirection of force, as no form of warlike activity was open to ships in that direction except blockade, for which Russia cared nothing. Such a negative result produced

QUARTER-DECK OF A FRIGATE, 1865

disappointment in England, where public ignorance of the true capabilities of a fleet had raised great hopes of some kind of decisive action, without clearly understanding what it was to be. They remembered Navarino and Acre, but failed to realize that these were decisive only on account of the power of a fleet to intercept transport vital to an enemy. Russian sea transport was non-existent, and land transport beyond naval reach. No country in the world is more impervious in fact to naval pressure, being self-contained strategically and commercially. Hence arose an absence of dramatic episodes on the sea, while the Army was distinguishing itself with great gallantry on the land; which obscured the truth that the ships had literally done everything that they were built to do. The allied fleets had first driven the Russians off the sea and scared them into scuttling their finest capital vessels as having no further use except as sunken obstacles. Next they had taken the allied armies and put them ashore to carry fire and sword on Russian soil; and all the while they were shielding their own countries so completely that although at war with the nation owning the largest army in the world, the British and French populations never even heard the sound of a gun; nor of all the thousands of ships carrying their commerce did any fall a Russian prize. Most of these services passed unrecognized, however, through not being accompanied by sensational incidents of the kind appealing to public sentiment, and even official authority failed to apply their teaching. Because the defences of Sevastopol withstood a whole year's siege the British Government of the day concluded that their own naval ports should be fortified on the same scale, and, blind altogether to the factor of blue water command which dominated the whole problem of national defence, they lavished prodigious sums on land fortifications; which after all were recognized in the end as not being worth the expense of arming, but still stand as grass-grown monuments of mis-spent millions.

Two more squadron actions fell to the Navy before 1865, though no capital ships were engaged. Japan was just emerging from centuries of rigid exclusion, and some of its powerful feudal chiefs were bitterly antagonistic to the change. Certain retainers of the Satsuma clan murdered an Englishman in 1862, and as the Japanese Government were unable to obtain satisfaction for the outrage, Admiral Kuper was requested by the British Minister to take his squadron to Kagosima, the clan capital, and demand reparation. None being forthcoming, he attacked the local forts in the teeth of a rising typhoon, which compelled him to run for shelter after half an hour's fighting, since it is no more possible for ships to engage in a typhoon than troops in an earthquake. In that time his squadron of one frigate and five smaller vessels suffered considerable damage and sixty casualties (including his flag-captain and commander, both killed), but inflicted enough retribution for the defenders to want no more and pay a heavy indemnity to avoid it. The other incident was provoked by a similar spirit of local intransigeance at another place, but this time retaliation was international. The great Chosiu clan, whose territory was on the Straits of Shimonosaki, took to cannonading every passing vessel under a foreign flag. Protests and parleys being unavailing, a British, French, Dutch, and American combined force of two frigates, six corvettes, and seven sloops, all acting under Kuper's general supervision, engaged the Shimonosaki batteries for the whole afternoon of September 3, 1864, before they were silenced; with seventy casualties and considerable damage to the squadron but complete success in stopping the trouble. These were the first Japanese encounters with European ships, and the experience was such a revelation as to influence their whole national policy thenceforward; one of their first acts being to request the loan of British naval officers as instructors.

Although no actions between fleets under weigh occurred in the early Victorian era the change from steam to sail entirely altered the principles of tactics. Close-hauled manœuvring for the weather gauge had gone, and increased certainty of movement led to advocacy of the ram. But in the absence of actual experience naval opinions differed so widely that no particular theory of steam battle formations found general acceptance for half a century. As regards gunfire the old idea of very close range where every shot was a hit still prevailed, and rapidity of fire was considered all-important in consequence. Drill was everything, accurate shooting mattered little.

On one adversary, however, guns had no effect. The sea is an enemy against which every ship has to be perpetually on guard, and even when its enmity is abated at times the peace is only superficial. Though the British Navy suffered comparatively little loss at the hands of human opponents in the reign of Victoria, it suffered more at the hands of the elements than any national service on land or water in the whole world. The ocean floors are strewn with the ribs of ships and the ribs of men who went down under the British pennant in the long Victorian age. Some simply vanished, leaving nothing to show how. Others were known to have foundered in stress of weather. Rocks, reefs, shoals, and ice added to a list including every class of vessel from capital ships down to the smallest brigs and gunboats. Fogs and collisions completed it. The total loss between 1827 and 1865 was 79 ships and 2,702 officers and men. Additional to the latter were some 750 lives lost in isolated fatalities caused by falls overboard or from aloft, capsized boats, gunnery accidents, engine-room accidents, cable accidents, &c. Thus the responsibilities of the Navy in that period exacted a tribute of about 3,400 victims to duty by violent deaths unconnected with the operations of war and unrecognized by decoration or reward.

Of all the world's armed forces on land or sea not one can lay claim to any form of achievement of such universal and outstanding benefit to humanity as that arising from the work of the hydrographic branch of the British Navy in surveying and charting the High Seas of the globe. Nineteen out of every twenty ships moving under any flag to-day are setting their course by a British Admiralty chart, and the great majority of those charts bear the date of an original Victorian survey undertaken at the expense of the British tax-payer, at whose charge they are still kept up to date as reefs and shoals change shape or crop up in new places. From the British Admiralty also come the 'sailing directions' and printed pilotage information regarding every navigable ocean, sea, gulf, bay, channel, strait, anchorage, harbour, and coast-line in this planet—a matter that always impressed Conrad. Every ship captain can understand and use an English hydrographic chart even if he cannot speak a word of English, and our enemies use them as well as our friends. And as a result England receives from all the great seafaring nations (except France) a form of undeclared but very real deference and priority in the realm of geography. For since on British charts the longitude is measured from the position of the Royal Observatory at Greenwich as a Prime Meridian or zero line, the navigators of all nations using such charts follow suit. Thus a ship under any important maritime flag (except the French) logs her daily position on blue water as being so many degrees north or south of nature's great dividing belt of the equator, and so many degrees east or west of a London riverside suburb.

The surveying ship has to face the risks of the pioneer. Her way lies off the beaten track and her duty is to search for dangers and make them known. Being thus employed it is inevitable that she sometimes falls a victim herself, like the minesweeper. Nine British ships met their end between 1827 and 1865 while at work on survey or exploration, of which the most important were the *Erebus* and *Terror*, lost with 110 officers and men while engaged under Sir John Franklin in investigating the arctic North-West Passage.

VII

THE ARMY

VII

THE ARMY

By JOHN FORTESCUE

It is impossible to treat of the condition of the Army at Queen Victoria's accession without a very brief recapitulation of its previous history.

The nucleus of the present army was the New Model army, called into being by the Parliament in 1645 for purposes of civil war. It was subsequently used by Cromwell for the military government of England and as such was cordially detested by the Royalists, and hardly less by the extreme Republicans of the Parliamentary party. At the Restoration a small portion of it was retained by Charles II, and a few additional regiments were raised to supply foreign garrisons. Regimental officers now purchased their commissions for money. The duties of the Army were the same as in Cromwell's time, namely, the work of police and of preventive service at home in time of peace, and in time of war, the manning of the fleet, defence at home, and aggression across the sea. Garrisons were as yet inalienably attached to their stations whether at home or abroad.

James II greatly augmented the Army with the idea of establishing absolute government; and this action made a standing military force as loathsome in the eyes of the old Parliamentary party as Cromwell had made it in the eyes of the Royalists. Thenceforward both political parties, Royalist Tories and Parliamentary Whigs, united in denouncing the evils of a standing Army at all times and seasons.

The disbandment of James's army after his expulsion was, however, averted by the need for employing it, and indeed augmenting it still further, to contend with France, which had espoused the cause of James. The war lasted from 1689 until 1697; and at its close Parliament behaved so infamously towards both officers and men, who had fought most gallantly under William III, that, but for the speedy advent of another war—that of the Spanish Succession—matters could hardly have ended otherwise than in a great military riot. All, however, were recalled to the colours in

1702, and then under Marlborough British troops rose to the highest reputation in Europe. Hostilities, through no fault of Marlborough's, were unduly prolonged. The country became sick of the war. Faction raged unceasingly. The soldiers were denounced as the plagues of the nation. Finally, the Tories came into power for a brief space, disgraced Marlborough, and patched up a shameful peace. They were speedily driven from high place. The House of Brunswick acceded to the throne upon the death of Queen Anne. But both parties remained unchanged in their hostility to a standing army.

To disband it completely, however, was out of the question. It was still required for its old duties; and, moreover, the Empire had been increased not only by natural growth in North America but by the acquisition of Nova Scotia across the Atlantic, and of Gibraltar and Minorca in the Mediterranean. These new garrisons, added to greater responsibilities in the West Indies, puzzled the English Government exceedingly. They could not make up their minds whether to attach troops to them permanently or to send out to them regiments from the standing Army. Ultimately they took a middle course, filling some stations with permanent garrisons and sending out regiments to others. One and all of these garrisons were shamefully neglected in the matter of shelter and provisions, and the troops dreaded service in them. At home, however, the soldiers were little better off. There were few barracks, except at the Tower of London and one or two like fortresses. The men were scattered about in the alehouses of countless little market towns, wherein the people at large never ceased to malign and to persecute them; magistrates abusing their powers to make their lives a burden to officers and soldiers, and the officers retaliating as they had opportunity.

The Army in fact was not an army but a collection of regiments. In the cavalry and infantry the officers, having bought their commissions, felt a pride in their property which they imparted to their men, thus building up a regimental spirit which is still a peculiarity of the British military force. The artillery and engineers were not subject to the law of purchase but received their commissions from the Board of Ordnance; and being well-trained soldiers they possessed a pride of their own. The cavalry and infantry

3RD HUSSARS: OFFICERS IN UNDRESS, 1830

By courtesy of Thomas H. Parker, Ltd.

were subject to the War Office; the artillery and engineers to the Board of Ordnance; the militia were subject to the Home Office; and transport and supply were the province of the Treasury. Thus there was division not only of regiments but of departments, which possibly was also an aid to survival; for each of them was subject to a political head, and politicians are slow to abolish offices of profit to themselves.

As to the general public, it knew little of what passed in time of war, having practically no information concerning it beyond what was vouchsafed by the *London Gazette*. They saw recruiting sergeants in the market-places and heard of bounties which they hoped might tempt some worthless lad, whom they disliked, to take the shilling. They could not be unconscious that trade was bad and taxation heavy, and therefore trusted that the war might soon end. They might be stung to fury by such a disaster as the loss of Minorca, and roused to pride by such a story as that of Minden, but they had no such sentiment about soldiers as is common now. Hundreds of sons of country squires must have fallen during the wars of the Austrian Succession, of the Seven Years, and of American Independence; yet you will rarely find a memorial to any one of them in a parish church. Occasionally some ghastly tragedy or noble action stirred the imagination of a poet; and Glover wrote *Hoosier's Ghost*—now long forgotten—and William Collins wrote (presumably with Fontenoy in his mind) in 1746

How sleep the brave who sink to rest,

which has found a place in many anthologies. But there are not many Englishmen who could enumerate the important actions fought by British troops between 1742 and 1748.

Then came the wars of the French Revolution and Empire, throughout its opening years from 1793 and 1801 a time of chaos and destruction. Millions of money and tens of thousands of lives were thrown away to no purpose by Pitt's false military policy. He tried to raise men by his father's most vicious methods and suffered the manhood of the country at large to evade its duties by enrolling themselves as volunteers. The war dragged on unprofitably until 1807 when Castlereagh took matters in hand, and a fitting sphere of action was found for the British Army in the Peninsula. Meanwhile Pitt had driven the Navy to mutiny in 1797, and had only averted a like catastrophe in the Army by granting the increase of pay for which military officers had been clamouring for years. Two great administrative changes, however, were accomplished by Pitt. First, barracks were built all over the kingdom, and the troops were no longer quartered in alehouses. Secondly, at the King's earnest importunity the Duke of York, against the wish of Ministers, was in 1795 appointed Commander-in-Chief, and the Army was thus in some measure delivered from political jobbery. The Duke improved the discipline of all ranks beyond estimation. He built up a most efficient staff at the Horse Guards. He founded the Royal Military College, the Staff College, as well as the Duke of York's School for soldiers' orphans. His hand, in fact, so far as the Army was concerned, worked everywhere for good.

When peace at last came in 1815 the British Army had since 1793 seen service in Holland, Belgium, sundry parts of Germany from the Ems to Stralsund, Denmark, southern France, northern France, northern Italy, southern Italy, Corsica, Sicily, Capri, Malta, and the Ionian Islands; in India from Attock to southern Mysore, in Ceylon, Java, Mauritius, and Bourbon; in Egypt, on the Red Sea, at the Cape of Good Hope; about the Great Lakes, Washington, and New Orleans in North America; in countless West Indian islands, and at Dutch Guiana, British Guiana, Monte Video, and Buenos Aires in South America. It had also furnished parts of the crews at the naval actions of June 1, 1794, St. Vincent and Copenhagen. Incidentally, it had conquered a new Empire.

Yet the attitude of Parliament towards the military forces in 1815 was exactly the same as it had been in 1713. Every war has its aftermath, and the aftermath of Waterloo was the consolidation of the new Empire, a task which kept the Army employed almost without intermission from 1815 until 1914. Yet Parliament could not or would not take account of this. Its zeal for economy was wholly laudable. The unreformed Parliament as husband of the public purse was incomparably superior to its degenerate successors of the twentieth century. But in its treatment of the Army its conduct can only be characterized as criminally imbecile. It grumbled at the cost of recruits and did its best to kill them off as rapidly as possible.

In the first place their barracks, conceived and distributed for purposes of police rather than of military duty, were ill-built, insanitary, and infamously overcrowded. There were instances of rooms 32 feet long, 20 feet broad, and 12 feet high, where twenty soldiers ate, drank, slept, and did everything but drill. Until 1827 the men were huddled together in all climates four in a crib; and when in that year the Duke of Wellington gave every man a bed to himself the space between beds often did not exceed 5 inches. The sanitary arrangements were unspeakable—it is literally impossible to set down the disgusting details—and until 1849, when some improvement was made, cases of typhus were frequent at the Tower of London. The water-supply was equally defective. In most barracks a single pump was considered sufficient for the needs of a whole battalion.

The meat supplied for the soldier at home was good beef; but there was no means of cooking it except a copper, so that his diet consisted of boiled beef and beef broth on every day of the year. His meals daily were two—breakfast at 7.30 a.m., dinner at 12.30 p.m.—so that he had nineteen hours in every twenty-four without food. Living always under unhealthy conditions the soldier never felt well, and naturally kept himself up with drink. The State by letting canteens to the contractor who tendered the highest sum for the tenancy ensured that the soldier should be supplied with the worst and most fiery poison that could be called spirit. Thereby it made a profit of £53,000 a year, and a probable loss of half a million sterling in destruction of good human material.

Such were the conditions at home; and it must be added that the only remedy for the misconduct which inevitably follows upon ill-treatment was ruthless flogging. Medals or rewards for good conduct were not unknown, but they were due wholly to the thoughtfulness and good will of regimental officers, the State having no part whatever in them.

Abroad the conditions were worse. The healthiest stations were the Cape of Good Hope, Canada, and Australia, and there the lowest annual rate of mortality was 13 per 1,000. In the British Isles it was 15 per 1,000. In the Windward Antilles, Ceylon, and India it was 71 per 1,000; in Jamaica it was 121 per 1,000; and on the west coast of Africa 75 to 80 per cent. Much of this destruction could have been averted if the men had been reasonably fed; but as a matter of routine, under the rule of the Treasury, unpalatable salt beef was served out, and the soldier was driven to drink. His dwellings also were gloomy and unwholesome. He had nothing whatever to do during the long hot days, and when the sun began to decline he sallied out to get drunk. In Mauritius he could do so for a penny; in the West Indies he could buy a quart of rum for sixpence; in all the Colonies he could intoxicate himself at a most reasonable rate. In the West Indies there was yellow fever, in India there was cholera, at Gibraltar and Malta there were local fevers to kill men already enfeebled by excess. And yet Parliament grumbled at the cost of the Army, which perversely persisted in dying.

Parliament itself hastened the process by granting far too small an establishment for the needs of the Empire, and keeping the great bulk of the infantry in unhealthy climates. Until 1822 the Commons were always cutting down the numbers of the Army, only perforce to augment them upon some alarm, and then cut them down again. At last in 1826 Palmerston pointed out that this perpetual increase and reduction was false economy, and declined to diminish the Army's numbers below 120,000. At that moment of eighty-three regiments of the line no fewer than fifty-one were abroad, twenty-three in Ireland, and four only in the United Kingdom. As to a second line, there was none. Castlereagh had brought the Militia to a high state of efficiency; but since the peace it had been utterly neglected and was fast falling into extinction. The Yeomanry it was that stood between England and anarchy in the troublous years that were immediately to come.

Throughout these years of trial to the Army it was as usual the regimental officers who did all that was done for the men. The Guards, enjoying the exceptional advantage of being always at home, took pride in providing the best hospitals for their men, gave them books to read and gardens to cultivate, and opened savings-banks for the thrifty. The line, less wealthy and always abroad, likewise provided savings-banks, also opening coffee-houses and furnishing light suppers to keep the men from drink, and even building up theatrical companies from the ranks to keep the soldiers interested and amused. The officers thought of their men in terms of human nature; Parliament, guided by the Treasury, thought of them in terms of pounds, shillings, and pence, and even so made a very poor business of them economically.

So matters drifted on until the accession of Queen Victoria, but before coming to the year 1837 it will be well to enumerate the wars undertaken for the consolidation of the Empire from 1814 onwards.

1. THE NEPAL WAR, 1814–16. This was an extremely difficult and troublesome campaign in pathless, mountainous country, in which final success was gained only at the cost of many petty reverses.
2. THE PINDARI WAR, 1816–19. A long and arduous campaign for the pacification of Central India, involving the employment of some 120,000 troops. Cholera appeared in the course of it for the first time since the British occupation of India.
3. THE KANDYAN WAR, 1818. A difficult mountain campaign against a contemptible enemy in a very unhealthy climate. The troops suffered terribly from sickness.
4. THE BURMESE WAR, 1824–6. A river campaign, which was to have lasted three months and actually lasted two years. Cholera supplemented the evils of a deadly climate. Of the European troops employed six out of seven perished, chiefly from sickness. Altogether it was a ghastly business.
5. THE ASHANTI WAR, 1824–6. A war which began with a great disaster to the British, and was ended after a really critical and savage action, in which the casualties upon both sides exceeded 6,000. Few white men long survived the evils of the climate.
6. THE KAFFIR WAR OF 1834–5. A very difficult contest against a brave and elusive enemy, but very well conducted without serious loss except from hardship and exposure.

The list is a tolerably long one and helps to explain why the great majority of the infantry regiments were always abroad. The establishment of the Metropolitan Police in 1829—and it must be noted that this force was composed at the outset chiefly of discharged soldiers—had relieved the

Army of some of its duties at home, otherwise it would have been imperative to increase its numbers. But the constant exile of so large a proportion of the infantry made the service very unpopular; and in 1836 it was resolved at last to alter the entire policy of the country towards the Army. In the first place the infliction of flogging was made less frequent and less severe. In the second, badges and additional pay for good conduct were instituted. In the third, the diet in the West Indies was greatly improved by the substitution of fresh for salt meat. In the fourth, it was arranged that regiments on foreign service should go first to the Mediterranean, thence to the West Indies, thence to Canada, and thence home, so that none should be detained for more than a certain time in unhealthy climates. The number of battalions abroad was still unduly large—82 out of a total of 103—but it was to be long before this evil should be cured. These improvements in the condition of the soldier were brought about by Lord Howick, grandson of a general who had earned great distinction in the American War of Independence and in the West Indies in 1794. Since they came into force in 1837 they may be reckoned as contemporaneous with Queen Victoria's accession.

Hardly was the young Queen upon the throne than a rebellion in Canada strained the military resources of the country almost to breaking point. There were in Canada only eight weak battalions, besides three more which were hurried down by sleighs in the depth of winter from New Brunswick. From England there could be spared only one battalion of the line, which had only left Canada four years before; and it was necessary to dispatch two battalions of Guards and two regiments of cavalry because there were literally no other troops to send. The withdrawal of a battalion from Gibraltar completed the reinforcement, which happily proved to be sufficient. The rebellion was but a petty affair, after all, and was speedily put down by the excellent dispositions of the Governor-General, Sir John Colborne, perhaps Wellington's ablest pupil. But it made a lamentable exposure of England's military weakness, and of Parliament's utter indifference to the needs of the Empire.

At home, likewise, there was acute distress, with its inevitable concomitants of unrest and disaffection. Hitherto, as has been told, the Yeomanry chiefly had stood between

England and anarchy ever since the peace. Troops had indeed been frequently called out to deal with troubles in the manufacturing districts, and the hardened veteran officers of the Peninsula had dealt with the unfortunate operatives in a spirit of gentleness and sympathy. Their men were disciplined and could be trusted not to break loose, no matter how trying the provocation. The Yeomanry were less patient and therefore more dreaded; but, in spite of this failing, they formed an efficient constabulary. Yet, strangely enough, the Whig Government chose this moment to diminish this force, choosing in particular (as is the way of faction) the troops and regiments commanded by Tories for reduction. The action of Ministers was the more strange since the Government of India was committed to a new and very dangerous adventure in Afghanistan which might easily require the dispatch of reinforcements from home. In all the circumstances the Government decided in 1840 to increase the Army from 110,000 to 120,000 men.

In the same year Parliament granted the munificent sum of £3,500 for schoolmistresses to educate the 10,000 children of soldiers who were to be found attached to all regiments at home and abroad. In the following year, 1841, the Government gave official sanction to the formation of regimental libraries and savings-banks, which had been (as already mentioned) instituted by regimental officers long before it occurred to the War Office to move a finger for the benefit of the soldier. On the other hand, the Commons did not allow enough money for the soldier to reap the full profit of former concessions for the improvement of his lot. It appeared that the country could not afford to give a good conduct medal to every soldier who had earned it, nor even so much as a good conduct badge. For the latter distinction he had to pay three shillings, so that, the better he behaved, the more heavily he was fined. Moreover, good conduct pay was withdrawn from private soldiers upon promotion to be sergeants or sergeant-majors, so that they were actually discouraged from seeking advancement.

Such petty measures did not make a military career more attractive; and always there hung over the infantry the sentence of perpetual exile. The succession of wars which raged almost without ceasing between 1839 and 1861 made the calls for British troops heavier than ever. First, there was the insane enterprise which is known as the First Afghan War, in which all military considerations were sacrificed to the whims of a handful of 'political' officers. This fatal policy was abandoned after the disastrous retreat of Elphinstone from Kabul; but meanwhile the native troops of the Indian Army, always frightened of penetrating beyond the Indus, had become so much demoralized that all serious fighting fell inevitably upon the British. Such a war was certain to have its aftermath, but since it was over and since Canada was completely pacified, Parliament insisted upon a reduction of the Army in 1843. In that year was fought the campaign in Sind, and the 'one day war' against the Mahrattas; while in the years 1841 and 1842 there had been war in China as well as in Afghanistan. But the years 1842 and 1843 were those of what were called the Rebecca riots—an insurrection against the maintenance of toll-gates in South Wales—and troops were sorely needed to do the work of police. In the dearth of trained soldiers, a Bill was introduced to enable the Government to call out Chelsea pensioners in aid of the civil power. There were endless declamations against it in the House of Commons, which suggested that the establishment of a military despotism was immediately imminent. These proceeded from the mouths of Cobden and Bright and of their followers who were known as the Manchester School. They were good and conscientious men, very zealous for peace—whatever peace may be—and fully persuaded that it could be attained by universal throwing open of the world's markets. It never occurred to them that it might be unpleasant for a pensioner to be suddenly torn away from his home; still less that it was a hardship to keep soldiers for fifteen, twenty, and even twenty-two years in India, and thus compel pensioners to be called out at home in their stead. Such things, even such trifles as the maintenance of public order, were of little account in their eyes, for, strangely enough, they did not associate order with peace.

In 1845 began the first Sikh war, the severest which we ever fought in India, and the most costly in British casualties. The Sikhs had more powerful artillery than the British; they were well-trained soldiers, and they entrenched themselves in strong positions. Moreover, whereas other enemies in India had fought bravely so long as they were behind defen-

ROYAL ARTILLERY IN ACTION, 1840

By courtesy of Thomas H. Parker, Ltd.

sive works of one kind or another, but had fled directly that the British had forced an entrance, the Sikhs were not dismayed when the redcoats had obtained a footing in their trenches, but brought up reinforcements and counter-attacked. The fighting consequently was very severe, and the whole brunt of it fell upon the European troops, for the native Indian troops were afraid of the Sikhs and behaved exceedingly ill. The British casualties in action alone during the first Sikh war amounted to 4,000, which signified a very heavy drain upon an army that was already too weak for its work.

Then in 1847 there came a more serious alarm of a rupture with France, and Ministers became really frightened, for, if a French army had invaded England, the English could not have raised 30,000 men to meet it. The peril passed away, but meanwhile a very able veteran of the Peninsula, Sir John Burgoyne, had addressed to the Duke of Wellington a memorandum upon the defencelessness of England, and the Duke had answered it confirming Burgoyne's views in every respect. The correspondence was private, but by some indiscretion the Duke's letter was, to his great annoyance, published and the public began to awake to its peril. The result was the introduction in 1847 of a Bill to alter the terms of service in the Army with a view to building up a reserve. It was introduced by Mr. Fox-Maule, later the Lord Panmure who became notorious during the Crimean War. The measure was exceedingly crude and ill-thought out, but the general idea was to limit the first period of enlistment in the infantry to ten years and in the cavalry to fourteen, and to allow men either to re-engage themselves for a further term, or to accept a small retaining pension which should ensure their service if called up within twenty-two years of the date of their discharge. But the root of the whole matter was the choice between old and young soldiers for the Army. If there were old soldiers there would be no reserve, and if there were a reserve there would be no old soldiers. All the leading officers declared in favour of old soldiers; and, though the Bill was passed, it was pretty certain that it would produce no reserve. Meanwhile no attempt was made to revive the Militia; and an elaborate scheme for the fortification of arsenals and dockyards, for which Parliament had voted a million, was damped by the belated discovery that forts and guns were useless without soldiers to man them. It was frequently necessary for military members to explain such elementary points to their simpler civilian colleagues.

Meanwhile the grievance of continued exile for the infantry of the line remained unremedied, and in this year a small party in the Commons proposed to remove it by getting rid of the Colonies themselves. The Colonies, as they pointed out, were a great expense and brought in little pecuniary profit. Indeed, if summed up in terms of pounds, shillings, and pence, instead of in terms of men, women, and children, the Empire was, for the present at any rate, demonstrably a very poor investment. All English ministries with good reason remembered the secession of the American Colonies when they were faced with the problem of Imperial Defence. The best that they hoped for was to part with the New Empire upon friendly terms. But Cobden and his followers urged, with perfect justice, that the Colonies which accepted self-government should accept also the responsibility for their own defence, naval and military, and bear the cost thereof. The question was brought up again in 1851, when Fox-Maule answered that the Colonies always raised an outcry if British troops were withdrawn from them. This was most true. Colonial tradesmen delighted to have English money spent among them; and, if they had had their way, there would have been no end of Kaffir and Maori wars. Nevertheless it was pretty clear that Cobden's arguments must ultimately prevail.

Meanwhile the end of 1848 and the opening months of 1849 had seen the beginning and end of the second Sikh war, with the usual heavy casualties among the British troops. For this reason the establishment of the Army was reduced by only 5,000 instead of 10,000 men in 1849, though 4,000 more were dispensed with in 1850. But Cobden and his followers were still unsatisfied. They now pressed for a decrease of officers, pleading that the Army was a mere refuge where idle scions of the aristocracy could live at the public expense. This was both mischievous and malignant. In not a few of our decisive actions the scale had been turned in our favour by the fact that there was a larger proportion of regimental officers in the British Army than in any other. Moreover, the British officer, having purchased his com-

BATTLE OF THE ALMA: THE GUARDS MOVING UP TO THE REDOUBT

By courtesy of Thomas H. Parker, Ltd.

mission, enjoyed very little pay beyond the interest upon its price. The actual salary of a lieutenant-colonel of the Guards, apart from this interest, would have been sneered at by a bank clerk. Then of course no account was taken of the officer's expenses—his uniform and the various regimental subscriptions which kept the regiment, or in other words the Army, together. Nor was the slightest regard paid to his long enforced residence in foreign and often most unhealthy stations. Regiments were not supposed to enjoy more than five years at home to every ten abroad; and the actual allowance was generally fifteen or twenty years abroad to four at home. That the officer frequently knew little more about his profession than a few parade-movements is likely enough; but the State did not give him men enough to interest himself in their training. Cobden and his crew in 1850 succeeded in drawing from the Horse Guards a regulation that ensigns and lieutenants should pass an examination in a terrifying list of subjects before promotion. There was sound sense in the principle; but how the unfortunate subalterns were to find the necessary books and teachers in foreign garrisons, and how, if these were supplied, they were to raise the energy to pursue their studies in the hurricane months of the tropics or during the summer in the plains of India, the Manchester School did not explain. The leaders of that school had many real virtues, benevolence and kindliness not the least of them. But their lack of imagination led them to encourage acts of inconceivable inhumanity.

At the close of 1851 a new Napoleon arrogated the absolute government of France, and the British Government became uneasy. Twice of late years, in 1843 and 1850, Palmerston had unnecessarily led England to the brink of war with France; and now it seemed high time to trifle no more with military matters. In 1852 the Whig Government increased the Army by 5,000 men and brought in a Bill to reconstitute the militia. They were presently driven from office, but a Tory Government, with Palmerston's support, introduced a new Bill for the embodiment of 80,000 militiamen in England, to be raised by voluntary enlistment or, if necessary, by ballot. The measure was passed in spite of violent opposition from the Manchester school; and by great good fortune a veteran general, Lord Hardinge, became Master-General of the Ordnance. He discovered that the artillery was on the point of dissolution. England possessed only forty field-guns and siege-guns within her own shores, and even of these the carriages were unserviceable. By great exertions he contrived to remedy these disgraceful defects before the Tories were driven to resign after ten months of office.

Meanwhile two more wars, one in South Africa and one in Burmah, had supplied further occupation for the British soldier. That in Burmah was necessarily rendered destructive by the climate. That in South Africa for a time threatened every white man in Cape Colony with extinction, but, through the great moral courage of Sir Harry Smith, a general insurrection of black against white was averted, and the troops following the Kaffirs into their wildest fastnesses forced them to submission. But they suffered much from hardship and exposure owing to the extreme ruggedness of the country, and there was inevitably much sickness. The campaign, however, is chiefly memorable for the introduction of a new weapon. The percussion cap, which wrought nothing less than a revolution in small firearms, had been adopted in the British Army in 1839. In 1852 there were served out for trial to the troops in Kaffirland a few specimens of a new rifle, called the Minié, with a spiral twist to the rifling grooves and a conical bullet. It was sighted up to 900 yards and quite efficient up to 500 or 600. It was still a muzzle-loader, but even so a far more effective weapon than had yet been handled by the British infantry. The old Duke of Wellington saw and approved it not long before his death in September 1852, though it is doubtful whether one was carried by any of the thousands of soldiers who followed him to his grave in St. Paul's Cathedral. With the Great Duke vanished not only the most prominent British general since the passing of Marlborough, but a great Englishman who had notably raised the standard of public duty.

The year 1853 was marked by a new departure. For the first time, except during a period of war, some 10,000 men were sent into camp at Chobham Common for training. Hitherto there had been but one quarter in the British Isles —Dublin—where troops enough were stationed even for a brigade field-day. The manœuvres, if so they may be called, revealed many defects, most notably in the artillery, which to some extent, but by no means fully, were remedied.

N.C.O.s OF THE COLDSTREAM GUARDS, 1856

By courtesy of Thomas H. Parker, Ltd.

Thereupon a large piece of ground at Aldershot was purchased for future manœuvres, but was very shortly turned to a very different purpose. For in 1854 the Government from sheer irresolution drifted into the Crimean War, and now the unfortunate Army had to pay for all the follies of Parliament during the past forty years. Wellington in the Peninsula had built up a most efficient system of transport and supply. He had tried hard to keep some nucleus of a wagon-train, but Parliament had ruthlessly swept it away. Latterly Parliament had even laid violent hands on the Commissariat, despite of the protests of the Treasury, which had pointed out that food was as necessary to the Army as ammunition. The Medical service had been paralysed by excessive formalities in the matter of requisitions for drugs and special food for the sick; the cost of these articles being charged to them in case of any deficiency. For forty years everything military had been regulated as a matter of money. Men counted for nothing in the national balance sheet.

The troops, English and French, were at first landed in Bulgaria in the expectation of meeting their enemy there. They fired not a shot and were little moved about, but were much enervated by the climate and thinned by cholera. Then suddenly they were ordered to land in the Crimea and besiege Sevastopol. They landed accordingly upon an open beach without a wagon or draught-animal of any kind, disembarked a certain quantity of supplies and stores, and took leave of the fleet upon which their very existence depended. By good fortune they captured a few wagons, advanced towards Sevastopol, and drove away a Russian army which had been posted in a strong position to stop them. Had they failed in this action and had the weather, which was very uncertain, been stormy, they could not have re-embarked and must have been captured to a man. However, they continued their advance, regained communication with the sea, and sat down before Sevastopol, with a strong garrison and a complete arsenal in their front, and the whole might of the Russian Empire in their rear. The entire plan imposed upon the Allied generals was simply insane, and they knew it to be such; but they loyally obeyed orders.

The operations of the siege did not prosper. There was a very able engineer in charge of the Russian defence. The Allies had indeed regained touch with the sea, but the harbours upon which they depended were not too safe, and that of Balaclava, which was assigned to the British, was far too small for its purpose. The distance from thence to the British camp was eight miles, and there were not men enough to spare for the work of making a road to it. The business of keeping the Army fed was still most difficult, for there was no forage on the spot to feed transport animals, and, despite of repeated urgent requisitions, the authorities at home were very slow to supply it. Lord Raglan, the British Commander-in-Chief, had asked in June 1854 for a land-transport corps to be sent out to him, but the Government never moved a finger towards that end until February 1855. Raglan was tortured by anxiety as to the possible plight of his army in the winter. He had not sat down before Sevastopol until the end of September, and he dreaded the consequences of wintering upon the bleak exposed plateau above the fortress. He brought the subject repeatedly to the notice of the Government, but could elicit no answer. Ministers were not ill-disposed, but their ignorance of war was beyond belief. They could understand that soldiers needed powder and shot, but they could not realize that soldiers require, as much as other men, clothing, shelter, food, and drink.

The autumn advanced with its usual inclemency. Apart from cholera, the men were overworked, and with greater exposure the more weakly broke down, throwing the more labour upon the stronger survivors. On the 5th of November the Russians delivered a great attack upon the Allies both from within and from without Sevastopol. It failed chiefly through the superb tenacity of the British, but it ought to have succeeded; and its success would have signified the annihilation of the Allied forces. As things stood, they were now the besieged rather than the besiegers, and were bound to spend the winter where they stood. On the 14th of November a violent storm laid the camp flat, turned the road to Balaclava into a sea of mud, and wrecked several ships on the coast. It became impossible to bring food, warm clothing, and shelter and fuel to the Army, and during the next three months the soldiers died by scores and hundreds daily of cholera, dysentery, diarrhœa, hunger, and cold. They did not complain. Those that survived were in the trenches—a sea of mud and water—for five and even six days out of seven; but they stuck to their work until relieved

CHRISTMAS DINNER ON THE HEIGHTS OF SEBASTOPOL

By courtesy of Thomas H. Parker, Ltd.

by death. Reinforcements, landed in November and December, perished even more rapidly than the men who had passed through the whole campaign.

Even when the disabled were removed from the plateau they were little better off. There was no room for a base hospital nearer than Constantinople, and owing to the cramped accommodation at Balaclava there was much suffering for sick and wounded before they could be embarked. Then came a voyage of 300 miles, and then Turkish military hospitals at Scutari. One of these had been early reduced to good order and system by the British medical authorities, but this would hold only 1,000 patients, and the wounded after the action of the 5th of November alone exceeded 2,000. So a new building was acquired, standing, after the Turkish manner, in a sea of sewage. There was no proper ventilation, no clean clothing, no facilities for washing or cooking, not, very frequently, even the simplest medical and surgical necessaries. The doctors, full of goodwill, were hampered by the dread of responsibility and of initiative, both of which they had been most carefully trained to avoid. The hospital orderlies had mostly died of cholera or of drink. The average mortality among the patients was forty-two in every hundred; and they might almost as well have been left to die on the plateau above Sevastopol.

All of this was nothing new. The horrors at Carthagena in 1741 exceeded those at Scutari in 1854. The sufferings of the troops at Quebec during the winter of 1759 and at Havana in 1762 could hardly have been less than at Carthagena. Perhaps the worst that a British army ever endured was during the retreat from Holland to the Ems in 1794. But of all these things the British public knew nothing. They did indeed in 1794 see some wretched wounded soldiers brought into the channel ports in 1794, laid upon the open deck without mattresses and without covering; and their hearts were instantly stirred to compassion. There were also some who in 1809 saw Moore's army land with all the filth and grime of the retreat to Coruña still upon them. But in 1854 there was a correspondent of *The Times* in the Crimea, who brought to notice all the shortcomings which had so long remained concealed. Mr. Sidney Herbert, the Secretary at War (not the Secretary *for* War), had already taken matters in hand, and by a stroke of genius dispatched Miss

Florence Nightingale and a staff of female nurses to Scutari. By sheer ability and force of will that wonderful woman overthrew all the obstacles of prejudice, reduced chaos to order, and not only improved the hospitals on the spot beyond recognition but set a new standard for hospitals and in particular for nursing all over the world. She could not bring back the thousands of dead to life, but she inspired the living with a new hope and with a trust in medical care which had hitherto been unknown whether within the Army or without.

The winter passed away. A railway from Balaclava to the camp overcame the difficulties of transport. Sevastopol fell in September 1855; and by the spring of 1856, just two years too late, the British Army was in really fine fettle for a campaign. Peace was then concluded; and the nation and Parliament busied themselves with the search for a scapegoat to bear sins which were wholly their own. Ministers, in the most cowardly fashion, tried first to blame Raglan and later certain members of his staff. Raglan defended both himself and his subordinates most effectively until he died; and after his death the Chief of his Staff, General Airey, demanded an inquiry and not only confuted but utterly crushed their accusers. Raglan and Airey were, as a matter of fact, far abler men than the average Cabinet Minister. Lord Panmure, who was at the War Office during the latter part of the war, evinced lamentable moral cowardice.

Altogether this Crimean war shed a very unpleasant light on the government of England whether by the Cabinet or the Press; and the efforts of certain private individuals, among them a delegate of *The Times* newspaper, to mitigate the sufferings of the troops, shone all the brighter against a background of hysteria and imbecility. The only names that will ultimately be remembered in connexion with it are those of Colonel Todleben, who defended Sevastopol, and of Florence Nightingale. Great administrative changes were made while the war was actually carrying on, and these shall be presently mentioned. But the great and lasting effect of the war was that the public discovered, through the medium of Miss Nightingale, that the British soldier was no idle, drunken, hard-swearing fighting man, but (as one great lady put it) a Christian and a gentleman, courteous, respectful of goodness and purity, grateful for the slightest care, and in-

SIEGE OF SEBASTOPOL: A QUIET NIGHT IN THE BATTERIES

By courtesy of Thomas H. Parker, Ltd.

finitely patient. It had taken 200 years for the English at large to find out that very simple and obvious truth. From sheer vindictiveness they had damned the soldier as a ruffian and done their utmost by ill-treatment to justify their damnation. They did not take the lesson fully to heart until the German war compelled all able-bodied men to become soldiers, when at last they recognized that the military could be an honourable profession.

Incidentally it must be remarked that recruits did not at first come forward readily for this Crimean war. Far too many boys were shipped over 3,000 miles of sea to be buried within a few weeks of their arrival. But the newly constituted militia patriotically volunteered to do the work of the Mediterranean garrisons and further furnished over 30,000 fine recruits to the Army. These numbers were, however, insufficient, and the Government actually went to work in the old fashion to raise foreign mercenaries, Swiss, Germans, Italians, and Americans, none of whom, however, went into action. The early years of Queen Victoria were really, in military matters, very near to those of George I.

Meanwhile in 1855 a few strokes of the pen had transformed the entire system of military administration. The Commissariat, the Board of Ordnance, the old office of Secretary at War, and the Militia were all absorbed under the control of the War Office. An Army Clothing establishment was formed, the colonels of regiments being compensated for the loss of their profits on clothing. Lastly, as the workmen at Birmingham showed a characteristic inclination to make undue profits out of the manufacture of rifles, the Government very rightly took the whole of its custom from them and set up a small-arm factory of its own. It was, of course, absurd to suppose that such far-reaching administrative reforms could take effect in a few weeks. They required in fact forty years for their full accomplishment, and in the end proved to be considerably more expensive than the old system. But it was of great advantage to gather the various military departments under a single head.

At the close of the Crimean War the establishment of the Army as voted by Parliament was nearly 250,000 men, including foreign mercenaries, though its actual strength was under 200,000. After the conclusion of peace the establishment was nominally reduced to 150,000 men, but, as a matter of fact, no men (except the mercenaries) were discharged, though on the other hand recruiting was totally suspended. We were already committed to a little war against Persia; and that had hardly been brought to a satisfactory end before, in May 1857, the Bengal army broke into mutiny. England was greatly stirred by the general danger, and even more by the massacres of white women and children. The establishment was at once raised to over 220,000. A second battalion was added to each of the first twenty-five regiments of the infantry of the line, and recruits were readily forthcoming. The spirit of the country, if vindictive, was at least good and sound.

Fifty or sixty years ago the Indian Mutiny was held up to youth as exhibiting British heroism at its brightest. In a sense this was true. There were many deeds of individual daring. There were not a few beleaguered garrisons which, with the prospect of massacre before them, defended themselves with a fine tenacity. Above all, the patience of both men and women, deprived of the most elementary comforts during the hot season in India, was exemplary. The mutineers had timed their outbreak well, so that the sun should be their most potent ally. Yet, speaking generally, the ease with which the outbreak made progress, owing to the fatuous disposition of the troops, was anything but creditable to the Indian Government; and the measures for its repression were very faulty. The centre of the insurrection was Delhi, and it was probably right to assail this point without delay. But the force sent there was weak, and for long remained weak, for it was reinforced only by driblets which left it no stronger than before. The Commander-in-Chief, General Anson, died in the first days of the Mutiny, otherwise matters might have been conducted with better sense; but his sound views were combated by the 'politicals'. The Governor-General was an excellent man, but irresolute and dilatory when he should have been swift and firm, and unyielding when he should have been conciliatory. The Council of India was incompetent and inactive. The leading military commanders with a few rare exceptions were of the second or third rank; though fortunately the enemy was so contemptible that the most elementary military precautions could be safely neglected.

The hero who was above all held up to admiration at the

THE PRESENTATION OF THE CRIMEAN MEDAL, HORSE GUARDS PARADE, 1855

By courtesy of Thomas H. Parker, Ltd.

time was Henry Havelock, a good soldier and a good man, but not of shining talent, who was already full old when he attained to high command. He had attempted to be the Napier of more than one Indian campaign, but had failed. But he was a Baptist, a man of strict principle and deep religious feeling, as hard to himself as to any of his men; and his virtues specially commended themselves to the Nonconformists who were for long a great political power in England. They made the most of Havelock, who was not really a man of outstanding ability; but if his name be now little known it is because the Nonconformists have ceased to exercise much influence whether in religion or—the arena which they preferred—in politics.

The commander whose ability was really eminent was Sir Hugh Rose, who in the spring and summer of 1858 marched a column of about 5,000 men a distance of 1,000 miles from Ujjein to the Jumna. He had no maps, and so had to reconnoitre the whole way for himself. But no fortress could resist him, no risk could daunt him, no enemy arrest him. None the less some of his marches during the hot weather were trying beyond endurance. Upon one occasion a brigade, being called upon for a great effort, cheerfully marched on through overpowering heat. It was such a day that the very dogs ran howling away, their skins slashed as if by sabre-cuts by the burning sun. There was no shade and no water. The transport bullocks dragged themselves painfully on at the rate of one mile an hour. The men dropped down first by twos and threes and then by scores. The litter-bearers had no strength to carry their loads. Officers were brought back to the rear shrieking or laughing in delirium. All staff officers were prostrated and the column struggled on without guides till it overtook a brigade which had marched before it. When the halting-place was reached it was long before water could be found; and only with difficulty were sufficient able men found to stand sentry over the well and preserve order while the water was distributed. On this day thermometers marked 130 degrees Fahrenheit and then burst.

Such was an extreme example of the trials to which the troops were subjected. The sun and the flies were far more dreaded than the mutineers. And even in the cooler intervals the fatigue suffered by the soldiers was intense. In the final work of hunting down a rebel leader over a country as large in area as England, one squadron of cavalry is reckoned to have covered 2,000 miles and another little less. Men after hours of riding in heavy rain simply dropped off their horses when halted for the night, were asleep before they reached the ground, and never moved from the mud in which they had fallen. Individual deeds of daring, it must be repeated, were many; but the cheerful endurance of hardship was the most significant quality of the soldier. Nor, despite the massacre of white women and children, was he unmerciful. 'You have fought against the strong,' wrote Sir Hugh Rose in his farewell order to his troops, 'and you have protected the rights of the weak and defenceless, foes as well as friends. I have seen you in the ardour of the combat preserve and place children out of harm's way. This is the discipline of Christian soldiers.'

The last embers of the rebellion in India had been hardly trampled out when, at the end of 1859, 14,000 men were sent from thence to China. There a very skilful little campaign was carried to a successful conclusion by Sir Hope Grant, and by October 1860 the Court of Pekin was brought to terms. In that same year trouble began with the Maoris in New Zealand, and desultory war continued until 1866, absorbing at one time as many as ten battalions. Meanwhile in 1863 the Indian Government had entangled itself in an awkward little mountain campaign about the Ambela pass, which lasted for three perilous months and cost nearly a thousand casualties. Lastly, in 1867–8 the Indian Government embarked in an expedition to Abyssinia, one of the most difficult and dangerous enterprises which the British Army ever carried to a successful issue. The base was on the Red Sea and to reach the objective the force had first to cross twelve miles of desert, then to ascend through fifty miles of mountain-passes to a height of 7,000 feet, then to advance over 350 miles of rugged mountain and valley to the fortress of Magdala, 10,000 feet above the sea. The preliminary arrangements made by the Bombay Government were abominable, and the casualties among the transport animals—elephants, camels, mules, ponies, and bullocks—consequently amounted to 25 per cent. On the other hand, the medical organization was excellent and the casualties among the troops were creditably low. The campaign is memorable as that wherein British soldiers for the first time carried breech-loading rifles and erected a field telegraph line.

And now, since we are approaching a crisis in the life of the Army, it may be well to recapitulate in tabulated form the wars in which that Army had been engaged since Queen Victoria's accession:

1839–42.	First Afghan War.
1841–2.	First China War.
1843.	Sind campaign.
1843.	The 'one day war'.
1845–6.	First Sikh War.
1845–6.	First New Zealand War.
1848–9.	Second Sikh War.
1851–2.	Kaffir War.
1852.	Second Burmese War.
1854–6.	Crimean War.
1857–9.	Indian Mutiny.
1860.	Second China War.
1860–6.	Maori War.
1863.	Ambela Campaign.
1867.	Abyssinian Expedition.

A glance at this table shows that for twenty years there was no breathing time in India, and not a great deal in the Empire at large. The Crimean War had shown the British Army to be full of defects, and the Indian Mutiny had proved that the whole administration of India was rotten to the core. We have seen how great reforms were hurriedly effected in the middle of the Crimean War in England. Similar violent changes were made in India. The government was transferred from the East India Company to the Crown, and the Company's regiments were absorbed into the Army, though owing to the folly of the Indian Government the absorption was barely accomplished without a mutiny.

Thus the year 1859 in a sense opened a new era for both Army and Empire; but Ministers had still no idea of providing an adequate military force. They took it as their principle that there must be always half as many battalions at home as abroad. Thus since India required fifty battalions and the Colonies thirty-seven, there must be not fewer than forty-four in the British Isles. But this was a most illiberal allowance; and although the establishment for the year was raised to 230,000 men, the numbers had only been kept up by drawing heavily upon the militia for recruits.

A foreign war, between France and Austria, came opportunely to silence those in Parliament who would have opposed so great an increase; and the vapourings of certain irresponsible French officers served to kindle the martial ardour of the nation generally. At the call of prominent public men from 60,000 to 70,000 men enrolled themselves as volunteers for the defence of their country. They deserved every credit for their patriotic action, but the Government should never have allowed them to come into being. Volunteers had been tried and found wanting in the last great war, and it was certain that they would fail upon a second trial. The national force for home defence was the militia, and the Government ought to have insisted that not the well-disposed only but that all alike should be liable for service in that force. In 1860 indeed a Bill was introduced for substantial increase of the militia, but still through voluntary enlistment. In truth successive Governments since 1815 had allowed the old militia to perish; and the steadily approaching ruin of agriculture forbade any re-establishment of it upon its old footing. In every way the repeal of the Corn Laws had made England's military condition more precarious.

In the Army itself, despite the work of Miss Nightingale and the report of a Sanitary Commission which visited the Crimea, the mortality among the soldiers from bad housing was shamefully high. Parliament voted huge sums to build a palace for itself and spacious prisons for convicts, but would do little to improve barracks or military hospitals. The average space allowed to convicts was 1,000 cubic feet, and to soldiers—even in military hospitals—from 300 to 400 feet only. There were barracks in use so ruinous that they had been condemned ten years before and were only prevented from falling down by props and shores, while the state of the latrines below them was unspeakable. The general result was that whereas the average annual death-rate of the civil population of military age was 9 per 1,000, that of the Guards was 20, of the line 18, and of the cavalry 18 per 1,000. The deaths from phthisis in the Army were 18 per 1,000—due to overcrowding—whereas those of the civil population were but 3½. Parliament, of its unspeakable

THE GRAND REVIEW OF VOLUNTEER RIFLE CORPS, 1860

By courtesy of Thomas H. Parker, Ltd.

wisdom, first voted bounties to tempt recruits and then proceeded to kill them off twice as fast as the rest of the population. Such was its idea of economy.

Nevertheless some good was done. In the matter of armament breech-loading cannon were introduced in 1860, and the first breech-loading rifle was issued in 1864. Next, the Crimean War decided that Aldershot should be used rather as a permanent camp than as a training ground, though the accommodation consisted of nothing better than huts constructed of green timber. It became a kind of squatters' village, and immediately alongside it there grew up a still viler village full of the undesirable population, male and female, which hangs about the skirts of a camp. All this was bad and foolish; but the mere concentration of a fairly large body of troops in one place was very beneficial. Both the training and the health of the troops were improved. The death-rate at Aldershot fell to 5 per 1,000, and since it was possible to buy groceries in bulk these could be more cheaply retailed to the soldier. Small sums were grudgingly granted for recreation rooms and gymnasia; and the allowance for lighting barrack rooms—two candles for one large room—was increased. Even the management of canteens, thanks to the exertions of regimental officers, was improved; and the Government wisely transferred the whole of that business to the direction of a committee in each regiment. Lastly, the advantages of central training grounds became so obvious that additional camps were established at Colchester, Shorncliffe, and the Curragh. Altogether the condition of the soldier at home was decidedly improved between 1860 and 1870, though there was much still lacking to him. Not till 1865 were there so many as one-third of the battalions of the line at home; and the fact was announced in Parliament with triumph instead of with shame.

And here it must be noted that even on passage abroad the soldier was none too safe. In those days the Admiralty had a certain number of steam troopships of its own of the very worst quality. One such was the *Megaera*, which started from the Downs for the Cape on January 3, 1852, caught fire twice and put into Plymouth on the 5th, was patched up and sent on its way on the 7th, and caught fire several times before she reached Capetown on March 24. Another ship, the *Transit*, bound for India, met a cyclone in the Indian

Ocean which so dangerously loosened her plates that, had she not fortunately run ashore in the Straits of Banca, she must have foundered in mid-ocean. Yet another ship, the *Urgent,* could not go even from England to Barbados without putting in twice for repairs on the way, after which, leaking continually, she fortunately reached her destination. On the other hand the stories of the *Sarah Sands,* when the soldiers fought a fire desperately for fourteen hours and brought the wreck of their vessel safely into Mauritius, and of the *Birkenhead,* which every child knows, are among the grandest testimonies to the discipline of the British soldier.

Throughout the early sixties, however, despite sporadic amelioration of the soldier's lot, the supply of recruits continued steadily to fail. Upon examination of the results of the measures taken to produce an Army of Reserve in 1847, it was found that the Reserve counted just 1,600 men. The scheme was naturally dismissed as a failure, but nothing was done until in 1867 Ministers found themselves confronted with imminent disaster. Discharges and casualties for the year amounted to 32,000 men; and the average number of recruits gathered in during the three previous years was but 14,000. Evidently something must be done, and done at once, to meet the emergency; and the immediate peril was averted by the increase, long overdue, of the soldier's pay. But the question of a Reserve was more serious. Expedients were put forward but proved to be an abject failure. The only way in which a reserve could be built up was by short service, by, in fact, parting with the old soldier. This vital step was taken in 1870. The purchase of commissions was abolished in 1871; and therewith the history of the Old Army came to an end, and the history of the New Army was begun.

These early years of Queen Victoria's reign furnish, so far as the Army is concerned, very strange reading. That unfortunate service was at once the puppet of the Sovereign and the abomination of the people. George IV was above all things a tailor. His idea of a soldier was a fine animal smartly dressed, and beyond a fine appearance on parade he asked for no more. His whims cost the officers hundreds of thousands of pounds in dress. William IV had a fanciful idea that all British soldiers should be clothed in scarlet, and further heavy fines were thus imposed on officers. Under

THE WRECK OF H.M.S. BIRKENHEAD

By courtesy of Thomas H. Parker, Ltd.

Queen Victoria those that had worn blue reverted to blue at further expense, but no practical change was made. Officers landed on the beach in the Crimea in coatee, cross-belts, and epaulettes, as if they had been going on guard at St. James's. After the Crimea there was a rage for following French fashions, and a shako of new pattern and the tunic were introduced—little more practical for field service than the discarded coatee. In India all ranks wore their European dress except that a puggaree (called a curtain) was fitted over the forage cap as a protection against the sun. During the Mutiny, however, khaki (then a stone-grey) made its appearance, as also the sun-helmet. In really rough campaigns, such as those against the Kaffirs, all ranks soon tore their clothes to pieces, and patched them with such make-shifts as they could find; so that they presented a most ruffianly appearance. Not until the end of Queen Victoria's reign did common sense assert itself, saving thousands of lives.

The matter of hair greatly exercised the soldier. In the Peninsula men had been clean shaven but for a very short patch of whiskers. But before the death of George IV huge whiskers had come into fashion and made their way into the Army. Moustaches were confined at first to hussars, then extended to all light cavalry, and finally, together with most exuberant whiskers, to the whole army. The heavy dragoons in particular affected a prodigious length of whisker. The men of course lagged not behind their officers. I have still a boyish vision of a battalion of the Grenadier Guards, about 1869—huge men all moustached and whiskered. All ranks wore their hair long, and the smart thing in the fifties for a soldier was to wind a long lock all round his forage cap. After the Crimea the Army's fashions reacted upon the civilian's. The troops returned from active service heavily bearded, whereupon the entire male population began to cultivate their beards. Presumably they hoped to be confounded with veterans and heroes, for men are very silly vain creatures.

Another institution of Queen Victoria's early years was the medal for military service. This was not altogether new. A little copper medal had been issued after the battle of Dunbar. A General in America had, in 1758, given a medal, at his own expense, to a small column of troops under his command. The East India Company from time to time gave medals. Regiments gave, towards the end of the eighteenth century, their own good-conduct medals at the officers' expense. Generals and commanding officers in the Peninsula and some other campaigns received a gold medal. A silver medal was served to all ranks for Waterloo. But the issue of medals upon a regular system was due to a curious accident. After the disgraces of the Afghan War the Governor-General tried to put a good face on a bad business by granting medals to all ranks. Thereupon veterans of the Peninsula cried out that they had done ten times as much work and had received nothing. Wellington, being consulted, declared that it was now too late to grant medals for service thirty years old, and that the Navy would justly ask for medals also. However, opinion prevailed against him and in 1847 medals, bearing Queen Victoria's head, were at last granted to Army and Navy for services in the great French war. Since that time, every campaign has brought with it its medal.

To these decorations Queen Victoria added, while the Crimean War was still continuing, a new one called the Victoria Cross. Officers of the old school disapproved of it. Thoroughly broken in to ill-treatment by their country they maintained that it was a soldier's business to display valour without thought of reward. In its early days it was little regarded and not unfrequently ill bestowed. Men were bidden to choose one of their number whom they should consider most deserving of the order; and more than one bullying old sergeant-major took care that the men should vote for himself. Gradually this state of things improved. Many crosses were awarded, and deservedly awarded, for acts of extraordinary courage; and now it is the most coveted decoration in the world. If a king desire it, he must earn it by outstanding valour in action, for it can be earned in no other way.

All of these rewards helped to raise the soldier somewhat in the popular esteem; but a full generation was to pass before the families of respectable labouring men should cease to look upon military service as a disgrace. A little discipline was in many cases the one thing wanted to turn a wild and wayward boy into a steady useful man; yet, if he enlisted, he was too often cast off by his relations, while his parents, afflicted to tears, pinched themselves to buy his discharge.

For this, Parliament by the example which it set to the nation was directly responsible. They had driven the Navy to mutiny at a most critical time, and it was not their fault that the Army had not mutinied a hundred times. At the opening of Queen Victoria's reign they were exactly as they had been at the opening of George I's. They were never more brutal and callous—no weaker words will suffice—than in the forty years that immediately followed after Waterloo. They persistently refused to maintain an army large enough for the Empire's needs, and worked the few soldiers that they kept in pay to death. They condemned them to constant exile, wrought all they knew to keep them in bad health and discontent, and yet looked to their officers—themselves shamefully underpaid—to hold them to obedience. Marvellous to relate, the officers did tide the Army over this as over all difficult times. They were not, most of them, professionally efficient, if tried by the standards of to-day. Many of them, from sheer want of men to command, were idle and unprofitable until sent on active service. But they cared for their men and were proud of their regiments, and for the honour of their regiments they shrank from no danger nor hardship. Few realized what those hardships could mean. In the later stages of the Sind campaign all marches were made by night, and the men lay quiet all day with wet towels round their heads. On one day in June, Sir Charles Napier, the Commander-in-Chief, and thirty-three English officers and men immediately about him were struck down by heat apoplexy. Napier recovered; every one of the thirty-three died within three hours. No great account was taken of it. They were soldiers.

VIII

THE MERCANTILE MARINE, 1830–65

§ 1. CROWDED WATERS.

§ 2. DESIGNS AND RIGS.

§ 3. LIFE AT SEA.

§ 4. PASSENGERS, EMIGRANTS, AND MAILS.

§ 5. THE ADVENT OF STEAM.

§ 6. SPEED AND THE TRADE ROUTES.

VIII

THE MERCANTILE MARINE, 1830–65

By BASIL LUBBOCK

§ 1. CROWDED WATERS

WE, in these days, though used to a crowded world, have no conception of a crowded sea such as our ancestors knew, when the English Channel teemed with shipping and the North Sea was red with the tanned sails of our fishing fleets.

From where I write on the Sussex coast, that great highway of ships which we call the Channel, and our Elizabethan ancestors called the British Sea, is bare to the horizon, except for one lonely smoke. Yet it used to be the most crowded traverse in the whole wide world—a veritable street of tall ships, some bound east, others west; some zigzagging to windward in long and short legs as the wind served, others running before it with stunsails alow and aloft; whilst inshore were the small fry, brown-sailed fishing luggers, bluff-bowed coasters with well-tarred bends—mostly snows and brigantines these—and perhaps a shapely fruit schooner racing with her cargo of oranges for the London market.

Not even in the war-days of the Napoleonic era were the British seas as deserted as they are now; for great convoys of the different trades—the East India trade, the West India sugar trade, the Straits currant trade, the Canary wine trade, and so on, escorted by flash frigates and saucy gun-brigs, often covered the horizon with from 200 to 300 sail, whilst lurking inshore were the French privateers, large three-masted *chasse-marées*, waiting to pounce on any ship which dared to proceed alone or dropped astern of her convoy; smuggling luggers, too, might be observed on moonlight nights playing their everlasting game of hide-and-seek with the revenue cruisers.

Within ten years of the peace, the British seas had become a veritable forest of sails, and a telescope from such a vantage point as Beachy Head or Plymouth Hoe showed such a panorama of our Mercantile Marine to the sea-side Briton as could not fail to set his heart beating with pride. Yet not the red ensign alone flew in the Channel at this date. Out in mid-channel, perhaps, a large black **X** on a cotton fore-topsail told of a Yankee packet bound up to London from New York; and closer at hand there might be a plunging Dutch galliot, deep-loaded with tiles, or a Prussian snow, flying light and homeward-bound to Hamburg, or, again, a Normandy Newfoundlander off to the Banks, or, possibly, a Scandinavian lumberman bound to a west-coast port with a deck-load of pit props. But the vast majority of the shipping and craft would be pronounced by any quick-eyed longshoreman to be 'built o' British oak and h'elm'. And, with finger slowly travelling through the degrees of the horizon, he would be able to give the trade and probable destination of every ship in sight—this one with the lofty rig and white band was a West India sugar drogher from Jamaica; that stumpy barque, with the crow's-nest where her fore-topgallant yard should have been parelled, a spouter bound to the South Seas; the next, a Straits vintager from Malaga, and in her wake a Geordie collier, a white bone in her teeth, as she thrust her bow, consisting of a solid balk of oak, through the short Channel seas; then a handsome barque with bright spars—a west-country copper-oreman, being overtaken by a low snaky craft with long skysail poles—a West African oil and ivory trader this last; there would be no mistaking the next vessel with her large tops and many white-painted deck houses—a grim Van Diemen's Land convict ship: note the red coat of the sentry—one can almost hear the clank-clank of the leg-irons; his next ship would, perhaps, be a Jersey potatoman, high-sided and dandy-rigged, or a Mediterranean fruiter, with her copper flashing in the sun as she heeled under a press of canvas to the off-shore wind. There would sure to be a pilot cutter in sight, with a black number and a large P in her mainsail, and any number of south coast fishing luggers.

The crowded state of our British seas a hundred years ago was nothing to the crowded state of our roads and harbours. In the golden age of sail, good roadsteads and handy refuge harbours, where ships held up by head-winds or bad weather could ride in safety, where passengers could be landed or embarked or anchors and cables brought off, were of very great importance. Of such in the great Channel fairway was St. Helen's Roads, where the outward-bound East Indiamen were wont to assemble; Plymouth Sound, a handy place to run back to from the chops of the Channel when beset by a south-west gale; and the Carrick Roads, Falmouth, the great port of call for a ship's final destination. But the most used of all roads were the Downs, that strip of shallow water between the Goodwins and the Kentish shore. Voyagers from London reckoned their days out from the Downs, and homeward-bounders considered they had arrived when they reached the Downs. In the winter of 1874, after a long period of westerly winds, there were between 800 and 900 sailing vessels lying at anchor in the Downs.

In January, eight years earlier, the Deal paper reported: 'Upwards of 500 vessels are riding at anchor in the Downs, presenting one of the grandest sights witnessed here for many months.' In January 1861 the same paper recorded: 'Upwards of 100 ships passed or anchored in the Downs in one day from all quarters of the globe, amongst others eleven from Calcutta, several from Australia, the East and West Indies, &c.' In five days, from March 31 to April 4, 1858, 225 sail left the Downs anchorage, only five of which were steamships. This was about the average at that date both in number and the percentage of steam to sail. A month later we find the week's sailings from the Downs numbering 208 sail and 9 steam. The statistics of steam to sail in 1865, were, according to the shipping returns, 4,936,776 tons of sailing craft to 823,533 tons of steamers.

Flitting about amongst the crowds of shipping in the Downs would be the famous Deal luggers and galley punts—open boats which cared no more for a gale of wind than a modern lifeboat, and were accustomed to launch from Deal beach on the smallest chance of making a few pounds, no matter whether the sky was dark with a snow blizzard, the sea torn into flying scud and soapsuds, and the beach screaming under the batter of the surf. In their hey-day their chief business was hovelling, recovering lost anchors and chains, bringing off passengers and stores, and anything wanted, up to an anchor weighing close on 50 hundredweight. They were invaluable as pilots in an emergency, and in early days it must be confessed that they were not above a bit of smuggling. Their biggest money, however, came from clever salvage work on the dreaded Goodwin Sands, where wrecks and strandings were of constant occurrence during the winter months. Then, indeed, the Deal boatman in his

40-foot, close-reefed lugger showed that he was a true Son of the Sea. Theirs was a poor living, full of terrible hardship, never ceasing risk to life and limb, and with but little reward in kind; yet the lives they saved in the bitter winter storms have only been numbered in the Recording Angel's book.

§ 2. DESIGNS AND RIGS

Let us take a galley punt and row round the anchored fleet.

The first thing to remark upon would be the fact that every vessel, without exception, was built of wood, if we go back to the year 1830, for the first iron sailing ship, the *Ironsides*, was not built until 1838, though the first iron steamer was the *Vulcan*, which was launched in 1819. The first iron war vessel was the gun-brig *Recruit*, built in 1846. The next cause for surprise would be the small tonnage of even such vessels as first-class Indiamen. A thousand tonner was considered a big ship in 1865, and in 1830 only the Honourable East India Company's vessels topped that tonnage. Yet though ships were so small, according to our modern ideas, so short, so tubby, so deep-draughted, and so over-masted, they were by no means ill designed when one takes into consideration the severe handicap of the 1733 tonnage law.

Except for a few scientific draughtsmen, such as the R.N. surveyors, who put their plans down on paper, most of the designers in the days of oak and hemp were simply master shipwrights, who built their ships mostly by eye, paring down a block of soft wood into the hull model that their experienced eyes told them was most suitable for the trade for which the ship was to be built. Such men were not the slaves of theory, nor yet were their ideas too much influenced by old practices. If one makes a close examination of old plans and models and compares them with the modern, one finds that the old shipwright, at any rate in the matter of sweetness of line, had little to learn from the modern architect.

What advance in ship design there is has been due in great part to change of materials. The change from wood to iron and steel allowed of ships whose only limit in size is due to draught. Ships built of steel plates can be riveted together by the mile. No wooden ship had two sections alike. There was one favourite rule, which exercised much influence upon the old shipwright—that was 'the cod's head and mackerel tail' rule, sometimes called 'cod's head and salmon tail'. Every shipwright, every seaman knew that timber—tree trunks—towed easiest butt or big end forward. Thus, if bows were bluff and apple-cheeked, with the greatest beam close under the catheads, the hulls tapered away in what was called 'a fine run', and this it was found made for good speed, especially with the wind aft. Many of the old collier brigs were hard to beat with the yards squared; they were shaped somewhat like a wedge, the bows—often a solid balk of oak—being the thick end. It was not until the clipper ship came into vogue that the greatest beam came aft of the foremast.

There were four great causes of progress and improved design in the early part of the Victorian era. These were:

(i) The non-renewal of the East India Charter in 1833.
(ii) The introduction of the steam-engine.
(iii) The repeal of the Navigation Laws and adoption of free trade in 1849.
(iv) The revocation of the old 1773 tonnage law in 1854.

The first gave a great fillip to private enterprise.

The second introduced the factor of the time-table into sea passages and, at the same instant, played its part in waking up the long dormant speed instinct. Steam's first success was in short distances, such as the Channel passages. Not even by 1865 had it won the long trade routes from the sailing ship, but by that date the battle between steam and sail was indeed a grim one. The repeal of the Navigation Laws and the adoption of free trade have been credited by Liberal politicians with Great Britain's overwhelming supremacy in world trade at the end of the nineteenth century. But it was the introduction of iron in ship-building and the close proximity of the ship-building yards to the collieries and iron foundries which were the real causes of our commercial success. No other country had such natural advantages. No wonder that we could afford to take off our protection duties. It was the other countries, such as America and Germany, who were obliged to put on protection duties in order to save their shipping and their commerce. In the forties, when nine-tenths of the merchant ships of the world were built of wood, the United States had a larger merchant marine than the British Isles, and quite half the world's shipping was being built on the

American and Canadian sea-board. This was simply because the Down Easter and the Canuk had the advantage of cheap and plentiful timber. It was the iron plate of northern Britain, not the repeal of the British navigation laws, which in the end killed the great American mercantile marine.

The revocation of the old tonnage law completed the havoc by releasing British shipping from an overwhelming handicap. The old law only taxed length and breadth; thus a vessel of good healthy dimensions, without inordinate depth, was knocked out by heavy tonnage dues. As soon as Moorsom's plan of internal measurement was adopted, both owner and designer gained.[1]

In appearance, the ship of the early Victorian was much more artistic and attractive to the sea-painter than that of the present day. Nearly all vessels had black topsides and copper bottoms, scraped spars and flax sails: wire rigging and the use of chains aloft were only becoming popular in the early sixties, and hemp shrouds and manila running rigging, which, to keep set up and tidy-looking, required the mate's constant attention, were considered by our conservative forefathers to be far superior to such new-fangled ideas as wire-standing rigging and chain sheets. The first vessel to be fitted with a set of wire-standing rigging was a clipper brig. When she sailed for New York every shell-back prophesied that she would speedily put back dismasted. She reached New York, however, but on the homeward passage her masts did go over the side, probably because her crew did not properly understand the inflexibility of the new material.

The wooden ship, being much shorter than her iron successor, had her masts much closer together. This meant not only that her fore and aft stays were more up and down, but that her running rigging, such as braces and bowlines, had to be carefully rove and tended to prevent endless chafing. Indeed, there have been instances of ships being lost through their fore- and main-yards interlocking. And when all the stunsail gear was added to—what must have seemed to the landsman—an immense tangle of ropes, one has to realize that the old tarpaulin had to be a skilled rigger. Indeed, 'the lord of the bunt and gasket' was the master of an art, which

[1] There was, perhaps, one other fillip to our sea trade in the thirties that should be mentioned, and that was the great interest shown by William IV, our sailor-king, in anything to do with shipping, whether naval or mercantile.

is now extinct to all practical purposes. In the two sciences of ship design and sail management our ancestors knew a great deal more than possibly we shall ever know. Our many sea inventions have saved us much muscle labour, but they have stultified our craftsmanship and atrophied our artistic sense.

Our improvements have nearly all been mechanical improvements, designed to lessen the need for man-power. Of such were patent sheaves, steam windlasses, patent reefing gears, screw steering gears, ball-bearings, and the like. Our mechanical genius has changed the face of the world, has brought luxury and comfort into our homes, but it has killed the old handicrafts and robbed thousands of skilled and unskilled workmen of their livelihood. And it has, alas, turned the romantic profession of the sea from an art into a drudgery. In the struggle for existence the sailing ship became the victim of the merciless economic factor, and the man before the mast had more and more put upon him in spite of labour-saving devices. A first-class Indiaman of 1830, such a vessel as the *Earl of Balcarres* or the *Thomas Coutts*, of between 1,300 and 1,500 tons burthen (old tonnage), carried a complement of 130 souls. Twenty years later, her successor, a Green or Wigram Blackwall frigate of the same tonnage, was considered amply manned with a crew of 70 men. Ten years later that crew of 70 had dropped to 50.

About this time, double topsails, instead of the old single topsails with their four rows of reef points, had been introduced in order to save labour, though every seaman admitted that they were less effective.[1]

Other labour-saving appliances, such as donkey engines and brace winches, gave sailing-ship owners a further opportunity of cutting down their crews, until at the last a 2,500-ton four-mast steel barque washed round the world with a complement of 28, and a watch of not more than 6 able seamen.

Such a rig was not known in early Victorian days. The most popular rig on our coasts, and probably in the world, in 1830, was the brig or snow—the distinction was only a slight technical one—these square-rigged two-masters were

[1] For a time also a sort of roller reefing gear, called Cunningham's patent, was adopted by many owners on their single topsails. This, on the whole, was not a success.

to be found in every part of the world; and the Symondite gun-brig, the first of which, the famous *Columbine*, was launched in 1826, was the destroyer of her day—the fastest all-round vessel in the British Navy. The brig was popular not only for her speed off the wind but for her handiness—she could be sailed forwards or backwards with the greatest ease; she could be boxed about in a narrow channel like a modern yacht; and her way could be stopped in an instant. The Geordie colliers, which had the long reaches of the London river to work up in all states of the tide, amidst such crowds of shipping as can hardly be imagined in these days, were all brig-rigged.

Next to the brig in popularity came the brigantine and topsail schooner. There were also two-topsail schooners, which carried two light yards on the main. These rigs were the speciality of our coasting trade. The revenue cruisers were all big powerful cutters, with square yards and stunsails (spinnakers had not yet been invented). All the larger North Sea and Channel smacks were also cutter-rigged. The ketch-rig, which afterwards became so popular at Yarmouth, Lowestoft, Ramsgate, and Brixham for trawlers, was in the eighteenth century the rig of the naval bomb-thrower known as a bomb-ketch, and dandy was a term just coming into fashion in the thirties for a yawl-rigged yacht. The ordinary fisherman's rig was the lugger, and all round the British coast, on every beach, scores of sturdy luggers might be seen hauled up in unfavourable weather. Each locality had some slight technical difference in design and rig, but the lugsail, that is to say the dipping lug, was the fisherman's sail. That aristocrat of the seas, the lordly East Indiaman, was, of course, ship-rigged. Barques, too, were plentiful enough in early Victorian days. It was a handy, economical rig, for a barque was always well balanced and never carried the hard weather helm, which was very common with some full-riggers in a fresh breeze.

Sail-cloth in British ships was made of flax; the Americans, being big growers of cotton, preferred that material for their merchant ships, though they used Dundee flax for their navy until well into the nineteenth century. Undoubtedly cotton sails looked better, being white in tint, and they often appeared to set better. It is very noticeable how baggy the sails in marine pictures of 100 years ago appear to be. Was this an

THE THOMAS COUTTS

WATERFORD LINE SCHOONERS

By courtesy of Thomas H. Parker, Ltd.

artist's licence or merely an exaggeration? It was neither. Flax sail-cloth used to be of a very loose description, both warp and weft being of a single thread; and the old sail-maker believed in plenty of flow, especially for square sails. It has generally been supposed that our ancestors cut their sails in bags because they did not know any better. Yachtsmen have lately discovered, with the invention of the parachute spinnaker, that running sails cannot be cut with too much flow or belly.

The sail-maker, until well into the nineteenth century, had great difficulty with his fore and aft sails, owing to the stretching of the flax, the openness of warp and woof, and its liability to shrink unevenly in damp weather, only the greatest care and watchfulness on the part of a deck officer kept jibs and staysails in shape. Leeches speedily became concave, the foot of the sail hollow, and the flow in streaks, or all in the wrong place. Great improvements were made in the manufacture and cut of sails during the first half of the nineteenth century. These improvements were chiefly due to two very famous sail-makers, George Rogers Ratsey and Richard Hayward. The great firm of Ratsey and Lapthorn, headed by Thomas W. Ratsey, one of the most brilliant lights in the yachting firmament, still leads the world in the art of sail-making.

§ 3. LIFE AT SEA

In considering life at sea during the period under review, we find the art of sailorizing, as it was called, at its zenith.

If muscle still reigned supreme, and strength on a capstan-bar or a halliard, or in picking up and muzzling a fighting sail, was a very necessary attribute in an able seaman; he also was a master craftsman, who could handle the tools of his craft, the fid and the marlinspike, the sail-needle and palm, with a skill, neatness, and efficiency that is not to be found afloat in these days of mediocrity, due to workers' unions, and of machines which do the skilled workman out of his job. The machine, even in 1865, was still an iron jumble of restive horses and far from being a really efficient servant, and it was the wind which gave breath and life to the ship and imbued even the paddle-wheeler with spirit and character.

Legislation in the days of sail gave absolute power into the hands of the sea-captain. There was no such thing as overtime. The watch below was only too often passed in stirring fight on a topsail foot-rope or on a flooded main deck. The ship came first and was the real seaman's only thought. He spent himself not only to preserve her, but to do her honour. A ship's deck was no place for the slacker or weakling—the mate's boot and the belaying-pin dealt freely with such. Yet, for the real man, the life was beyond comparison. He had time to work, he had time to play, and he had time to think. He knew a physical health which can only be obtained by sea air, muscle fitness, and a tight belt. Besides being a loose-limbed athlete, he was a care-free happy child, who sang at his work and romped at his play. Nor was his life in any way dull or humdrum, for there were still new coasts to chart, new seas to fathom, new peoples to encounter. And the life-stream of mankind was not so overcrowded and moved less swiftly—the two factors of time and speed still counting for very little, whether ashore or afloat. Speed, indeed, did not become a vital force at sea until the yellow specks in a Californian creek sent the gold fever coursing through the veins of every adventurous male.

The time needed to make a first-class seaman in the golden age of sail was from five to seven years. The two great nurseries for foremast hands were the colliers and the coasters. On the east coast a man was not allowed to ship as A.B. until he had passed a viva voce examination set by grey-headed leading seamen of the local sailors' guild.

A man who could boast that he had served his time in a Geordie collier was considered to be true blue—for there was no harder training in the whole wide world. Owing generally to drink, the skipper and mate were often brutally cruel, especially to the wretched ship's boy. A Geordie captain had no education, frequently he could neither read nor write. He felt his way about the North Sea with the lead-line. After taking soundings, one sniff at the arming gave him his exact position. Winter and summer, hot or cold, the Geordie skipper wore the same rig-out, a tall chimney-pot hat, a sleeved vest, fearnought pilot-cloth trousers, and nothing on his feet, except when ashore. A gangway ladder for a Geordie in port was an unheard-of luxury. You went aboard by swarming up the chain cable.

Of the many ways in which sea-life was carried on, the

chief were 'Blackwall Fashion', 'Geordie Fashion', and 'Packet Ship Fashion'.

The characteristics of 'Blackwall Fashion' were: good treatment, easy work with plenty of men to do it, a certain smartness both of ship and person, and all that was expressed by the sea term 'full and plenty'.[1]

'Geordie Fashion' was a way of sea-life that was of a toughness scarcely imaginable, whilst 'Packet Ship Fashion' was one in which 'belaying-pin soup' and 'knuckle dusters' played a large part. This was not a British sea fashion, but an American one. It was due to the Down East American officer's attempt to enforce discipline in crews of absolutely wild, almost untameable, Liverpool Irishmen.

There were thus three distinct types of merchant seamen: the Geordies who despised the lordly Sou-Spainers, the Sou-Spainers who jeered at the uncouth bear-like Geordies, and the packet rats who despised every kind of sailor except themselves. They were, without doubt, the hardest men in the world, the most reckless, the most lawless, and, in some cases, the most fearless. As regards hardness, they were accustomed to go aboard a small Black Ball or Swallow Tail packet in Liverpool for the winter trip to the westward with nothing but the clothes they stood up in, consisting, as a rule, of nothing but a canvas jumper, a pair of patched dungaree trousers, a leather belt, and a sheath knife—no boots, no shirt, no bedding, no plate or pannikin, not even a canvas cap. These Liverpool Irish packet rats prided themselves on their toughness, they would rather fight than eat, every penny they earned went in drink. And the carpenter's first task on a packet towing to sea was to grind the points off the sheath knives of her fo'c'sle crowd.

As regards sailorizing, they were at their best when sail fisting—a winter south-west gale at its worst brought out their best qualities, but they had little patience for the leisurely arts of high-class marlinspike seamanship such as the Sou-Spainers delighted in.

The crew were not all packet rats. Some of them were first voyagers, either yokels and farmers' sons making their first essay at sea-life or else some unfortunate townsmen 'shanghaied' aboard by such a heartless boarding-house master as

[1] 'Shipshape and Bristol Fashion' was a sailor's description which came down from the Elizabethans.

Paddy West. These raw hayseeds and errand-boys were known by the Yankee slang term of 'joskins'. They were bullied unmercifully by the mates and used as slaves by the packet rats, who blacked their eyes and stole their clothes and made them do all the dirty work of the ship. Sometimes these joskins developed into packet rats, sometimes they left the sea with a curse and went back to the farm. But whatever course they steered, one voyage was sufficient to turn each one of them into a man or a beast. There was no happy mean possible.

If it was sometimes difficult to find foremast hands for the American packets in Liverpool, it was easy enough with any ships bound south of the Line. There were no shipping offices in 1830. The hour for shipping, which would probably be 11 a.m., was posted up in the ship's main rigging a few days beforehand.

From an early hour on the day named a crowd of some 200 or 300 prime seamen would be gathered on the quayside—all desperately eager to ship. Practically all the men were in debt to their boarding-house keepers, who would also appear on the scene in order to do their best to get their own men shipped. Most of these latter were Hebrews, the most prominent being the runners of Hart, the Jew, a noted slopshop keeper and cashier of advance notes at exorbitant rates at that date.

The scale of wages for able seamen was 35*s*. per month, and two months' advance out of this went to the boarding-house keeper. The man who shipped in an Indiaman—was bound for a warm climate, and the saying was that he could put his clothes in a stocking.[1]

But if he lacked a sea-chest, he always had his ditty-bag, containing amongst other sea-tools his marlin-spike, pricker, palm and needles, and bullock's horn of grease.

In appearance the seaman of the early Victorian era could not be mistaken for the landsman. To begin with he was usually much bigger, his shoulders occupying the space of two ordinary men. Both in length and breadth of limb he was a giant compared to the puny landsman of the period. His bright, fearless eyes had the wrinkled corners of a man

[1] The Commander of an Indiaman was a man of great dignity, and he seldom showed aboard before his vessel came to an anchor off Gravesend on her way to sea. The crew were picked by the first and second officers, who rarely made a mistake in judgement.

who spent his time looking at a distant horizon in a bright sun. His half-shut hands had the grip of a grizzly bear, and his handshake was something to be avoided by the delicate or small-boned. His dress was peculiar to his calling. In cold weather he wore a watch coat, a short, blue pilot-cloth pea-jacket, over his striped cotton shirt, and changed his thin calico trousers for, perhaps, an oiled tarpaulin skirt. Jack used to be fond of a gaily coloured neckerchief, but after the death of Nelson this was always black. On his feet he sported pumps with big brass buckles, and on his head a man-of-war straw, a black sou'wester, or perhaps a knitted French cap. The true Jack Tar of the early nineteenth century was a bit of a dandy and took a great pride in his appearance, thus his shirts and jumpers were often decorated with the most elaborate embroidery in coloured silks. Both the man-of-war's man and merchant jack cut out and made all his own clothes in those days.

§ 4. PASSENGERS, EMIGRANTS, AND MAILS

It was not until the discovery of alluvial gold in California and Australia that the great wave of emigration to the Antipodes set in. Until 1848 the chief long-distance passenger routes were those round the Cape to India and across the Atlantic to the New World. The crack passenger ships sailed from London in the Indian and China trade. Until 1834 these were first-class Indiamen, which were specially taken up, as it was called, by the Honourable East India Company, and only made one round voyage every other year. The passengers on such ships were divided into three categories: Indian Civil Servants and planters, troops, and last, but not by any means the least important, the fair sex.[1] First of all there was the fiery, old, yellow-faced Nabob—an Indian civilian of top rank, who always travelled with a large retinue of native servants, bearers, khidmutgars, sweepers, &c. Then there were the prospective nabobs, called griffins, young adventurous sparks, going out to be writers or cadets in the East India Company's employ. There was sure to be a red-faced, short-tempered, loud-voiced Colonel, and a number of obsequious subalterns and mischievous ensigns.

[1] Such books as *The Greenhorn*, by George Cupples, or Clark Russell's *My Shipmate Louise* give one a very vivid idea of the inmates of an Indiaman's cuddy.

The cheroot-smoking planter, in his pongee silk sack-coat, would also be much in evidence. The chief of the ladies would be an Anglo-Indian matron, who spoke Hindustani in a hard, raucous voice to a cringing ayah. But the most popular person in the ship would be the shy young thing, with golden hair and speaking eyes, who would hold court in a ring of worshipping subalterns, griffins, and midshipmen, when she was not patrolling the deck on the arm of the Captain himself.

In an Indiaman, passage money amounted to a little over £100 for the run out to Bombay or Calcutta. For this the intending passenger received a small empty cubicle or cabin (the term state-room only came in with Mark Twain and the Mississippi stern-wheelers) which he was obliged to furnish himself. He would also have to provide himself with bedding and linen; and if he was a Sybarite he might hand over a stock of hams to the chief steward. But this was not really necessary, for he messed with the Captain, who provided what we abstemious people of the present day would call a groaning table, which would include every kind of wine from champagne to claret, from port to Madeira. The passenger ship of the thirties, whether East Indiaman or Western Ocean packet, had her decks completely lumbered up with pig-pens, chicken, geese, and duck coops, and cow stalls, whilst the long-boat often proved a convenient receptacle for half a dozen sheep. Emigrants were strangers to Indiamen, but troops, hard-featured long-service men of the Kipling type, with mahogany complexions and amazing thirsts, and callow, raw-faced recruits, all tightly buttoned up in red tunics and pipe-clayed belts, usually filled the lower, or troop, deck.

First-class passengers had a comfortable enough time; troops, if well looked after by their officers, had little to complain about, but the wretched emigrants in the Yankee and Australian packets travelled in such hardship, such squalor, and such misery as it is hard to believe. Even when the hatches were open, the ventilation was so bad in the average packet of even the fifties that a 'tween-deck lantern—the only form of light—burnt with a blue flame. Then, directly the ship began to roll and pitch, very nearly every man, woman, and child was utterly and awfully sick. There was no one to attend upon the sea-sick, and as for those who were ill or hurt—well, the doctor made his rounds once a day. There was no one to cook for the emigrants if they could not do it themselves. The third mate served out water in the first dog watch, but if a man or woman was not there to receive it, on the wet and windy deck, he or she could neither cook nor wash for the next twenty-four hours. Cases were not rare of delicate women practically dying of starvation aboard these packets.

Epidemics, too, raged, and took toll of the emigrants to the tune, sometimes, of forty or fifty lives. In the autumn of 1853, when the emigration boom across the Atlantic was at its height, every packet arriving in New York reported so many deaths from cholera. The *Washington* had close on 100 deaths, and 60 serious cases besides, on arrival.

Sometimes in bad weather water got below, then the hard-used emigrants had the further tragedy of wet bedding, spoilt food, and smashed-up boxes. Other ships encountering the emigrant packets in the winter gales reported hearing the most heart-rending cries coming from them and mingling with the wild oratorio of the storm. Indeed, for the first few days at sea, it was no uncommon thing for the women to scream from sheer fright for hours on end.

Most of these trans-Atlantic emigrants were Irish, fleeing from the potato famine. Poverty stricken, shiftless, ignorant, few of them made any preparations for the voyage, and many of them believed that New York was within a day's sail or so of Liverpool. Often and often, these little emigrant packets, through no fault of their own, took sixty days on the passage, beating to windward without a let up against the merciless Westerlies.

Before the gold boom the emigrant ships to Australia were quite as bad as the Atlantic packets in their callous treatment of their passengers. The British Government regulations regarding emigration which were in force in the forties might have been framed for a traffic in hell. Even the convicts in Somes's convict ships had no worse time than the average government-assisted emigrant. Yet those hardy emigrants, whose descendants at the present time form the backbone of Australia, stuck it out and, undismayed, started out to clear the unknown wild for their homesteads, after surviving an experience which would have unhinged the brain and broken the nerve of the modern traveller.

There was one other way of travelling in the thirties besides taking it easy in an Indiaman or roughing it in a British or American emigrant ship, and that was by taking passage in one of His Majesty's packets which carried the mails. The greater number of these R.N. mail packets sailed for the Peninsula and West Indies from Falmouth.

These little Falmouth packets had had a long and adventurous history, many having fought to the death to preserve His Majesty's mails from the enemy. They were established as far back as 1688, but it was not until 1823 that they were taken over by the Admiralty, in order to provide employment for the many naval officers thrown out on half-pay at the end of the Napoleonic wars.

During the 1830's there were as many as twenty-four packets based on Falmouth. These were fast-sailing brigs and brigantines, specially designed for the purpose by the Surveyor of the Navy, and each one in charge of a naval officer. Others supplied the cross-channel services from Dover, Weymouth, Holyhead, and Liverpool. Two of the most famous of the packets were the *Pandora* and the *Pantaloon*. *Pandora*, a little brigantine of 318 tons, built at Woolwich in 1833, began life as a West Indian mail packet, and ended up, after many years of surveying all over the world, as an arctic explorer. The beautiful little brig *Pantaloon*, of about the same size, in 1832–4 was an express packet to Lisbon. This vessel was specially designed by Sir William Symonds, the Surveyor of the Navy, as a gun-brig yacht for the Duke of Portland, and after she had proved her speed against the smartest vessels in the Experimental Squadron, she was bought by the Admiralty. After a few years as a Lisbon packet, she was made tender to the Royal Yacht *Royal George*, and she ended her life as a slave-catcher in the Bight of Benin. By 1830 the short-distance mail packets were beginning to be replaced by paddle-boats, but the Admiralty compelled private companies to carry a naval lieutenant aboard every ship with mails, as His Majesty's agent.

§ 5. THE ADVENT OF STEAM

The shallow-draft, wooden paddle-wheel steamer, with tubular boiler and beam or oscillating engines, was chiefly developed on the Clyde by the famous engineer David Napier and the builders Wood and Denny. The first regular paddle-wheeler on the Thames was the *Marjery*, of 70 tons, built in 1813–14 by J. & C. Wood of Port Glasgow, and brought south by a syndicate of London merchants.[1]

In the same year the *Argyle* was built by J. & C. Wood and run on the Clyde between Glasgow and Greenock; after a few months she also was bought by the London merchants and sent south under the new name of the *Thames*. She was slightly larger than the *Marjery*, her dimensions being: length 65 ft., beam 14 ft. 6 in., draught 3 ft. 6 in., horse-power 16. Her burthen was 74 tons, her paddle-wheels were 9 ft. in diameter, and her speed 9 miles an hour. She put into Portsmouth on her way round the coast. A court martial was sitting at the time of her arrival, on board the *Gladiator*, but such a novelty was she, that the whole court rushed off to inspect her. On these early steamboats the funnel was so tall that it was used to set a gaff-sail upon. The *Thames* advertised a 'choice library, backgammon boards, draught tables, and other means of amusement'.

The General Steam Navigation Company, which claims to be the oldest steamship company in existence, began running paddle-wheelers to Margate and Ramsgate in 1824. These steam packets were by no means popular at first. Old people were afraid to trust themselves aboard the smoking monsters. The inhabitants of Margate hated them, and it is recorded that when the famous engineer Brunel arrived there by a packet, he was refused a bed at the York Hotel. The Thames watermen also viewed them with suspicion and charged exorbitant fares to take people off to them: it was this short-sightedness that chiefly led to the introduction of floating piers on the London river.

Besides the G.S.N. Co., there were other steam-packet companies on the Thames in the 1830's. The chief of these was the 'Woolwich and Watermen's Steam Packet Company', whose first vessel was the *Fairy*, launched in 1835, by Seaward of London, of 93 tons gross, with engines of 36 h.p. and a reported speed of 14·75 miles per hour. This vessel's coal capacity and daily consumption was 4 tons. Then there was the Greenwich Steam Packet Company, which was founded by

[1] There has been some contention as to which had the first passenger steamers running, the Thames or the Clyde. The supporters of the London river contended that a man named Dawson ran a steamer between London and Gravesend in 1813.

John Penn, the marine engineer, and whose first packet was the *Greenwich*, built by Fletcher and Fearnell at Limehouse, and launched on April 15, 1835. Both these companies were well managed and very popular with the public.[1]

We must now trace the progress of the steam-propelled ships on deep water. In 1817–18 a full-rigged steamer, called the *Rising Star*, was built under the superintendence of the famous Lord Cochrane for service in the liberation of Chile. Her propelling apparatus was some sort of a wheel contrivance which we are told operated through an aperture in the bottom of the vessel. The *Rising Star* was the first steam vessel to enter the Pacific.

The first steamer to reach Calcutta was the *Enterprise*, of 470 tons and 120 h.p. She left England in 1825 and was 103 days under steam and 10 days refuelling. The pioneer steamer in the mail service between Bombay and Suez was the *Hugh Lindsay*, of 411 tons and 160 h.p., built at Bombay in 1829.

The *Meteor* made the first steamship trip from Falmouth to Malta and Corfu with mails. This was in 1830, ten years before the Peninsular and Oriental Steam Navigation Company extended its service from Gibraltar to Malta and Alexandria. As far back as the early twenties two Englishmen named Wilcox and Anderson had a few small sailing vessels trading to the Iberian peninsula. Their first steamer, the *William Fawcett*, of 206 gross tons and 60 h.p., was launched in 1829; she was followed by the *Royal Tar*, of 308 tons and 260 h.p., in 1832, the *Jupiter*, of 610 tons and 210 h.p., in 1835, and the *Iberia* and *Braganza*, of about the same size, in 1836. With these vessels they began running the mails between London, Lisbon, and Gibraltar in 1837, under contract to the British Government and under the name of the Peninsular Company. In 1840 this Company was incorporated by Royal Charter under its present name. The best known of its early ships was the *Hindostan*, of 2,017 tons and 520 h.p., which left England for India and China via the Cape in September 1842. Two years later the Company undertook the mail service between England and China via Alexandria and Suez.

[1] The Thames Steam Towing Company began operations with a tug-boat named the *Thames*, of 53 tons gross, built at Newcastle in 1832. Her engines were described as 'Grasshopper single' of 25 h.p. She had a coal capacity of 8 tons and a speed of 6 knots. She was followed in 1836 by the paddle-tugs *Black Eagle*, *Joseph Somes*, and *London*.

P. & O. S.S. HINDOSTAN

S.S. ARCHIMEDES

By courtesy of Thomas H. Parker, Ltd.

The history of the first steamships on the Atlantic has been written over and over again: first came the *Savannah* in 1819, an American production which trusted mostly to her sails. She was followed by the Canadian *Royal William* fourteen years later. Then in 1838, the same year that the first screw steamer *Archimedes* was built at Blackwall, the paddle-wheeler *Sirius*, of 700 tons and 250 h.p., arrived in New York, on April 23, 18 days out. But she was beaten by the *Great Western*, of 1,320 tons and 450 h.p., which was designed by Brunel, and did the passage in 14 days. In 1840 the *Britannia*, of 1,140 tons and 440 h.p., with engines by Robert Napier, arrived in Boston on July 18, having taken 14 days 8 hours, at an average speed of 8½ knots and a fuel consumption of 38 tons per day. This paddle-steamer was the first of four vessels named by Samuel Cunard, George Burns, and Robert Napier in their tender for the American mail contract which was accepted by the British Government.

This was the foundation of the Cunard Line and the beginning of the battle of the Atlantic steamship companies. The American Collins Line and the British Inman Line were floated in 1850, then in 1856 came the Anchor and Allan Lines. They were followed by the Guion steamers in 1863, the White Star in 1870, and so on.

The pioneer ship of the Royal Mail Steam Packet Company to the West Indies was the paddle-steamer *Clyde*, of 1,840 tons, launched February 25, 1841. The Company, which inaugurated its service with fourteen barque-rigged paddle-boats, had great difficulty in ousting the Admiralty and their old Falmouth packet brigs, and it only succeeded by agreeing to place naval officers in command of its steamers.

The P.S.N. Co. was founded by William Wheelwright, who in 1829 commanded a smart Baltimore-built schooner named *La Veloz Manuela*, sailing as a packet between Valparaiso and Cobija, the chief port of Bolivia, and earning a great reputation for speed and good treatment of passengers. The firm's first steamers were the *Chile* and *Peru*, paddle-wheel brigs, which started opening up the Pacific trade in 1839.

The Bibby Line was started in Liverpool in 1851 with the object of wrestling the Mediterranean currant and orange trade from the beautiful little fruit schooners. Its success was undoubted from the first. One by one the schooners were driven out of the Mediterranean and were obliged to confine themselves to the Azores. Numbers of them, too, went across to Newfoundland and joined in the fish trade to Oporto, Lisbon, and the Italian ports. The pioneer ships of the Bibby Line were the *Tiber* and the *Arno*, screw-barques. They were the first screw-steamers seen in the Mersey. The Bibby Line was amongst the earliest supporters of the great Belfast ship-building firm, Harland and Wolff. The Union Line, the first steamship line to South Africa, for the Castle Line were first of all sailing ships, was started at Southampton in 1853.

It will be noticed that all these new lines of steamships catered entirely for passengers: it was not until well after the half-century that steam began to invade the realms of the cargo carrier—the tramp-steamer had not yet arrived on the scene of the world's trade. In its early days the steamship was looked upon not only with disfavour but with scorn by most sailors.[1] They vented all their sarcasm and wit upon its ungainly paddles, its absurd bridge, which looked so fragile that a few sprays would seem sufficient to set it adrift, and, lastly, its towering chimney. The old seaman could not abide ugliness, and to his eyes the paddle-wheeler was abominably ugly; but his chief complaint was that she was not seaworthy. Marine engineers were not seamen, and some of their 'contraptions', as Jack called them, were very far from being shipshape. There were also lesser drawbacks which were a continual irritation to the old sailors.

To begin with, the steamer was always dirty. Her ill-consumed smoke poured down on her decks in a black pall which spread its soot and smuts everywhere and drove a keen mate to distraction. It was in vain that the first smoke stacks reached as high as the main-top—the heavy smoke blew down and spoilt the mate's clothes as well as his temper. Secondly, the 'Puffing Billy' was always noisy, with an unceasing clanging of metal against metal, of paddle-floats against sea-water; and she was always hissing steam, and her raucous voice, the steam whistle, invaded the high seas, where before only the thunder of guns, the clatter of canvas, and the hauling cries of men pulling on brace and halliard were heard. Thirdly, she was so hot in her ill-ventilated engine-rooms and stoke-hold that stokers, and even engi-

[1] It was not until 1853 that the Royal Yacht Squadron did away with their rule prohibiting the steam-engine in all R.Y.S. yachts.

neers and greasers, collapsed before a tropical watch was out. Finally, most steamers were like diving-bells in a sea-way, for neither forward nor aft were they given enough bearing. Such designing was good enough for smooth waters like the Thames and the Clyde, but more than alarming in an Atlantic gale.

The advantage of speed, however, overcame every opposition, and the marine engineer went gaily ahead with his wonderful mechanics.

In 1850 the Collins liner *Atlantic* crossed the Western Ocean in 9 days 17 hours. On the Channel passages the *John Penn*, on her maiden trip in 1859, averaged 15·2 knots between Dover and Calais; this was beaten the following year by the Holyhead–Kingston boat *Connaught*, which averaged 18·2 knots. The P. & O. *Himalaya*, which was built in 1853 to inaugurate the taking over of the Suez-Bombay mail service from the East India Company and at that date the biggest steamship in the world, registering 3,438 tons and 2,050 h.p., on being taken up for trooping purposes to the Crimea in 1854, averaged 13·5 knots whilst crossing the Mediterranean.

But even as regards speed, machinery did not succeed in conquering sail until the titanic struggle had gone on for the greater part of the nineteenth century.

§ 6. SPEED AND THE TRADE ROUTES

Those of us who can remember the days before the invention of the internal-combustion engine and the spectacular advent of the first motor-car with its red-flag man walking a few yards ahead, can easily envisage our ancestor's outlook as regards what constituted speed. On land a galloping saddle-horse marked the extreme limit. The express coach corresponded to the express train; and the motor-bus between country towns and villages was represented by a wagon, whose speed was no more than that of a South African ox-wagon. In the eighteenth century, and during the first few decades of the nineteenth, a man who was in a hurry was an unusual object. He made elaborate preparations and saw to it that horses were available for a relay of galloping stages. In this way Lieutenant Lapenotière, of the schooner *Pickle*, brought the news of the victory of Trafalgar. He changed horses nineteen times between Falmouth and London. He landed about 11 a.m. on November 4 and drew up before the Admiralty at 11 a.m. on the 6th, a matter of 48 hours for 266 miles.

The first type of vessel to which the term clipper was applied was the Baltimore schooner. Other vessels, until the middle of the forties, were generally designated as sharp, medium, or full built.[1]

As slavers, pirates, and smugglers, Baltimore brigs and schooners were the outlaws of the seas in the nineteenth century; in the eighteenth, their chief guise was that of the privateer, the express cruiser, and the Navy dispatch vessel. The design was not very suitable for a bigger ship and, so far as I know, only three full-rigged ships were built on Baltimore lines. These were the *Hannibal*, 809 tons (American), built in 1810, and captured and taken into the British Navy under the name of *Andromeda*; the *Ann McKim*, of 493 tons (American), built in 1832 for the American shipowner and merchant Isaac McKim; and the *Architect*, of 520 tons (American), built at Baltimore in 1847 for the China tea trade.

Baltimore designs were specially favoured by all illegal trades. One of the chief of these trades in the nineteenth century was that of smuggling opium into China. Between 1830 and 1860 the opium clippers, as they were called, were renowned beyond all other trades for their speed and seaworthiness, as well as for their fighting capabilities, for besides Mandarin junks they had to out-sail, or else out-fight, the pilong, or Chinese pirate, as well as the Malay.

Being smugglers, or at any rate illicit traders, they earned huge dividends and were run without regard to expense, and the service, being both exciting and well paid, was much sought after by adventurous seamen. Indeed, the opium trade was held up as one of the finest nurseries for training officers in the Merchant Marine in early Victorian days.

[1] There has been much controversy as to how the famous Baltimore design was evolved, for the model which served to inspire the Baltimore shipwrights was a very long way ahead of its times. Some trace it back to the old fast-sailing Jamaica sloop of the buccaneers, which in the eighteenth century had been modified and improved in the Bermuda shipyards, and from thence found its way to Virginia, and was to be seen in many of its best features in the Virginia pilot-boat. Others trace it to Swedish, others again to French, and a small number to New England influences. Probably the type evolved in the brain of some long-forgotten Baltimore genius, who was able to combine the best characteristics of the Jamaica and Bermuda sloops, French luggers, Scandinavian fishermen, New England pinkys, and even the Mediterranean xebecs.

The opium clipper had to beat up and down the China Sea against the prevailing monsoon. This difficult traverse, amidst uncharted shoals and coral heads and against fierce squalls and strong currents on wild unknown coasts, with pirates lurking and ready to pounce from behind every headland, could never be accomplished by the old East Indiamen of the Honourable John Company, who always arranged their passages so as to have the favourable monsoon each way.

In 1829, however, a little barque of 253 tons was built in the Howrah Dock, Sulkea, Hooghly river, by Captain William Clifton, a retired lieutenant R.N. and East Indiaman commander; this was the *Red Rover*, the first vessel to beat up to the Canton river against the strength of the north-east monsoon. Now the interesting fact about the *Red Rover*, which was known as the first of the opium clippers, was that she was built on the lines of an old American privateer, called the *Prince de Neufchatel*. This vessel, a schooner of 18 guns and 135 men, was captured after a hard chase in blowing weather by the frigates *Leander*, *Newcastle*, and *Acasta*, when they were searching for the *Constitution*. Sir George Collier, the commander of the squadron, was so impressed by the beautiful lines of the *Prince de Neufchatel* that he sent her home with dispatches, and the Admiralty, equally pleased with her, ordered her lines to be taken off and preserved at Deptford. Here, somehow or other, Captain Clifton got hold of them, and the result was the *Red Rover*. This little barque was the first of the Calcutta-built opium clippers, which included such famous vessels as the barques *Waterwitch*, *Sylph*, and *Cowasjee Family*, the brig *Antonio Pereira*, the brigantine *Poppy*, and the schooners *Nymph* and *Psyche*.[1]

The opium clippers never conformed to a special type like the Baltimore clippers; and this added to the interest, for every type of fast ship was thus seen competing together. In 1835–6 three were built by the Parsees in the Bombay Dockyard. These were the brig *Lady Grant* and the barques *Sir H. Compton* and *Ardaseer*. Naval men compared the *Lady Grant* unfavourably with the *Red Rover*, declaring that she was too sharp and narrow, and overmasted for the vicious

[1] Though all the others were inspired by the *Red Rover* in their model, the *Sylph* and *Cowasjee Family* came from the board of the Surveyor of the Navy, Sir R. Seppings, and were built on his diagonal method of construction.

squalls of the monsoon. Overmasting, indeed, led to many a disaster in the ranks of the opium fleet, but, taken on the whole, their performances in bad weather, and especially in weathering out typhoons, were astonishing and the admiration of all seamen. This was due in part to the superb seamanship of their officers, in part to good building and easy lines.

Some of the early opium cracks were ex-slavers, such as the brig *Ann* and the schooners *Syed Khan* and *Black Joke*; some again were ex-fruiters, bought because of their speed in the 'dry and green fruit trades' as they were called. The best known of these was the schooner *Time*. Then there were some old R.Y.S. yachts, such as the flagships of Lord Yarborough, *Falcons I* and *II*, *Anonyma*, a 427-ton brig, once the property of the Hon. R. F. Greville, and the schooner *Royalist*, once the famous yacht of Rajah Brooke. Following the yacht model, were a number of schooners, built by White of Cowes—the *Denia*, *Nina*, *Eamont*, and *Wild Dayrell*.[1]

It was not until after 1860 that the sailing clipper in the opium trade had to give way to steam. In that year the Thames Shipbuilding Company launched the racing steamer *Ly-ee-moon* for Dent & Co. This pioneer vessel was designed by James Ash, registered 1,001 tons, and had oscillating engines of 350 h.p. which developed a speed of 17 knots. Following her came a fleet of racing steamers, specially designed for carrying opium from India to China.

That there were other fast ships, both British and American, in the thirties and forties, has been rather lost sight of through the wide advertisement given to their successors, the American, Aberdeen, and Clyde clippers of the fifties.

The most noted of these early free-traders to the East was the tea-ship *John o' Gaunt*, of 449 tons, built at Liverpool in 1835 and owned by the Gladstones. Under Captain John Robertson she made such quick and regular voyages to China and the East that her famous master was requested by the Admiralty to submit his track charts, especially of the China Seas, for their inspection. Her chief British rivals

[1] The American-built clippers in the opium trade mostly belonged to the firm of Russell. These included schooners built on the New York pilot-boat model, such as *Anglona*, *Spec*, and *Mazeppa*; and some very fine designs from the well-known board of Sam Hall at Boston, the schooner *Zephyr*, the brig *Antelope*, and the barque *Coquette*.

were the London ship, *Alexander Baring*; Bates's *Euphrates*, a Liverpool ship; the *Richard Cobden* of 461 tons, also from Liverpool; the *Foam*, 628 tons, the first tea-ship built on the Clyde for James Findlay, afterwards the owner of such famous vessels as *Serica*, *Taitsing*, *Spindrift*, and *Windhover*; Green's frigate-built *Monarch*; and several Aberdeen-built craft, such as the *Reindeer*, *Emperor*, *John Bunyan*, &c.

These vessels had to contend against some very smart Americans, the best known of which, if we leave out the famous *George*, a Calcutta trader, known throughout the world as the 'Salem Frigate', was the *Ann and Hope* of Providence, a vessel of 450 tons (American), which had a passage of 95 days from New York to Canton to her credit as far back as 1809. Then there was the *Nautilus*, which, under Captain Charles Pearson, was 95 days to Batavia on her second voyage and 97 days to China on her third.

The critics of British ship designers contended that the Americans were superior in every way to their British rivals, both in lines of hull, method of rigging, and cut of sails. Certainly American designs, even of the thirties, were easier to drive, and faster all round than the British; also they worked easier, neatness aloft being rather overdone in British ships, which for that cause forced large ropes through small blocks, whereas Americans believed in big blocks and small running-gear. Another factor which helped American designs was the give and take of their soft-wood hulls, but this was not a good financial merit, for such hulls in a few years became strained and water-soaked; thus American ships only lasted half the time of British hard-wood ships. An exception to this statement must be made in the case of the Salem frigate *George*. This remarkable vessel made no less than twenty-one successful voyages between Salem and Calcutta from 1815 to 1836. Of 328 tons, she was built from a model by Christopher Turner by an association of Salem shipwrights, who were thrown out of employment by the war. Finished in 1814, she was intended for a privateer but never sailed, and when the peace came Joseph Peabody bought her, added another deck, and sent her into the Indian trade, where she proved a marvel in light winds, though she never succeeded in logging more than 250 miles in the twenty-four hours.

The first British ships which were honoured by the name of

clipper, if we except the opium craft, were those built on the Aberdeen model. This Aberdeen model was chiefly notable for what was known as the Aberdeen bow. There is no mystery about this bow, which our ancestors considered such a remarkable advance in ship designing. It was merely the rounding in of the planking forward so that it was butted into the stem from the rail down, thus doing away with the old open head, which was very vulnerable to the attack of the sea. The first vessel launched by Alexander Hall of Aberdeen with this improved bow was the topsail schooner *Scottish Maid*, of 142 tons. She was built in 1839 as a coaster running between Aberdeen and London with passengers and cargo, and from the first she proved a remarkable success.

In those early days intending passengers to distant parts of the United Kingdom generally found it more comfortable, and even quicker, to take ship instead of coach. The *Scottish Maid* was followed by a number of clipper schooners, which ended by cutting out the famous Leith smacks which ran to London and were cutter-rigged. The best known of these Aberdeen clippers were the *Aberdonian, London, Rapid, Non-such,* and *Swift,* all built between 1840 and 1843. Hall's first ship-rigged clipper was the *Glentanner*, built in 1842 for Yale, Wylie & Co. of Liverpool. She was followed the same year by the *Humayoon* for James Findlay of Greenock, 530 tons. In 1845 the barque *Alexander Hall* was launched for Donaldson, Rose & Co. Other well-known Hall-designed vessels of this period were *Bon Accord*, ship, 380 tons; *North Star*, ship, 384 tons; *Pilot Fish*, ship, 302 tons; *Peruvian*, barque, 413 tons; and *Reindeer*, ship, 328 tons. This vessel, commanded by Captain Anthony Enright, distinguished herself in 1850 by making the round voyage out to China and back in 7 months 28 days.

In that year Hall launched the ship *Stornoway*, of 527 tons, built to the order and under the supervision of Captain John Robertson, late of the *John o' Gaunt*, and generally known as the first of the British tea-clippers. On her maiden voyage she went out to Hong Kong in 102 days and came home from Whampoa in 103 days. These times put heart into the British shipowner, who for the previous five years had been obliged to watch whilst the Americans carried off the pick of eastern cargoes and received the top freights. This conquest of the tea trade by the Americans in the forties was due to more than just superiority in design of some half-dozen ships.

American masters were highly educated men of good social position, whilst British officers, except in the first-class passenger trade, were ill-educated bears, poor navigators, slack watch officers, and not seldom drunkards, to whose devotion to the bottle was due a high percentage of the little round blobs on the yearly wreck chart. The American mate, though he bore a bad reputation for treatment of his men, was invariably a superb seaman, who kept his ship in apple-pie order; whereas the British mate was too often slow, stupid, and slovenly—perhaps the three worst faults a seaman could have. As regards the men before the mast there was not much to be said, each, Jonathan and John Bull, were without compare as masters of sea-craft—if the one was smart and quick in the uptake, the other was slow and sure—both were reliable in accident or stress of weather, and they both held a great pride in their ships. But by the end of the forties both merchant navies were being invaded by foreigners of every nationality, who certainly were not of the same high standard, whether in efficiency or reliability.

It was not until Great Britain's adoption of free trade in 1849 that the merchant marines of the two countries really came to grips. Before that date British shipowners were sunk in a state of stagnant complacency, content to carry on their business in the same old antiquated way and with the same old tub-like vessels. But this fool's paradise was rudely disturbed when the new American clipper *Oriental* hauled into the West India Docks on December 3, 1850, only 97 days out from the Canton river with 1,118 tons of prime tea in her hold—the first tea to be landed in England from a vessel under a foreign flag. This clipper belonged to the well-known American firm of A. A. Low and Brother, and had received a freight of £9,600—about three-quarters of her cost.

It was the famous commander of the medium-built American ship *Paul Jones*, Captain Nat Palmer, who induced Messrs. Low to order three sharp ships of unusually fine lines, and on a design advocated by himself, from the New York builders, Brown and Bell. These were the *Houqua*, of 706 tons, named after the Canton Hong merchant, and launched in 1844; the *Samuel Russell*, of 940 tons, named after the founder of Russell & Co., and launched in 1847;

and the *Oriental*, of 1,003 tons, launched in 1849. These three vessels were undoubtedly much faster than any British ships of the forties. Each in turn was commanded by Captain Palmer, whose influence on American clipper-ship design has never been sufficiently appreciated. The Low clippers had only three rivals in speed in the eastern trade and these were American-built like themselves, namely, the Baltimore clipper *Architect*, and the Howland and Aspinwall clippers *Rainbow* and *Sea Witch*.

The *Rainbow*, which was built from the designs of a draughtsman in Smith and Dimon's drawing-loft, named Griffith, has generally been called the first of the Yankee clippers. She was the first vessel to be built with hollow lines. Controversy raged round her whilst she was on the stocks. Old sailors declared that she was being built inside out and would never be safe. Other critics went so far as to say that she was built contrary to nature, with her concave-bow lines and knife-like entrance. She cost 22,500 dollars to build, registered 750 tons (American), and was launched in January 1845. On her second voyage she went out to Canton from New York in 92 days and came home in 88, bringing the news of her own arrival out East. These times were better than others, British or American, but for one exception—that was the *Natchez*, a full-pooped, flat-floored old New Orleans packet, which, under a young captain named Robert H. Waterman, actually reached New York, in 1845, 78 days 6 hours out from the Macao Anchorage, and in the following year in 83 days for the same passage. This led to the building, in 1846, of the *Sea Witch*, of 907 tons, an improved *Rainbow*, put on the stocks by Smith and Dimon specially for Captain Waterman. This wonderful little ship made three tea passages to New York in 1846–8 of 81, 78, and 79 days, under the now famous 'Bully' Waterman, as he was called.

These passages spread the fame of the new American hollow-line design far and wide. Shipping experts raved about the beauty of the new clippers. Their one criticism was that the ships were too light in construction.

This lightness was soon to be remedied when the two great ship designers, William H. Webb of New York and Donald McKay of East Boston, entered the lists in 1850.

That year marks the beginning of the boom in American clipper-ship building, which did not collapse until the outbreak of the North and South war. It was also the beginning of the battle between the Down East and British shipyards, between the hard-wood clippers flying the red ensign and their soft-wood rivals under the stars and stripes. There were many factors contributing to this shipping boom. First of all came the opening of the British markets to the world; next came the discovery of gold in California, quickly followed by the equally important discovery in Australia, and, lastly, there was the enterprising spirit of the starving peasants in Ireland and Europe, which led them to bravely shoulder their bundles and take ship into the unknown.

As usual, the demand produced both the men and the ships on both sides of the Atlantic—men of genius and ships of a beauty, speed, and power never previously known. The rivalry amongst the designers and the shipwrights was intense: British against American and, do not let us forget, Canadian; Aberdeen against the Clyde; the Mersey against the Thames; and, on the other side, New York against Boston; New Brunswick against Nova Scotia, and so on.

The clippers and emigrant ships grew larger by leaps and bounds; in the forties 1,000 tons was a big ship; larger ships, indeed, there were, but they found it a slow matter filling their holds. Cargo came down to the ports in small lots, a lighter or a sampan at a time. There were no steam derricks, and every bale, barrel, or case had either to be humped aboard on human backs or hoisted over the side by means of a block and tackle from spencer gaff or yard-arm. Nor was merchandise shot into a ship's hold like so much coal, as it is to-day. Stevedoring was still an art. A ship was packed like a lady's trunk, and the placing of weights, whether high or low, was a matter of much consideration on the part of the mate and the head stevedore. It was some years before the simple cargo carrier grew to any size: the big wooden clippers of the fifties were all passenger and emigrant ships, and, what is more, they were nearly all American or Canadian built.

As soon as the news of the gold discovery in California spread to the Eastern States and the Continent, every kind of craft that would just float was pressed into service and advertised as a new clipper of amazing speed, which guaranteed to reach the Golden Gate by way of Cape Horn in under 100 days. Along South Street, New York, or on the Liverpool landing-stage, men of every walk in life were to be seen, already fully dressed in the miner's red shirt and jack-boots, and intent on seeing an extraordinary pile of unsuitable baggage safely deposited aboard some ancient, patched-up barque, which displayed in her rigging a board announcing that she was about to sail—to receive dispatch was the usual expression—for the El Dorado of the West. Some of these overloaded, worn-out has-beens foundered, with all hands, amongst the Cape Horn greybeards. Others limped in through the Golden Gate with their pumps clanking and a gush of clear water pouring through the lee scupper holes. Others, again, came in under a press of sail and, instead of anchoring, ran straight up on the mud flats of Mission Bay, where they were speedily deserted by passengers, officers, and crew. Only the real cracks were able to replace their crews and go on to China for a tea cargo or back round the Horn again. Very few of these, it must be confessed, belonged to British ports. The greater number by far were brand-new Yankee clippers, superb craft with inspiring names, such as the *Flying Cloud*, *Sovereign of the Seas*, *Westward Ho*, *Witch of the Wave*, *Neptune's Favorite*, *Golden Gate*, *Winged Racer*, *Romance of the Seas*, *Witchcraft*, *Comet*, *Swordfish*, *Tornado*, *Whirlwind*, *Ocean Telegraph*, *Twilight*, &c., &c. The *Flying Cloud* held the record for the Horn passage of 89 days, made in 1851, which she repeated in 1854. Many of these glorious sailing ships of Uncle Sam continued their spectacular careers by crossing the Pacific in record time, notably the *Swordfish*, which covered the 7,200 miles to Shanghai in 32 days 9 hours.

As soon as the tea shippers saw these mighty racers, which were over twice the size of the little clippers from Aberdeen and Sunderland, they hastened to offer them freights at much higher rates. This was not surprising, for the difference in capacity, power, and speed was plain to see. On the one side there were the low-sided, delicate-looking Aberdeen clippers, such as the *Stornoway*, *Chrysolite*, *Cairngorm*, *Vision*, and *Robin Hood*, and the early beauties, built by Steele of Greenock, such as *Kate Carnie* and *Ellen Rodger*; the Sunderland-built *Crest of the Wave* and *Spirit of the Age*; Scott's iron heeler, *Lord of the Isles*; Chaloner's of Liverpool first *Fiery Cross*, and Dicky Green's gallant little *Challenger*, not one of which came near topping the thousand tons; and on the other, such renowned American cracks as *Challenge*, *Celestial*,

Nightingale, *Surprise*, *Sea Serpent*, *Witch of the Wave*, *Comet*, *Ringleader*, *Quickstep*, and *John Bertram*.

A race which aroused much interest at the time was that of the *Challenge* and *Challenger*, in 1852, for a wager between the owners of the former, N. L. and G. Griswold (known in America as 'No Loss and Great Gain'), and Dicky Green, the builder and part owner of the latter, which was to be the losing ship. Unfortunately, the two ships loaded at different ports. *Challenger* got away first on July 27, but leaving Shanghai she had at least a week's sail farther to go than *Challenge*, which did not leave Whampoa until August 5. All accounts seem to agree that the two vessels were together in Sunda Straits, though the shipping reports gave September 4 for *Challenger* signalling Anjer and September 12 for *Challenge*. It is possible that *Challenger* was held up in the Straits. She reached London on November 19, three days ahead of her huge rival, and the story goes in the Blackwall yard that the American-built *Result* was bought with Green's winnings.[1]

This was by no means the first international tea race, nor yet the last; but, on the whole, it must be confessed that the Americans had the best of it. In 1852 *Witch of the Wave* was only 90 days to the Downs; in 1853 *Architect*, with 107 days, carried off the premium of an extra pound per ton on the freight for the first ship home; in 1854, after a great race, the little *Chrysolite* managed to reach Deal one day ahead of *Celestial*—*Cairngorm* took the premium that year; but in 1855 *Nightingale* made the magnificent record of 91 days home from Shanghai. In 1856 the most interesting race was between the iron *Lord of the Isles* and a lovely American clipper barque, the *Maury*. Both arrived in the Downs on the same day, October 15, but *Maury* had the best passage by 4 days. Curiously enough, the following year, *Lord of the Isles* sailed a dead heat from Shanghai with *Celestial*. But the former will always be remembered for an 89-day run in 1858, when she left Shanghai on November 29 and was off Dover on February 26, having averaged 320 knots for 5 days crossing the Indian Ocean trades.

War with China closed the Canton river in 1857 and 1858;

[1] The *Challenge* ended her days under the name of *Golden City* and the British flag. She was wrecked near Ushant at the end of the sixties. It was certainly an unequal race, for the *Challenge* registered 2,000 tons against the *Challenger's* 699 tons. The former crossed a 90-foot main-yard and spread 12,780 yards of canvas, and she was some 60 feet longer.

and numbers of ships were held up at Hong Kong. It was the end of American competition in the English tea trade. Financial depression and the North and South war practically wiped out the wonderful merchant marine of the U.S.A.

America began selling ships to Great Britain in the early days of free trade, and Canada for many years before that. Liverpool shipping people were the chief buyers of these soft-wood ships, many of which came over to be coppered, re-fastened with copper bolts, and to be artistically finished off. Others brought timber; for throughout the Victorian era Liverpool was the entrepôt for Canadian lumber. Liverpool owed her status as a premier world port almost entirely to her transatlantic trade. From the year 1816, when the American Black Ball Line commenced monthly sailings with the four little 500-ton packet ships, *Amity, Courier, Pacific,* and *James Monroe,* the port was the chief embarkation point for all passenger and emigration traffic to the United States.

Then, when the discovery of gold at Ballarat in 1851 set the tide of emigration in the direction of the Antipodes, such enterprising men as James Baines, James Beazley, Henry Threlfall Wilson, and Gibbs, Bright & Co. saw a chance to compete successfully with the first-class London ships of Green, Wigram, T. & W. Smith, Joseph Somes, and Duncan Dunbar, by buying some of the big ships which were being built across the water.

The London ships were hard-wood ships, beautifully built and known far and wide by the proud title of the 'Blackwall Frigates'. Though they were the successors of John Company's East Indiamen, few of them exceeded 1,000 tons, and they were built on the lines of a serving mallet, without sheer, with apple-cheeked bows, and heavy quarter-galleried sterns. The largest of these frigates at the beginning of the fifties, such as Green's *Prince of Wales* and *Monarch,* Wigram's *Queen,* and Smith's *Marlborough* and *Blenheim,* none of which exceeded 1,500 tons, were considered fit to rank as 50-gun frigates in the Royal Navy, should the occasion to arm them arise, but they had no chance of sailing level with an American clipper; and this gave Liverpool her opportunity in the emigrant trade, where the comfort of fastidious passengers had not to be considered.

James Baines, who founded the Liverpool Black Ball Line,[1] began his successful career by purchasing the *Marco Polo*, a three-decked New Brunswick ship of 1,625 tons register. This vessel, on her first voyage to Australia in 1852, was commanded by Captain James Nicol Forbes, known in shipping circles as 'Bully' Forbes. He took 930 government emigrants out to Melbourne in 68 days, a record. The whole voyage only took 5 months and 21 days, and as the *Marco Polo* came up the Mersey on Sunday, December 26, a waterman called out to James Baines on the street: 'Sir, the *Marco Polo* is coming up the river.' 'Nonsense, man,' returned the little man; 'she has not arrived out yet.'

But *Marco Polo* it was; and Forbes knew how to advertise. As she hauled into the Salthouse Dock a huge strip of canvas between the fore and mainmasts announced in 2-foot black letters: 'The fastest ship in the World.' There were soon many rivals to dispute that statement. In 1853 the *Sovereign of the Seas* came across to Liverpool with her designer and builder on board. The result was an order for four record breakers, given by James Baines to Donald McKay.

Nor was Wilson of the White Star Line letting the ground grow under his feet. McKay's four giant clippers, *Lightning*, *Champion of the Seas*, *James Baines*, and *Donald Mackay*, were countered by the purchase of *Red Jacket* from Jackson's yard at East Boston and the *White Star* and *Shalimar* from St. John's.

These monster emigrant clippers (*Donald Mackay*, the largest, registered 2,408 tons) are the only sailing vessels which have ever run 400 sea miles in the twenty-four hours: *Lightning* holds the record with 436 miles made on March 1, 1854, when crossing the Atlantic, and 430 miles on March 19, 1857, when running her easting down to Melbourne. *James Baines*'s best was 423, *Donald Mackay* logged 421, *Shalimar* 420, and *Red Jacket*'s best were 417 and 413. For the greatest speed through the water *James Baines* claims the record, her log entry stating, 'going 21 knots with mainskysail set'.

The chief cause for these wonderful speeds was not so much the fine lines of these big ships, but their size, high sides, light live cargoes, tall sail plans, and power of being driven through any weather. It must be confessed, however, that in spite of

1 Not to be confounded with the American Black Ball Line of Marshall & Co., though it flew the same flag, a black ball on a red ground.

moonsails at the main and any number of flying kites, they were not fast in light winds, and it was the crossing of the tropics which so often spoilt their passages.

The only two chances which British designers had of building wooden ships of the size of these great American and Canadian clippers both came the way of Alexander Hall of Aberdeen.

In 1854 he built the *Schomberg* of 2,284 tons for James Baines. This unfortunate vessel was wrecked on her maiden passage, without having accomplished any noteworthy burst of speed owing to light weather. In 1866 Hall had his second chance with the *Sobraon*, of 2,131 tons, the largest composite clipper ever built. Though undoubtedly a very fast ship all round and one of the most successful passenger ships in the Australian trade, *Sobraon* never got near the big 24-hour runs of the Black Ball and White Star clippers.

With the advent of the sixties, iron began rapidly to take the place of wood in British ship-building. But there were certain trades where iron hulls were tabooed, as being bad for the cargo. One of the chief of these trades was the China tea trade. Builders overcame this objection by putting teak planking over iron frames, a method of construction which was termed composite by Lloyd's. The first vessel built on this plan is said to have been the schooner *Excelsior*, launched in 1850, her designer being a man named John Jordan. Then Bilbe and Perry of Rotherhithe built the *Red Riding Hood*, of 720 tons, in 1857. Numbers of ships were built with iron beams, but iron frames did not really come into fashion until about 1863, when the tea clippers *Taeping*, *Black Prince*, *Eliza Shaw*, and *Pakwan* were all built on this principle.

Owing to the growing popularity of iron plates, composite construction only had a short vogue, about the last vessel to be built on this plan being the famous Adelaide passenger ship *Torrens*, which was launched at Sunderland in 1875 by James Laing.

The most beautiful examples of composite construction were the tea clippers of the sixties, whose annual races from China were followed by the British public with an interest which almost equalled that excited by horse-racing. No more lovely craft were ever built than Robert Steele's masterpieces, *Ariel*, *Sir Lancelot*, and *Titania*; Connell's *Spindrift*, nicknamed the giblet pie, because she was all legs

P. & O. S. S. HIMALAYAN

THE RACE: TAEPING AND ARIEL

By courtesy of Thomas H. Parker, Ltd.

and wings; Stephens' *Forward Ho*; Pile's *Undine*; Linton's *Cutty Sark*; *Leander* and the record breaker *Thermopylae*, both designed by Bernard Waymouth, secretary of Lloyd's Register; and *Black Prince* and *Norman Court*, designed by Rennie. These little clippers, none of which exceeded 1,000 tons register, were as delicately fashioned, as perfectly finished, as beautifully kept as the smartest yachts in the Royal Yacht Squadron, and their races down the China Sea, across the Indian Ocean, round the Cape, up the Atlantic, and through the narrow waters of the Channel to the gates of the East and West India Docks, were as closely contended as those of small raters round the Solent and Spithead buoys.

The most famous tea race of all was that of 1866 when *Ariel*, *Taeping*, and *Serica*, after crossing the bar of the Min river together, all docked on the same tide, 99 days out from the Pagoda Anchorage, with the first teas of the season. After much argument it was agreed that the stakes and the premium for first ship to dock should be divided between *Ariel* and *Taeping*, *Ariel* being the first ship to take her pilot off Dungeness; but *Taeping*, owing to drawing less water, the first vessel to haul into dock.

The art of sail navigation and seamanship reached its zenith in these tea races of the sixties.

By the end of the early Victorian era the science of mechanics had made considerable strides in harnessing the forces of nature to the will of man, in easing the burden on human muscle, and in freeing sea life of much of its old cruelty and hardship; but, already, though the British Mercantile Marine was developing rapidly in every direction, the stress of competition and the strain of economic laws were growing severe. At sea 'yer fair whack and nae mair' was replacing the old style 'full and plenty' and the daily tot of rum. Even the ships themselves were being stinted by the soulless limited companies, which were stepping into the shoes of the old shipowner, who loved each vessel of his fleet as he loved his own children. In early Victorian days the joints of civilization, which are now screaming for want of oil, had hardly begun to creak. Life at sea, if strenuous, was also joyous; if lacking in many amenities, was yet a career of adventure with new worlds to conquer and new seas to chart. The sailor was still a craftsman, delighting in his craft, strong-nerved, robust, and facing life with open eyes and smiling lips, and there were still some fifty years to go before the eclipse of that age-long sea-craft, which had slowly developed from the pre-historic day when the first deer-hide was spread to catch the favouring breeze and save the paddle of some weary ferryman.

PRINTED IN
GREAT BRITAIN
AT THE
UNIVERSITY PRESS
OXFORD
BY
CHARLES BATEY
PRINTER
TO THE
UNIVERSITY

36-37

38-41

41-8

59-6

210

36-7

394

41-42